25

D0081700

The Italian Crusades

THE ITALIAN CRUSADES

The Papal–Angevin Alliance and the Crusades
against Christian Lay Powers, 1254–1343

NORMAN HOUSLEY

CLARENDON PRESS · OXFORD

OXFORD
UNIVERSITY PRESS

Great Clarendon Street, Oxford OX2 6DP

Oxford University Press is a department of the University of Oxford.
It furthers the University's objective of excellence in research, scholarship,
and education by publishing worldwide in

Oxford New York

Athens Auckland Bangkok Bogotá Buenos Aires Calcutta
Cape Town Chennai Dar es Salaam Delhi Florence Hong Kong Istanbul
Karachi Kuala Lumpur Madrid Melbourne Mexico City Mumbai
Nairobi Paris São Paulo Singapore Taipei Tokyo Toronto Warsaw

with associated companies in Berlin Ibadan

Oxford is a registered trade mark of Oxford University Press
in the UK and in certain other countries

Published in the United States
by Oxford University Press Inc., New York

© Norman Housley 1982

The moral rights of the author have been asserted
Database right Oxford University Press (maker)

Special edition for Sandpiper Books Ltd., 1999

All rights reserved. No part of this publication may be reproduced,
stored in a retrieval system, or transmitted, in any form or by any means,
without the prior permission in writing of Oxford University Press,
or as expressly permitted by law, or under terms agreed with the appropriate
reprographics rights organization. Enquiries concerning reproduction
outside the scope of the above should be sent to the Rights Department,
Oxford University Press, at the address above

You must not circulate this book in any other binding or cover
and you must impose this same condition on any acquirer

British Library Cataloguing in Publication Data

Data available

ISBN 0-19-821925-3

1 3 5 7 9 10 8 6 4 2

Printed in Great Britain
on-acid free paper by
Bookcraft (Bath) Ltd.,
Midsomer Norton

For my wife

List of Abbreviations

The full title is not given here if the work is listed in the bibliography.

AA., Arm. C	Archivum arcis, Armadio C
ASN	Archivio di Stato, Naples
ASPN	*Archivio storico per le provincie napoletane.*
ASV	Archivio segreto Vaticano
BDSPU	*Bollettino della Deputazione di storia patria per l'Umbria*
EHR	*English Historical Review*
I et E	Introitus et exitus
Instr. misc.	Instrumenta miscellanea.
Mélanges	*Mélanges d'Archéologie et d'histoire publiés par l'École française de Rome.*
MGH	*Monumenta Germaniae historica inde ab anno Christi quingentesimo usque ad annum millesimum et quingentesimum auspiciis Societatis aperiendis fontibus rerum germanicarum medii aevi,* ed. G. H. Pertz *et al.* (Hanover–Weimar–Berlin–Stuttgart–Cologne, 1826 ff.).
MGH, Const.	*Constitutiones et acta publica . . .,* ed. L. Weiland *et al.*
MGH, Epist. pont.	*Epistolae saeculi xiii e regestis pontificum romanorum,* ed. C. Rodenberg.
MGHS	*MGH Scriptores.* 32 vols. (Hanover–Leipzig, 1826–1934).
QFIAB	*Quellen und Forschungen aus italienischen Archiven und Bibliotheken.*
Reg. Vat.	Registra Vaticana.
RCAR	*I registri della cancelleria angioina ricostruiti,* ed. R. Filangieri di Candida *et al.*
RHC	*Recueil des historiens des Croisades,* ed. Académie des inscriptions et belles-lettres. 14 vols. (Paris, 1841–1906).
RHGF	*Recueil des historiens des Gaules et de la France,* ed. M. Bouquet *et al.* 24 vols. (Paris, 1737–1904).
RIS	*Rerum italicarum scriptores,* ed. L. A. Muratori. 25 vols. (Milan, 1723–51).
RISNS	*Rerum italicarum scriptores,* new series, ed. G. Carducci *et al.* (Città di Castello-Bologna, 1900 ff.).
RQ	*Römische Quartalschrift.*

Preface

In the thirteenth century the Kingdom of Sicily consisted of the island of Sicily and the Italian mainland as far north as the frontier of the Papal State, with the exception of the papal enclave of Benevento.[1] By the terms of the treaty of Caltabellotta in 1302 the island of Sicily became independent of the mainland and was held as a papal fief by an Aragonese prince. To spare papal sensibilities, however, it became known as the Kingdom of Trinacria, while the mainland provinces retained the name Kingdom of Sicily. To avoid confusion I have adopted the term 'Kingdom of Naples' to describe the mainland kingdom in the fourteenth century. Both it and the unified kingdom of the thirteenth century are occasionally referred to by the convenient Italian term *Regno*. A more intractable problem of terminology, for which I have been unable to find a completely satisfactory solution, concerns the duration of a crusade. Was there, for example, one crusade against the rebel Sicilians during the War of the Vespers, or was there a series of crusades, each of them beginning with the release of a fresh crusade bull? The problem arises from the fact that the popes rarely used the term 'crusade' in this period, referring in their letters only to the plenary indulgence that was to be granted to crusaders. Technically, a crusade lasted as long as the indulgence was proferred and accepted. But it would be pedantic and fruitless to argue whether the issue of a new crusade bull cancelled the previous indulgence, and hence the previous crusade, or simply extended them. Fortunately this does not affect any of the practical aspects of the crusade.

All proper names are transliterated into their English equivalents unless it seems to me that there is an established usage to the contrary (thus John Amiel and John of Joinville, but Giovanni Orsini and Giovanni Villani). For the rare occasions on which Arabic names appear I have adopted the system of spelling used by the contributors to *A History of the Crusades* (editor-in-chief K. M. Setton). For monetary equivalents I have used the rates of exchange compiled by K. H. Schäfer in

---

[1] The full description was *Regnum Siciliae Ducatus Apulie et Principatus Capue*. See, e.g., *RCAR*, i, Reg. 1, nos. 1–2. This was sometimes abbreviated to *Regnum Apulie et Siciliae*. See, e.g., Ptolemy of Lucca, 'Tractatus . . . super regnum Apuliae et Siciliae'.

Die Ausgaben der apostolischen Kammer unter Johann XXII., pp. 38*–131*.

This book is a revised version of a dissertation which was accepted for the degree of Ph.D. in Cambridge in 1979. Many institutions have helped and encouraged me in the work for the dissertation and for the book. The Faculty of Archaeology, History, and Letters in the British School at Rome elected me to a Rome Scholarship in Medieval and Later Italian Studies, which facilitated nine months of research at Rome and Naples in 1976–7. Girton College earned my gratitude by electing me to a Research Fellowship in 1978, thus enabling me to continue my research without financial hardship. The Vatican Archives allowed me free access to papal records, and I also worked in the Vatican Library, the libraries of the British and French Schools at Rome and the Biblioteca nazionale at Naples. The staff of Cambridge University Library has shown inexhaustible patience and skill in finding books for me and answering my enquiries. I also acknowledge the assistance of the Twenty-Seven Foundation in providing a grant towards the cost of publication.

There are innumerable debts of gratitude to individuals. In particular, I should like to thank Dr D. S. H. Abulafia, Dr R. C. Smail, Dr A. T. Luttrell, Professor C. N. L. Brooke, Professor W. Ullmann, and the Reverend H. E. J. Cowdrey for their criticisms and suggestions. I have benefited from conversations on Italian history with Dr L. A. Ling. My Italian supervisor, Professoressa Jole Mazzoleni, allowed me to use the material in the *Ufficio della Ricostruzione angioina* in the State Archive at Naples and gave me much help and guidance in doing so. My two greatest debts are to my supervisor in Cambridge, and to my wife. To Professor Jonathan Riley-Smith I owe more than I can say. He taught me medieval history as an undergraduate and suggested that the crusades against Christian lay powers would be a fruitful field of research. Those who have been taught by him know how invaluable are his knowledge, enthusiasm, and kindness. My wife has tolerated the daily intrusions of the popes and their Angevin vassals for four years; her moral and financial support has been of inestimable worth.

Girton College, Cambridge   Norman Housley

Contents

Maps

Introduction

This is a study of the use of the crusade against Christian lay powers in Italy between 1254 and 1343. Crusades of this type were responses to what the papacy believed were attacks on its temporal possessions and rights, or those of its allies and vassals. It is important to make a clear distinction between such crusades and crusades against heretics. In some ways they were similar. In the crusades against the Albigensians and the Hussites, for instance, the crusaders were also engaged in a struggle with secular powers and their political institutions.[1] It is also the case, as we shall see, that the charge of heresy played a very large part in the crusades against lay powers. The crucial difference lies in the fact that, whereas in the crusade against heresy the involvement of secular authorities was incidental to, and arose from, the determination of the Church to stamp out heretical beliefs, in the crusade against lay powers political opposition to the Church was the primary reason for the crusade. It is, however, misleading to interpret the difference between the two crusades in terms of the distinction between a 'religious' motivation and a 'political' one. The papacy's lands and rights were important because they were believed to buttress and express its unique position in the Christian Republic; from the papal viewpoint, the crusade against Christian rulers was as closely related to the defence of the Faith as was that against heretics. The term 'political crusade' is therefore a misnomer.

Like many important developments in the crusading movement, the use of the crusade against Christian lay powers originated in the reign of Pope Innocent III. In November 1199 Innocent declared a crusade against Henry VI's seneschal, Markward of Anweiler, who was guilty of opposing papal rights

[1] See P. Belperron, *La Croisade contre les Albigeois et l'union du Languedoc à la France (1209–1249)*, *passim*; F. G. Heymann, 'The Crusades against the Hussites', in K. M. Setton (ed.), *A History of the Crusades*, iii, *passim*.

in the Papal State and the Kingdom of Sicily.[2] Thereafter crusades against Christian rulers became common. At least eight popes in the thirteenth century declared crusades against their lay opponents,[3] and crusades of this type remained an important weapon in the hands of the popes of the fourteenth and fifteenth centuries: as late as 1512 Pope Julius II issued a crusade indulgence to the English army setting out to fight the French.[4] The powers against whom these crusades were launched were very varied. They included Aragonese kings, German emperors, English rebel barons, French mercenary companies, and, during the Great Schism, rival popes. This book does not aim to encompass all these crusades; if it did, it would be at least double its present length. Nor does it deal with all the crusades planned or declared against Christian lay powers in the ninety years studied. The short-lived crusade of 1265 against the rebellious English nobles, for instance, is mentioned only in passing. I have concentrated on the series of crusades waged by the papal Curia in conjunction with the Angevin kings of Sicily and Naples and the other Guelf powers in Italy, notably Florence. There are several good reasons for narrowing the range to the period 1254–1343. First, as will become obvious in the first chapter, it is very rich in crusades against Christian rulers. Secondly, the crusades declared in support of the Guelf cause, particularly on behalf of its cornerstone, the papal–Angevin alliance, possess a unity and continuity denied to others, either within the same period or outside it. The principles of Guelfism influenced the way they were represented by the popes, while the resources of the exponents of the *parte guelfa* dictated the military and financial nature of the crusades. On the other hand, the crusades in Italy can be considered as broadly representative of the crusades against Christian lay powers. Because most of the papacy's lands and

---

[2] See *Patrologiae cursus completus. Series latina*, comp. J. P. Migne, ccxiv, no. 221, cols. 780–2; E. Kennan, 'Innocent III and the First Political Crusade: a Comment on the Limitations of Papal Power', *Traditio*, xxvii (1971), *passim*. This is the first such crusade for which there is convincing documentary evidence. For a possible twelfth-century precedent, see D. P. Waley, 'Papal Armies in the Thirteenth Century', *EHR*, lxxii (1957), 25.

[3] Not five, as stated by Kennan, 'Innocent III', p. 231.

[4] See *Calendar of State Papers and Manuscripts relating to English Affairs existing in the Archives and Collections of Venice and in other Libraries of Northern Italy (1202–1558)*, ed. R. Brown, ii, no. 169; J. J. Scarisbrick, *Henry VIII*, p. 29.

rights lay in Italy, most of the crusades either took place in the peninsula or, like those against Frederick II in Germany and Peter II in Aragon, were directed against rulers who were actively pursuing political goals there.

The crusades against Christian rulers form one of the most neglected aspects of the history of the crusading movement. During the first great period of scholarly research on the crusades, which lasted from the 1840s to the First World War and witnessed a proliferation of works of seminal importance, the only book which dealt with them was Henri Pissard's *La Guerre sainte en pays chrétien*, a cursory and disappointing study of their juristic origin and development which appeared in 1912. Since then the situation has improved only slightly, despite suggestions in 1963 and 1977 that more work should be done on the subject.[5] Individual crusades, such as those against Markward of Anweiler, the Staufen, and the Aragonese, have been described, but in brief and generally unsatisfactory form.[6] There is still no detailed study of these crusades in any language, no analysis of how they were justified, preached, organized, and financed, what response they achieved or how they were regarded by contemporaries.

This startling lacuna has to be explained largely in terms of prejudice. Crusade historiography has traditionally centred on the crusades to the Holy Land. Crusades which occurred elsewhere have been considered as at best curious anomalies, at worst the misuse of a spiritual weapon for political ends. The crusades against Christian lay powers, many of whom were not even accused of heresy, have been regarded as the outstanding example of such misuse, and distaste has bred neglect. In a sense, it is a great tribute to the effectiveness of the propaganda of the papacy's enemies that hundreds of years after they first attacked the crusades against them as an unscrupulous perversion of the crusade ideal, this approach is still adhered to by most historians. Thus the German scholar Adolf Gottlob wrote of the 'political derailment of the crusade indulgence', and, in a

---

[5] See J. A. Brundage, 'Recent Crusade Historiography: some Observations and Suggestions', *Catholic Historical Review*, xlix (1964), 506; F. Cardini, 'La crociata nel Duecento. L' "Avatāra" di un ideale', *Archivio storico italiano*, cxxxv (1977), 130.

[6] See J. R. Strayer, 'The Political Crusades of the Thirteenth Century', in Setton (ed.), *History of the Crusades*, ii; *id.*, 'The Crusade against Aragon', *Speculum*, xxviii (1953); Kennan, 'Innocent III'.

short article characteristically entitled 'Les Déviations de la Croisade', Pierre Toubert attacked the crusades against Christian rulers as 'the degradation of the crusade', and the 'degeneration of the institution', and considered them to be 'a complete politicisation' of the crusading movement.[7] Steven Runciman wrote that as a result of the crusades against the Greeks, the Cathars, and finally the Staufen and their successors, 'the Holy War was warped to become a tragic farce'.[8] The moralization implicit in this approach has recently been challenged by Maureen Purcell, who saw the crusades against the papacy's political enemies as only the expansion and exploitation by a hard-pressed Curia of an inherent dichotomy in the crusade movement, 'a real stress between crusade seen in terms of the immediate Christian objective, and crusade accommodated to a longer, more complex view of the Christian economy of salvation'.[9] There remains in Purcell's own approach a deep-seated grain of dissatisfaction with crusades against Christians which reflects the older attitudes even though cloaked in a historicist treatment of events. But her book is at least a sign of a new open-mindedness, for since 1945 historians have increasingly perceived the inadequacy of defining the crusade in terms of its geographical objective. If the meaning of the word 'crusade' has become open to question and the concept of crusading itself is disconcertingly confused, these trends have at least made possible a more dispassionate portrayal of crusades taking place outside the Holy Land.[10]

The crusades against Christian lay powers have, indeed, never been without their defenders. At the end of the nineteenth century Edouard Jordan wrote that Pope Clement IV's insistent presentation of the crusade against Manfred as a mere preface to a crusade to Latin Syria was sincere and was reflected in papal policy, while Élie Berger defended the legitimacy of the

---

[7] A. Gottlob, *Kreuzablass und Almosenablass. Eine Studie über die Frühzeit des Ablasswesens*, p. 165; 'Les Déviations de la Croisade au milieu du xiiie siècle: Alexandre IV contre Manfred', ed. P. Toubert, *Le Moyen Âge*, lxix (1963), 392, 395–6.

[8] S. Runciman, *A History of the Crusades*, iii. 471–2.

[9] M. Purcell, *Papal Crusading Policy. The Chief Instruments of Papal Crusading Policy and Crusade to the Holy Land from the Final Loss of Jerusalem to the Fall of Acre, 1244–1291*, p. 4. See also pp. 19 ff., 69–86, 97–8, for treatment of crusades against Christian lay powers.

[10] On the definition of the crusade, see H. E. Mayer, *The Crusades*, pp. 281–6; J. S. C. Riley-Smith, *What were the Crusades?*, *passim*; Mayer, review of *What were the Crusades?*, *Speculum*, liii (1978), 841–2.

crusade against Frederick II and the very heavy taxation associated with it in terms of the threat which the Emperor was
believed to pose to the Church.[11] It is significant that both
these men had edited the registers of thirteenth-century popes
(Clement IV and Innocent IV), and had therefore had a
chance to examine the justification of the crusades *in extenso*. In
the early 1920s the German historian Paulus also argued for a
more sympathetic approach to these crusades.[12] These tentative attempts at reinstatement were, however, handicapped by
the idea that the crusades against the pope's political enemies
were diversions of the crusade and had to be defended. Such an
approach was attacked with vigour by Carl Erdmann in his
great study of the origins of the crusading idea, which appeared
in 1935. Erdmann claimed that the concept of a holy war
against enemies within the Church, not only heretics but also
excommunicates and rebels, developed before that of a holy war
against pagans. He also maintained that it was the holy war
which, in the hands of the Reform papacy, and in particular
Gregory VII and Urban II, was transformed into the crusade.
Consequently Erdmann concluded that although the crusades
against Christian lay powers followed the first crusades against
pagans chronologically, they preceded them in the development of curialist thinking on violence; they could not be considered as diversions or aberrations of the crusade ideal, for 'the
"aberrations" had long been there, and the "genuine" crusade
proceeded from them far more than from a supposed change in
the condition of pilgrims and of the city of Jerusalem'.[13]
Erdmann's own approach has been criticized for undervaluing
the importance of factors other than the holy war in the genesis
of the crusade movement.[14] Perhaps as a consequence, neither
his comments on the crusades against Christian lay rulers nor
the sympathetic treatments of his predecessors have been ex-

[11] See E. Jordan, 'Notes sur le formulaire de Richard de Pofi', in *Études d'histoire du
Moyen Âge dédiées à G. Monod*, pp. 332–3; É. Berger, *Saint Louis et Innocent IV. Étude sur les
rapports de la France et du Saint-Siège*, pp. 3, 237, 267, 297. On the threat posed by Frederick
II, see R. Brentano, *Rome before Avignon. A Social History of Thirteenth-Century Rome*, p. 167;
G. Digard, *Philippe le Bel et le Saint-Siège de 1285 à 1304*, i. xxiii; Waley, 'Papal Armies', pp.
25–6.
[12] N. Paulus, *Geschichte des Ablasses im Mittelalter vom Ursprunge bis zur Mitte des 14.
Jahrhunderts*, ii. 29–30.
[13] C. Erdmann, *The Origin of the Idea of Crusade*, p. xxxiii, and cf. p. 265.
[14] See Erdmann, *Origin*, pp. xxi–xxx.

panded into a thoroughgoing analysis of such crusades. Nevertheless, Erdmann's claim that the crusades against the internal enemies of the Church had a respectable juridical lineage has never been refuted; indeed, Jonathan Riley-Smith has recently stressed that they were a logical and coherent extension of the papacy's interpretation of the crusade movement generally.[15]

Curiously, although these crusades have attracted very little notice in themselves, their importance has always been recognized. Attention has been fixed, however, not on their justification and their operation as crusades, but on their results, which have been described with regularity as being entirely detrimental both to the papacy and to the crusading movement. In general, critics have made four accusations. First, it has been asserted that the employment of a spiritual weapon in defence of political holdings or claims aroused a storm of indignation from contemporaries,[16] diminished the papacy's authority and popularity, and greatly impaired its ability to act out its role as spiritual leader of Christendom. As Kennan wrote of Innocent III,

He committed the last and most powerful instrument of spiritual leadership to destroy a political enemy . . . The popes . . . attracted to themselves dangerous enmity and excoriating scorn for perverting their spiritual trust. Ultimately disgust at political diversion of the crusade contributed to that contempt for papal spirituality which proved so nearly fatal in the fourteenth century.[17]

Palmer Throop too wrote of 'the decaying prestige of a papacy too inclined to use spiritual weapons for apparently secular aims',[18] and Runciman even claimed that the Sicilian Vespers constituted 'the ruin of the Hildebrandine Papacy'.[19]

---

[15] See *What were the Crusades?*, pp. 27–8.

[16] Runciman writes of 'constant and vociferous criticism'. See his 'The Decline of the Crusading Idea', in *Relazioni del X Congresso internazionale di Scienze storiche. Storia del medioevo, iii*, p. 645.

[17] 'Innocent III', p. 231.

[18] P. A. Throop, *Criticism of the Crusade: a Study of Public Opinion and Crusade Propaganda*, p. 49.

[19] *The Sicilian Vespers. A History of the Mediterranean World in the Later Thirteenth Century*, p. 286. For similar comments see e.g. W. Ullmann, *A Short History of the Papacy in the Middle Ages*, pp. 261–3; J. K. Hyde, *Society and Politics in Medieval Italy. The Evolution of the Civil Life, 1000–1350*, p. 125; G. Leff, *Heresy in the Later Middle Ages. The Relation of Heterodoxy to Dissent c. 1250–c. 1450*, i. 23–4.

Obviously this argument is valid only if it can be shown that public opinion was uniformly or at least overwhelmingly hostile to the use of the crusade against Christian lay powers. Joseph Strayer was doubtful if this could be proved, and he narrowed his criticism of the crusades to the claim that it was papal taxation for the crusades, and not the crusades themselves, which did the most harm to the prestige and authority of the Holy See. Not only did clerical opposition to the taxes levied by the popes weaken the internal solidarity of the Church, but the continual granting of clerical tenths to secular powers which supported the papacy in the crusades undermined the Curia's relationship with these powers and facilitated the growth of lay control over the Church. The conflict between Pope Boniface VIII and Philip IV of France which this brought about resulted in the disaster of Anagni and the exile of the papacy at Avignon.[20] A slightly different interpretation of events was put forward by the distinguished English historian, F.M. Powicke, who wrote that the taxation of the Church by the popes for purposes which were patently temporal simply provided a precedent which was followed by the secular powers.[21]

The third common criticism rests on the connection between the crusades in Italy and the collapse of the Christian states in Palestine and Syria at the end of the thirteenth century. It has been argued that the papal Curia continually diverted crusade resources, at a time when they were desperately needed in the East, in order to fight its wars in Italy. Vows taken to crusade in the Latin East were commuted so that the *crucesignati* fought in Italy instead, and clerical tenths, alms, and legacies collected on the pretext of a crusade to the Holy Land were spent on the Italian crusades. The belief, implicit in these actions and explicitly stated by the popes, that the wars in Italy were more important than the defence of the Holy Places or the fate of the Christians in the East, is said to have aroused furious public hostility. In the course of a recent attempt to analyse popular reactions to the fall of Acre in 1291 the Swiss historian Stickel

---

[20] See 'Political Crusades', pp. 373–5, and 'The Crusade against Aragon', p. 113. For Strayer's views, see also 'The First Western Union', in his *Medieval Statecraft and the Perspectives of History. Essays*, ed. J. F. Benton and T. N. Bisson, pp. 336–8, 340, and his *The Albigensian Crusades*, pp. 43 ff.

[21] See 'Pope Boniface VIII', in his *The Christian Life in the Middle Ages*, p. 61. Cf. T. S. R. Boase, *Boniface VIII*, p. 141.

stated that 'anybody who still cherished the battle for the Holy Land and the fight against Islam in his heart must have regarded the use of the sign of the cross in a war against Christians as the prostitution of a holy object.'[22]

The fourth accusation commonly made against the crusades also relates to the crusading movement generally. The crusades in Italy are said to have been one of the factors which led to a decline in crusade enthusiasm in Western Europe after about 1250.[23] Several reasons have been adduced for this connection. The scandal of Christians taking the cross to kill other Christians led, it has been claimed, to disillusionment with crusading and to a growing disbelief in the efficacy of the indulgence.[24] The Christian conscience, aroused by bad news from the Latin East and by papal crusade bulls on behalf of the Holy Land, was continually paralysed in practice by postponements of the crusade to the East in order that the Curia could concentrate on some new development in Italy. Thus scepticism grew and fewer people responded with sincerity to the call to crusade.[25] The French monarchy, moreover, was numbed and humiliated by the failure of the crusade against Aragon in 1285, and abandoned under Philip IV its traditional interest in the crusades.[26]

These are serious criticisms and they relate to some of the most important problems of late medieval history: why the Christian West failed to hold or to recover the Holy Land; why the papacy was unable to maintain its prestige among the European monarchies or its position as acknowledged arbiter of Christendom; why the secular powers of Western Europe were increasingly able to assert their grip on the revenues of their churches, to the detriment of the papacy. It is all the more important, therefore, that they should be considered in the context of a detailed examination of the crusades against Christian lay powers and of contemporary reaction to them. It should be stressed that in order to undertake such an examina-

---

[22] E. Stickel, *Der Fall von Akkon. Untersuchungen zum Abklingen des Kreuzzugsgedankens am Ende des 13. Jahrhunderts*, p. 185. Cf. Throop, *Criticism*, p. 284.
[23] See, e. g., Runciman, 'Decline', pp. 644 ff.
[24] See, e.g., Cardini, 'La crociata', pp. 130, 139.
[25] Cf. 'Les Déviations', p. 391.
[26] See Strayer, 'Political Crusades', p. 375.

tion one does not have to become an apologist for the papacy or the *parte guelfa*. While the papal approach to the crusades will be described at length, it will, I hope, be balanced by a fair representation of the viewpoint of the enemies of the Curia as well as that of powers with interests in the Latin East who felt and argued that these interests were being sacrificed to the needs of the pope or his allies. In the end, the judgement of the issue must be left in the hands of contemporaries. Did they take the cross to fight in these crusades, did they attack the Curia and its officials, did they manifestly lose faith in the power of the indulgence and the spiritual authority of the Holy See?

First then, it is necessary to understand how the papacy represented its crusades against Christian rulers and what arguments it used to rouse the Christian Republic. After a chapter establishing the chronology of the crusades between 1254 and 1343, these arguments will be set out in chapter 2. The Latin East played a large part in these arguments, and there was a sharp and unavoidable collision of interests between the two fields of crusading activity; consequently the chapter on justification will be followed by a consideration of how papal policy reacted to the various pressures applied to it. Chapter 4, on the preaching of the crusades, will show where, how, and by whom the preaching was carried out, what privileges and obligations were enjoyed and incurred by the *crucesignati*, and what efforts were made by the papal Curia to organize those who took the cross so that their contribution could be most effective. It is followed by a chapter which uses the available evidence in contemporary chronicles to evaluate the effect of the preaching and to describe the peculiar ethos which distinguished the crusade armies in the field. The final two chapters deal with the financial burdens imposed by the crusades on the European clergy, the problems and consequences of taxation, and the collection and mobilization of the crusade funds to finance the crusade armies. An attempt will also be made to assess the influence of the measures taken to finance the crusades on the development of papal financial policy generally.

ii. THE SOURCES

By far the most important source for the crusades against

Christian lay powers is the papal registers.[27] The registers contain substantial lacunae, partly because of losses suffered by the Vatican Archives and partly because many bulls were not inscribed in the first place. The letters of Martin IV and Clement V incurred exceptional losses, but other pontificates were affected. To give one example, ninety-seven letters dispatched by Clement IV to Simon of Brie during his legation in France escaped registration at the chancery; as they do not reflect well on the pope or his office it is possible that the omission was deliberate. Only the fortuitous survival into the eighteenth century of copies of these letters allows us to reconstruct the details of Simon's troubled legation, in particular the enormous problems faced by the Curia in financing Charles of Anjou's invasion of the Kingdom of Sicily in 1265–6.[28]

For all their faults, the registers present an incomparable picture of papal government at work. The letters in the registers not only display the official papal viewpoint on the crusades, their justification and defence; they also contain the numerous mandates and directions, diplomatic, financial, and military, which were necessary for their organizaton. The registers of the thirteenth-century popes and of Benedict XI, Clement V, and Benedict XII have now been published in full or in calendared form by the French School at Rome or, in the case of Clement V, by the Benedictines.[29] Unfortunately, many of the bulls for the crusades against Christian lay powers were only calendared. In these cases I have consulted and cite the original registers. The French School has not, moreover, completed its publication of the registers of John XXII (1316–34), one of the most important popes in the history of the crusades against Christian rulers. Mollat completed the enormous undertaking of calendaring all his *lettres communes* and Coulon and Clémencet published his secret and curial letters on French affairs (which include some Angevin material because they cover Provence),

[27] See W. Ullmann, *Law and Politics in the Middle Ages. An Introduction to the Sources of Medieval Political Ideas*, pp. 148–9; L. E. Boyle, *A Survey of the Vatican Archives and of its Medieval Holdings*, pp. 103–13.

[28] See the comments of J. Guiraud and E. Jordan in their editions of the registers of Urban IV, iv.3, and Clement IV, i. 445–6. See also below, pp. 15, 26, 31.

[29] On the French School publications, see R. Fawtier, 'Un Grand Achèvement de l'École française de Rome. La publication des registres des papes du xiiie siècle', *Mélanges*, lxxii (1960), *passim*.

but the unpublished body of letters is still vast, extending to many of the letters on the crusades, crusade taxation, and Italian affairs generally. When these letters have not been published or adequately calendared by scholars such as Theiner, Schwalm, Riezler, or Bliss, or the various compilers of the *Annales ecclesiastici*, it has been necessary to refer to the registers themselves, volumes 109–17 of the Vatican series in the Vatican Archives.

The Vatican Archives contain other documentary sources which are valuable for the study of the Italian crusades. Various volumes in the series *Introitus et exitus* record the expenditure by the authorities of the Papal State on the crusades of the 1320s, and many notarial acts testifying to the preaching of the crusade have survived in the series *Instrumenta miscellanea* and *Archivum arcis*. From the 1280s onwards the records of the central fiscal administration of the Holy See, the *camera*, become more abundant and give a fairly detailed picture of the financial aspects of the crusades. The submitted accounts (*rationes*) of papal collectors from the time of Gregory X onwards illustrate the organization of crusade taxation and, to some extent, the problems and obstacles encountered by the collectors. Many of these, particularly in the case of the Italian collectorates, have been published, as have many of the documents relating to papal income and expenditure in the reigns of John XXII and Benedict XII.[30]

Until 1943 the archives of the Angevin kings at Naples formed a collection of documents as wide-ranging and rich in detail as those of their papal lords. But on 30 September of that year the entire collection of 378 registers, 332 of which covered the reigns of the first three Angevin kings, was destroyed by German troops.[31] From the point of view of the reconstruction

---

[30] See, e.g., the series of accounts of the Italian collectors published as *Rationes decimarum Italiae* in *Studi e testi*, nos. 58, 60, 69, 84, 96–8, 112–13, 128, 148, 161–2. Lombardy and Piedmont have unfortunately not been covered by this series. For cameral records generally, see *Les Archives de la Chambre apostolique au xive siècle*, ed. J. De Loye.

[31] There is an account of the disaster in 'Documents from the Angevin Registers of Naples: Charles I', ed. E. M. Jamison, *Papers of the British School at Rome*, xvii (1949), 87–9. For the surviving holdings of the Archivio di Stato, Naples, on the Angevin period, see J. Mazzoleni, *Le fonti documentarie e bibliografiche dal secolo x al secolo xx conservate presso l'Archivio di Stato di Napoli*, pp. 31–52.

of the economic and social history of the *Regno* the loss of the registers represents an insuperable obstacle. For the study of the Angevin contribution to the crusades, however, the difficulties are much less grave. The majority of the documents relating to the crusades or to papal–Angevin affairs generally had been transcribed before the disaster either to make up published collections of documents (*codici diplomatici*), or for use in books and articles on analogous subjects. A stay of some weeks at Naples in the winter of 1976–7 resulted in the discovery of only a few transcriptions which had not been so used. For the period 1265–81 and 1285–90 scholars of Angevin affairs now possess the magnificent reconstruction of the registers by Riccardo Filangieri and the Neapolitan archivists.[32] For the period not yet reached by the *ricostruzione* I have used a wide range of *codici* and secondary works.[33]

Documents issued by other governments and individuals involved in the crusades in Italy are mainly available in published form. The *Layettes du trésor des chartes* and volumes xxi–xxii of the *Recueil des historiens des Gaules et de la France* contain many relevant French records. Most of the documents for the involvement of the English crown are contained in Rymer's *Foedera*, those for Germany and the empire generally in the volumes of *Constitutiones* of the *Monumenta Germaniae historica*. Interesting documents from Florence are printed in Ficker's *Urkunden*. The *Acta aragonensia* of Heinrich Finke is a valuable source for the period 1290–1327, not only for the Aragonese documents which it contains, but also for the reports of Aragonese proctors at the Roman Curia. If not always entirely objective in their assessment of current events, these reports give a clear and powerful impression of the political pressures under which the popes worked and of the factions within the college of cardinals.

The period 1254–1343 is an extremely rich, if somewhat uneven one for narrative sources. Matthew Paris, Salimbene de

---

[32] See *RCAR*, i–xxv, xxviii–xxx. See also reviews by J. Longnon in *Journal des savants*, 1959, 1970, 1974.

[33] For bibliographies on the Angevins, see G. M. Monti, 'Gli angioini di Napoli negli studi dell'ultimo cinquantennio', in his *Nuovi studi angioini, passim*; Mazzoleni, *Fonti documentarie*, pp. 53–8; P. Herde, 'Carlo I d'Angiò', in *Dizionario biografico degli Italiani*, 20, pp. 224–6; A. Nitschke, 'Carlo II d'Angiò', ibid., p. 235; C. De Frede, 'Da Carlo I d'Angiò a Giovanna I (1263–1382)', in E. Pontieri *et al.* (eds.), *Storia di Napoli iii: Napoli angioina*, pp. 325–32.

Adam, and Giovanni Villani, for example, all wrote about part of the period at least. There was much to attract them in the crusades which the popes were waging in Italy and they described the principal events with zest and colour. But they are often disappointing on the finer details, in particular the results of the crusade preaching. It has also to be borne in mind throughout that most of the chroniclers were partisan. This presents few problems with fanatical Guelfs like Andrew of Hungary, the title of whose work, 'A description of the victory which the Roman church enjoyed by the arm of the magnificent Lord Charles, most victorious King of Sicily', will lead no one to expect impartiality. Similarly, it is clear that Matthew Paris's complaints about papal exactions in England were the product of a strong personal prejudice. But, as Carlo Merkel revealed in his important essay on the chroniclers' treatment of Charles of Anjou's expedition of 1265–6, while most chroniclers displayed their feelings in less direct fashion, they nearly all had political affiliations of some kind, with the result that the narrative sources are less useful as an index of popular opinion than one might expect or hope. Although I have attempted to read all the relevant chronicles, I have relied on them as little as possible; I have also tried to indicate the political bias involved if it has bearing on the validity of the text as historical evidence.

A final important source for the crusades in Italy is the crusade memoirs and projects of the period. Although they deal primarily with the problems of organizing a crusade to the Latin East, the 'Directorium ad passagium faciendum',[34] Peter Dubois's *De recuperatione terre sancte* and Marino Sanudo Torsello's 'Liber secretorum fidelium crucis' all throw light on various aspects of papal thought about the crusade movement in general as well as reflecting the views of some contemporaries on the Italian wars and their wider significance. The ideas and opinions expressed in Marino Sanudo's memoir were expanded in detail in his letters, a surprising number of which have survived, forming a vivid commentary on the clash of interests

---

[34] The authorship of the 'Directorium' is currently in dispute. See D. Geanakoplos, 'Byzantium and the Crusades, 1261–1354', in Setton (ed.), *History of the Crusades*, iii, pp. 52–3.

which developed between Pope John XXII's Italian crusades
and the need for a crusade to defend the Latin East.[35]

[35] For the letters, see *Gesta Dei per Francos, sive orientalium expeditionum et regni Francorum Hierosolymitani historia*, ed. J. Bongars, ii. 289–316; 'Studien über Marino Sanudo den älteren mit einem Anhange seiner ungedruckten Briefe', ed. F. Kunstmann, *Abhandlungen der historischen Classe der Königlich bayerischen Akademie der Wissenschaften*, vii (1855); 'Lettres inédites et mémoires de Marino Sanudo l'ancien (1334–1337)', ed. C. De la Roncière and L. Dorez, *Bibliothèque de l'École des chartes*, lvi (1895); 'Nuove lettere di Marino Sanudo il vecchio', ed. A. Cerlini, *La Bibliofilia*, xlii (1940). The most important is the long letter to Bertrand du Poujet, written in April 1330 ('Studien über Marino Sanudo', pp. 755–89).

Chapter 1

The Papal–Angevin Alliance and the Italian Crusades

The chronology of the crusades against Christian lay powers in Italy has been approached by many historians with great inexactitude. Thus, crusaders are described as being present at the battle of Montaperti in 1260, whereas there is no evidence for crusade preaching against Manfred between 1256 and 1261. Martin IV is said to have declared a crusade against Peter of Aragon in 1284, whereas he really declared it in 1283. The crusade against the Emperor Louis IV is dated to 1327, whereas it was really declared in 1328.[1] In defence of such errors it must be said that an exact chronology of the crusades is, in some cases, impossible; there are too many omissions from the papal registers, and the chroniclers sometimes describe crusades for which there is no evidence in the documentary sources. A chronological framework of sorts is nevertheless a necessary preliminary to an analysis of the justification and structure of the crusades. Similarly, the crusades cannot be understood outside the context of the political and military situation which led to their use, or of the political alliance of which they were the peculiar instrument and expression.

All the crusades waged in Italy between 1254 and 1343 were concerned to some degree with the establishment and defence of the temporal power of the papacy. With few exceptions, the popes of this period were fully committed to the policy of recuperations laid down by Innocent III at the end of the twelfth century.[2] But within this broad interpretation two well-defined phases are discernible. In the first, which lasted from 1254 to 1302, the Curia was fighting to enforce and then to

---

[1] See Purcell, *Papal Crusading Policy*, p. 81; *Kaiser, Volk und Avignon. Ausgewählte Quellen zur antikurialen Bewegung in Deutschland in der ersten Hälfte des 14. Jahrhunderts*, ed. O. Berthold *et al.*, p. 29; Throop, *Criticism*, p. 282. Other errors can be found in J. Heers, *Parties and Political Life in the Medieval West*, p. 46.

[2] See Ullmann, *Short History*, pp. 208 ff.

maintain its claims to sovereignty in the Papal State and to suzerainty in the Kingdom of Sicily against Manfred and Conradin of Staufen and the Aragonese kings and princes who inherited the Staufen claim to the *Regno*. In the second phase, from 1302 to 1343, the crusades were directed against the Ghibelline revival in central and northern Italy and, although papal claims to sovereignty were still involved, the struggle centred on the connection between Ghibellinism and heresy.

When Conrad IV died in May 1254 a curious hiatus ensued in the life-and-death struggle between the papacy and the Staufen. The crusade against Conrad was not immediately switched to his half-brother Manfred, as it had been to Conrad soon after the death of their father at the end of 1250.[3] Manfred's position in the Kingdom of Sicily was insecure owing to his illegitimacy, and at first there were hopes of a settlement with the Curia, based on the recognition by the Staufen party of papal rule in the kingdom, and on Manfred's tenure of his apanage of Taranto.[4] Negotiations with England on the cession of the *Regno* to Edmund, the younger son of Henry III, were delayed, and Pope Innocent IV refused to commute Henry's vow to crusade in the Holy Land to one of conquering the kingdom in Edmund's name.[5] But in October 1254 Manfred rose in rebellion against Innocent and took refuge at Lucera, the Muslim colony founded by his father in the province of Capitanata. The conflict between the papacy and the Staufen thus entered a new phase, based on Manfred's power and ambitions in southern Italy and beyond.[6]

The first crusade against Manfred was preached early in 1255, at Naples and elsewhere in Italy. An army composed of crusaders and mercenaries, and led by the Florentine Cardinal Octavian degli Ubaldini, marched against Lucera and was

---

[3] Pope Innocent IV, *Registres*, ed. E. Berger, nos. 5031, 5036.

[4] Ibid., nos. 8023–4.

[5] *Foedera, conventiones, litterae, et cuiuscunque generis acta publica, inter reges Angliae et alios quosvis imperatores, reges, pontifices, principes vel communitates*, ed. T. Rymer *et al.*, i, pt. 1, p. 304.

[6] See *Acta imperii inedita seculi xiii. et xiv. Urkunden und Briefe zur Geschichte des Kaiserreichs und des Königreichs Sicilien in den Jahren 1198–1400*, ed. E. Winkelmann, ii, no. 1044 (Manfred's excommunication, March 1255). The best narrative account of the struggle between Manfred and the papacy is Runciman, *The Sicilian Vespers*, pp. 31–95. E. Jordan, *Les Origines de la domination angevine en Italie*, is fundamental.

defeated in the summer.[7] After this initial setback the Curia was unable to hinder Manfred's rise to power, and in August 1258 he was crowned King of Sicily at Palermo. Alexander IV continued to issue indulgences for the war, but his measures lacked the drive and single-mindedness of his great predecessor. The cross was preached in England in the autumn or winter of 1255, and in October 1256 the people of L'Aquila were encouraged to resist Manfred's siege with promises of the crusade indulgence for all who had died, or should die, while defending the city.[8] In May 1261 the cross was preached in the city and diocese of Alatri, in Campagna, again in an attempt to rally local opposition to Manfred and his supporters, and to prevent him enforcing his claim to become Senator of Rome.[9] Alexander's one success was in the March of Treviso, where between 1255 and 1260 a crusade was successfully preached against the Ghibelline tyrants Ezzelino and Alberich of Romano.[10] But the overthrow of the Romano brothers was only achieved at the cost of the aggrandizement of the power in Lombardy of Oberto Pallavicini, another, if less obnoxious, Ghibelline *signore* and vicar of King Manfred.[11]

Alexander's successor, Urban IV, adopted a more vigorous policy towards the threat posed by Manfred; indeed, by the end of 1261 Manfred's incursions into the Papal State, and his alliances with Ghibellines in Tuscany and Lombardy, made a more forceful approach imperative if Guelfism was not to suffer a total eclipse. In July 1263 the Archbishop of Arborea was told to preach the crusade throughout Sardinia to help a Guelf noble

---

[7] Saba Malaspina, 'Rerum sicularum libri sex', *RIS*, viii, cols. 794–6; 'Annales de Burton', ed. H. R. Luard, *Annales Monastici*, Rolls Series xxxvi, i. 352.

[8] *Antiquitates italicae medii aevi, sive dissertationes de moribus, ritibus . . . italici populi post declinationem romani imperii ad annum usque MD*, ed. L. A. Muratori, vi, cols. 516–17. For the preaching in England, see Matthew Paris, *Chronica maiora*, v. 521–2. This must have occurred after the arrival of Rostand in England, about Michaelmas 1255 (see W. Lunt, *Financial Relations of the Papacy with England*, i. 259).

[9] See 'Les Déviations', pp. 397–9 and *passim*.

[10] See *Codice diplomatico eceliniano*, ed. G. Verci, in his *Storia degli Ecelini*, iii, nos. 225, 236–7; Salimbene de Adam, 'Cronica', *MGHS*, xxxii. 364–7; Martino da Canale, 'Cronaca veneta', in *Archivio storico italiano*, viii (1845), 436 ff.; O. W. Canz, *Philipp Fontana, Erzbischof von Ravenna—ein Staatsmann des xiii. Jahrhunderts (1240–1270)*, pp. 59–75; G. Marchetti-Longhi, *Gregorio de Monte Longo patriarca di Aquileja (1251–1269)*, pp. 135–63. Brief account in English in J. K. Hyde, *Padua in the Age of Dante. A Social History of an Italian City-State*, pp. 202–3.

[11] Jordan, *Les Origines*, pp. 131–7.

and his forces to overthrow Manfred's rule there.[12] The following year was a critical one for Urban: Manfred organized an
ambitious threefold campaign in the Papal State with the probable aim of capturing the Pope himself at Orvieto. In March
the papal vicar at Rome, the Bishop of Bethlehem, was told to
preach the cross there to oppose Manfred's ally, Peter di Vico,
and in the summer a crusade was preached in the Papal State
and in the patriarchates of Grado and Aquileia to fight his
lieutenant Percival Doria.[13]

In 1262 and 1263 negotiations had been conducted by
Urban's notary, Albert of Parma, for the transfer of the Sicilian
crown to Charles, Count of Anjou and Provence and youngest
brother of King Louis IX of France.[14] The project was from the
start designated a crusade; even in the abortive negotiations of
1253 it had been agreed that if Charles accepted the papal offer
he and all who came to Italy with him would receive the crusade
indulgence.[15] In the negotiations of 1263 Urban granted
Charles's request that the cross be preached in France,
Provence, the imperial dioceses which lay between France's
eastern border and the Kingdom of Germany, Lombardy,
Tuscany, and the Papal State.[16] Simon of Brie, Cardinal-priest
of St. Cecilia, was sent to France as papal legate in May 1264 to
conclude the negotiations with Charles and was told to organize
this preaching. Pope Clement IV renewed Simon's commission
at his accession in 1265, and as late as November 1265 he issued
a very detailed crusade bull to the legate and to the French
secular clergy and Orders of friars.[17] He also sent Geoffrey of
Beaumont, papal chaplain and Chancellor of Bayeux, to preach
the crusade in Lombardy, and decreed preaching in the March
of Ancona and the patriarchate of Grado.[18] The Angevin army

[12] Pope Urban IV, *Registres*, ed. J. Guiraud, no. 321; Jordan, *Les Origines*, pp. 142–3, 456.
[13] Urban IV, *Reg.*, nos. 633, 778, 860, 870, 2991. See also K. Hampe, *Urban IV. und Manfred (1261–1264)*, pp. 44–61; D. P. Waley, *The Papal State in the Thirteenth Century*, pp. 172–3.
[14] Full account in Jordan, *Les Origines*, pp. 370 ff.
[15] Innocent IV, *Reg.*, nos. 6812–14.
[16] *Thesaurus novus anecdotorum*, ed. E. Martène and U. Durand, ii, cols. 21–2.
[17] *Thes. novus*, ii, cols. 70–2, 113, 196–9 (only the first part of the bull; the rest was published by R. Sternfeld in *Ludwigs des Heiligen Kreuzzug nach Tunis 1270 und die Politik Karls I. von Sizilien*, pp. 318–20); Pope Clement IV, *Registres*, ed. E. Jordan, no. 240.
[18] Ibid., nos. 161, 168, 1751.

set out from Lyons in October 1265 to march to Rome. It recruited substantial Guelf contingents *en route* and joined Charles of Anjou in Rome about 15 January 1266, a few days after his coronation as King of Sicily in St. Peter's. Desperately short of money, Charles began the invasion at once, and was fortunate enough both to defeat and kill his rival at the battle of Benevento on 26 February. News of the victory was either slow to reach Clement at Perugia, or reached him in a garbled form, for on 5 March the Pope issued a last crusade bull against Manfred, sending it to the Cardinal-bishop of Albano, his legate in the Kingdom of Sicily.[19] It was not needed: opposition to Charles collapsed after Benevento and the whole kingdom was soon under Angevin control.

The dramatic attempt by Conrad IV's young son, Conradin, to regain control of the *Regno* in 1267–8 led to a brief crusade against him. In April 1268, when he was making his descent through central Italy, Clement IV ordered the Franciscan guardian at Perugia to preach the cross against him in the diocese; similar mandates were sent to other ecclesiastical authorities, and crusading forces opposed Conradin's troops and supporters in Tuscany and, possibly, Sicily.[20] In February 1268 Rudolf of Albano was told to preach the cross against the Muslims of Lucera and their 'false Christian' allies, who had rebelled against Charles I and were being besieged at Lucera by an Angevin army.[21] Conradin was defeated at the battle of Tagliacozzo in August 1268 and captured soon after. He was executed at Naples in October, but the garrison at Lucera held out until August 1269, when it was forced by starvation to surrender. The fall of Lucera brought to an end almost thirty years of crusades against the Staufen and their supporters.

Relations between Charles I and the popes in the 1270s were marked by disputes and disillusionment. The price to be paid for the release of the papacy from the threat of Staufen domination was a preponderant Franco–Angevin influence at the

---

[19] Ibid., no. 297.

[20] See *Regesta pontificum romanorum inde ab anno post Christum natum 1198 ad annum 1304*, ed. A. Potthast, ii, no. 20318; *Thes. novus*, ii, col. 532; Giovanni Villani, *Cronica*, i. 350. For Conradin's expedition, see K. Hampe, *Geschichte Konradins von Hohenstaufen*, pp. 169–295.

[21] *Thes. novus*, ii, cols. 575–6.

Curia.[22] In February 1281 Charles I's machinations resulted in the election of a fervent French patriot and Angevin supporter, Simon of Brie, as Pope Martin IV. It was this rather unimpressive pontiff who had to deal with the Sicilian revolt against Angevin rule in March 1282 and the Aragonese intervention which followed.[23] It has been claimed that Martin's response was more violent than was necessary for the maintenance of papal power in Italy, especially since the revolt did not pose a threat to the Papal State itself, and that a reduction in the strength of a dangerously ambitious and domineering vassal had its advantages for the Curia.[24] But Martin's policy owed less to his undoubted loyalty to Charles I than to the belief, prevalent at the Curia, that papal suzerainty in the *Regno* was a *sine qua non* of the effective functioning of papal authority throughout Europe. Moreover, the Pope's actions reveal an approach based, at least at first, on caution and moderation. The documentary evidence suggests that Martin did not declare a crusade against the Sicilians until 13 January 1283, some months after Peter II of Aragon greatly increased the seriousness of the revolt by assuming its leadership and committing the substantial resources of the Aragonese crown to the enforcement of his claim to the kingdom.[25] The bull of 1283 was also restricted to the Kingdom of Sicily, where the crusade was to be preached by the papal legate, Gerard Bianchi, Cardinal-bishop of Sabina.[26] It was not until April 1284, two years after the outbreak of the rebellion, that the crusade was extended to northern Italy, and even then, curiously, most of the Papal State appears to have been excluded.[27] According to Salimbene de Adam there was no actual preaching because of

[22] But see Waley, *Papal State*, pp. 174–5.

[23] See Runciman, *The Sicilian Vespers*, pp. 214 ff.

[24] See Strayer, 'Political Crusades', pp. 370–1.

[25] For the Aragonese intervention and its background, see J. N. Hillgarth, *The Spanish Kingdoms 1250–1516. Volume I. 1250–1410. Precarious Balance*, pp. 233–86.

[26] Pope Martin IV, *Registres*, ed. F. Olivier-Martin *et al.*, no. 301. According to Bartholomew of Neocastro, who was present, there were crusaders at the siege of Messina in 1282. See his 'Historia sicula', *RISNS*, xiii³, p. 27.

[27] The crusade was to be preached by the Cardinal-bishop of Porto in his legatine area, which covered Italy north of the Papal State, together with the province of Romagna. Preaching was extended to Sardinia and Corsica in June 1284. See Martin IV, *Reg.*, nos. 570, 591.

the deaths, early in 1285, of both Martin IV and Charles I.[28] A bull authorizing crusade preaching in France, in connection with the transmission of the Kingdom of Aragon to Charles of Valois, was also issued in the early months of 1284.[29]

From the beginning the crusade against the Sicilians and the Aragonese was dogged by failure. The Catalan chronicler Raymond Muntaner commented that the Angevins and their French mercenaries and supporters were defeated in every engagement.[30] The Aragonese crossed the Messina straits and advanced into Calabria in the spring of 1283; their brilliant admiral, Roger of Lluria, inflicted continual defeats on the Angevins at sea. In June 1284 Charles of Salerno, the heir to the throne, was captured in a sea battle off Naples, and in January 1285 Charles I died at Foggia. Nor were the French any more successful in their attempt to win the Aragonese crown for Charles of Valois. Philip III's invasion of Aragon in 1285 was a humiliating failure.[31] Nevertheless, crusade preaching and recruitment continued through what were, for the Angevin monarchy, the darkest years of the war, when Charles of Salerno was in captivity in Catalonia and the co-regents, Robert of Artois and Gerard Bianchi, continued to suffer defeats in Sicily and southern Italy. Crusaders were thus present at the invasion of Sicily in 1287 and at the relief of Gaeta in August 1289.[32] Crusade preaching against Aragon was also continued in France in 1286, probably as a defensive measure against Aragonese attacks.[33] There is, however, no extant crusade bull against the Sicilians or the Aragonese, to my knowledge, between June 1284 and August 1290, when Pope Nicholas IV promised the Bishop, clergy, and people of Gaeta that if their town was again besieged by James of Aragon and they resisted the attack with determination, they would receive the crusade indulgence.[34] In May 1291 Nicholas renewed

---

[28] 'Cronica', p. 564.

[29] See C. V. Langlois, *Le Règne de Philippe III le Hardi*, pp. 151–2, 448.

[30] *Chronicle*, i.294.

[31] See M. Amari, *La guerra del Vespro siciliano*, i, pp. 291–404; Strayer, 'The Crusade against Aragon', *passim*; A. Lecoy de la Marche, 'L'Expédition de Philippe le Hardi en Catalogne', *Revue des questions historiques*, xlix (1891), *passim*; Langlois, *Le Règne de Philippe III*, pp. 154–65.

[32] See Bartholomew of Neocastro, 'Historia sicula', pp. 86, 109. See ibid., p. 78, for the use of the crusade indulgence in 1286.

[33] Pope Honorius IV, *Registres*, ed. M. Prou, Introduction, pp. lvii–lviii.

[34] Pope Nicholas IV, *Registres*, ed. E. Langlois, no. 3017. See also ibid., no. 4711.

crusade preaching throughout the Kingdom of Sicily, copying Martin IV's bull of 1283, with the necessary alterations of names.[35]

The death of Nicholas IV in April 1292 led to a papal vacancy of two years, during which there are signs of a crisis in the Curia's commitment to the war. It was now a decade old. The Siculo–Catalan advance in Calabria had been held at a defensive line on the frontier of the Principato, but the military position of the Angevin monarchy was still poor, its revenues depleted, and its morale low.[36] King Charles II, who had been released from prison in 1288 and crowned by Nicholas IV in 1289, was prepared to abandon Sicily, at least for the rest of his own lifetime, in order to secure the mainland provinces of his kingdom and to concentrate on other political objectives, in particular the negotiation of an Angevin succession to the Hungarian throne. Many of the cardinals had doubts about the wisdom of continuing the war at a time of disasters in Latin Syria. Fortunately for the papal–Angevin alliance, the ruling family of Aragon also wanted to end a war which was unpopular with the Aragonese nobility, and both Alfonso III and James II negotiated willingly with Charles II for an Aragonese withdrawal from the struggle. The central decade of the war (1286–95) produced more treaties than battles, and was distinguished by diplomatic bargaining of great complexity.[37]

With the election of Boniface VIII in December 1294 the war entered its last phase. Boniface's election represented the success of the pro-Angevin war-party at the Curia; from this point onwards the driving force behind the war was the new pope's rigid determination to recover Sicily. In the summer of 1295 he achieved the diplomatic coup of realigning James II on the papal–Angevin side. By the terms of the treaty of Anagni, James

---

[35] Ibid., no. 6702.

[36] The best account of the war is still Amari, *La guerra*, but it should be supplemented by the work of E. Pontieri, 'Un capitano della guerra del Vespro: Pietro (II) Ruffo di Calabria', *Archivio storico per la Calabria e la Lucania*, i (1931), *passim*; and C. Carucci, 'Le operazioni militari in Calabria nella guerra del Vespro siciliano', *Archivio storico per la Calabria e la Lucania*, ii (1932), *passim*; and *Codice diplomatico salernitano del secolo xiii*, ii, *passim*.

[37] See Digard, *Philippe le Bel*, i.20–221; L. Klüpfel, *Die äussere Politik Alfonsos III. von Aragonien (1285–1291)*, *passim*; H. E. Rohde, *Der Kampf um Sizilien in den Jahren 1291–1302*, *passim*.

agreed to withdraw Aragonese troops from Sicily. Negotiations with James's younger brother Frederick, his governor in Sicily, were less successful. Frederick assumed leadership of the rebels and was crowned King of Sicily at Palermo in March 1296.[38] It was necessary once again to resort to arms. Boniface VIII renewed the crusade against the Sicilians in 1296, 1299, and 1302; he also employed the crusade against the Colonna cardinals, the allies of Frederick of Aragon and personal enemies of the Pope, in 1297–8.[39] With the help of James II the Angevins were able to take the offensive. They cleared Calabria in 1297–8 and in 1299 won their first major naval victory at the battle of Cape Orlando. But despite the aid of the Aragonese and, subsequently, that of a French contingent led by Charles of Valois, the island could not be reconquered. The treaty of Caltabellotta, in August 1302, recognized the occupation of Sicily by Frederick of Aragon, though not by his heirs, who were to surrender the island to the Angevins in return for other lands or a sum of money.[40]

The War of the Sicilian Vespers and the treaty which ended it substantially altered the balance of power in Italy. Between the battle of Benevento and the revolt of 1282 the Guelfs in general and the papal–Angevin alliance in particular had enjoyed a virtually unchallenged hegemony in the peninsula, and the blow which had been dealt to Angevin power and papal prestige weakened Guelfs everywhere. Sicily under its Aragonese kings became a major Ghibelline power posing a constant threat to the truncated Angevin kingdom. Shortly after the treaty of Caltabellotta Ghibelline strength also revived in northern and central Italy as a result of the Italian expedition of the Emperor-elect Henry VII (1310–13). Guelfism as it had been established in the years of Charles of Anjou's crusade against Manfred had fairly firm roots in the alliance between the papacy, the Angevin monarchy, and Florence. Until the intervention of Louis IV in 1323 the new Ghibellinism lacked this coherence. It consisted of various locally-based *signorie*

---

[38] See Pope Boniface VIII, *Registres*, ed. G. Digard *et al.*, no. 184; Boase, *Boniface VIII*, pp. 68–71; Amari, *La guerra*, i, pp. 473–89.

[39] Boniface VIII, *Reg.*, nos. 1575, 2375–6, 2383, 2878, 3072, 4625.

[40] Ibid., no. 5348 (papal ratification of the treaty, May 1303). For the last stage of the war, see Boase, *Boniface VIII*, pp. 211–14, 222, 269–92.

united only by their opposition to the claims of the popes and the influence of Naples. Thus in the Papal State Count Frederick II of Montefeltro organized and co-ordinated revolts against papal authority at Urbino, Spoleto, Osimo, Recanati, and other towns in the March of Ancona and the Duchy of Spoleto. At Mantua and Verona Raynaldo Passarino Bonacolsi and Can Grande della Scala established spheres of influence, while the Estensi consolidated their lordship in Ferrara and, most importantly, Matthew Visconti and his large family of capable sons built up an extensive territorial *signoria* based on Milan.[41]

Ironically, the first crusade waged in northern Italy in the fourteenth century for which documentary evidence survives was not declared against any of these Ghibelline powers, but against the Commune of Venice, which had, as its rulers said in their defence, always been a relatively faithful daughter of the Church.[42] The bone of contention was Ferrara, a city of great importance both to the popes and to Venice because of its geographical location on the border of Romagna and its great commercial potential. The death of Azzo VIII Este in 1308 led to a disputed succession; Venice supported Azzo's natural son, Fresco, while Azzo's brother, Francesco, appealed to and received the backing of Pope Clement V. The Pope appointed two nuncios to reassert the authority of the Holy See in Ferrara, and in April 1309 he sent Arnaud of Pellegrue as Cardinal-legate to lead military opposition against the Venetians. A crusade was declared against Venice in June and was preached throughout Italy. Venice submitted in the following year, but the government of Ferrara itself remained a serious problem for the Curia, especially after an Estensi regime hostile to the popes was restored in 1317.[43]

Apart from issuing orders for the arrest of Venetians in his

[41] See W. M. Bowsky, *Henry VII in Italy. The Conflict of Empire and City-State, 1310–1313*, *passim*; 'Eretici e ribelli nell'Umbria dal 1320 al 1330 studiati su documenti inediti dell'Archivio segreto Vaticano', ed. L. Fumi, *BDSPU*, iii–v (1897–9), *passim*; G. Mollat, *The Popes at Avignon 1305–1378*, pp. 76–7.

[42] G. Soranzo, *La guerra fra Venezia e la Santa Sede per il dominio di Ferrara (1308–1313)*, pp. 133–4. Cf. *Rationes decimarum Italiae. Apulia–Lucania–Calabria*, ed. D. Vendola, pp. 362–3.

[43] Pope Clement V, *Regestum*, ed. cura et studio monachorum Ordinis S. Benedicti, nos. 5081–2, 5084; Soranzo, *La guerra, passim*; A. Eitel, *Der Kirchenstaat unter Klemens V.*, pp. 170–201; Mollat, *Popes at Avignon*, pp. 70–6.

lands, for the confiscation of their goods, and for an embargo on trade with the city, the new Angevin king, Robert, did not play an active role in the crusade against Venice; he had no personal interest in the conflict and it seriously damaged the thriving commercial links between Venice and Apulia.[44] Soon, however, the need for constant military activity compelled the Curia to call on Angevin aid to help enforce its policies in Lombardy and in the Papal State. In 1317 Pope John XXII confirmed his predecessor's bull giving Robert an imperial vicariate in northern Italy, and in the decade 1320–30 papal–Angevin collaboration reached a level comparable to the crusades against Manfred and the Sicilians, though it was now complicated by the fact that the Curia maintained its own forces in the field under the command of powerful cardinal-legates. Once again this sustained Guelf offensive was backed up by the full spiritual armoury of the Church, and John XXII employed the crusade with frequency in what he saw as a struggle against rebellion and heresy.[45]

John XXII's first crusades against the Ghibellines were declared at the end of 1321. On 8 December crusade bulls were issued against Frederick of Montefeltro and his brothers, Guido and Speranza, together with the communes which supported their rebellion in the March of Ancona and the Duchy of Spoleto: Osimo, Urbino, Recanati, and Spoleto.[46] Thanks primarily to the help of Guelf communes and *signori* such as Perugia and the Malatesta of Rimini, the crusade was a striking success. Frederick was driven back to Urbino and killed, Osimo and Recanati were taken in 1322, Spoleto in 1324.[47] But the

[44] See 'Notizie storiche tratte dai documenti conosciuti col nome di *Arche in carta bambagina*', ed. R. Bevere, *ASPN*, xxv (1900), p. 259; G. Yver, *Le Commerce et les marchands dans l'Italie méridionale au xiii* et au xiv* siècle*, pp. 254–65. See also below, p. 195.

[45] The Italian policies of John XXII and their broader context are handled best by G. Tabacco, *La casa di Francia nell'azione politica di papa Giovanni XXII, passim.* See also Mollat, *Popes at Avignon*, pp. 76–110, and P. D. Partner, *The Lands of St Peter. The Papal State in the Middle Ages and the Early Renaissance*, pp. 304–26. For the Angevin contribution, see R. Caggese, *Roberto d'Angiò e i suoi tempi*, ii, *passim.*

[46] 'Eretici e ribelli', iii.471–81; Pope John XXII, *Lettres communes*, ed. G. Mollat, nos. 16125–7, 16180, 16183, 16189. See also *Sacrorum conciliorum nova et amplissima collectio*, ed. G. D. Mansi *et al.*, xxv, cols. 595–7.

[47] See G. Franceschini, *I Montefeltro*, pp. 201–20; M. P. Fop, *Il comune di Perugia e la Chiesa durante il periodo avignonese con particolare riferimento all'Albornoz*, pp. 16–18, 98–9; W. Heywood, *A History of Perugia*, pp. 126–32.

crusade did not lead to the restoration of papal authority. Ghibelline resistance was maintained and encouraged by the March towns of Fermo and Fabriano and by the Ghibelline *signore* and Bishop of Arezzo, Guido Tarlati. A crusade was declared against Fermo and Fabriano in 1324, but papal and Angevin efforts to restore order in Umbria were frustrated, and in 1327 the *Romzug* of Louis IV gave the rebellion a larger significance and further diminished papal power in central Italy.[48]

Crusades were also declared at the end of 1321 against Matthew Visconti and the Estensi. It is not possible to date them exactly because the crusade bulls seem to have evaded the chancery clerks who transcribed the bulls into the registers, but we can be fairly accurate. Papal representatives sent to tell Matthew Visconti about the crusade which had been declared against him, in order to give him a final chance to submit before preaching was set in progress, entered the Visconti *signoria* on 1 January 1322.[49] Allowing two weeks for the bull to travel from Avignon to the headquarters of the papal forces in Lombardy, at Piacenza,[50] this would suggest that the bull was released at roughly the same time as the crusade bull against Frederick of Montefeltro. The same probably applies to the crusade bull against the Estensi and their supporters in Ferrara; this crusade was being preached at Parma in February 1322.[51]

The mission to Milan was unsuccessful, and Bertrand du Poujet, Cardinal-bishop of Ostia and papal legate in Lombardy, started to preach the crusade against Matthew Visconti

---

[48] See *Documenti per la storia della città di Arezzo nel medio evo*, ed. U. Pasqui, ii, nos. 715, 725, 728, 735, 738, 741, 745; R. Sassi, 'La partecipazione di Fabriano alle guerre della Marca nel decennio 1320–1330', *Atti e memorie della R. Deputazione di storia patria per le Marche*, series 4, vii (1930), *passim*. For the crusade against Fermo and Fabriano, see 'I registri del ducato di Spoleto', ed. L. Fumi, *BDSPU*, iv (1898), 149.

[49] H. Otto, 'Zur italienischen Politik Johanns XXII.', *QFIAB*, xiv (1911), 214–15.

[50] Two weeks would have been a reasonable travelling time if the bull was sent by special courier. See Y. Renouard, 'Comment les papes d'Avignon expédiaient leur courrier', *Revue historique*, clxxx (1937), 29.

[51] 'Chronicon parmense', *RISNS*, ix⁹. 165. For crusade preaching against the Estensi, see also *I libri commemoriali della republica di Venezia Regesti*, ed. R. Predelli, i.241–2.

and his sons on 13 or 14 January.[52] Crusading forces joined his army and the Angevin troops under Raymond of Cardona in an attack on Milan, and by the summer the Visconti *signoria* had collapsed and Matthew himself had died. The Guelf armies concentrated at Monza in the following year, hoping to deliver the death-blow to Matthew's sons, but the dramatic intervention of Louis IV's ambassadors in May led to a Ghibelline revival, and Milan was relieved in July.[53] Memories were strong at Avignon of how much the War of the Vespers had cost the Church and how little had been gained by it, and an influential peace-party, led by Napoleon Orsini, Peter Colonna, and James Caetani, pressed the Pope to agree to a compromise settlement with the Ghibellines and not to act against Louis IV or his ambassadors. The Pope was aware of the dangers involved in creating or sanctioning another papal–imperial conflict and agreed with Napoleon Orsini that papal policy in Italy was not proving a success. But he also took the view that the Ghibellines were heretics whose defeat and submission were essential for the good of the Church, and that if Louis supported them he was guilty of the crime of aiding heresy.[54] There were fierce arguments in consistory, but the Pope's will prevailed. In March 1324 Louis was excommunicated and a crusade was declared against the sons of Matthew Visconti. Two months later the crusade against the Estensi and the Commune of Ferrara was renewed, and in July a crusade was declared against Raynaldo Bonacolsi of Mantua.[55]

Neither these crusades nor the extension (*prorogatio*) of the Visconti crusade for another year in April 1325 could revive

[52] *Acta aragonensia. Quellen zur deutschen, italienischen, französischen, spanischen, zur Kirchen-und Kulturgeschichte aus der diplomatischen Korrespondenz Jaymes* II. *(1291–1327)*, ed. H. Finke, i, no. 254. See also ASV, Reg. Vat 111, f. 155ʳ⁻ᵛ, nos. 643–4; L. Ciaccio, 'Il cardinal legato Bertrando del Poggetto in Bologna (1327–1334)', *Atti e memorie della R. Deputazione di storia patria per le provincie di Romagna*, series 3, xxiii (1905), 491–2; *I libri commemoriali*, i.239–40; *Sacr. conc. coll.*, xxv, col. 597.

[53] See *MGH, Const.* v, nos. 742, 753, 780.

[54] *Acta arag.*, i, nos. 262, 265; ii, no. 393; Pope John XXII, *Lettres secrètes et curiales relatives à la France*, ed. A. Coulon and S. Clémencet, no. 1445; *MGH*, Const. v, no. 881.

[55] *MGH, Const.* v, no. 881; *Annales ecclesiastici*, ed. C. Baronio *et al.*, ad ann. 1324, nos. 7–11, xxiv. 242–5; *Codex diplomaticus dominii temporalis Sanctae Sedis*, ed. A. Theiner, i, no. 710; *Urkunden zur Geschichte des Römerzuges Kaiser Ludwig des Baiern und der italienischen Verhältnisse seiner Zeit*, ed. J. Ficker, no. 32.

the flagging Guelf fortunes.[56] In March 1325 Azzo Visconti captured Borgo San Donnino. In September the Florentines were defeated at the battle of Altopascio, and the threat posed in Tuscany by Castruccio Castracani, the Ghibelline *signore* of Lucca, led the commune to call in King Robert's eldest son, Charles of Calabria, as *signore* in 1326.[57] Charles was unable to deal effectively with Castruccio, the most able military commander of the age, but Bertrand du Poujet achieved some successes in Emilia and Romagna in 1326–7, albeit at enormous financial cost.[58] The situation was balanced and unpredictable when Louis IV began his long-awaited *Romzug* in January 1327. The last of the great medieval conflicts of empire and papacy, this has often been described as an anachronistic episode, a pale reflection of its predecessors.[59] To Guelfs throughout Italy, however, the danger was real enough; Louis was able to co-ordinate the Ghibelline opposition in Lombardy, Tuscany, and the Papal State, and in 1328 an invasion of the Kingdom of Naples, with the aid of Frederick of Sicily, seemed imminent. The Curia was surprisingly slow to react to this threat. It was not until January 1328, when Louis was already installed at Rome, that a crusade was declared against him.[60] It was, however, an anticlimax. Lack of money and food supplies, and the failure of Frederick of Sicily to send the ships he promised, compelled Louis to abandon his invasion plans and to leave Rome in August. On 3 September Castruccio Castracani died and the Ghibelline coalition disintegrated rapidly.[61] In 1329

---

[56] For the extension of the Visconti crusade, see ASV, Reg. Vat. 113, ff. 174ᵛ–175ʳ, no. 1033.

[57] For Charles's *signoria* at Florence, see 'La signoria di Firenze tenuta da Carlo figlio di re Roberto negli anni 1326 e 1327', ed. R. Bevere, *ASPN*, xxxiii–xxxvi (1908–11), *passim*; R. Davidsohn, *Geschichte von Florenz*, iii. 753 ff. For Castruccio Castracani, see F. Winkler, *Castruccio Castracani Herzog von Lucca*, *passim*; *Castruccio Castracani degli Antelminelli. Miscellanea di studi storici e letterari edita dalla Reale Accademia lucchese*, *passim*.

[58] See *Die Ausgaben der apostolischen Kammer unter Johann XXII. nebst den Jahresbilanzen von 1316–1375*, ed. K. H. Schäfer, pp. 13*–14*, 31*.

[59] See, e.g., H. S. Offler, 'Empire and Papacy: the Last Struggle', *Transactions of the Royal Historical Society*, 5th series, vi (1956), 22; Ullmann, *Short History*, p. 284. For the *Romzug* in general, see A. Chroust, *Beiträge zur Geschichte Ludwigs des Bayers und seiner Zeit. I. Die Romfahrt*, *passim*; W. Altmann, *Der Römerzug Ludwigs des Baiern. Ein Beitrag zur Geschichte des Kampfes zwischen Papsttum und Kaisertum*, *passim*.

[60] *Thes. novus*, ii, cols. 716–23. Original letters in ASV, Reg. Vat. 114, ff. 226ᵛ–230ʳ, nos. 259–63.

[61] Altmann, *Der Römerzug*, pp. 104 ff.

Azzo Visconti and the Estensi changed sides and in June the crusade against Louis was renewed to rally Milanese and Lombard opposition to the Emperor.[62] Louis left Italy in 1330 and never returned.

The papal–Angevin alliance was now in a stronger position than it had held since 1322, but John XXII destroyed all his own gains by lending papal support to the scheme of John of Bohemia, the son of Henry VII, to found a kingdom in Lombardy, to be held as a fief from the Pope. Attractive as such a project appeared as a solution to Lombardy's anomalous political status, it was as great a threat to Florence and the Angevin monarchy as it was to the Ghibelline *signori* of Lombardy, and in September 1332 the league of Ferrara was formed to oppose the combined forces of John of Bohemia and Bertrand du Poujet. Led by the Visconti and Florence, the league had at least tacit Angevin backing, and constituted a revolution in Italian politics, a breakdown of the system of alliances which had functioned for seventy years. When John XXII died at the end of 1334 all the gains made by Bertrand du Poujet in Lombardy and Emilia-Romagna had been lost.[63] John's successor, Benedict XII, adopted a conciliatory policy which eventually restored the traditional Guelf–Ghibelline alignment, but without a militant papal leadership, and without employing the crusade.[64] Benedict's successors at Avignon, in particular Innocent VI and Urban V, returned to the policies of John XXII and declared several crusades against the Ghibellines and the mercenary companies threatening papal lands.[65] Guelfism, however, was never again to be as powerful a

---

[62] *Thes. novus*, ii, cols. 777–82. See also ASV, Reg. Vat. 115, ff. 18ᵛ–19ʳ, no. 128; *Die Ausgaben*, p. 510.

[63] See Mollat, *Popes at Avignon*, pp. 101–10.

[64] Benedict did, however, permit the crusade to be preached against Louis IV in 1337. See his *Lettres closes et patentes intéressant les pays autres que la France*, ed. J. M. Vidal, no. 1609. For his Italian policy, see Mollat, 'Benoît XII et l'Italie', in J. M. Vidal's edition of Benedict's *Lettres closes et patentes*, ii, *passim*; H. Otto, 'Benedikt XII. als Reformator des Kirchenstaates', *RQ*, xxxvi (1928), *passim*; G. Tabacco, 'La tradizione guelfa in Italia durante il pontificato di Benedetto XII', in P. Vaccari and P. F. Palumbo (eds.), *Studi di storia medievale e moderna in onore di Ettore Rota, passim*.

[65] See *Codex dipl.* ii, nos. 324, 375, 400, 410, 467; Matteo Villani, *Cronica*, ii. 72–3; *Thes. novus*, ii, cols. 848 ff.; *Ann. eccles.*, ad ann. 1368, nos. 1–3, xxvi. 150–1; Pope Gregory XI, *Lettres secrètes et curiales intéressant les pays autres que la France*, ed. G. Mollat, no. 3736; Pope Gregory XI, *Lettres secrètes et curiales relatives à la France*, ed. L. Mirot et al., no. 3296.

force in Italian politics as it had been in the reign of John XXII. The death of Robert of Naples in January 1343 and the civil war which ensued in the *Regno* meant that the Angevin monarchy could play a much less imposing role in the rest of Italy, while the former Guelf allies had too many differences to act in complete unison. Within a generation Florence herself, a power with a Guelf tradition as old as that of Naples, and with the closest financial ties to Avignon, would be at war with the Church.[66]

Even from this brief narrative survey it is clear that the Italian crusades followed a certain pattern in their inception. They were usually declared when opposition to papal policy in Italy had led to a military or financial crisis which could only be overcome by tapping the resources which the use of the crusade afforded: resources consisting primarily of crusaders, but also of money and the subtler, moral advantages of waging a holy war. This was equally true whether the crusade was declared in response to an unexpected and sudden crisis, such as Manfred's invasion of the Papal State in 1264, or Boniface VIII's clash with the Colonna in 1297, or was a measure incorporated into a scheme of long and complex gestation, such as the negotiations with Charles of Anjou leading up to his invasion of the Kingdom of Sicily. Of course there were exceptions to this rule. It has been suggested plausibly that the use of the charge of heresy against Matthew Visconti, and the declaration of a crusade against him, were diplomatic moves intended, by lifting the struggle in Lombardy onto the plane of a holy war, to prevent the French monarchy pressing the Ghibelline cause at Avignon.[67] But in general the use of the crusade was dictated by the situation in Italy rather than by events outside the peninsula.

Linking the cause of God and the Christian Faith to the vicissitudes and complexities of the papacy's wars in Italy involved an obvious danger. The political and military situation in Italy was notoriously unstable, as the popes themselves

[66] For the deterioration of relations between Florence and Avignon, see P. D. Partner, 'Florence and the Papacy, 1300–1375', in J. Hale *et al.* (eds.), *Europe in the Late Middle Ages*, *passim*; G. A. Brucker, *Florentine Politics and Society, 1343–1378*, *passim*.

[67] See F. Bock, 'Kaisertum, Kurie und Nationalstaat im Beginn des 14. Jahrhunderts', *RQ*, xliv (1936), 193–4. See also Tabacco, *La casa di Francia*, pp. 204–6.

complained.[68] Allegiances were changed without moral qualms and apparently stable coalitions dissolved and reformed with extraordinary rapidity. This could lead to anomalies dangerously at variance with the moral certainties needed for the waging of a crusade. In 1259, for example, the excommunicated Ghibelline *signori*, Oberto Pallavicini and Boso of Dovara, together with the Ghibelline Commune of Cremona, executed a skilful and dramatic diplomatic volte-face by allying themselves with the Guelf crusading army in Lombardy and helping to bring about the final destruction of Ezzelino of Romano; they even persuaded a religious to grant them absolution of their sins for so doing. Pope Alexander IV hastened to declare that the absolution was invalid and that the Ghibellines were to remain excommunicated, unless they should reveal signs of genuine repentance.[69]

This was, however, a minor anomaly and one which was easily rectified. More serious was the situation which arose in the early years of the reign of Pope Clement V, when the *parte guelfa* was fragmented in the wake of the disruptive policies of Boniface VIII. Early in 1306 Clement sent Napoleon Orsini to Italy as his legate to pacify the dissident Guelf factions in Tuscany and Emilia. It was a disastrous choice. His authority rejected by Florence and his person abused at Bologna, Napoleon responded in 1307 by preaching the crusade against the two communes.[70] There is no evidence that he had papal authority to do so.[71] Nevertheless, the declaration of a crusade, even without the requisite authority, against communes noted in the past for their support for papal aims in Italy, was an event of grave significance. It was impossible to believe that Florence in particular, which only recently had supplied 'athletes of Christ' for the Church's struggle against the Sicilian rebels and the Colonna heretics, was now a genuine enemy of the Faith.

---

[68] See *MGH, Epist. pont.* iii, no. 503; Partner, 'Florence and the Papacy', pp. 78–9.

[69] *MGH, Epist. pont.* iii, no. 503. See also Jordan, *Les Origines*, pp. 118–40, with interesting comments at pp. 122–3, 137 ff.; *Poesie provenzali storiche relative all'Italia*, ed. V. De Bartholomaeis, ii. 198–202.

[70] C. A. Willemsen, *Kardinal Napoleon Orsini (1263–1342)*, pp. 44, 174; Davidsohn, *Geschichte*, iii. 338; Partner, *Lands of St Peter*, p. 299. See Willemsen, pp. 25–52, for the legation generally.

[71] Most of Clement V's secret letters have however been lost. See Y. Renouard, 'Les Papes et le conflit franco-anglais en Aquitaine de 1259 à 1337', *Mélanges*, li (1934), 276–7.

The declaration of a crusade against Florence and Bologna could only damage the popular beliefs which were essential if the crusades against Christian rulers were to be seen as the cause of God and the indulgence valued.

But the situation which arose in 1307 was the result of a unique combination of factors: the division of the Guelfs into 'White' and 'Black' factions, the Ghibelline propensities of Napoleon Orsini, and, above all, the poorly defined and vacillating Italian policy of Clement V. Most of the crusades waged in Italy after 1254 had certain common features which made it possible for contemporaries to see the papacy's struggle against its enemies as a religious one. They were fought on behalf of an identifiable Guelf cause, at the heart of which lay the common interests of the papacy and the Angevin monarchy. The interests of the two powers were not so close that they co-operated in all the crusades. The Angevins played little part in the crusade against Venice and even less in that against the Colonna.[72] Nor was a crusade declared on all occasions when the Angevin crown was in danger; there was, for example, no crusade against Henry VII, who in 1312 represented a greater threat to Naples than did Louis IV in 1328.[73] Similarly, the Curia adamantly refused to permit another crusade against the Sicilians after 1302.[74] But the list of crusades which were waged by the papacy and its royal vassals together remains striking. In the crusades against the last Staufen, the Sicilians and the Aragonese, the Ghibellines and Louis IV, a very close political and financial partnership was formed between them.

The papal–Angevin alliance was a constant feature of Italian political life for three generations after 1265, a continuity all the more impressive when viewed against the confused politics of the period. Continuity was, indeed, an aspect of the alliance prized by both partners. Granting Robert of Naples a clerical tenth in March 1328 to help him resist Louis IV's planned invasion of the *Regno*, John XXII referred with gratitude to the services of his grandfather sixty years earlier:

[72] For the Angevins and the crusade against the Colonna, see 'Documenti sulle relazioni tra la corte angioina di Napoli, papa Bonifacio VIII e i Colonna', ed. F. Scandone, *ASPN*, NS, xli (1962), *passim*.

[73] For papal relations with Henry VII, see W. M. Bowsky, 'Clement V and the Emperor-Elect', *Medievalia et Humanistica*, xii (1958), *passim*.

[74] See ASV, Reg. Vat. 113, f. 60ʳ⁻ᵛ, no. 461. See also f. 59ʳ, no. 453, and below, p. 36.

When it is brought back to our attention and to the grateful memory of the Apostolic See how your grandfather Charles, King of Sicily, endured such grave dangers and such oppressive and burdensome toil with calmness and willingness, in order to drive off the ragings of the various tempests by which the Roman church was then hard pressed . . . then we realize that it is fitting that the Apostolic See should give you its favour and its generous support in your necessities.[75]

In a famous letter to Philip V of France in 1318, Robert of Naples too looked back to the days of Charles I, 'who entered Apulia as the champion of the Catholic Faith and the defender of the Holy Roman church, crushed the pride of the Ghibellines and tamed the wilderness'.[76]

The papal–Angevin alliance survived so long partly because of mutual interest in the maintenance of the settlement of 1265–8, partly too because of the survival of an aggressive and vengeful Staufen–Ghibelline tradition. The Guelfs were not the only ones who remembered Benevento and Tagliacozzo. In 1327, for instance, the Angevins claimed that Louis IV was hostile to Naples 'because of the old hatred arising from the war and destruction of Conradin'.[77] The 'old hatred', and the rival political traditions which fed it and were maintained by it, served to bind together the crusades waged by the popes and the Angevin kings in Italy. In 1328 as in 1268, the defence of the Church was synonymous with the defence of the Angevin dynasty in the Guelf political outlook. This is reflected in the wills of two men who had taken the cross to fight in the crusades in Italy and who did not wish to die intestate. The first, Jourdain IV of l'Isle Jourdain, a Gascon noble, made his testament at Perugia in 1266, 'whilst travelling to Apulia in aid of the Holy Roman church and of Lord Charles, illustrious

---

[75] 'Dum nostris et apostolice sedis grata commemoratione refertur obtutibus quanta clare memorie Carolus rex Sicilie avus tuus pro submovendis diversarum tempestatuum procellis quibus illis temporibus Romana premebatur ecclesia pericula gravia et ingentium laborum onera intrepida voluntate pertulerit . . . decens fore conspicimus ut tibi in supportandis apostolice sedis favorem et generosum auxilium impendamus.' ASV, Reg. Vat. 86, f. 127^r, no. 1474. The formula was repeated by Benedict XII when he granted Robert a tenth in 1339. See ASV, Reg. Vat. 127, f. 139^v, no. 199.

[76] *Acta imperii inedita*, ii, no. 1120.

[77] *Italienische Analekten zur Reichsgeschichte des 14. Jahrhunderts, (1310–1378)*, ed. T. Mommsen and W. Hagemann, no. 159, and cf. no. 160.

King of Sicily'.[78] The second, Boniface Caetani, had taken the cross against Louis IV 'in the service and honour of the Roman church and of King Robert, against the damned Bavarian, who is attacking the said Roman church and the said King Robert'.[79] These men were setting out to fight for a cause which in essence remained the same.

At the level of political action, the *raison d'être* of the crusades in Italy was thus the implementation of papal aims there and, on the many occasions when they converged with these aims, the defence of Angevin interests. But in this sense the crusades were no different from the other wars fought by the popes and the Angevin kings in this period. It was at the level of theological and juridical thought and argument that the papacy attempted to transform the wars from ordinary military campaigns into crusades, fought not simply in the pursuit of papal and Angevin aims in Italy, but in defence of the Christian Faith itself.

---

[78] P. Durrieu, *Les Gascons en Italie. Études historiques*, p. 5. For Jourdain, see below, pp. 156, 228–9.

[79] *Regesta chartarum. Regesto delle pergamene dell'Archivio Caetani*, ed. G. Caetani, ii. 59–60.

Chapter 2

Papal Justification of the Italian Crusades

The belief that it was licit to employ force against Christians who were guilty of rebelling against or attacking the Church had a rich juridical tradition behind it. In the eleventh century Pope Gregory VII and his supporters expounded the duty of all Christians to defend the Church against its enemies, and in the *Decretum* Gratian used texts from St. Augustine and Gregory I to establish the justice of such a war.[1] On one level, this just war was converted into a crusade by the simple mechanism of using the crusade indulgence as an encouragement to recruitment. As a recent historian of the just war succinctly put it: 'it was when the doctrine of indulgences was linked to the just war that the juridical theory of the crusades was born'.[2] But in order to launch an effective crusade more than a juridical theory was required. Arguments had to be adduced which would persuade people to take the cross or to contribute money. Furthermore, the Curia was acutely aware of the need to avoid being attacked by its enemies for misusing the crusade indulgence and to prevent its being attached to political causes of dubious moral worth. This awareness is well illustrated by a letter from Pope Clement IV to Charles I in October 1266. Charles, launching his policy of sustained hostility towards the revived Greek empire of Constantinople, had petitioned the Pope to grant him the crusade indulgence for an expedition against the Greek-held island of Corfu, on the grounds that the Greeks were schismatics. But Charles was intervening in Corfu on behalf of the sons of Philip Chinardo, who had been Manfred's admiral and an excommunicated enemy of the Church. Clement replied that:

It would be neither plausible nor judicious to grant the indulgence which you ask for helping the sons of that most excommunicated of

---

[1] See F. H. Russell, *The Just War in the Middle Ages*, pp. 72–6; I. S. Robinson, 'Gregory VII and the Soldiers of Christ', *History*, lviii (1973), *passim*. For the contribution of Gregory VII and his supporters, see also Erdmann, *Origin*, pp. 214–15, 253–6, 262–4.

[2] Russell, *Just War*, p. 204.

men, the late Philip Chinardo. I know that the Greeks are hateful to us. But it would be like granting the indulgence to the Tartars for helping to fight the Saracens, or to the Greeks themselves for helping against the Tartars or the Saracens, which nobody in his right mind would suggest . . . The indulgence cannot be granted in this manner to all and sundry, or what is intended as a means of salvation will be exposed to disbelief and derision.[3]

The papal Curia knew that the dangers inherent in declaring a crusade against Latin Christians were even greater than in the case of a crusade against the Greeks. If the cause was not a strong one the crusade could rebound against the Holy See. In 1325, for example, Pope John XXII turned down an Angevin request for a renewal of crusade preaching against the Sicilians, on the grounds that it would be unbecoming and injurious to papal authority, as the offences of King Frederick of Sicily had not yet reached the stage which permitted the use of the Church's ultimate weapon.[4] This caution was based on the fact that a crusade against Christian lay powers was paradoxical: how could the soldiers of Christ fight and kill baptized Christians? 'Since they are Christians, tyrants are signed with the cross. Consequently they must not be overthrown by those signed with the cross (*crucesignati*).'[5]

At least two leading contemporary political thinkers, the canonist Hostiensis and Augustinus Triumphus, addressed themselves to this paradox, and they adopted a similar approach. According to them, the fact that Christian rebels and tyrants owed allegiance to the pope did not extenuate their crimes; it aggravated them. They were worse than pagans, Muslims, or Jews because, as baptized members of the Church, they could do her more harm. 'When Christians sin, they must be punished more severely than pagans or Jews.'[6] This was a logical argument, and one which had been used many times

---

[3] *Thes. novus*, ii, col. 409. See also S. Borsari, 'La politica bizantina di Carlo I d'Angiò dal 1266 al 1271', *ASPN*, NS, xxxv (1956), 320–3.

[4] ASV, Reg. Vat. 113, f. 60^{r-v}, no. 461.

[5] Augustinus Triumphus, *Summa de potestate ecclesiastica*, Quaestio XXVI, Art. v 'Utrum papa debeat contra tyrannos sibi resistentes crucesignatos destinare', p. 158.

[6] Ibid., pp. 158–9. Cf. Hostiensis, *Summa aurea*, III, 'De voto', xix. 296^v–297^r, and Martin IV, *Reg.*, no. 587. On Hostiensis, see M. Villey, 'L'Idée de la Croisade chez les juristes du Moyen Âge', in *Relazioni del X Congresso internazionale di Scienze storiche. Storia del medioevo*, iii. 565–94, esp. 574–7, and *La Croisade. Essai sur la formation d'une théorie juridique*, pp. 256–62.

before, most notably by eleventh-century polemicists such as Manegold of Lautenbach and Bonizo of Sutri.[7] But both Hostiensis and Augustinus Triumphus knew that it lacked the simple emotional appeal of the argument employed by their opponents. Hostiensis acknowledged that 'the simple' would still prefer to go on crusade to the Holy Land, and revealed that when he had been in Germany he had encountered protests against the use of the crusade against the Staufen.[8] Augustinus admitted that the crusades against tyrants (by which he meant the Ghibelline *signori*), 'scandalized' some people, including the *inferiores de Ecclesia*, but he asserted that it was better for the Church to endure scandal than to allow terrible crimes to go unpunished; the tyrant was, after all, being attacked not as 'the follower of the Christian cross', but as 'the despiser of the vicar of Christ and the persecutor of the limbs of Christ'.[9] The incongruity of Christians being attacked and killed by *crucesignati* was skilfully employed as a form of attack on the papacy by such enemies as Ezzelino of Romano, Conradin of Staufen, the Emperor Louis IV, and, above all, Marsilius of Padua.[10] Other critics of the papacy, such as Dante and Peter Dubois, regarded the crusades against Christian rulers, and the use of other ecclesiastical weapons in a political cause, as examples of the misuse of the power of the Keys.[11] The papacy's reply to this attack is to be found in the crusade bulls themselves, together with bulls levying clerical taxes in aid of the crusades, as well as the processes of excommunication and heresy which were linked to the employment of the crusade. In such bulls the Curia undertook the double task of at once countering the attacks of its enemies and critics, and rousing the Christian Republic to take the cross on its behalf.

[7] See Erdmann, *Origin*, pp. 236, 251–2.

[8] *Summa aurea*, loc. cit. Hostiensis was attached to the German legation of Hugh of St. Cher in 1251 and thus witnessed the preaching of the crusade against Conrad. See C. Lefebvre, 'Hostiensis', in R. Naz (ed.), *Dictionnaire de droit canonique*, v, col. 1213.

[9] *Summa*, Qu. XXVI, Art. v, p. 158.

[10] See *Codex Italiae diplomaticus*, ed. J. C. Lünig, ii, col. 939; *MGH, Const.* vi, pt. 1, no. 436; Marsilius of Padua, *Defensor pacis*, Dictio II, Cap. xxvi. 16, pp. 508–11; Rolandino Patavino, 'Chronica', *MGHS*, xix. 133. See also Bartholomew of Neocastro, 'Historia sicula', p. 87.

[11] Dante, *Inferno*, xxvii. 85–120; Peter Dubois, *Summaria brevis et compendiosa doctrina felicis expedicionis et abreviacionis guerrarum ac litium regni Francorum*, pp. 12–13.

Using these bulls presents certain problems. Many, for instance, contain little or no justification. Of these, some are simply *littere executorie*: letters sent out to the secular clergy, friars or papal legates, commanding them to preach the cross.[12] In the fourteenth century the latest papal process against the guilty was included, and in the bulls against Frederick II there was a brief comment on his persecution of the Church and the duty of all Christians to defend it. But there was no reasoned résumé of the argument as to why the crusade was being preached. The bulls against Frederick II are particularly disappointing in this respect: not one contains real detail on his crimes against the Church.[13] In view of the fact that the bulls must have supplied the raw material for crusade sermons, this presents an interesting problem; perhaps those who preached against the Emperor were expected to use instead the rich detail contained in the decree on Frederick's deposition at the First Council of Lyons. The Curia also considered that once a cause had been established as worthy of a crusade there was no need to repeat the justification at length, unless there was an emergency or preaching was proving unsuccessful. Thus in June 1299 Boniface VIII, renewing crusade preaching in the *Regno* against Frederick of Aragon and the Sicilians, commented that it was neither expedient nor necessary to refer to all of their crimes against the Holy See and its Angevin vassals, and recounted only the most recent events.[14]

Nor were the crusade bulls which did contain detailed justification always consistent. The Curia was very adept at tailoring its arguments and appeals to make them more effective for the particular audience before which they were to be read or interpreted. In the Papal State, for example, the bulls associated the Guelf cause with civic liberty and independence in a way which foreshadowed the efforts of the later Florentine Guelf apologists. The Perugians were to be exhorted in 1264 to defend the Church and the Faith against Manfred—but also their own liberty and homeland; in 1322 they received the Pope's thanks for coming so readily 'to the defence of the orthodox Faith and the protection of the liberty of your

---

[12] See, e.g., *MGH, Epist. pont.* iii, no. 188.
[13] See *MGH, Epist. pont.* ii, nos. 199, 247, 456, 585, 630.
[14] ASV, Reg. Vat. 49, f. 177^{r-v}, no. 192.

country'.[15] In 1324 the Commune of Bologna too was reminded that it had offered to send cavalry 'for the protection and conservation of your homeland's liberty'.[16] The people of the Roman Campagna were to be told in 1261 that if Manfred became senator at Rome there would be danger 'not just for the Church but also for themselves'.[17] Particularly interesting is a crusade bull of Alexander IV of 1256 in which the Pope commended the people of L'Aquila for resisting Manfred in defence of their liberty and in accordance with the fealty which they owed the Church.[18] Urban IV's letter to the French clergy in May 1264 asking them to pay a tenth for Charles of Anjou's expedition contained appeals to the patriotism as well as the piety of the 'most renowned and most Christian realm' of France, with apposite references to Pepin and Charlemagne. A letter written at the same time to Louis IX asking him to support Simon of Brie's legation also referred to 'the most Christian king' of France and 'the most Christian house' of Capet.[19] This appeal to the historic role of the French crown as defender of the papacy and of the Christian Faith found frequent echoes in French and Guelf chronicles, perhaps the most abstruse one being Andrew of Hungary's comparison of Charles of Anjou both to Charlemagne and to Constantine, a reference to the fact that he was to recover for the Church lands originally given her by these emperors, but also, possibly, a pun on the name of Constance, the Norman heiress through whose marriage to Henry VI in 1186 the *Regno* had passed into Staufen hands.[20] In 1283 Pope Martin IV appealed to French nationalism by asking the French clergy to consider 'the damage to the Faith, the cost to Christianity, and the injuries to your own nation', which the Sicilian revolt entailed.[21] In a more

---

[15] 'ad defensionem fidei orthodoxe et protectionem patrie libertatis', ASV, Reg. Vat. 111, f. 320^r, no. 1286. For the bull of 1264, see ASV, Reg. Vat. 28, f. 121^{r-v}, no. 156.

[16] 'pro tuenda et conservanda patrie libertate', ASV, Reg. Vat. 112, f. 71^r, no. 335. See also Reg. Vat. 115, f. 18^v, no. 128.

[17] 'Les Déviations', p. 398.

[18] *Antiq. ital. medii aevi*, vi, col. 517.

[19] Urban IV, *Reg.*, nos. 804, 809.

[20] Andrew of Hungary, 'Descriptio victoriae a Karolo Provinciae comite reportatae', *MGHS*, xxvi. 562–3. On this theme, and the use made of it by Capetian propagandists, see J. R. Strayer, 'France: the Holy Land, the Chosen People, and the Most Christian King', in T. K. Rabb and J. E. Seigel (eds.), *Action and Conviction in Early Modern Europe*, *passim*.

[21] Martin IV, *Reg.*, no. 457.

general sense, the concentration on the 'blasphemous alliance' of Manfred with the Muslim inhabitants of Lucera is a typical example of the Curia stressing the features which it believed would most horrify the audience at a crusade sermon.

All this only shows that the crusade bulls were not polished pieces of theological or juridicial thought but instruments designed to arouse the consciences and anger of Christians. Indeed, they made an important contribution to the propaganda battle which had accompanied the quarrels between papacy and empire since the Investiture Contest, reaching its height in the thirteenth century.[22] If local needs are emphasized and national pride appealed to, this does not constitute the debasement of the crusade ideal described by Toubert;[23] the broader charges against Manfred and his successors were, after all, dealt with elsewhere. If the Muslims of Lucera were employed as propaganda, they also epitomized, for the popes, Manfred's crimes against the Church. Above all, it is not difficult to separate themes brought in with recruitment in mind from the arguments which represent curialist reasoning for the use of the crusade in the first place. There were many·such arguments, but they were all variations or expansions of two themes of central importance: the defence of the Christian Faith, and the needs of the Christian East.

i. THE DEFENCE OF THE FAITH

The most impressive common feature of all the crusade bulls which deal in some depth with justification is their defensive tone and content. Each one is very largely a recital of the offences committed against the Church and the threat posed to Christianity itself. To some extent this was due to the crusade bull format of *narratio-exhortatio*, which was above all suited to a defensive cause. But the papal chancery was also concerned to prove that it was fighting a just war in defence of the Faith. Obviously a crusade, which was by definition the cause of God,

---

[22] See Ullmann, *Law and Politics*, pp. 212–13, 259–61; O. Vehse, *Die amtliche Propaganda in der Staatskunst Kaiser Friedrichs II, passim;* H. Wieruszowski, *Vom Imperium zum nationalen Königtum. Vergleichende Studien über die publizistischen Kämpfe Kaiser Friedrichs II. und König Philipps des Schönen mit der Kurie, passim.*

[23] In 'Les Déviations', pp. 395–6.

could not be unjust. Consequently many of the enemies of the Church attempted to show that the Pope was fighting an unjust war in Italy in order to discredit his crusades there. The Sicilians claimed that the popes were fighting an unjust war against them because it was inspired by their love for the French.[24] Similarly, the author of the 'Annales mediolanenses', who was a supporter of the Visconti regime, inquired,

whether Pope John XXII waged a just war against the city of Milan. It can be seen that he did not, because the pope should not interfere in wars, but only in spiritual matters. Besides, nobody behaves justly when he attacks the possession of another, and the pope has no right over the city of Milan, so he behaved unjustly by attacking the city.[25]

Marsilius of Padua described John XXII's crusaders as 'invaders and unjust attackers of a country belonging to others', and their Ghibelline opponents as 'people defending their own country and observing the fealty which they owe to their true and rightful lord'.[26] To answer such criticisms effectively the Curia had to prove that its cause was just, that it was indeed related to 'spiritual matters', and that it was for these reasons the cause of God.

One of the ways in which the Curia did this was through the skilful use of traditional crusading vocabulary. The crusades in Italy were described at various times as 'the business of the cross', 'the service of the crucified one', 'the cause of the Faith', 'the cause of God', 'the business of God and the Church', 'the businesses of Christ and Christianity', and, in one bull of Martin IV, 'the businesses of the Faith, the Church, the [Holy] Land and Christianity'.[27] In 1322 the Rector of the March of Ancona described the crusade against Frederick of Montefeltro as 'the business of our Lord Jesus Christ and his vicar on earth, of holy mother Church and the Christian Faith'.[28] Again, a phrase employed by Martin IV, Nicholas IV, and John XXII at the start of their crusade bulls called on God to defend his

---

[24] See Bartholomew of Neocastro, 'Historia sicula', pp. 87, 112.

[25] 'Annales mediolanenses', *RIS*, xvi, cols. 697–8. See also C. Capasso, 'La signoria viscontea e la lotta politico-religiosa con il papato nella prima metà del secolo xiv', *Bollettino della Società pavese di storia patria*, viii (1908), 289; Mollat, *Popes at Avignon*, p. 81.

[26] *Defensor pacis*, Dict. II, Cap. xxvi, 16, p. 510.

[27] See 'Les Déviations', p. 398; Urban IV, *Registres*, no. 633; Martin IV, *Reg.*, nos. 457, 570, 591; *Foedera*, i, pt. 1, p. 301; *Thes. novus*, ii, col. 384.

[28] *Acta imperii inedita*, ii, no. 1122.

cause, and the same popes prefixed their grant of the crusade indulgence with the reminder that 'in these matters we are engaged on the cause of God'.[29] Some of the crusade bulls of Martin IV and Nicholas IV against Peter and James of Aragon consisted largely of a series of rhetorical questions asking if the attacks on the Church, the Angevin monarchy and, indirectly, the Holy Land, did not constitute the cause of God.[30]

The skilful employment of violent language also helped to create an impression of persecution and of the evil nature of the Church's opponents. By November 1247 the struggle with Frederick II had reached such a pitch that the Emperor was being termed 'the limb of the Devil, the servant of Satan, the miserable precursor of Antichrist'.[31] This was extreme language even for a papal–imperial dispute.[32] Manfred too was 'the son of iniquity, the foster-child of perdition'.[33] His persecutions were by 1264 'suffocating' the Church, so that 'because of these oppressions the Church can scarcely breathe'.[34] By April 1283 Peter of Aragon was 'a manifest persecutor of God and of the Church', and his son James inherited the title.[35] The Staufen tradition of opposition to papal aims in Italy, which ran from Frederick II to the Aragonese rulers of Sicily in the fourteenth century, was extremely useful in this respect because it gave continuity to the persecution and also because it enabled the Curia to attribute this persecution to a hereditary streak of evil. Thus Manfred 'imitated his father's evil actions from his early years, and we have seen how much further he has gone in savagery'. Conradin, it was hoped, was the 'sole, last glimmer' in the line, but a generation later 'the root of the serpent' brought forth the persecution of Frederick of Aragon.[36] Though

---

[29] ASV, Reg. Vat. 41, f. 110ᵛ, no. 36, Reg. Vat. 46, f. 164ᵛ, no. 13, Reg. Vat. 73, ff. 6ʳ–7ᵛ, no. 28; 'Eretici e ribelli', iii. 471, 480.

[30] ASV, Reg. Vat. 41, ff. 110ᵛ–111ʳ, no. 36, Reg. Vat. 46, f. 164ᵛ, no. 13; Martin IV, *Reg.*, no. 570.

[31] *MGH, Epist. pont.* ii, no. 456.

[32] Kennan ('Innocent III', pp. 246–7), sees the crusade against Markward of Anweiler as the first use of such abusive terms of attack. There were eleventh-century precedents, but they were usually restricted to attacks on ecclesiastics. See, e.g., I. S. Robinson, *Authority and Resistance in the Investiture Contest. The Polemical Literature of the Eleventh Century*, pp. 173–4.

[33] Urban IV, *Reg.*, no. 633.

[34] Ibid., no. 809.

[35] ASV, Reg. Vat. 45, f. 63ʳ, no. 328; Martin IV, *Reg.*, no. 460.

deprived of the Staufen tradition, John XXII showed himself to be no less inventive than his predecessors in describing his enemies' faults. Frederick of Montefeltro was termed a 'rebel, heretic, idolater, excommunicate, corrupter of the Catholic Faith, open enemy and adversary of God, manifest persecutor and foe of the said Church', and roughly the same list of pejoratives was applied to the Visconti.[37]

Accusations and assertions were, of course, not enough. Every contemporary ruler, including the enemies of the pope, claimed that he was fighting a just war, and that God was intervening on his behalf. During the War of the Sicilian Vespers the Sicilians and Aragonese were convinced that their remarkable victories were proof of divine aid. Bartholomew of Neocastro wrote that the Virgin Mary appeared in person in 1282 to help the rebels against the Angevin forces, and Raymond Muntaner believed that the Angevin naval defeat of 1284 was ample evidence of God's disfavour: 'Against the will and power of God no man can stand. And so the power and will of God was and is with the Lord King of Aragon and with his people; wherefore King Charles and the Prince were as nothing against him'.[38] Similarly, in a letter in which he reported the defeat of the French crusaders of 1285, Peter of Aragon wrote that they were 'the enemies of God' and God, not the Aragonese, had defeated them.[39] The Curia had to prove that the Church really was being persecuted in Italy, the person of Christ affronted through his bride, the Christian Faith itself threatened. To do this it resorted to detailed, often very long explanations of the nature of the persecution and of the course which it was taking. These explanations can usually be divided into two sections: harm done to the possessions and rights of the Holy See in Italy, and harm done to the Italian church and to the Faith in general.

First among the papacy's own possessions was the Papal State itself, established effectively for the first time by Pope Innocent III and threatened with partition or dissolution

---

[36] *Thes. novus*, ii, col. 196; Clement IV, *Reg.*, no. 427; Boniface VIII, *Reg.*, no. 2886.

[37] 'Eretici e ribelli', iii. 480. Cf. ASV, Reg. Vat. 111, f. 155ʳ, no. 644, f. 158ʳ, no. 653; *Ann. eccles.*, ad ann. 1324, no. 11, xxiv. 245.

[38] Bartholomew of Neocastro, 'Historia sicula', pp. 26–7; Raymond Muntaner, *Chronicle*, i. 279.

[39] See Langlois, *Le Règne de Philippe III*, p. 164.

almost throughout the thirteenth and fourteenth centuries, first from without by the Staufen, and subsequently from within by rival families in the Roman Campagna and by Ghibelline *signori* and communes.[40] Several of the crusades against Christian rulers in Italy were direct responses to these threats. In 1261 Alexander IV declared a crusade against Manfred when he attempted to seize the senatorship at Rome; this crusade was renewed three years later when he launched a campaign aimed at the conquest of the state. Boniface VIII declared a crusade against the Colonna cardinals at the end of 1297 when open warfare broke out between the Colonna and Caetani families for domination of the Campagna, and the justification for the crusade against Venice in 1309–10 was that the city had attempted to establish control of Ferrara, in defiance of papal sovereignty there dating back to Mathilda of Tuscany's donations in 1077–1102.

It is clear from the contemporary sources that there were three separate reasons for the importance which was attached to the Papal State by all the successors of Innocent III. For the popes of the thirteenth century the state was a defensive bulwark, within whose frontiers the Curia could operate without fear of secular interference. Thus in the summer of 1264 Urban IV complained that he could not combat the rising tide of heresy because Manfred had cut off the communications of the Curia with the outside world, 'so that nobody can come to us and we can send nobody out from our court'.[41] Consequently,

Since recourse cannot be had to us, and to the Church, the mistress of true dogma and of the Catholic Faith, and the guardian of ecclesiastical liberty, heresies are springing up, and the heretics are spreading their errors and poison on all sides without encountering any resistance, while ecclesiastical liberty is trampled under foot with impunity.[42]

The state was also intended to prevent the enemies of the Holy See from capturing the pope and his court; it was thus regarded as the most important and most vulnerable part of the Christian Republic. In March 1264 Urban IV described Manfred 'plung-

---

[40] For the Papal State in the period covered here, see Partner, *Lands of St Peter*, pp. 257–331; Waley, *Papal State, passim*; Eitel, *Der Kirchenstaat, passim*.

[41] Urban IV, *Reg.*, no. 809.

[42] Ibid., no. 633.

ing his savage hands into the bowels of the Church'.[43] Since Manfred employed his Muslim troops in this campaign the Curia was able to paint an exceptionally vivid picture, rich in the language of papal supremacy.

For behold the heathens have entered the inheritance of the Lord, they are polluting and profaning the churches and other sacred and pious places . . . Behold the followers of the law of Mahomet daring to invade and shake the Church, the bride of Christ, and the Catholic Faith, in their very foundations . . . Continually they attack the vicar of Christ, the successor to the prince of the apostles, the rector of the Faith, the father of all Christians, the pilot of Peter's bark.[44]

But the importance of the Papal State to the popes cannot be seen solely in terms of their personal safety or of the functioning of their court, if only because after 1304 they were resident outside Italy. Yet in the crusade bulls against the rebels in the state in the 1320s their rebellion against papal authority was described in detail and was obviously considered by the Curia to play a large part in the justification of the crusades against them.[45] No doubt part of the reason for this was that the popes were simply determined to defend their lands with whatever weapons lay at their disposal. But the Curia also felt particularly sensitive about the wider repercussions of events in the state: a blow to the papacy's political power in central Italy was regarded as a blow to its temporal magistracy throughout Christendom. For while the reasoned justification of the authority of the papacy in the Christian order was expressed in theological or theocratic terms, the day-to-day functioning of this authority was visualized in terms of prestige and respect, qualities which the popes felt that they could not enjoy or attract if they could not control the Papal State. As some of the cardinals asked at the time of Benedict XI's death, in 1304, 'How can we rule in other lands if we cannot dominate and pacify our own?'[46]

Thirdly, the Papal State resembled the Holy Land in that it had certain religious associations which made its defence

---

[43] Ibid., no. 778. Cf. ibid., no. 859, where the hands are those of Manfred's Muslim troops, the bowels those of Christ.

[44] Ibid., no. 859.

[45] See, e.g., 'Eretici e ribelli', iii. 472–4.

[46] *Acta arag.*, i, no. 116. See also Waley, *Papal State*, pp. 297–303.

against the enemies of the Faith of paramount importance. One of these associations was the city of Rome. As the second most holy Christian city, the scene of death of St. Peter, St. Paul and innumerable other saints and martyrs, Rome was 'the geographical expression of "Christianitas"'.[47] As early as the eighth century the popes had used its unique appeal to secure Frankish aid against the Lombards; not surprisingly, it played a significant part in the justification of the Italian crusades. It is probable that it was Frederick II's attack on Rome in 1240 which first led Gregory IX to preach the crusade against him, in an emotive scene which skilfully employed the city's relics.[48] In 1264 even the pilgrims were to be called upon to defend Rome against Manfred, and the immediate occasion for the use of the crusade against the Colonna was their threat to Rome and the Campagna at the end of 1297.[49] In his account of Boniface VIII's deposition of the Colonna cardinals in May 1297, one German chronicler made the Pope narrate the events of 1240, in connection with the treachery of John of Colonna on that occasion. According to this account, the enthusiasm displayed in 1240, when Gregory IX's own vestments had been torn up to make crusade crosses for the crowd, had entered into folk memory, for Boniface expected his audience either to have witnessed it or to have heard about it from their fathers.[50] The sanctity of Rome was cleverly turned against the Pope by Louis IV in April 1328. By associating 'this most sacred people and city of Rome' with the imperial cause, he was able to claim that they too were the victims of the crusade which John XXII had declared against himself and his supporters: 'He is preaching the cross against this, Christ's own people, just as if they were traitors.'[51]

The city of Rome was of course exceptional in this respect, but the Papal State as a whole had a special religious signifi-

[47] W. Ullmann, *The Growth of Papal Government in the Middle Ages. A Study in the Ideological Relation of Clerical to Lay Power*, p. 63. Cf. ibid., p. 65: 'Defence of this one church redounds to the good of all Christianity.'

[48] See, e.g., 'Annales placentini Gibellini', *MGHS*, xviii. 483. See also Gregory's own account in *Historia diplomatica Friderici secundi*, ed. J. L. A. Huillard-Bréholles, v, pt. 2, pp. 776–9.

[49] ASV, Reg. Vat. 48, f. 384^{r–v}, no. 76; Urban IV, *Reg.*, no. 778.

[50] 'Gesta Boemundi archiepiscopi Treverensis', *MGHS*, xxiv. 477.

[51] *MGH, Const.* vi, pt. 1, no. 436.

cance which, while it lacked the popular appeal of the sanctity of Rome, influenced the policy of the Curia. The development of the concept of the papal vicariate of Christ led to the increasing identification of the person and possessions of the pope with those of Christ. 'For all practical purposes, and as far as mankind is concerned, the pope is Christ himself.'[52] Thus the state was Christ's property, 'the inheritance of the Lord', or 'the patrimony of the crucified one', and to attack the pope was to attack Christ.[53] Typical of this trend is a phrase in a letter which Urban IV wrote in 1264 to Thomas Agni of Lentino, Bishop of Bethlehem and papal vicar at Rome, thanking him for displaying zeal and energy in preaching the cross against Manfred and his followers, 'for by this action Jesus himself is defended, whom these sons of Belial wanted to crucify again'.[54]

The second major temporal claim of the papacy in Italy was suzerainty over the Kingdom of Sicily. This claim rested on a hotchpotch of legal foundations: the widespread estates held in southern Italy and Sicily by the popes before the eighth century, the donations of Constantine and the emperors of the ninth, tenth and eleventh centuries, and the terms of the treaty of Melfi of 1059.[55] Although papal interventions in southern Italy were dictated by the need to secure a neighbour who would respect the territorial integrity of the Papal State and the enclave of Benevento, the papacy took a deep interest in the internal affairs of the *Regno*, whose rulers paid a large annual *census* to their feudal overlords. The kingdom was regarded as part of the Church's patrimony second only to the Papal State, its inhabitants the 'favoured sons' of the Roman church.[56] From the crusade against Markward of Anweiler onwards the suzerainty of the Holy See in southern Italy played a leading role in the justification of the Italian crusades. In 1248 Frederick II was attacked, among other things, for destroying

---

[52] M. J. Wilks, *The Problem of Sovereignty in the Later Middle Ages. The Papal Monarchy with Augustinus Triumphus and the Publicists*, p. 360.

[53] See, e.g., Boniface VIII, *Reg.*, no. 2388. For the Papal State as the *patrimonium crucifixi* and the *hereditas domini* see Matthew Paris, *Chronica maiora*, iii. 390; Urban IV, *Reg.*, no. 859 (quoted above, p. 45).

[54] Hampe, *Urban IV. und Manfred*, p. 88–9.

[55] See Partner, *Lands of St Peter*, pp. 119–20, and, for a contemporary explanation of the claim, Ptolemy, 'Tractatus', *passim*.

[56] *MGH, Epist. pont.* ii, no. 585. Cf. Boniface VIII, *Reg.*, no. 4127.

the former economic prosperity of the kingdom, and was compared to Pharaoh oppressing the Israelites.[57] After the death of the Emperor at the end of 1250 Innocent IV even tried to convert the papacy's suzerainty into direct control of the kingdom, and he sent the Archbishop of Bari to bring back the inhabitants of the *Regno* 'to fidelity to the Apostolic See', authorizing him to preach the cross against Frederick's sons and their supporters if they should resist.[58] Innocent's plan was frustrated first by the descent of Conrad and then by Manfred's rebellion. Manfred's subsequent illegal occupation of the kingdom was described in the same terms as his father's: 'The towns are burnt, the villages destroyed, the security of the highways violated, travellers robbed, Saracens and schismatics given precedence over Christians.'[59]

The aid given to the Angevin monarchy between 1282 and 1302 was also placed in the context of papal suzerainty in the *Regno*, an approach facilitated by the fact that the Aragonese had inherited Staufen claims there.[60] It is a fundamental misinterpretation of the War of the Vespers to regard the Curia as timidly granting enormous financial subsidies for the waging of an Angevin war. To contemporaries, including the popes, the conflict seemed at least as much the Church's business as that of the Angevin monarchy. In 1284 Martin IV wrote that he considered the Sicilian revolt to be 'our own affair and that of the Church', and in 1301 Boniface VIII described the war as a 'private matter' of the Church.[61] The same argument was put forward by the great Angevin jurist, Bartholomew of Capua, in an attempt to avoid paying back the money borrowed from the papacy in the course of the war, although his gambit met with no success.[62] For four years a papal legate, Gerard Bianchi,

---

[57] *MGH, Epist. pont.* ii, no. 585.

[58] Innocent IV, *Reg.*, no. 5339. See also C. Rodenberg, *Innocenz IV. und das Königreich Sicilien 1245–1254*, pp. 95–113.

[59] Urban IV, *Reg.*, no. 809.

[60] For the war as a continuation of the struggle with the Staufen, see Martin IV, *Reg.*, no. 276.

[61] See P. M. Amiani, *Memorie istoriche della città di Fano*, ii, pp. lxiv–lxv; Boniface VIII, *Reg.*, no. 4127.

[62] See 'Carlo II e i debiti angioini verso la Santa Sede', ed. G. M. Monti, in his *Da Carlo I a Roberto di Angiò. Ricerche e documenti*, pp. 123 ff., esp. 124, 126–7, and below, p. 244. See also *RCAR*, xxviii, Reg. 4, no. 92; 'Die Reden des Logotheten Bartholomäus von Capua', ed. A. Nitschke, *QFIAB*, xxxv (1955), 271.

ruled the kingdom jointly with Robert of Artois, and the papacy rejected a series of treaties which it regarded as prejudicial to its rights in the *Regno*; even the treaty of Caltabellotta was rejected at first by Boniface VIII.[63] Nor did papal suzerainty in the kingdom entirely disappear from the justification of the crusades after 1302. In 1328 Louis IV's planned invasion of the *Regno* was cited against him in the crusade bulls sent to the papal legates in Italy.[64]

The extension of papal political rights in Italy was completed by the decretal 'Si fratrum', issued in March 1317, which asserted that in an imperial vacancy, such as had existed since the death of Henry VII, jurisdiction throughout the empire devolved onto the pope, 'to whom in the person of St. Peter God himself committed the rights both to the earthly and to the heavenly empire'.[65] This was not a new claim: the authority of the pope as a supreme court of appeal during an imperial vacancy had been asserted by Innocent III and exercised in the Angevin interest by Clement IV and Clement V.[66] But John XXII pressed the claim with unprecedented vigour, using it to undermine the legal bases of signorial rule in northern Italy. The charge of rebellion was used in the crusade bulls of 1321 and 1324 against the Visconti, and Bertrand du Poujet was told to advertise the penalties against the supporters of Matthew Visconti 'both by apostolic and also by imperial authority'.[67] The Pope also called on all who owed the Emperor feudal

---

[63] See Honorius IV, *Reg.*, no. 814; Nicholas IV, *Reg.*, nos. 107, 560–2, 1389; Boniface VIII, *Reg.*, no. 5071. For the legation of Gerard of Sabina, see P. Herde, 'Die Legation des Kardinalbischofs Gerhard von Sabina während des Krieges der Sizilischen Vesper und die Synode von Melfi (28. März 1284)', *Rivista di storia della Chiesa in Italia*, xx (1967), *passim*; id., 'Gerardo Bianchi', in *Dizionario biografico degli Italiani* , 10, *passim*; Runciman, *The Sicilian Vespers*, p. 257. E. G. Léonard (*Les Angevins de Naples*, pp. 161–72), describes the period 1285–9 as 'the salvation of the kingdom by the papacy'.

[64] *Thes. novus*, ii, col. 722.

[65] *MGH, Const.* v, no. 401. The legality of the decretal was denied by the Ghibellines. See the 'Ann. mediolanenses' quoted above, p. 41.

[66] See Wilks, *Problem of Sovereignty*, p. 255; F. Baethgen, 'Der Anspruch des Papsttums auf das Reichsvikariat. Untersuchungen zur Theorie und Praxis der potestas indirecta in temporalibus', *Zeitschrift der Savigny-Stiftung für Rechtsgeschichte*, xli, *Kanonistische Abteilung*, x (1920), 172–247.

[67] 'tam apostolica quam imperiali auctoritate', ASV, Reg. Vat. 111, f. 155ʳ, no. 643. Cf. ibid., f. 158ʳ, no. 653. For the use of the charge of rebellion in 1324, see *Ann. eccles.*, ad ann. 1324, no. 11, xxiv. 245.

service in northern Italy to serve in his army against the rebels.[68]

The Curia could thus show that its Italian wars were just, since they were being fought in defence of lands over which the Holy See possessed some form of political or jurisdictional authority, against attack or rebellion. There were, however, few if any crusades which were declared on this basis alone.[69] In general, damage to the lands or rights of the papacy was not considered to be an adequate justification for the use of the crusade. There were two reasons for this. First, there was a strong conservative tradition within the Church and in society at large which frowned on the popes shedding Christian blood to defend their material status alone. Thus the English clergy, asked in 1244 to supply Innocent IV with a subsidy against Frederick II, declared that the secular arm should not be used against the occupiers of Church lands, but only against heretics.[70] This was a dubious claim historically, and it probably arose from unwillingness to pay a papal subsidy rather than from genuine moral scruples, but the fact that it was made suggests that it had at least some popular sympathy behind it, and while the Curia might disagree with the argument, the crusade was an instrument which depended too much on popular support for it to be ignored. Secondly, the cause of the church of Rome was not automatically felt to be that of the Church as a whole. Respect for the office of the pope and full acceptance of his authority within the Church was often tempered by scepticism about the wider significance of his policies in Italy. The fact that attempts to preach the crusade against Manfred in England in 1255 met with derision shows that there was at least sometimes the popular impression that the pope was fighting for himself rather than for the Church or the Christian Faith.[71]

---

[68] ASV, AA., Arm. C, no. 1030; Otto, 'Zur italienischen Politik', pp. 220–1. See also Baethgen, 'Der Anspruch', pp. 247–61.

[69] A possible exception was Clement V's crusade against Venice, which appears to have been justified solely on the basis of the Venetian occupation of Ferrara. See Clement V, *Reg.*, no. 5081.

[70] See 'Ann. de Burton', p. 265. Cf. Matthew Paris, *Chronica maiora*, iv. 39.

[71] See Matthew Paris, *Chronica maiora*, v. 521–2. It should be noted that the preaching was associated with an unpopular royal policy and with heavy clerical taxation.

In the case of the clergy the Curia was able to counter such arguments and doubts with effectiveness. When appealing to the national churches, it claimed that injuries to 'the mother church, the acknowledged head and mistress of all the churches', always affected the Church in general, if only because the pope was compelled to tax the Church in order to counter them.[72] Similarly, when he wrote to the French church in 1264, Urban IV assured it that, quite apart from the other 'innumerable and discernible benefits . . . both spiritual and temporal . . . not only for the Roman, but also for the universal Church', which would result from Charles of Anjou's conquest of the Kingdom of Sicily, one consequence would be that Rome would no longer need to appeal so often for financial aid to the churches across the Alps: the revenue from the Papal State and the *census* payments from the *Regno* would be enough for all her needs.[73] Behind such appeals and assurances there was the implicit argument that a Holy See restored to its full temporal power would be in a stronger position to defend ecclesiastical privileges and exemptions against secular encroachments. In the case of the laity, however, such arguments as these were of little use. When faced by their conservatism or scepticism the papal Curia had substantially to broaden the basis on which the crusades were justified in order to prove that its enemies also posed a genuine threat to the Christian Church and Faith.

Damage to the Church was considered in the form of offences against the ecclesiastical liberties of the Italian episcopate, clergy and Orders. Such offences were a constant theme in the crusade bulls against the Staufen. In the excommunication of Frederick II in 1239 and in his deposition in 1245 he was attacked for several infringements of the privileges of the Church in the *Regno*, in particular for interference with ecclesiastical elections, the imposition of taxes on the clergy, and the subjection of the clergy to secular courts of justice.[74] Charges such as these were levied against many contemporary rulers, but Manfred was accused of more serious crimes: the occupation and misuse of churches and monasteries, the exile, imprisonment, and murder of clerics and prelates, the expro-

---

[72] Boniface VIII, *Reg.*, no. 3917.
[73] Urban IV, *Reg.*, no. 804.
[74] Pope Gregory IX, *Registres*, ed. L. Auvray, no. 5092; *MGH, Const.* ii, no. 400.

priation and spoliation of religious lands, possessions, and revenues. By 1264 he was described as having already killed the Church in the *Regno*, and as being engaged in sucking the marrow from the bones.[75]

None of these charges were made in the War of the Vespers, presumably because the Aragonese received the support of the Sicilian clergy and so did not need to pursue an anti-clerical policy on the island.[76] They were, however, revived when the Ghibelline resurgence in the years after Henry VII's death led to the abuse of ecclesiastical liberties in many parts of northern and central Italy. Matthew Visconti and his sons were accused of every conceivable crime against the established Church: of levying illegal taxes on the clergy, stopping clerics going to Avignon, preventing chapter meetings and synods, driving prelates into exile, imprisoning and killing clerics, and raping nuns.[77] They were especially severe in their confiscation of Church revenues. The seizure of Church money and property was, indeed, practised by most of the Ghibelline *signori*. In the crusade bull of May 1324 against the Estensi, for instance, the Curia alleged that 'they have plundered and are plundering all the churches and monasteries and religious houses in the said cities and dioceses of their ecclesiastical revenues and incomes, subjecting them to tyrannical savagery'.[78] While the main reason for this was no doubt the wealth and vulnerability of the clergy and the religious Orders, it also represented Ghibelline reaction to the fact that, since the pope controlled an increasing number of provisions and appointments, many beneficed clerics were potentially papal agents and propagandists.[79]

The Curia argued that this wholesale looting of Church property and abuse of ecclesiastical privileges led, inevitably, to the neglect of the Church's pastoral duties towards the Italian population. Because of the harassment of the clergy and the confiscation of the means by which they lived, the Church was unable to minister the sacraments or preach the true Faith, and

[75] Urban IV, *Reg.*, nos. 804, 809.

[76] The charges may however have been used in crusade preaching. See Bernard Desclot, *Chronicle of the Reign of King Pedro III of Aragon. A.D. 1276–1285*, p. 218.

[77] See *Ann. eccles.*, ad ann. 1324, nos. 7–9, xxiv. 242–4; R. Michel, 'Le Procès de Matteo et de Galeazzo Visconti', *Mélanges*, xxix (1909), 307–26.

[78] *Codex dipl.* i, no. 710.

[79] See Y. Renouard, *The Avignon Papacy 1305–1403*, p. 100.

this resulted in the growth of heresy and schism. This argument played a large role in the justification of the Italian crusades. In 1264, for example, Urban IV wrote that 'almost everywhere in Italy heresies are springing up, divine worship is diminished, the orthodox Faith is suppressed, the position of the faithful depressed and oppressed, ecclesiastical liberties enslaved, clerical rights trampled underfoot'.[80] Not only was heresy allowed to spread, but the Inquisition was prevented from travelling freely to deal with it, and bishops were unable to visit and correct monastic houses. This last point was taken up by John XXII in the context of northern Italy:

Because of these scandalous oppressions the prelates of the churches have encountered many obstacles in visiting the clergy and others subject to them in their cities and dioceses, in correcting those who need correcting, in preaching the word of God, and in exercising the other spiritual duties of their pastoral office. As a result of which heresies have sprung up and are springing up in those parts, schisms have arisen, divine worship has diminished and the souls of the faithful have been exposed to damnation.[81]

It has often been argued or assumed that the Curia used the charge of heresy more or less indiscriminately in its political struggles in Italy in the thirteenth and fourteenth centuries.[82] In this the heresy charge has been compared to the crusade itself; the author of the most recent comprehensive study of medieval heresy claimed that 'the vague use of heresy charges ran hand in hand with the debasement of the crusade to attain political ends for the popes within christendom, the accusations being a part of the propaganda against offending rulers and a justification for military action against them'.[83] In reality the connection between heresy and the crusades in Italy was much more complicated than this would suggest, and a strong case can be made for the argument that the papal Curia proceeded with great tact and caution.

[80] Urban IV, *Reg.*, no. 809.

[81] *Ann. eccles.*, ad ann. 1324, no.9, xxiv. 244. Cf. John XXII, *Lettres secrètes*, no. 2904.

[82] See, e.g., Throop, *Criticism*, pp. 48–9; Partner, *Lands of St Peter*, p. 314; J. Larner, *The Lords of Romagna. Romagnol Society and the Origins of the Signorie*, p. 190. F. Bock, in 'Studien zum politischen Inquisitionsprozess Johanns XXII.', *QFIAB*. xxvi (1937). 21–2, 31, 61 and *passim*, takes the view that the inquisition only became 'politicized' under John XXII. See also Russell, *Just War*, p. 206.

[83] M. D. Lambert, *Medieval Heresy. Popular Movements from Bogomil to Hus*, p. 172.

It is true that heresy played a large part in the justification of the crusades. Those against Ezzelino of Romano, the Colonna and the Ghibelline *signori* in the 1320s all had heresy as their chief, though not their only, justification. Ghibellinism and heresy had many points of contact. They were united by their common hostility towards the papacy, more specifically by their denial, open in the case of heretics, usually tacit but sometimes open in that of Ghibellines, of the power of the Keys. In addition, the Staufen and Louis IV were able to make propaganda use of the imperial tradition of acting as reformers of a degenerate and materialist Church, which enabled them to attract the support of heretics such as the *fraticelli* who wanted a return to the poverty and humility which they believed had characterized the early Church. Just as many heretics thus embraced the imperial or Ghibelline political programme, furthering its objectives through their preaching and writings, so many Ghibellines could not avoid sliding into religious heterodoxy, as their contempt for the Holy See widened into contempt for the Church generally. Some of the enemies of the Curia, such as Frederick II and Conrad, claimed that they were opposed to heresy and that they were taking active steps against it; Frederick, indeed, was noted for his harsh decrees against heresy. But others, in particular Ezzelino of Romano, Manfred, and the Visconti, kept convicted heretics in their entourage and deliberately harassed the work of the secular clergy and the in-quisition.[84] This was a dangerous policy because of the penalties laid down by the Fourth Lateran Council decree, 'Excommunicamus', against rulers who aided heretics. 'Excommunicamus', drawn up at a time when heresy was very deeply interlocked with social and political forces in Languedoc, established that if a temporal lord neglected to purge his land of heretics when he was asked and required to do so by the Church, he was subject to excommunication and, after a year, his vassals were to be absolved of their oaths of allegiance and his lands offered to true Catholics, who would receive the indulgences and privileges of crusaders for driving out the

---

[84] See *Cod. dipl. ecel.*, no. 183; Urban IV, *Reg.*, no. 809; Matthew Paris, *Chronica maiora*, vi. 301–2; G. Volpe, *Movimenti religiosi e sette ereticali nella società medievale italiana secoli xi–xiv*, pp. 127–34. For Frederick II's decrees against heresy, see Leff, *Heresy*, i. 41–2.

heretics. All who were guilty of receiving, defending or aiding heretics were to be excommunicated and, after a year's contumacy, to be deprived of public office and professional status.[85]

On the other hand, there was a strong temptation for the pope to consider any political opposition to himself as heretical and to declare that any Ghibelline was *ipso facto* a heretic. 'Excommunicamus' established that all those excommunicated on suspicion of heresy who did not submit to the Church in a year were to be condemned as heretics, a ruling quoted by Hostiensis in justification of the crusades against Christian rulers.[86] Similarly, a secular ruler who was responsible for the imposition of an interdict on his lands laid himself open to the charge of aiding heresy, because the cessation of services and preaching enabled heterodox preachers to step into the gap. Consequently, as Hostiensis remarked, 'there is no schism which does not lead to heresy'.[87] Nor could a ruler escape the trap by compelling his clergy to celebrate the divine offices, for this led to the charge of contempt for the Keys; one of the heresy charges against Conrad was that he had the divine offices celebrated during an interdict.[88] To observe the interdict was to acknowledge the justice of the pope's cause, and to break it was to show contempt for the pope's spiritual authority.[89]

The temptation for the papal Curia to equate Ghibellinism with heresy which was created by the strong connections between the two and by the sanctions decreed in 'Excommunicamus' was strengthened by the growing trend in canon law to consider any attack on the established Church and its liberties as heretical.[90] Heresy was said to display itself as much in political hostility to the pope and the Church as in the expression of heterodox beliefs. Ezzelino of Romano, for instance, was condemned as a heretic *ex moribus*, while Urban IV wrote of

---

[85] *Sacr. conc. coll.* xxii, cols. 987–8.

[86] Ibid.; Hostiensis, *Summa aurea*, III, De voto, xix. 297ʳ.

[87] *Summa aurea*, loc. cit.

[88] See Matthew Paris, *Chronica maiora*, vi. 300.

[89] For the contrasted approaches of Louis IV and Frederick of Sicily towards this problem, see F. Testa, *De vita, et rebus gestis Federici II, Siciliae regis*, pp. 297–8; *Acta arag.*, ii, no. 452; *MGH, Const.* vi, pt. i, no. 727. See R. C. Trexler, *The Spiritual Power. Republican Florence under Interdict, passim*, for an interesting study of the workings and consequences of the interdict in the fourteenth century.

[90] See Volpe, *Movimenti religiosi*, pp. 135–54.

Manfred that 'he may be given the name of Christian, but his life and habits do not agree with the Christian religion and he is showing himself to be estranged from it in every way'.[91] This approach was taken up with enthusiasm by Guelf communes such as Orvieto, which passed statutes laying down the same penalties for both Ghibellines and heretics, as if the terms were interchangeable.[92] It was an identification which permeated Guelfism at the popular level and was expressed at its clearest in the function and character of the Guelf Orders and confraternities. Established from the 1230s onwards with the primary aim of combatting catharism in Lombardy and Tuscany, these *societates* soon widened their basis to include the defence of ecclesiastical liberty, so becoming the ideological and political spearhead of the *parte guelfa* in the Italian cities.[93] The most famous of the new groups was the Militia of Jesus Christ, a full-scale religious Order which originated at Parma in 1233, and had as its aim 'the extermination of the depravity of heresy, the observance of justice and the defence of ecclesiastical liberty'. A similar anti-heretical Order was the Militia of the Blessed Virgin Mary, which was founded in 1261. The members of its Third Order were popularly known as the 'jovial friars' (*frati gaudenti*) and came to enjoy an unsavoury reputation for luxurious living, as well as for joining the Order solely to avoid paying taxes.[94] Other *societates* included the Society of St. Hilary, which originated at Parma in 1263, and the Consortium of Faith and Peace, which was founded at Cremona and Piacenza in the wake of the battle of Bentevento. Some of the confraternities became noted for their participation in the struggle against the Ghibellines. In the 1250s the Piacenzan Company of the Cross fought Oberto Pallavicini in Lombardy, and in 1269 Charles I wrote to the Society of Bearers of the Cross (*Societas cruxatorum*) at Parma to thank it for its services to himself and to the Roman church, sending it a banner in token

---

[91] *Cod. dipl. ecel.*, no. 183; Urban IV, *Reg.*, no. 633.

[92] See Volpe, *Movimenti religiosi*, p. 125.

[93] A confraternity for the defence of the Catholic Faith 'contro ogni sorta di eretici e miscredenti' was founded at Piacenza as late as 1460. See G. M. Monti, *Le confraternite medievali dell'alta e media Italia*, i. 99, and *passim* for Italian confraternities generally.

[94] See Salimbene, 'Cronica', pp. 467–9; Dante, *Inferno*, xxiii. 103–8; J. Guiraud, *Histoire de l'Inquisition au Moyen Âge*, ii. 476–7; W. M. Bowsky, *The Finance of the Commune of Siena, 1287–1355*, pp. 81–2; Jordan, *Les Origines*, pp. 365–6.

of his friendship and esteem.[95] Salimbene de Adam even believed that the society had been founded at the instigation of
Charles himself, because Parma was a faithful Guelf city and its
citizens good soldiers. The standing and authority of the society
in Parma were certainly helped by the Angevin conquest; a
series of statutes and ordinances was passed in the city in 1266
granting the members of the confraternity valuable juridical
and financial privileges and exemptions.[96] The Guelf Orders
and confraternities are of particular interest because their
members shared the special juridical status of crusaders and
were granted the plenary indulgence, thus completing the link
between Ghibellinism, heresy, and the crusade. The Society of
the Faith, which St. Peter Martyr founded at Florence in 1244,
had banners consisting of a red cross on a white field, which
resembled the cross displayed by people who made crusade
vows to fight the Ghibellines.[97]

In view of all these connections between Ghibellinism and
heresy it is surprising to find that the Curia not only did not
make an automatic association between the two, but seems to
have avoided making it in cases where the charge of heresy
might be construed as a 'political' one. Frederick II was declared to be suspect of heresy at the Council of Lyons in 1245,
both because of his contempt for the Keys and because of his
notorious tolerance of and friendship with the Muslim inhabitants of his kingdom,[98] but this charge never appeared in the
crusade bulls against him, although fiercer terms of deprecation
were used. Even in the case of Manfred, his own suspected
heresy was played down, and the stress was on his persecution
of the Church and its heretical results. Most important of all,
heresy only once made its appearance during the War of the
Vespers, when Martin IV claimed in 1284 that Peter of Aragon
was sheltering heretics in Sicily by preventing the Inquisition

---

[95] See *RCAR*, ii, Reg. 8, no. 273; Volpe, *Movimenti religiosi*, pp. 170–1; Guiraud, *Histoire*, ii. 549–51.

[96] Salimbene, 'Cronica', p. 375; *Statuta communis Parmae digesta anno MCCLV*, pp. 467–8, 471–2, 478.

[97] Guiraud, *Histoire*, ii. 489; Monti, *Le confraternite*, i. 150–3; Davidsohn, *Geschichte*, ii. 294; *Forschungen zur älteren Geschichte von Florenz*, ed. R. Davidsohn, iv. 426–7. Cf. Salimbene, 'Cronica', p. 467; Monti, *Le confraternite*, i. 9. For the cross worn against the Ghibellines, see below, p. 137.

[98] *MGH, Const.* ii, no. 400.

from going there.[99] In a letter of April 1289 in which he established the Inquisition in southern Italy to deal with the growth
of heresy there, Nicholas IV did not even mention the war or its
effects.[100]

This conservative approach towards the association of heresy
and Ghibellinism was in marked contrast to the forthright
attitude of the Hostiensis, for whom political opposition to the
Holy See could not but entail heresy. The legalism of the papal
supremacist was in fact significantly modified by the Curia
itself in response to a more conservative public opinion, just as
his assertion that the rebellious and disobedient could and must
be punished because they had been baptized and lay within the
Church's jurisdiction was altered to a defensive view: that the
faithful, the *populus christianus*, must be protected against them.
Thus the heresy of Ezzelino of Romano lay as much in his
notorious cruelty towards his subjects as in his heterodox
beliefs. Innocent IV, in language bitter even for him, accused
Ezzelino of harbouring the nature of a brute beast beneath a
human form, and of being the enemy of the human race.[101] This
is not to deny that heresy could be the result of political opposition to the pope, once that opposition voiced itself as denial of
his office or its attributes. When the Colonna cardinals denied
Boniface VIII's papal status they made the use of the charge of
schism and heresy against them inevitable; not to have used it
would have been to admit the justice of their cause.[102]

In the case of both Ezzelino of Romano and the Colonna the
charge of heresy can be described as a 'political' one only if an
excessively fine distinction is drawn between religious heterodoxy and political opposition to the Holy See. This is true also of
the crusades waged by John XXII, in which the use of the
heresy charge against lay powers reached its most elaborate
development. The Inquisition in northern Italy worked in very

---

[99] Martin IV, *Reg.*, no. 587. Cf. Salimbene, 'Cronica', p. 564.
[100] Nicholas IV, *Reg.*, no. 892.
[101] *Cod. dipl. ecel.* no. 183. See also M. Rapisarda, *La signoria di Ezzelino da Romano*, p.
115, and the comments of Salimbene, 'Cronica', pp. 195, 367.
[102] This is clear from Boniface VIII, *Reg.*, no. 2389. See also W. Ullmann, Historical
introduction to H. C. Lea, *The Inquisition of the Middle Ages, its Organization and Operation*,
p. 50. There is a striking precedent for Boniface's crusade against the Colonna in Leo
IX's war against the deposed pope, Benedict IX, and his Tusculan partisans in
1049–50. See Erdmann, *Origin*, pp. 119–20.

close collaboration with John's legates, especially after 1327, when both Bertrand du Poujet and Giovanni Orsini were given overall charge of the Inquisition in their legatine areas.[103] The very large number of trials for heresy and the level of efficiency reached by the Inquisition are apparent in the processes which survive against those who were suspected of heresy or of aiding heretics, some of which were analysed and published by Friedrich Bock.[104] John XXII's crusades represent the papal response to an unprecedented fusion of heresy and Ghibellinism, with the stress on their mutual denial of the legality of the Pope's election, and of papal power in general. The background to this was a serious revival of religious heterodoxy around the turn of the century. Clement V was compelled to declare a crusade against the 'pseudo-apostles' of Fra Dolcino, who claimed that 'all that spiritual power which Christ gave in the beginning to the Church has been translated to the sect of those who call themselves the apostles', and the *béguins*, who were more numerous than the followers of Dolcino, also denied the spiritual powers of the Church, representing John XXII as Antichrist.[105]

These ideas constantly recur in the papal and inquisitorial processes against the Ghibellines. Thus in 1324 Galeazzo Visconti was said to have spoken out against the Keys and 'to have it preached in the presence of all by certain of his clerical and religious supporters that the sentences of excommunication and the other sentences directed against him were not to be feared'.[106] The papal register even emphasizes this point with a little drawing of the keys of St. Peter.[107] Witnesses claimed that Galeazzo also declared that John XXII was not a true pope and that the Ghibellines should elect a new one.[108] The Estensi, too,

---

[103] ASV, Reg. Vat. 114, f. 46ᵛ, no. 228. See also f. 62ᵛ, no. 342.

[104] See 'Studien zum politischen Inquisitionsprozess', *passim*; 'Die Beteiligung der Dominikaner an den Inquisitionsprozessen unter Johann XXII.', *Archivum Fratrum Praedicatorum*, vi (1936), *passim*; 'Der Este-Prozess von 1321', *Archivum Fratrum Praedicatorum*, vii (1937), *passim*.

[105] See Bernard Gui, *Manuel de l'inquisiteur*, i. 88, 110, 148–52. For the heresy of the 'pseudo-apostles', see R. Orioli, *L'eresia dolciniana, passim*; Salimbene, 'Cronica', pp. 255 ff., 619–20; Lambert, *Medieval Heresy*, pp. 193–5; Leff, *Heresy*, i. 191–5. For the crusade against them, see Bernard Gui, 'De secta illorum qui se dicunt esse de ordine apostolorum', *RISNS*, ix⁵ 26–8.

[106] *Ann. eccles.*, ad ann. 1324, no. 8, xxiv. 243.

[107] ASV, Reg. Vat. 112, f. 120ᵛ.

[108] Michel, 'Le Procès', pp. 308–9, 313.

were accused of declaring that John was not a true pope, and of openly expressing their contempt for the ecclesiastical sentences against them.[109] It was claimed that the Ghibellines of Recanati denied that it was sinful to celebrate the divine offices while under interdict, or even to kill priests who refused to do so.[110] Ghibelline adoption of heretical ideas was reinforced by personal contacts and friendships between Ghibellines and heretics; at Ghibelline Spoleto, for example, three citizens convicted of heresy by the Inquisition, one of whom had been condemned to life imprisonment, were given offices in the commune.[111] The Curia also seized eagerly on the fact that many Ghibellines were experimenting in astrology and black magic. The crusade bull of 1321 against Frederick of Montefeltro, which accused him of 'obscene operations and sordid iniquities', and allegiance to 'the most wicked cult of idolatry', was typical of others against the Visconti and the rebels in the Papal State.[112]

The celebrated dispute over Christ's poverty thus only confirmed and brought to the surface what was already a deep undertone of heresy in the Italian opposition to John XXII's political aims. Its importance should not however be underestimated. Not only did it give a specious doctrinal respectability to the beliefs espoused by the Ghibellines, but it was a particularly attractive doctrine for the rebels in the Papal State because it challenged the very basis of papal authority there. Moreover, it effectively crippled a highly important executive arm of the pope, the Order of friars minor. It is significant too that the controversy began at the end of 1321, when John XXII was told about the still serious dissension amongst the Franciscans on the exact nature of Christ's poverty. John might not have reacted with such authoritarianism had he not just ordered the first of his crusades against the Ghibellines. Denial of papal authority was one of the keynotes of their resistance; it

---

[109] 'Der Este-Prozess', pp. 44, 54 ff.; *I libri commemoriali*, i. 241. See also *Codex dipl.* i, no. 710.

[110] See 'Eretici e ribelli', v. 207.

[111] Ibid., iii. 482.

[112] Ibid., 477. See also Giovanni Villani, *Cronica*, ii. 239; G. Biscaro, 'Dante Alighieri e i sortilegi di Matteo e Galeazzo Visconti contro papa Giovanni XXII', *Archivio storico lombardo*, 5th series, xlvii (1920), *passim*; Volpe, *Movimenti religiosi*, pp. 195–8 ; K. Eubel, 'Vom Zaubereiunwesen anfangs des 14. Jahrhunderts', *Historisches Jahrbuch*, xviii (1897), *passim*.

was therefore essential to lay down a ruling on evangelical poverty which would reassert that authority both within and outside the Order of St. Francis.[113] The bull 'Cum inter non-nullos', issued in November 1323, rapidly added to the identification of the imperial–Ghibelline cause with heresy, since Louis IV put himself forward as the champion of those who refused to accept John's controversial ruling. In May 1324, in his Sachsenhausen manifesto, Louis declared John to be a manifest heretic.[114] In the same year appeared Marsilius of Padua's *Defensor pacis*, which poured scorn on the crusade indulgence granted by the Pope to those who fought in Italy, declaring that the crusaders would gain not eternal bliss but eternal damnation: 'they are the soldiers not of Christ, but of the Devil'.[115] The *fraticelli* now added their condemnation of the Pope to that of the *béguins*, and numerous entries in the papal registers record their continual infringement of the interdict, open attacks on papal power, and collusion with the Ghibellines in the late 1320s.[116] In May 1328 the Franciscan Spirituals *de opinione*, led by the Minister General, Michael of Cesena, left the papal cause, taking shelter under the imperial wing of Louis's invading forces, and completing the internal chaos of the Order of St. Francis.[117]

There can be no doubt that John XXII was insensitive to the depth of feeling in the Franciscan Order on the issue of Christ's poverty, that he saw the issue almost entirely in legal terms, and that he resolved the problem by a heavy-handed use of his plenitude of power. His attitude is summed up by the much quoted dictum in his bull 'Quorumdam exigit': 'Poverty is great, but blamelessness is greater, and obedience is the greatest good'.[118] But it should be noted in his defence that at this

---

[113] D. L. Douie's explanation of the dispute, in *The Nature and the Effect of the Heresy of the Fraticelli*, pp. 153 ff., is still the clearest. Leff (*Heresy*, i. 162–6, 206–7), shows a sympathetic insight into the dilemma of the Pope and a rare appreciation of his character. See also M. D. Lambert, *Franciscan Poverty. The Doctrine of the Absolute Poverty of Christ and the Apostles in the Franciscan Order 1210–1323*, pp. 208–45.

[114] *MGH, Const.* v, nos. 909–10.

[115] *Defensor pacis*, Dict. II, Cap. xxvi, 16, p. 510.

[116] See, e.g., ASV, Reg. Vat. 111, f. 104ʳ, no. 419; Reg. Vat. 113, f. 280ʳ⁻ᵛ, no. 1653; Reg. Vat. 114, f. 42ʳ⁻ᵛ, no. 209, f. 211ʳ, no. 1147; Reg. Vat. 115, f. 3ʳ⁻ᵛ, no. 18, f. 34ʳ⁻ᵛ, no. 216, f. 46ᵛ, no. 1260; *Vatikanische Akten zur deutschen Geschichte in der Zeit Kaiser Ludwigs des Bayern*, ed. S. Riezler, no. 772.

[117] See Douie, *Nature and Effect*, pp. 168–76.

[118] See comments by Leff, *Heresy*, i. 208.

time the single overriding concern of the Curia was the struggle with heresy and, in 1328–30, with schism. Heresy was so much the most important consideration in judging the crimes of the Pope's enemies in the 1320s that Raynaldo Bonacolsi was thought worthy of a crusade in 1324 on the basis of his alliance with convicted heretics, and in June 1328 Florence pleaded for the same criterion to apply to the commune's arch-enemy Castruccio Castracani, who was aiding the heretical Louis IV by besieging Pistoia.[119]

Whether they used the charge of heresy or not, the popes were able, by reference to the persecution of the Italian church and its heretical consequences, to relate the crusades more closely to the needs of Christendom than they could have done by describing simply their own grievances, however great and far-reaching these might be. For this reason the papal vicar at Rome in 1246 was told to stress in his crusade preaching against Frederick II the Emperor's persecution of the clergy: 'for how long he has poured out the strength of his savagery against the clergy, with what mad fury he rages continually against them', the aim of this being to convince the audience that Frederick's actions threatened 'not just the Church, but almost all the Christian people'.[120] Frederick, Manfred, and the Ghibelline enemies of John XXII were all accused of wanting to destroy the Christian Faith itself; Manfred was even said to have made an alliance with the Muslims of Lucera solely in order to facilitate his attacks on the Church.[121] These were extreme claims, and they show the importance which the Curia attached to proving the universal relevance of its cause.

ii. 'CRUX CISMARINA' AND 'CRUX TRANSMARINA'

Although their primary justification was the defence of the Faith in Italy, the Italian crusades were frequently related also to the defence of the Latin East. This relationship between Italy and the Levant was expressed in two ways. One was the priority of defending the Church in Italy over the defence of the Holy

---

[119] *Urkunden*, nos. 32, 127. Cf. 'Studien zum politischen Inquisitionsprozess', xxvi. 31–2.

[120] *MGH, Epist pont.* ii, no. 247.

[121] ASV, Reg. Vat. 112, f. 49ᵛ, no. 222ᵃ; *MGH, Epist. pont.* ii, no. 456; *Thes. novus*, ii, col. 196.

Places or the Christians in the East, and the diversion of crusade resources which the enemies of the Curia were thus bringing about; the other was the importance of the Kingdom of Sicily and its rulers in the organization and direction of a successful crusade to the East.

The priority of the crusade in Italy over that to the Holy Land was stated by Hostiensis in terms of Christ's mission on earth.

If it seems correct that we should promote the crusade overseas (*crux transmarina*), which is preached in order to acquire or recover the Holy Land, then we should use all the more vigour in preaching the crusade on this side of the sea (*crux cismarina*), against schismatics, which is aimed at the preservation of ecclesiastical unity . . . For the son of God did not come into the world or suffer the cross to acquire land but to redeem the captive and to recall sinners to repentance . . . [122]

Like Hostiensis's views on heresy, this argument was too extreme for the Curia to employ in this form in its crusade bulls. It was therefore substantially modified. First, the enemies of the Holy See in Italy were equated with the Muslims in their common desire to harm the Church. If anything, the former were more savage in their hostility. Thus when Clement IV wrote to the Hospitallers in the *Regno* in 1267 exhorting them to take the cross against Conradin's supporters in Sicily, he assured them that the custom of their Order which forbad them to fight anybody but Muslims could be ignored in this instance because 'they differ little from the Saracens, and indeed some are worse than the Saracens'.[123] Secondly, the threat to the Church and the Faith from the rebel Christians was greater than that from the Muslims, for reasons of geography.[124] Common sense dictated that the nearer danger should be dealt with first, and that the crusade against the Muslims must be delayed until the Church was secure from attack at home.

Such arguments naturally rested on a certain interpretation of the historical function of the crusade, in particular that it represented the Church's way of combating its enemies on

---

[122] *Summa aurea*, III, De voto, xix. 297ʳ.
[123] *Thes. novus*, ii, col. 532. The Pope was probably referring to a Hospitaller ruling (*esgart*) of c. 1239. See *Cartulaire général de l'Ordre des Hospitaliers de S. Jean de Jérusalem (1100–1310)*, ed. J. Delaville le Roulx, ii, no. 2213, p. 543.
[124] See, e.g., 'Ann. de Burton', p. 352; Urban IV, *Reg.*, no. 860.

whichever 'front' they fought, that only a pope could declare a crusade, and that only he could decide where a crusade was most needed. Certain aspects of this interpretation can be traced back to the second crusade, if not to the very beginning of the crusade movement.[125] Other aspects owed their plausibility largely to the innovations and organizational genius of Pope Innocent III and to the skill of his successors in taking advantage of the precedents which he established.[126] While this approach towards the crusade and its function enabled the Curia to justify employing the crusade in the implementation of its Italian policy, it also made it vulnerable to the attacks of its enemies. For since the crusade movement was treated as a unified entity controlled and directed by the Holy See, the failure of the crusades in the Latin East could be laid at the Pope's door. As we shall see, the Ghibellines consistently claimed that the disasters in Latin Syria and in other areas where Christians were exposed to the attacks of non-believers were the direct result of the system of priorities ruthlessly adhered to by the Curia.[127] In order to counter or anticipate such attacks, the crusade bulls asserted that it was not the Holy See, but its enemies, who were impeding the crusade to the East, by creating the need for crusades in Italy. This was a charge first used by Innocent III against Markward of Anweiler, and constantly reiterated during the struggle with the Staufen; in 1239, for example, Frederick II was accused of 'impeding the business of the Holy Land and of Romania'.[128] It was during the War of the Vespers that the charge of diverting crusade resources received its fullest treatment at the hands of the Curia, obviously because of the Christian losses in Syria at this time. Much more than in the cases of the crusades against the Staufen or the Ghibelline *signori*, the crusade against the Aragonese and the Sicilians was justified in terms of the needs of the Latin East.[129]

[125] See Riley-Smith, *What were the Crusades?*, pp. 34 ff.; G. Constable, 'The Second Crusade as seen by Contemporaries', *Traditio*, ix (1953), 220, 223–4 and *passim*; Villey, 'L'Idée de la Croisade', pp. 578–81.

[126] See Mayer, *The Crusades*, pp. 205 ff.; H. Roscher, *Papst Innocenz III. und die Kreuzzüge, passim*.

[127] See below, pp. 78–9.

[128] See *Patr. curs. comp.* ccxiv, no. 558, col. 514; Gregory IX, *Registres*, no. 5092. By 'Romania' the Pope meant the Latin empire of Constantinople.

[129] See below, pp. 75–6.

Although the papal Curia was generally content to put the
offences of its enemies in this respect in terms of unconscious
and indirect aid to the Muslims, it occasionally employed the
canonical concept of *impium foedus*, a blasphemous alliance with
other enemies of the Church in order to do her more harm. In
1245 Frederick II was attacked for his treaty of 1229 with the
Muslims in Syria, and for exchanging messengers with the
Sultan. Matthew Visconti was accused of making alliances with
the King of Tunis and the Emperor of the Greeks, and of
sending messengers to Muslim leaders asking them for money
with which to defeat the papal troops.[130] In his Maundy Thurs-
day process of 1300 Boniface VIII remarked of Frederick of
Aragon and the Sicilians that 'they are showing themselves to
be the allies and associates of the enemies of the cross of Christ
and the foes of the Christian Faith'.[131] The outstanding example of *impium foedus* was the Staufen tolerance of and active
employment of the Muslim colony of Lucera. Useful as the
Curia found the colony to be in propaganda terms, the existence
of such an outpost of Islam, less than 200 miles from Rome, and
the tolerance with which the Staufen permitted it to observe all
the laws and customs of that faith, even the daily call of the
muezzin, seems to have genuinely appalled the popes; Boniface
VIII was delighted at its final destruction in 1300.[132] Lucera
certainly struck the imagination of others. Charles of Anjou
disdainfully called Manfred 'the sultan of Lucera', and in 1258
the English nobles at the parliament of London considered that
all vows taken to go to the Holy Land should be commuted to
help Henry III to conquer the Kingdom of Sicily, 'which can be
done with honesty because of the town of Lucera in Apulia,
which is inhabited by infidels'.[133]

Both the general charge of diverting crusade resources from
the East and the specific accusation of *impium foedus* played a

[130] *MGH, Const.* ii, no. 400; Michel, 'Le Procès', p. 323. See also *MGH, Epist. pont.* ii,
no. 456.

[131] Boniface VIII, *Reg.*, no. 3879.

[132] See P. Egidi, 'La colonia saracena di Lucera e la sua distruzione', *ASPN*,
xxxvi–xxxix (1911–14), *passim*; F. Gabrieli, 'Le ambascerie di Baibars a Manfredi', in
Studi medievali in onore di Antonino de Stefano, passim. R. Bevere ('Ancora sulla causa della
distruzione della colonia saracena di Lucera', *ASPN*, NS, xxi (1935), p. 224), stresses
that the Angevins destroyed the colony in 1300 partly in order to please Boniface VIII
in the Jubilee year.

[133] Giovanni Villani, *Cronica*, i. 325–6; Matthew Paris, *Chronica maiora*, v. 680–1.

much smaller part in the justification of the crusades waged by John XXII than they had done in the thirteenth-century crusades. There was no lack of material for the charge: the Visconti were accused of preventing the despatch to Avignon of clerical taxes intended for the crusade to the Holy Land, and in 1322 John XXII complained that the crusade against Matthew Visconti constituted a serious obstacle to the recovery of the Holy Places.[134] But the crusade bulls rarely strayed beyond the themes of rebellion, persecution of the Church, and heresy; nor did the Latin East appear in Augustinus Triumphus's justification of crusades against Christian lay powers, as it had in that of Hostiensis. The charge of heresy against the Ghibellines was no doubt considered to be serious enough to justify a crusade against them without introducing extra charges, while the loss of the Latin states in Syria made it more difficult for the Pope's enemies to assert that his crusades in Italy were impeding an immediate passage to the East.[135]

Like so many of the arguments examined here, the idea that a crusade in Italy not only took priority over a crusade to the Holy Land, but could also act as an essential preliminary to it, had its origins in the crusade which Innocent III declared against Markward of Anweiler. In 1199 Innocent wrote that if Sicily was held against the Church by Markward and his Muslim allies, no hope would remain of recovering the land lost in Palestine. If the island was regained, on the other hand, 'it will be possible to come to the aid of the Holy Land more easily'.[136] The Pope was clearly thinking not of Sicilian crusaders, but of logistical factors of transport and supplies. The eastern ports of the *Regno*, Bari, Barletta, and Trani, were amongst the most popular embarkation points for the crusade, while Sicily was a convenient stopping-off point for French contingents. The *Regno* was also one of the most important sources of supplies of food and horses for the Latins of the East. Thus, when Henry III expressed his desire to commute his vow of going to the Holy Land to one of conquering the Kingdom of Sicily, his request

---

[134] ASV, Reg. Vat. 111, f. 155ᵛ, no. 644; Biblioteca Vaticana, MS Vat. lat. no. 3937, pp. cxvi–cxvii; Michel, 'Le Procès', pp. 311, 314.

[135] But see below, p. 79.

[136] *Patr. curs. comp.* ccxiv, no. 221, col. 782. See Kennan, 'Innocent III', p. 231, for a different interpretation of this passage.

was refused, at first, because 'when the Kingdom of Sicily has been won, you will be able the more easily, conveniently, and efficaciously to help the Holy Land'.[137] Martin IV exempted merchants carrying supplies to the East from the ban on trade with the rebel Sicilians which he imposed in November 1283, and in June 1284 he accused Peter of Aragon and the Sicilians of deliberately preventing the transport of food to the Holy Land, which depended very heavily on the island for supplies.[138]

In attributing such importance to the Kingdom of Sicily the Curia was reflecting contemporary practice and feeling. The first three Angevin kings wrote numerous letters to their customs and port officials ordering them to allow the military Orders to export food and horses to the Latin East, sometimes without paying the normal duty.[139] In 1267 Louis IX expected his brother to supply his forthcoming crusade with food, livestock, and horses.[140] The loss of Sicily does not seem to have seriously affected this role. When Benedict XII spent 10,000 florins on a cargo of cereals to be exported to the famine-stricken Armenians, it was to Apulia that he turned for the grain, although King Robert would only waive export duty on two-fifths of it.[141] The author of the 'Directorium ad passagium faciendum', writing in 1332, could still praise the potential of both Apulia and Sicily as sources of food supplies for a crusading expedition, and John XXII also expected the *Regno* to help supply the expedition.[142] Contemporaries also agreed with the Curia on the importance of the kingdom's ports as crusade embarkation points. For the reconquest of Constantinople, lost to the Latins in 1261, the use of the Apulian ports, indeed the active involvement of the kingdom and its rulers, was a *sine qua non*, a consideration which explains the rapidity with which the exiled Latin emperor, Baldwin II, an ally of Manfred, changed

---

[137] *Foedera*, i, pt. 1, p. 304.

[138] Martin IV, *Reg.*, nos. 587, 482. Cf. Salimbene, 'Cronica', p. 564.

[139] See, e.g., *RCAR*, i, Reg. 6, nos. 398, 402, 410–11; *Annali delle Due Sicilie dall'origine e fondazione della monarchia fino a tutto il regno dell'augusto sovrano Carlo III. Borbone*, comp. M. Camera, ii. 198–200; 'Notizie storiche', p. 261; *Syllabus membranarum ad regiae Siclae archivum pertinentium*, ed. A. A. Scotti *et al.*, ii. 213–14, iii. 22.

[140] Sternfeld, *Ludwigs des Heiligen Kreuzzug nach Tunis*, p. 322.

[141] Y. Renouard, 'Une Expédition de céréales des Pouilles en Arménie par les Bardi pour le compte de Benoît XII', *Mélanges*, liii (1936), *passim*.

[142] 'Directorium ad passagium faciendum', *RHC, Documents arméniens*, ii. 403; John XXII, *Lettres secrètes*, no. 5392.

his allegiance to Charles of Anjou after Benevento.[143] In the 'Directorium', which was written for the crusade planned by Philip VI of Valois in the 1330s, it was claimed that peace between Robert of Naples and Frederick of Sicily was essential for the success of the crusade, because it required the ports, ships, and sailors of southern Italy and Sicily.[144] The plan of the author of the 'Directorium' was to conquer Constantinople and use it as a base for the reconquest of Palestine, so it was inevitable that he should envisage a crusade departure from southern Italy. But Philip VI's advisers, who in general rejected the suggestions of the 'Directorium', also advocated the departure of at least Philip himself from Naples, so that Italians from Tuscany and Lombardy would join the crusade, and he could obtain the advice of his relation Robert.[145]

The papal Curia also saw the Angevin kings of Sicily as potential crusaders in the Latin East; indeed, the Angevin candidature for, and conquest of, the kingdom, made the traditional crusade role of the *Regno* even more striking, for they were seen in terms of the well-known zeal of the Capetians for crusading overseas. Though it was not stated in the treaty by which Charles of Anjou was enfeoffed with Sicily, it was accepted by both sides, as well as by many contemporaries, that the conquest of the kingdom was only the prelude to a crusade either to reinforce the Latins in Syria, or to reconquer Constantinople. Both of these projects, Urban IV wrote, depended on the success of the Guelf cause in Italy.[146] Crusading enthusiasts saw this as a commitment to which Charles I was morally bound, and in 1267 and 1277 Louis IX and the French poet Rutebeuf pressed the King to take part in an expedition to the East.[147] Once associated in this way, Italy and the Latin East remained locked together in papal policy. At the turn of the century Boniface VIII attempted to recreate the successful alliance of the 1260s with his plan for Charles of Valois to settle

---

[143] See D. J. Geanakoplos, *Emperor Michael Palaeologus and the West 1258–1282. A Study in Byzantine–Latin Relations*, pp. 194 ff.

[144] 'Directorium', pp. 403–5.

[145] See J. Delaville le Roulx, *La France en Orient au xive siècle*, ii. 9–11.

[146] Urban IV, *Reg.*, no. 813. Cf. *Thes. novus*, ii, col. 72. See also Jordan, *Les Origines*, p. 406; Borsari, 'La politica', p. 319.

[147] See Sternfeld, *Ludwigs des Heiligen Kreuzzug nach Tunis*, p. 321; Rutebeuf, *Onze poèmes concernant la Croisade*, p. 121.

disputes in Italy and then lead a general passage to the East.[148] They were even associated in the legatine commission of Archbishop Bertrand of Embrun in October 1333. The Archbishop was to intervene between Bertrand du Poujet and the dissident Guelfs in Lombardy, to reform the Papal State, and to organize the defence of the Latins in Greece against the Turks.[149]

iii. CONCLUSION

The most important aim of the papacy in justifying the Italian crusades was to present the struggle in Italy as an issue which affected all Christians. Thus Clement IV claimed that as a result of the conquest of the *Regno* by Charles of Anjou 'the kingdom itself will enjoy its longed-for peace, Italy will rejoice, freed of its wars and internal upheavals, the status of the Roman empire will be restored, and the Holy Land will be relieved by a strong hand'.[150] Urban IV had been even more expansive in his letter to the French clergy in May 1264, when he asserted that the Angevin candidature involved 'not only the relief of the Roman and universal Church, but also the exaltation and promotion of the Faith, the salvation of souls, the strengthening of the standing of the faithful, the weakening of that of the unfaithful, and the expansion of divine worship'.[151] Such statements are sometimes taken as examples of the aggressive nature of the papal monarchy in this period, or of the radicalism of curialist thought; 'a succession of Italian civil wars of the thirteenth and fourteenth centuries', as they have recently been called,[152] were thus represented as somehow involving all Christendom. In fact, the most striking aspect of the papacy's justification of its crusades in Italy is its conservatism, which was dictated by the conservatism of public opinion. The internal structure of the crusade bulls, in particular the careful progression from a detailed description of the harm sustained by the Curia and its allies to one of the harm which had been

---

[148] See Boniface VIII, *Reg.*, no. 3917.
[149] ASV, Reg. Vat. 117, ff. 255ᵛ–257ᵛ, nos. 1305, 1308–11, 1314–18. See also Otto, 'Benedikt XII.', pp. 61–2. Cf. B. Guillemain, *La Cour pontificale d'Avignon (1309–1376). Étude d'une société*, pp. 286–7, on the career of John Amiel.
[150] *Thes. novus*, ii, col. 197.
[151] Urban IV, *Reg.*, no. 804.
[152] J. Sumption, review of Riley-Smith, *What were the Crusades?*, *Times Literary Supplement*, no. 3930 (8 July 1977), p. 825.

done, and could be done, to the Church as a whole, shows clearly that the popes looked on the wider significance of their Italian wars as something to be proved, not assumed. This is evident when we compare the crusade bulls with the short passage in Hostiensis. In considering both the connection between political opposition to the Church and heresy, and the relationship between the crusade in Italy and that in the East, the Curia toned down the claims of the great canonist. It avoided charges of heresy which might be construed as overtly political, and it argued not that the threat in Italy was of a higher order than that in the East, but simply that it was more serious because of its proximity to the Holy See. Even then it took pains to link the crusade in Italy to a forthcoming general passage. In addition, far from ruthlessly expanding the basis of the crusade's justification, to cover attacks on the papacy's political status, the Curia tended to use existing justifications, in particular, to relate its Italian crusades to the threat of heresy or the needs of the Holy Land. The result of this conservatism is that papal justification of the crusades in Italy is remarkable more for its continuity than for its development or change.[153] Once the principal arguments had been set out in the crusades against Markward of Anweiler and Frederick II they changed very little. There were interesting minor fluctuations in the papal approach to the crusades: whereas in the 1240s Innocent IV justified the crusade against Frederick II in terms of the Emperor's persecution of the Church, John XXII deliberately held back the use of the crusade against Louis IV until he had been convicted of heresy, despite his impassioned boast in consistory, in 1323, that he would teach Louis's German followers what ferocity was.[154] But on the whole the crusades were fought on principles which remained remarkably stable.

---

[153] Cf. the conclusion of J. A. Watt on the canonists' treatment of papal monarchy in the thirteenth century, in *The Theory of Papal Monarchy in the Thirteenth Century. The Contribution of the Canonists*, p. 138: '. . . the really fundamental positions, at least as far as applications were concerned, remained the same'.

[154] See *Acta arag.* i, no. 262.

Chapter 3

Papal Crusade Policy in Practice

A collision between the interests of the papal Curia and its allies in Italy and those of the Christians in the East was inevitable: both required the undivided resources of the crusade, in terms both of crusaders and of money. We have seen how the Curia tried to avoid receiving the blame for this collision and its consequences, and even attempted to turn them to its own advantage by representing the Italian crusades as essential preliminaries to effective expeditions to relieve the Latin East.[1] But this approach encountered powerful obstacles. Papal policy was opposed both by the propaganda of the pope's enemies in Italy and Europe generally, and by the arguments and diplomatic pressure of enthusiasts for the crusade to the East. The aim of this chapter is to examine this opposition and see what modifications, if any, it succeeded in forcing on the approach of the Holy See.

i. THE CONFLICTING NEEDS OF ITALY AND THE CHRISTIAN EAST

For almost exactly a half of the period 1254–1343 the papacy was engaged in waging crusades against Christian rulers in Italy. Unfortunately for the Curia, these crusades nearly always coincided with periods of crisis in the Latin East, or at least with periods of enthusiasm in western Europe for a crusade to the Holy Land. The series of coincidences began with the crusade against the Staufen. Innocent IV resumed Gregory IX's crusade against Frederick II in June 1246, when King Louis of France was already promoting crusade preaching and collecting revenue on behalf of his own crusading expedition.[2] The

---

[1] Pope Gregory XI provided a concise definition of this approach in a letter to the King of Hungary in 1372, when he wrote that 'depositio tyrannorum est dispositio passagii contra Turchos'. *Vetera monumenta historica Hungariam sacram illustrantia*, ed. A. Theiner, ii, no. 267.

[2] *MGH, Epist. pont.* ii, no. 199; J. R. Strayer, 'The Crusades of Louis IX', in Setton (ed.), *History of the Crusades*, ii. 490–2.

crusade against the Emperor, and subsequently against Conrad, reached its height during Louis's crusade, imprisonment in
Egypt, and sojourn in Palestine. The tension caused by these
conflicting crusades relaxed with the return of the French King
from Acre in 1254 and the relatively passive policy adopted
by Pope Alexander IV in Italy while he concentrated on the
abortive negotiations with Henry III. But this period of calm
did not last long; after 1260 events became critical both in Italy
and in the Latin East. In Italy Alexander's negligence meant
that by the Pope's death in May 1261 Manfred had established
a virtual stranglehold on the papacy's lands in central Italy.[3]
In the East the crisis was twofold. The great Mamluk Sultan,
Baybars, started to execute systematic military campaigns
against Latin Syria, and the Greek Emperor of Nicaea, Michael
Palaeologus, succeeded in routing his rival, the Despot of
Epirus, at the battle of Pelagonia in 1259, and in capturing
Constantinople from the Latins in 1261.[4]

At his election in August 1261 Urban IV was thus confronted
with three very urgent threats to Christendom, all of which
were by now associated with the crusade. The most difficult
aspect of this tripartite crisis was the clash between the crusade against Manfred and the crusade planned to relieve the
Christians in Palestine. Inexorably their planning and organization conflicted. In January 1263 a five-year crusade
hundredth was levied in the Kingdom of France and the diocese
of Cambrai, and Archbishop Giles of Tyre was given a commission to collect it and to preach a crusade to the Holy Land;
preaching was also set in motion in many other parts of
Europe.[5] In the following year the negotiations with Charles of
Anjou were brought to a successful conclusion and Manfred
launched his deepest plunge yet into the Papal State, an action
which led to widespread crusade preaching against him. At the
same time as preaching was at its height in France for the
expedition of Charles of Anjou, and the expedition itself was

---

[3] See Jordan, *Les Origines*, pp. 262–70.

[4] See Geanakoplos, *Emperor Michael Palaeologus*, pp. 59–115.

[5] Urban IV, *Reg.*, nos. 203, 373–97; *Reg. Cam.*, nos. 310–32; V. Cramer, *Albert der
Grosse als Kreuzzugs-Legat für Deutschland 1263–4 und die Kreuzzugs-Bestrebungen Urbans IV.*,
passim.

taking place, Baybars was achieving a spectacular string of victories in Palestine, including the captures of Caesarea and Arsuf in 1265, and Safed and Toron in 1266.[6]

The crusade against the Aragonese and the Sicilians coincided with a similar series of losses in Latin Syria. The news of the capture of Lattakieh in 1287, of Tripoli in 1289, and Acre and the other surviving mainland towns in 1291, reached Europe at a time when several of the powers traditionally associated with the crusade, including France, Aragon, Sicily, and the papacy, were preoccupied by the War of the Vespers. Throughout the last ten years of the conflict over Sicily the Curia was keenly aware of the need to mount a crusade to regain the Holy Land before the emotional shock of its loss ceased to make itself felt. The years that followed the treaty of Caltabellotta were of crucial importance in this respect. Clement V entered into crusade negotiations with various secular powers, and placed the Hospitaller crusade of 1309 on an equal footing with the crusade against Venice.[7] Nor did the crusade proposals presented and discussed at the Curia lack popular support. After 1313, when Philip IV and his three sons took the cross, there was a wave of crusading zeal in France; Philip's successors, in particular Philip V, Charles IV, and Philip VI of Valois, all threw the weight of the French crown behind the planning of a crusade to regain the Holy Places.[8] The election of John XXII in August 1316, after an interregnum of more than two years, was therefore an event of potential significance in the history of the crusades. Not only did there appear to be enough crusade enthusiasm in the West to organize and launch a crusade to the Latin East, but the Curia was not hindered by the obstacle of a major war in Italy.

At first it seemed that the new pope would take advantage of this situation. Shortly after his coronation, on 14 September

---

[6] See S. Runciman, 'The Crusader States, 1243–1291', in Setton (ed.), *History of the Crusades*, ii. 575–6.

[7] *Acta arag.*, iii, no. 97. See also L. Thier, *Kreuzzugsbemühungen unter Papst Clemens V. (1305–1314)*, pp. 92–3 and *passim*.

[8] See 'Continuatio chronici Guillelmi de Nangiaco, a monacho benedictino abbatiae S. Dionysii in Francia', *RHGF*, xx. 607; *Acta arag.* i, no. 308; A. De Boislisle, 'Projet de Croisade du premier duc de Bourbon (1316–1333)', *Annuaire-bulletin de la Société de l'histoire de France*, ix (1872), *passim*; Delaville le Roulx, *La France en Orient*, i. 78–102.

1316, he presided over an impressive ceremony at Lyons, at which the crusade was preached and it was announced that Louis of Clermont and more than 5,000 French nobles had taken the cross. A general passage was arranged to take place in March 1318.[9] In July 1317 John registered a personal triumph by securing a truce of three and a half years between Robert of Naples and Frederick of Sicily. He pressed Robert to come to Avignon to discuss the details of a crusade to the Holy Land with himself, Philip V, and Charles of Valois, or their representatives.[10] But from the very start of the Pope's reign the position of the Guelfs in Italy deteriorated, and events moved towards renewed papal intervention on their behalf. The most serious clash came over Genoa, a city crippled by internal conflict between Guelfs and Ghibellines, but possessing a great fleet and substantial interests in the eastern Mediterranean. John XXII saw the establishment of a stable and reliable regime in Genoa as the essential prerequisite for his planned crusade.[11] The exiled Genoese Ghibellines, led by the Doria and Spinola families, were supported by Matthew Visconti and the Ghibelline league, while the Guelfs vested the *signoria* of the city in Robert of Naples and the Church in July 1318.[12]

There are signs that in 1318 the Pope still hoped that the situation at Genoa would not seriously impede the crusade,[13] but in the course of the next two years he took steps which added up to a postponement of the general passage until the political situation in Italy could be settled to the Guelf advantage. The most important of these were the appointment of Bertrand du Poujet as legate in July 1319, and the papal backing given to the unfruitful intervention of Philip of Valois in Lombardy in 1320. The key document on John XXII's approach at this time is a letter which he wrote to Philip V between September 1319 and the summer of 1320. In it he wrote that there was no chance of a crusade because all of

[9] *Acta arag.* i, no. 145. See also Tabacco, *La casa di Francia*, pp. 63–7.

[10] See John XXII, *Lettres secrètes*, nos. 365, 480, 508, 667, 829.

[11] See, e.g., John XXII, *Lettres secrètes*, no. 1227; R. St. Clair Baddeley, *Robert the Wise and his Heirs 1278–1352*, pp. 509–10.

[12] See Mollat, *Popes at Avignon*, pp. 76–82.

[13] See ASV, Reg. Vat. 109, ff. 172ᵛ–173ʳ, no. 669, f. 186ᵛ, no. 706; St. Clair Baddeley, *Robert the Wise*, p. 508.

Christendom was entangled in wars and disputes: England against Scotland, Robert of Naples against Frederick of Sicily, Cyprus against Armenia, Guelf against Ghibelline, the German princes amongst themselves. In addition, the Spanish kingdoms were fully occupied with fighting the Muslims on their borders, and the Hospitallers were crippled by debts of over 360,000 florins.[14] Few of these powers had ever co-operated fully with the Pope in planning a crusade; it was Italy, which tied down the Curia, Naples, and France, which was really responsible for the Pope's pessimism. From this point onwards the suppression of French crusade enthusiasm was to be a constantly recurring feature of John's reign. In 1323 Charles IV was diverted from his project for a crusade by the papal offer of support for a French candidature to the empire, and in 1330–1 Philip VI was briefly deflected from his crusade plans by the tempting offer of a kingdom in Lombardy.[15] By the time the Curia was sufficiently free of Italian commitments to give its full backing to the crusade aspirations of the French crown, the outbreak of the Hundred Years War made them no longer practicable.

ii. THE CHALLENGE TO PAPAL POLICY

This series of coincidences was not necessarily detrimental either to the efficacy or to the popularity of papal crusade policy. Given the right circumstances, a crisis in the Latin East could give credence to the standard papal claim that the enemies of the Church were impeding a crusade to the East. In September 1283 Martin IV complained that the Sicilian revolt had prevented Charles I invading the Byzantine empire at a time when conquest would have proved easy because of the King's detailed preparations and the rumoured disputes between the Emperor Michael VIII Palaeologus and his sons. He also warned that unless the rebellion was quickly suppressed, all the crusading plans still current from the time of the

---

[14] John XXII, *Lettres secrètes*, no. 1227. For the dating of this letter, see Tabacco, *La casa di Francia*, pp. 222–3. On Hospitaller debts, see A. Luttrell, 'The Hospitallers at Rhodes, 1306–1421', in Setton (ed.), *History of the Crusades*, iii. 290–1.
[15] Tabacco, *La casa di Francia*, pp. 218, 304–5.

Second Council of Lyons would be frustrated: 'All the work done, not just by our predecessor Pope Gregory X of happy memory and his brothers, but by the universal Church . . . for the preparation of aid for the Holy Land, will be denied any fulfilment.'[16] Similarly, in 1300 Boniface VIII was able to make political capital out of the news that the Mongols, who had defeated the Mamluks in December 1299 with Armenian and Cypriot aid, were offering Jerusalem to the Christians. That the West could not respond to this offer was, Boniface maintained, partly the fault of the Sicilian rebels. It was they who were responsible for the loss of the Holy Land in the first place, and it was their continued obstinacy which was preventing Christendom from taking advantage of this new opportunity to regain the Holy Land, 'which divine mercy has recently liberated from the hands of the Saracens, as if by a miracle'.[17]

In most cases, however, bad news from the Latin East, or a renewal of crusade enthusiasm in the West, led to pressure on the Holy See to make peace with its Christian enemies in order to concentrate on the crusade overseas. This pressure increased significantly if the papal claim that the crusade in Italy was an essential preliminary to an expedition to the East was obviously without foundation. It was plausible that Charles of Anjou's expedition against Manfred was such a 'preliminary' crusade; similarly, Charles's campaigns against the Sicilians, in 1282–5, could be seen as a prelude to his crusade against the Greeks. But such a claim could hardly be advanced in the period after 1285, when Charles I had died, Angevin power had reached its nadir, Charles of Salerno was a prisoner, and much of the *Regno* was occupied. At times such as these the Curia was especially vulnerable to pressure to reverse its priorities and make peace overtures and concessions to its Christian enemies.

Such pressure came from several sources. First, it was exerted by Christian powers in the Levant. From the time of the Second Crusade onwards newsletters and delegations from Latin Syria had arrived with frequency in the courts of western Europe

[16] Martin IV, *Reg.*, no. 457.
[17] Boniface VIII, *Reg.*, no. 3879. Cf. ibid., no. 3917.

asking for men and money.[18] In the thirteenth and fourteenth centuries the Christians in the East, whether in Syria, Cyprus, Greece, or Armenia, identified the preoccupation of the papacy with Italy as one of the reasons why the West was not responding to such requests. They saw their own needs as being more important than the recovery of papal lands or rights, and did not fail to say so. Thus in 1262–3 Baldwin of Courtenay, the exiled Latin Emperor of Constantinople, placed pressure on the Curia, both by his own arguments and by his influence at the French court, to make peace with Manfred in order to mount a crusade to regain Constantinople.[19] Bartholomew of Neocastro recounted a dramatic but implausible story of a Templar messenger from the Holy Land appearing at the Curia in 1289 to blame Nicholas IV and the war against the Sicilians for the loss of Tripoli.

You could have relieved the Holy Land with the power of the kings and the strength of the other faithful of Christ, and you would not have had to bear so many wrongs from the heathen. But you preferred to attack a Christian king and the Christian Sicilians, arming kings against a king to recover the island of Sicily, which took up just arms in the struggle against oppression.[20]

Unless he made peace with the Sicilians and sent help at once Acre too would fall. In 1298 the Patriarch of Armenia, Gregory, wrote to Boniface VIII begging him to pacify Europe and send help to Cilician Armenia, and in 1327 ambassadors came from King Leon V of Armenia to make the same request of John XXII.[21] It is possible that such arrivals caused consternation at the Curia, which regarded the protection of the Latin Christians in the East as a responsibility of the Roman church, but they lacked the diplomatic weight effectively to alter papal policy. They were invariably promised aid once the Curia was freed of its Italian commitments, and sometimes supplied with funds to help them in the meantime. These were not insubstantial: the

---

[18] See R. C. Smail, 'Latin Syria and the West, 1149–1187', *Transactions of the Royal Historical Society*, 5th series, xix (1969), 3–4 and *passim*.

[19] See Jordan, *Les Origines*, pp. 384–90. The Latins in Syria were represented in these negotiations by John of Valenciennes, lord of Cayphas.

[20] Bartholomew of Neocastro, 'Historia sicula', pp. 108–9.

[21] ASV, Reg. Vat. 114, ff. 93ᵛ–94ʳ, no. 535; Boniface VIII, *Reg.*, no. 2663.

Armenian ambassadors who approached John XXII secured at least 52,393 florins.[22]

A second source of pressure was made up of the papacy's own enemies in Europe. From the Emperor Frederick II onwards a tradition of propaganda developed amongst the Ghibelline powers, which learnt to use the news of disasters in the Latin East as a diplomatic weapon to try to compel the Curia to make peace.[23] Their comments centred on two themes. One was that by directing the crusade resources of Christendom against them the papacy was directly responsible for the events in the East. Thus in May 1290, on hearing details of the fall of Tripoli, Alfonso III of Aragon wrote a letter to the Master of the Templars criticizing the popes, who had decreed a 'general preaching of the cross' against him, and who were 'diverting the preaching of the cross, which used to be used to help the Holy Land, and the treasure of the Church, which was collected from all corners of the globe for its liberation, to the acquisition of our realm'.[24] The Aragonese and Sicilian chroniclers, particularly such staunch exponents of the Ghibelline cause as Raymond Muntaner and Bartholomew of Neocastro, were more forthright in their condemnation of papal policy. In one of his most delightfully arrogant passages, Raymond Muntaner claimed that Honorius IV privately disapproved of his predecessor's pursuit of the war against Aragon—'God forgive Pope Martin who cast them out of the Church'—on the grounds that only the

---

[22] The Introitus et exitus registers record a total of 35,722 florins. It includes travelling expenses for the Armenian messengers, but the actual subsidies amounted to over 30,000 florins. See K. H. Schäfer, 'Geldspenden der päpstlichen Kurie unter Johann XXII. (1316–1334) für die orientalischen Christen, insbesondere für das Königreich Armenien', *Oriens christianus*, iv (1904), *passim*; *Die Einnahmen der apostolischen Kammer unter Johann XXII.*, ed. E. Göller, pp. 401–3; *Die Ausgaben*, p. 440. To this must be added 16,671 florins which were sent between 1324 and 1328 but are not recorded in the I et E registers; they formed part of a promised sum of 30,000 florins. See *Chypre sous les Lusignans. Documents chypriotes des archives du Vatican (xiv⁰ et xv⁰ siècles)*, ed. J. Richard, pp. 36–49. If the entire 30,000 were in fact sent, the total would reach over 65,000 florins. Even if they were not, the documented sums entail a revision of the traditional view (for which see, e.g., A. Luttrell, 'The Crusade in the Fourteenth Century', in Hale *et al.* (eds.), *Europe in the Late Middle Ages*, pp. 134–5), that John XXII's subsidies to the Christian East were totally inadequate.

[23] For precedents, see the attacks on the popes and the clergy by the Provençal troubadours during the Albigensian crusade, as analysed by Throop, in *Criticism*, pp. 28–42.

[24] *Acta arag.* iii, no. 5.

Catalans could have defeated the Muslims. He also wrote that the day on which Charles of Anjou was granted the Kingdom of Sicily was 'an accursed day for Christians, for, chiefly by this grant, was all the land beyond sea lost, and all the Kingdom of Anatolia, belonging to the Turks . . . Wherefore it may be said that that day was one for weeping and grief'.[25] Bartholomew of Neocastro even included a long passage in which a Sicilian hermit visited Nicholas IV in 1289 to tell him that God had instructed him to order the Pope to bring peace to the world and help the Holy Land.[26] Ghibellines in Italy, or Italians with Ghibelline leanings like Dante, also blamed the popes for events in Syria. In the *Paradiso* Dante made his ancestor Cacciaguida refer to his service under Emperor Conrad III in the Second Crusade and lay the blame for the loss of Palestine on the shoulders of the Pope.[27] Nor did the loss of the Holy Land entirely rob the enemies of the Pope of this basis for criticism. In 1328 Louis IV attacked John XXII for ignoring the Muslim threat to Armenia and the Prussian threat to north-east Germany.[28]

The second criticism frequently employed by the Pope's enemies was that the Curia was preventing them going on crusade in person. This was a claim made with regularity, and appears to have originated with Frederick II. In 1238 Frederick asserted that, far from standing in the way of a crusade to the Holy Land, as the Pope claimed, he himself was ready and willing to lead one, 'as is shown by the letters he has written in reply to kings of the world and to crusaders in France, who chose him as the lord and rector of the army'.[29] It is probable that Manfred claimed that he would help Baldwin of Courtenay regain his empire if he could secure a truce with the Curia, and James of Aragon, commenting on the threat to Acre in 1289–91, in a letter to William of Beaujeu, declared that 'if only it would please our most holy father, our lord the high pontiff, to admit us mercifully into the bosom of his grace, compassion and pity! If we could obtain his favour we would go to the aid of the Holy

---

[25] Raymond Muntaner, 'Chronicle', i. 85, ii. 375.
[26] Bartholomew of Neocastro, 'Historia sicula', pp. 111–14.
[27] See *Paradiso*, xv. 139–44. Cf. ibid., ix. 124–6, and *Inferno*, xxvii. 85–90.
[28] *MGH, Const.* vi, pt. 1, no. 436.
[29] *Hist. dipl.* v, pt. 1, pp. 256–7. Cf. Matthew Paris, *Chronica maiora*, v. 99.

Land, nobly and in strength, following in the footsteps of our fortunate predecessors.'[30] In 1287 the three orders of Aragon promised the college of cardinals that if Alfonso was pardoned he would continue the traditional struggle with the Muslims in the Iberian peninsula, and Frederick of Sicily told the author of the 'Directorium ad passagium faciendum' that he wanted 'nothing so much in the world as to spend the rest of his life on crusade, if he was offered a secure and suitable peace'.[31] Matthew Visconti too asserted that he was prepared to go on crusade, and in October 1336 Louis IV included amongst the peace terms to be presented to Pope Benedict XII a generalized promise to crusade overseas as a form of penance, for as long as the Pope considered proper.[32] Marino Sanudo Torsello numbered the 'very great longing' which Louis had to go on crusade in the Holy Land and to recover the lands held there by the Muslims amongst the reasons why, in his opinion, Benedict should pardon the Emperor.[33]

Some of these claims and promises were obviously more sincere than others. The crown of Aragon, for instance, had a traditional interest in the crusades, both in Spain and in the eastern Mediterranean, which lent plausibility to the promises and assertions of James, Alfonso, and Frederick; two of James I's illegitimate sons had led a brief crusade to Acre in 1269, and James II himself sent five galleys to Acre in 1290.[34] In other instances, such as Henry VII's promise in 1309 to go on crusade if Clement V would consent to his coronation at Rome, it is clear that the offer was intended as a powerful bribe, a neat solution to the problems both of the empire and of the crusade.[35] Crusading zeal, real or pretended, could be a weapon as well as a bribe, and the promises of Ghibellines like Matthew Visconti were intended not for papal ears, but for

---

[30] *Papsttum und Untergang des Templerordens*, ed. H. Finke, ii, no. 1. For Manfred, see Runciman, *The Sicilian Vespers*, pp. 135–6.

[31] Digard, *Philippe le Bel*, ii. 226–7; 'Directorium', pp. 404–5.

[32] *Vat. Akten*, no. 1841 (also in *Kaiser, Volk und Avignon*, no. 37). The crusade was suggested as one of a number of possible penitential acts. For Matthew Visconti, see below, pp. 84–5.

[33]. 'Lettres inédites', pp. 31–2, 41.

[34] See Runciman, *History of the Crusades*, iii. 330–1, 409.

[35] See *MGH, Const.* iv, pt. 1, no. 294. In 1313 Henry attacked Robert of Naples for holding up the crusade by opposing him. See ibid., pt. 2, no. 946.

those of other secular rulers with genuine crusading aspirations and enough political influence at the Curia to press the Ghibelline cause there.

For by far the most powerful pressure on the popes to make peace in Italy came from other western European powers with crusade projects of their own. The most important of these was the French monarchy. Papal policy on the crusades placed it in an ambivalent position. Traditionally, the French crown saw itself as the principal defender of the Holy See, an image which popes like Urban IV and Martin IV took pains to encourage. It therefore had much sympathy for the attempts of the Curia to defend its possessions and rights in Italy, especially when the Kingdom of Sicily was conquered by a cadet house. But it also had a great crusading reputation and a deep commitment to the defence of the Latin states in the East, a commitment reinforced by the fact that papal approval of a crusade project led to the granting of lucrative crusade taxes levied on the French church. Continual appeals for aid from the Christians in the East did not leave the French court unmoved. Twice in the period under discussion the French crown nearly compelled the papacy to abandon its order of priorities, and on a third occasion it could be argued that it did so.

The first difference of opinion between the papacy and France arose during the crusade against the Staufen. Although there is little evidence that Louis IX disapproved of the crusade against Frederick II in itself, he was anxious that it should not interfere with his own expedition. To avoid an open conflict Innocent IV was driven to subterfuge. In July 1246 he told his legate, Odo of Châteauroux, to stop all preaching for the Holy Land while the cross was being preached against Frederick, but to keep the move a secret.[36] Nevertheless, Louis must have been suspicious. It was at his request that, in October 1247, Innocent ordered that preaching for the Holy Land in the imperial dioceses on France's eastern border should not be impeded, and that no vows should be commuted there.[37] In the following month, however, the vows of five French crusaders and fifteen Germans were commuted at the request of William

---

[36] Innocent IV, *Reg.*, no. 2935.
[37] Ibid., no. 3384.

of Holland, and preaching against Frederick II was stepped up throughout Germany and the empire.[38] There was considerable opposition in France to this clear subordination of the King's crusade to the exigencies of the papal struggle with Frederick, and it increased when Louis's crusade met with defeat and the King was captured. In the summer of 1250 Alphonse of Poitiers and Charles of Anjou arrived back from the crusade with the plea that the Pope would make peace with Frederick II so that he could go to aid their brother. In 1251 Blanche of Castile, infuriated at the continuation of the conflict with the Staufen at a time when her son desperately needed more men and money, issued the famous edict that the lands of any royal liegemen who took the cross against Conrad should be confiscated: 'Let those who fight for the pope be fed by the pope's officials, and let them go, never to return.' Her example was followed by many of the French barons whose lands lay on the borders of France and the empire.[39]

Such opposition should not be overestimated. Much of the evidence for it is derived from Matthew Paris, whose work was notoriously unreliable and who was bitterly prejudiced against the papacy.[40] Nevertheless, Louis IX had shown himself to be less than fully satisfied with the way the Holy See approached the needs of the Latin East. This made it essential to get his support for the infeudation of his brother with the Kingdom of Sicily and for the preaching of the crusade against Manfred in France. At first there were problems. Louis was attracted by Baldwin of Courtenay's plan for Manfred to do penance for his offences against the Church by helping the exiled Emperor to recover Constantinople. He put pressure on the Pope to use this idea as the basis for negotiations with Manfred. Some negotiations took place in the autumn and winter of 1262–3, but by Easter 1263 Urban IV was convinced of Manfred's insincerity.[41] Louis's support still hung in the balance, and the situation was eased, if not saved, by a stroke of luck for Charles and Urban in July 1263. Baldwin, worried that Louis was turning against Manfred, wrote to him urging him to send a

---

[38] Ibid., nos. 3433, 4060, 4062. See also Berger, *Saint Louis et Innocent IV*, pp. 231–7.
[39] See Matthew Paris, *Chronica maiora*, v. 174–5, 260–1.
[40] See R. Vaughan, *Matthew Paris*, pp. 130–6, 140–1, 263.
[41] See Urban IV, *Reg.*, no. 151; Hampe, *Urban IV. und Manfred*, pp. 86–8.

messenger to the French court to assure Louis of his good intentions. The letter thus established the close collaboration between Baldwin and Manfred, of which the French King was unaware. It was intercepted by the Guelf *podestà* at Rimini, and the Pope sent it to his notary, Albert, at Paris. It was enough to sway Louis in favour of his brother's plans, and he supported the candidature. Plans for the reconquest of the Eastern empire were put aside, and negotiations pursued with Michael VIII Palaeologus.[42]

With the backing of Louis IX, Urban IV and Clement IV were able to assert their order of priorities on the crusade with vigour. When Simon of Brie was sent to France as legate in May 1264 to complete the negotiations with Charles, several aspects of his commission gave him clear superiority over the legation of the Archbishop of Tyre on behalf of the Holy Land. He was allowed to suspend the general passage to the East for a year, and was told to inform the Archbishop that the latter was not to exercise his rights of procuration since they would overlap with his own and prove too burdensome for the French church. The Archbishop was to hand over the papal letters assigning him these rights and to employ money from the French hundredth for his expenses instead.[43] Although he urged the Archbishop to continue to promote the crusade to the Holy Land, Clement IV assured Charles of Anjou in July 1265 that the crusade to the East would not be allowed to impede the crusade against Manfred, even though the news from Palestine showed that the Holy Land was 'in the greatest danger'.[44] Ottobuono Fieschi, who was sent to preach the cross against the rebel barons in England in 1265, was allowed to commute vows made to crusade in the Holy Land, but not those made in support of the Sicilian venture.[45] *Crucesignati* who were unable to draw on the clerical tenth because it was being collected for Charles of Anjou were allowed alternative sources of financial support. Alphonse of Poitiers, for example, was advised to approach

---

[42] See *Thes. novus*, ii, cols. 23–6; Urban IV, *Reg.*, nos. 295, 322–6, 748, 848. For the whole paragraph, see Jordan, *Les Origines*, pp. 378–409.

[43] Urban IV, *Reg.*, no. 815; *Thes. novus*, ii, col. 81.

[44] Clement IV, *Reg.*, no. 826; *Thes. novus*, ii, col. 153.

[45] *Calendar of Entries in the Papal Registers relating to Great Britain and Ireland. Papal Letters 1198–1342*, ed. W. H. Bliss, i. 427–8.

King Louis and Giles of Tyre for money from the crusade hundredth, while Bocard, Count of Vendôme, was permitted to collect all the money raised over a two-year period from the redemption of crusade vows, crusade legacies, and obventions, within the city and diocese of Le Mans.[46]

The deep and prolonged involvement of the French crown in the War of the Sicilian Vespers meant that it did not make any vociferous objections to the crusade against the Aragonese and the Sicilians, and it was not until the 1320s that French crusading fervour again presented the Curia with diplomatic problems. Philip V and his brother Charles did not believe that it was necessary to postpone the crusade to regain the Holy Land while John XXII defeated the Ghibellines in Lombardy. Matthew Visconti sent them ambassadors and letters pleading his willingness to go on crusade with them and, as a more tangible incentive for their intervention, he suggested that Lombardy's political problems would be solved by the establishment there of a French *signoria*.[47] In April 1321 Philip V openly took Matthew Visconti, his sons, and the Ghibelline league under his protection, and in the following month a legation led by Henry of Sully presented a series of French proposals to the Pope at Avignon. They started by invoking the traditional loyalty of the French crown to the Holy See, then revealed that Philip and Charles were still intent on a crusade. 'Amongst the other things which they [the kings of France] have most desired in this century and have most at heart is the holy voyage overseas, and the pursuit of all the things which are profitable for the holy voyage, and the removal, as far as their strength permits, of all the obstacles which could impede and disturb it.'[48] One of the chief obstacles to the 'holy voyage' was the dispute between the Church and Robert of Naples, on the one hand, and Matthew Visconti, his sons and allies, on the other. Unless a reconciliation was effected between them 'the passage could never be securely made'. Charles of La Marche

---

[46] *Thes. novus*, ii, col. 313; Clement IV, *Reg.*, nos. 80–1.

[47] This was one of several attempts to bring the French crown into Lombardy on the Ghibelline side. See C. W. Previté-Orton, 'Marsilius of Padua and the Visconti', *EHR*, xliv (1929), *passim*; *Acta arag.* i, no. 320; John XXII, *Lettres secrètes*, nos. 859–60, 1407; Tabacco, *La casa di Francia*, pp. 189–208, 289–90.

[48] Bock, 'Kaisertum', p. 211.

had refused the *signoria* which had been offered to him 'several times' because he knew that his acceptance would offend the Pope and Robert of Naples, but John XXII was asked to offer Matthew Visconti absolution. Once this had been done the French crown would help achieve a political settlement in Lombardy and Matthew Visconti would participate, 'by sea and by land', and 'with a very great retinue', in the planned crusade.[49]

Such a plan, which involved not only a compromise settlement with the Ghibellines, but also the establishment of a permanent French presence in Lombardy in the Ghibelline interest, was anathema to John XXII. By dexterous diplomacy he was able to avoid implementing it; indeed, the dispute escalated. At the end of the year the crusade was used against Matthew Visconti and in March 1322 he was convicted of heresy. But the Ghibellines continued to make attempts to persuade the French crown to intervene on their behalf by appealing to French crusading enthusiasm. In February 1322 a leading Genoese Ghibelline exile, Simon Doria, asked John XXII to help secure peace at Genoa, 'so that such a respectful city as Genoa, so necessary and useful for the passage to the Holy Land, if it takes place, should not suffer more of this destruction'.[50] The Pope was no longer open to such arguments, but Simon Doria and his companion, Nicholas Spinola, had arrived at Avignon from the French court, and had evidently used similar arguments there. Charles IV wrote to John on their behalf, and the Pope was forced to write a letter in April presenting the Guelf view of how the struggle had developed.[51] Charles was still not persuaded, and in June 1322 John wrote him a stronger letter, reminding him that Matthew Visconti was now a convicted heretic, dedicated, like all heretics, to the poisoning of the mystical body of the Church and to the destruction of the Christian Faith and Catholic Church. Not only could there be no political settlement until Matthew had recanted his heterodox beliefs, but the French kings themselves had a historic role as the suppressors of heresy. Charles was asked to continue this tradition by actively intervening in Italy on the

---

[49] Ibid., pp. 211–12. See also *Acta arag.* i. no. 317.

[50] *Acta arag.* ii. no. 376.

[51] John XXII, *Lettres secrètes*, no. 1407.

side of the Church. 'Rise up, therefore, dearest son, in aid of the Church of Christ, rise up, and crush the audacious undertakings of the said heretic and of his defenders and allies . . . knowing beyond all doubt that if you assume the cause of Christ, he will assume yours.'[52] Until this heresy was destroyed, John implied, there was to be no crusade to the East.

In the spring of 1323 the opposition of Charles IV to the crusades in Italy reached its height, as negotiations were resumed between the papal Curia and the French court on the organization of a passage to the East. For a time it seemed as if Charles, together with the substantial group of cardinals who were hostile to John XXII's Italian policy, might succeed in making the Pope alter his plans, especially as news was reaching the West of mounting Mamluk pressure on Cilician Armenia. A crusade was in fact preached in 1322–3 to aid Armenia and Cyprus; trunks were ordered to be placed in cathedrals and other churches to collect the offerings of the faithful, and there were detailed suggestions from the cardinals as to how a crusade led by Charles IV could best be organized and financed.[53] It was on the familiar problem of finance that the crusade foundered. In the autumn of 1323 Charles IV claimed that £1,600,000 *Tours* were needed each year if the crusade army was to be effective, and that the French kingdom could not be expected to provide it all.[54] Before the end of 1323 Charles had been diverted by the suggestion of a French candidacy to the empire, and in 1324 there was renewed war with England. Charles thus failed to prevent the increasing papal military and financial involvement in Italy which characterized the mid-1320s.[55]

Soon after his accession in 1328 Philip VI of Valois also showed himself to be an avid crusader. A two-year tenth for the crusade was levied in France in 1330, and the King took the

[52] John XXII, *Lettres secrètes*, no. 1445.

[53] See John XXII, *Lettres communes*, nos. 17742, 18089–92, 18097, 18141–9, 18174–5; John XXII, *Lettres secrètes*, nos. 1692–1709, 1571–3. Crusade indulgences were also issued in 1322–3 for the defence of Achaea and Chios against the Greeks and the Turks. See John XXII, *Lettres communes*, nos. 16672, 16977.

[54] *Acta arag.* i, no. 329.

[55] For the events recounted in this paragraph, see also N. J. Housley, 'The Franco-Papal Crusade Negotiations of 1322–3'. *Papers of the British School at Rome* (1980).

cross two years later.[56] Once again the Curia found itself subject to French pressure to negotiate peace in Italy.[57] This time it appeared to respond to it: from 1330 papal expenditure on the Italian crusades declined dramatically, while papal correspondence on the crusade to the East increased.[58] Tentative plans to move the seat of the Curia to Bologna were shelved to facilitate discussion of the crusade with Philip VI and his advisers. An apposite example of the way in which priorities had changed by September 1333 is the fact that Bolognese ambassadors at Avignon had to wait for an interview with the Pope until talks on the crusade had been concluded.[59] On the other hand, the reversal of crusade priorities which these measures represented should not be attributed entirely to French pressure. The Guelf alliance in northern Italy collapsed in 1331–2 and by October 1333 the Pope accepted that his Italian policy was a failure.[60] With Venice also pressing for papal and Angevin help in the organization of a naval league against the Turks, there was no longer any justification for postponing any crusading effort in the Latin East in order to concentrate on Italy.[61]

The other western power which used its influence at the Curia to try to persuade it to alter its approach to the crusades was the English crown. King Edward I, like St. Louis before him, retained considerable interest in the affairs and needs of the Christians in Syria as a result of time spent there on crusade.[62] Between 1284 and 1289 Edward applied substantial diplomatic pressure on the Curia to bring about a peaceful settlement of the Sicilian question in order to help the Latins in Syria. In January 1284 he wrote to the Abbot of St. Denis announcing his intention of personally intervening in the dispute, 'because of the love which we bear, and must bear,

---

[56] See Delaville le Roulx, *La France en Orient*, i. 86–8; A. S. Atiya, *The Crusade in the Later Middle Ages*, pp. 95 ff.; J. B. Henneman, *Royal Taxation in Fourteenth Century France. The Development of War Financing 1322–1356*, pp. 90–2, 97, 103–7. See also John XXII, *Lettres secrètes*, nos. 5207–5227. Philip had already taken the cross once, in 1313.

[57] See, e.g., John XXII, *Lettres communes*, no. 61324, p. 234.

[58] See *Die Ausgaben*, pp. 13*–14*, 31*.

[59] ASV, Reg. Vat. 117, f. 258ᵛ, no. 1326. Cf. Ciaccio, 'Il cardinal legato', pp. 528–9.

[60] See Mollat, *Popes at Avignon*, p. 108.

[61] For the naval league, which achieved some minor successes in 1334, see P. Lemerle, *L'Émirat d'Aydin, Byzance et l'Occident. Recherches sur 'La Geste d'Umur Pacha'*, pp. 89–100; Luttrell, 'Hospitallers', p. 293.

[62] See Runciman, *History of the Crusades*, iii. 335–8.

towards the said kings [of Sicily, France, and Aragon], and also because of the state of the Holy Land and the said kings, and besides that for the good of all Christianity'.[63] In July 1286, with tentative papal backing, he secured the conditions for a truce between France and Aragon, and asked Pope Honorius IV to ratify them for the sake of Christians both in the West and in the East.[64] Honorius would not accept the truce, and the treaty of Oleron, drawn up in July 1287, which was intended to effect the release of Charles of Salerno, met with the same fate in March 1288.[65] Finally, in October 1288, the treaty was revised at Canfranc, and Charles was released after four years of imprisonment.[66] Behind all these negotiations and treaties lay the consciousness of what was happening in the Holy Land. In 1284 Edward announced his intention of again taking the cross, and when he did so, in 1287, he became the focus of European crusading enthusiasm. He also used his crusading friend and adviser Odo of Grandison as his chief envoy to the popes. As in the case of the French crown, it is difficult to know how much pressure Edward applied, or was prepared to apply, on behalf of his crusade plans, which were motivated at least in part by his desire to tax the English church. Certainly the efforts of Odo of Grandison and William of Hotham to secure help for the Christians in the East after the fall of Tripoli were instrumental in bringing about the truce of Gaeta in August 1289, but little diplomatic muscle was needed since both Charles II and James II wanted to break off hostilities.[67]

Owing to the relative paucity of documentary evidence on the subject, it is impossible to examine in detail the arguments which were used by the French and English envoys at the Curia to try to persuade the popes to disengage their crusade resources from the Italian wars. We do, however, possess a

[63] *Foedera*, i, pt. 2, p. 637.

[64] Ibid., pp. 670–1; Honorius IV, *Reg.*, no. 920, and *Addenda*, pp. 938–9. See also Digard, *Philippe le Bel*, i. 29–30.

[65] *Foedera*, i, pt. 2, pp. 677–8; Nicholas IV, *Reg.*, nos. 560–1, 7413.

[66] *Foedera*, i, pt. 2, pp. 687–8. See also Amari, *La guerra*, i. 427–31; W. Kienast, 'Der Kreuzkrieg Philipps des Schönen von Frankreich gegen Aragon', *Historische Vierteljahrschrift*, xxviii (1933–4), 680–6 and *passim*.

[67] See *Foedera*, i, pt. 2, pp. 641, 674–5; *RCAR*, xxx, 'Additiones', Reg. 5, nos. 2–5. Digard (*Philippe le Bel*, i. 72–9, esp. 75), believed that the news of the fall of Tripoli did make a considerable difference to negotiations at Gaeta.

detailed and critical commentary on papal crusade priorities in the shape of the letters of the Venetian crusade theorist and propagandist, Marino Sanudo Torsello.[68] Marino's wide knowledge and experience both of Italian politics and of the situation in the Latin East enabled him, to a degree unequalled by any other figure in the period, to understand how they interrelated. His original analysis of the problems of organizing a crusade to the East was laid out in his book, the 'Secreta fidelium crucis', which he wrote between 1306 and 1321. In 1321–3 he travelled to Avignon and Paris and presented copies to John XXII, Robert of Naples, and Charles IV, all of whom still seemed to be interested in a crusade to the East.[69] He was appalled at the widespread escalation of European conflicts in the 1320s, 'most of all in Lombardy, Tuscany, and almost all of Italy', which were preventing John XXII from turning his attention to the liberation of the Holy Places, the relief of the embattled Armenians, or the defence of Latin Greece from Turkish naval raids.[70] In many of the forty-one extant letters which he wrote between 1324 and 1337, most of them to persons with influence at the French, papal, and Angevin courts, he attempted to show how events in Italy were impeding such projects and how their clashing needs could be reconciled.

In October 1334 Marino Sanudo remarked of a prospective settlement between the Pope and Louis IV that 'if this peace was made, I believe and do not doubt that, with the aid of our lord Jesus Christ, a passage would succeed, and that the land subject to the sultan would be acquired together with Asia Minor and many other lands'.[71] There were several reasons why he attributed such importance to the papal–imperial conflict and the Italian wars which he anachronistically believed to be simply its extension. They tied down the military and financial resources of two of Christendom's leading crusade powers, the papacy and the Angevin monarchy; the Angevin court in particular had commitments in Greece and the East which it was neglecting.[72] They also had serious repercussions

---

[68] For Marino Sanudo, see A. Magnocavallo, *Marin Sanudo il vecchio e il suo progetto di crociata*, *passim*; Atiya, *Crusade*, pp. 114–27.

[69] See 'Studien über Marino Sanudo', pp. 787–8; *Gesta Dei*, ii. 310.

[70] Ibid., ii. 290, 304.

[71] 'Studien über Marino Sanudo', p. 809.

[72] See *Gesta Dei*, ii. 292, 298, 305; 'Studien über Marino Sanudo', pp. 778–9.

outside Italy. The commerce of the whole of Europe was adversely affected, since the traditional trade routes were disrupted and pirates were permitted to make the seas unsafe.[73] The spiritual as well as the economic well-being of Christendom deteriorated, as so many Christians died as excommunicates.[74] The Italian wars were, in fact, the principal cause of the disunity of the Christian Republic, a disunity which could lead to its downfall at the hands of its Muslim and pagan enemies. In a long memorandum to Bertrand du Poujet in 1330 Marino Sanudo wrote that Latin Christians constituted only a tenth of the inhabitants of the world; the rest were Greeks and Muslims. If the Christians continued to be divided amongst themselves they could easily be overrun. Italy was being depopulated rapidly by the wars, and the population of Germany was stagnant. The Mongols had already surged to the frontiers of Hungary; if they burst through, they would invade and subjugate Italy, Germany, and France, just as their ancestors had done in the Dark Ages. There was a similar threat from the Muslims in Spain and the Turks, 'the worst of the Saracens', in the eastern Mediterranean.[75]

The Mongol threat had, of course, long aroused apocalyptic fears—William of Montahagol had said in 1258 that unless they united in a crusade against the Tartars, all the Christian princes would lose their lands.[76] Marino Sanudo's originality lay in the fact that he carried the analysis further by suggesting that a united Christendom could engage in a form of expansionist holy war. Though numerically inferior to their enemies, the Latin Christians were better and more skilled soldiers. Thus, 'if God would pacify the Christian faithful, and in particular establish peace between the Church and the empire, as it should be by right, then not only would these dangers cease, but the entire world would be conquered in the name of Christ'.[77] This was both a more worthy and also a more profitable alternative to the wars being fought by the Curia in Italy, for the revenue which the Holy See would be able to draw from its lands in Italy and

---

[73] See ibid., pp. 770–1; *Gesta Dei*, ii. 293, 314.
[74] See ibid., ii. 310. For similar comments by Peter Dubois, see his *De recuperatione terre sancte*, p. 25, and *Summaria brevis*, pp. 12–13.
[75] See 'Studien über Marino Sanudo', pp. 779–81.
[76] See Throop, *Criticism*, pp. 78–9.
[77] 'Studien über Marino Sanudo', p. 788. Cf. *Gesta Dei*, ii. 306, 310.

elsewhere in times of peace would be worth three times what it was gaining at the moment.[78] The crusade to the East was not only the manifestation of a united Christendom, it was also the best way of securing that unity in the first place, as many who were opposed to the Pope would return to obedience once they saw that a crusade was being planned and set in motion.[79] The alternative was to continue to fight destructive wars in Italy which, owing to the instability of Italian politics and the strength of the imperial–Ghibelline tradition, the Church could not hope to win.[80]

Marino Sanudo's warnings and suggestions fell on deaf ears.[81] Why was it that such detailed arguments, the predictions and fears of which were regularly confirmed and reinforced by messengers from the Latin East begging for western aid, and which were backed up by the diplomatic pressure of the French and English crowns, failed, on all but perhaps one or two occasions, to persuade the Curia to alter its crusade policy? There are several explanations. The Curia genuinely believed that its Italian crusades would quickly triumph and that the Holy See, its prestige renewed, its revenues restored, and its commitments reduced, would then organize aid to the East. Again, crusades waged in Italy were much more inviting prospects than those in the Latin East: they were less expensive, could be controlled more easily by the Church, and had political objectives which could be more readily achieved and contributed more directly to papal power and authority. Most importantly, enthusiasts for a crusade to the East expected the Church to make the necessary political concessions to its enemies to secure peace in Italy. The Curia could never accept Marino Sanudo's suggestion that the Church should submit to her enemies on temporal disputes, 'which is not to submit, but to exalt'.[82] The whole mental and juridical cast of the later medieval papacy was opposed to the abandonment of the Church's rights or possessions, let alone reconciliation with

---

[78] See 'Studien über Marino Sanudo', p. 788.
[79] See Marino Sanudo, 'Liber secretorum fidelium crucis', p. 48; *Gesta Dei*, ii. 289, 290, 293.
[80] See 'Studien über Marino Sanudo', pp. 782–4; *Gesta Dei*, ii. 306–7.
[81] See Bertrand du Poujet's reply to the memorandum of 1330, 'Studien über Marino Sanudo', pp. 789–90.
[82] Ibid., p. 784.

excommunicates and heretics, which this would have entailed. As for the argument that the Church should imitate the humility which Christ displayed on the cross, Augustinus Triumphus replied that Christ showed humility to liberate man from 'the pride of the tyrants', and that he intended his cross to be employed as a weapon to drive out demons and tyrannical rulers alike.[83]

This is not to say that the Curia did not feel embarrassed by the fact that its Italian crusades collided so often with setbacks and disasters in the Levant, which made it vulnerable to the propaganda of its enemies. This was particularly true of the War of the Vespers, when the last Latin settlements in Syria were falling. Unable to sacrifice its policy in Italy, the Curia at least tried to link the two areas of urgent Christian need in the form of a number of interesting peace settlements which were proposed on the basis of rapid and substantial Aragonese, Sicilian, and Angevin help to the East. The first such set of proposals was presented to James of Aragon in 1290 or early in 1291 by a friar sent by Nicholas IV. James replied that in return for a papal guarantee of a truce during his absence, and the lifting of the sentence of excommunication and interdict from all who participated in or aided the expedition, he would lead forty galleys and a large force of soldiers to Acre for one year; the cost would be 40,000 gold ounces.[84] Bartholomew of Neocastro wrote that it was James who broke off the negotiations, after listening to the advice of a Sicilian, Pandolf di Falcone, who reminded him of what had happened during Frederick II's absence on crusade—papal troops had invaded the Kingdom of Sicily.[85]

Negotiations at about the same time with James's brother Alfonso were more productive. The treaty of Tarascon-Brignolles, signed in February 1291, established that Alfonso would go to the Holy Land as penance for his sins: 'In order to show his own devotion, for the honour of God and of the Roman church, for the salvation of his own soul and of the souls of his ancestors, and to make amends for the wrong done by himself or by his father, he offers to return to the Holy Land for a suitable

[83] Ibid., p. 785; Augustinus Triumphus, *Summa*, Qu. xxvi, Art. v, p. 159.
[84] *Acta arag.* i, no. 2.
[85] Bartholomew of Neocastro, 'Historia sicula', pp. 114–18.

period of time and with a good following, as it pleases the Roman pontiff to direct him.'[86] Four months later Alfonso died, and negotiations were resumed with James, although they were complicated by the loss of the Syrian ports and strongholds. In August 1293 the Aragonese drew up a variation of the 1290 plan. James was to marry the sister of the King of France and to keep Sicily for the rest of his life, to contribute a force of twenty galleys for four months each year, over a period of four years, to the defence of Cyprus and the harassment of Muslim shipping, and to accompany the next general passage East for two years with forty galleys and four hundred knights. Frederick of Aragon was to marry a daughter of Charles II and receive Sardinia as a papal fief, together with 50,000 gold ounces from the papal *camera* to help him conquer it; alternatively, he could wed Catherine of Courtenay, titular heiress to the Latin empire of Constantinople, and use the 50,000 ounces to wrest Constantinople from the Greeks.[87] A few months later the treaty of Figueras also assigned the Eastern empire to Frederick, promising him Aragonese and Angevin help, 'with the aid of the Roman church and of crusaders', to conquer it.[88]

With the accession of Pope Boniface VIII at the end of 1294, and more particularly after the treaty of Anagni in 1295, these tortuous negotiations finally bore fruit. The outstanding single aim of Boniface's pontificate was the achievement of peace in Europe in order to mount a crusade to regain the Holy Places.[89] Thus of all the popes between 1254 and 1343 it was Boniface who most insistently and most skilfully asserted the traditional papal approach to the crusades, in particular the belief that 'the relief of the Holy Land depends for the greatest part on the recovery of the island of Sicily'.[90] The war for the recovery of Sicily was Boniface's 'most important concern'; but the con-

---

[86] *Foedera*, i, pt. 2, p. 745. For optimistic views of the feasibility of this plan, see Digard, *Philippe le Bel*, i. 123; *Annali*, ii. 23. The compiler, Camera, remarked of Alfonso's death that 'because of this misadventure the French failed to retake Sicily, the Christians to regain Palestine'.

[87] *Acta arag.* iii, no. 11.

[88] *Aus den Tagen Bonifaz VIII. Funde und Forschungen*, ed. H. Finke, p. xii.

[89] See, e.g., F. L. Cross and E. A. Livingstone (eds.), *The Oxford Dictionary of the Christian Church*, pp. 187–8; Digard, *Philippe le Bel*, i. 206; J. A. McNamara, 'Simon de Beaulieu and *Clericis laicos*', *Traditio*, xxv (1969), 155. For a different interpretation, see Boase, *Boniface VIII*, pp. 224–7; F. Giunta, *Aragonesi e Catalani nel Mediterraneo*, ii. 94–6.

[90] Boniface VIII, *Reg.*, no. 3871.

sideration which both compensated Boniface for his own 'immense mental efforts and sleepless nights' and justified the 'innumerable expenses' involved was that Sicily was a stepping-stone to Palestine.[91]

The lynchpin of the Pope's plans for settling the Sicilian war and retaking the Holy Land was the series of separate agreements which made up the treaty of Anagni. Again, it was proposed that Frederick would marry Catherine of Courtenay and use Aragonese and Angevin soldiers and ships to recapture Constantinople. Writing to Catherine in August 1295, Boniface warmly commended the marriage to her, claiming that it would not only lead to the recovery of her empire but would also constitute 'a very great benefit' for the Holy Land; it was this *maxima utilitas* which furnished the justification for using all the Templar and Hospitaller possessions in the kingdoms of Aragon and Valencia as the guarantee for the payment of the 100,000 silver marks which were to form the dowry of James II's Angevin bride and compensate him in part for surrendering Sicily.[92] Boniface also adopted and realized the idea of sending Aragonese help to the Holy Land as a form of penance. In January 1296 James II was appointed 'standard-bearer, captain, and admiral-general of the Church' for life, with the 'special and express mandate' of sailing in relief of the Holy Land with sixty galleys, at the Church's expense, when a general passage was ordered. It is only the phrase 'in aid of the Holy Land, or against any of the enemies or rebels of the said Church', which shows the reader that the crusade was to be preceded by the reconquest of Sicily.[93]

These plans to divert Aragonese expansion from Sicily to the eastern Mediterranean were not as chimerical as they appear. The Aragonese court was tempted at least to some extent by the idea of establishing an Aragonese political presence in the Levant to support and further Catalan commercial expansion there.[94] In 1289 Hugh of Brienne, a vassal of Charles II of Naples who had a claim to Cyprus, attempted to interest

[91] Ibid., nos. 2663, 3871.
[92] Ibid., nos. 809, 5567–8.
[93] V. Salavert y Roca, *Cerdeña y la expansión mediterránea de la Corona de Aragón, 1297–1314*, ii, no. 19.
[94] See Giunta, *Aragonesi e Catalani*, ii, *passim*.

Alfonso III in a plan to conquer the island and place it under Aragonese suzerainty, and in September 1295 Charles II himself hoped to fob off James II of Aragon with his rights to the Kingdom of Jerusalem, should he prove unable to persuade Pope Boniface VIII to cede Sardinia and Corsica to the Aragonese king.[95] In 1315 James married Mary of Lusignan, daughter of King Hugh III of Cyprus. Had Mary, who died childless in 1322, given birth to a son, the crowns of Cyprus and Jerusalem would have reverted to Aragon, a possibility which had led the Hospitallers to promote the match.[96] Clearly such projects would not have been pursued had no encouragement been forthcoming from Barcelona.

As the great struggle for Sicily continued into Boniface VIII's last years, so the attempts to link it with the Latin East multiplied. In July 1299 a plan was evolved to marry Frederick to a daughter of Charles II, giving him the Kingdom of Jerusalem as his dowry and the island of Rhodes, to be held as a fief of the Church, or alternatively, with the assent of his brother James, the islands of Corsica and Sardinia.[97] In 1300–2 the Pope actually put into practice his most ambitious project of all. Charles of Valois married Catherine of Courtenay and was issued with a comprehensive papal commission to 'pacify' Tuscany, win the Sicilian war, and then reconquer the Eastern empire.[98] Nor did the war's conclusion bring an end to its association with the Latin East. In July 1307, when negotiations were in progress at Poitiers about the repayment of the money owed to the Holy See by Charles II as a result of the debts contracted in the war, Pope Clement V outlined a plan for its repayment partly in the form of Angevin aid to the East. A third of the massive sum of 366,000 gold ounces was to be remitted outright, 'out of the pure generosity and simple compassion of ourselves and of the Roman church'. For the other two-thirds Charles II or one of his sons, or Robert of Calabria or one of his sons or brothers should Charles die in the meantime,

---

[95] See 'An Offer of the Suzerainty and Escheat of Cyprus to Alphonso III of Aragon by Hugh de Brienne in 1289', ed. E. Lourie, *EHR*, lxxxiv (1969), *passim*; Salavert y Roca, *Cerdeña*, ii, no. 18.
[96] See Luttrell, 'Hospitallers', pp. 287–8; Giunta, *Aragonesi e Catalani*, ii. 126–35.
[97] Boniface VIII, *Reg.*, no. 3398.
[98] Ibid., no. 3917; Boase, *Boniface VIII*, pp. 269 ff.

was to go to the Holy Land with 300 knights in the next general passage, and to remain there after the end of the crusade, 'as long as the Church considers it useful, until the remainder of the above debt has been repaid', in order to act as a garrison to protect the newly regained settlements. In addition, Charles was to keep twenty galleys afloat in the eastern Mediterranean for four months each year, during and after the general passage. If, before the crusade took place, the Mongols were to repeat their achievements of 1299–1300 and offer the Holy Land, or part of it, back to the Christians, and the offer was accepted by the Pope, Charles was to send a hundred knights and five galleys as a garrison and protective naval force. A rate of twenty florins for the equipment of a knight, and a hundred gold ounces for the maintenance of a galley at sea for a month, was agreed upon, and the *servitium* was to cease as soon as the 240,000 gold ounces had been repaid. It was also not to be demanded until a period of three years had passed, because of the post-war exhaustion of the *Regno*.[99]

Unfortunately we do not know what action was taken on this very interesting proposal.[100] But for many years to come the connection established between the Angevin–Aragonese duel and the affairs of the Latin East was to persist, both because of the achievements of the Catalans in Greece and also because the Angevin court continued to propose territorial compensation in the eastern Mediterranean for Frederick of Sicily in return for giving up his island kingdom. In the treaty of Caltabellotta it was laid down that Frederick's heirs should receive Cyprus, Sardinia, or a kingdom of similar status, or 100,000 gold ounces, as compensation for surrendering Sicily at his death.[101] Not all such proposals concerned the Latin East; it was in fact a question of searching the entire Mediterranean littoral for lands, preferably holding the status of a kingdom, which could be represented as having a value roughly equivalent to that of Sicily. Thus in 1301 or 1302 it was suggested by James II that Frederick could exchange Sicily for either Sardinia and Corsica, or the kingdoms of Murcia and

---

[99] Clement V, *Reg.*, no. 2269. Clement's plan also envisaged additional Angevin military *auxilium* in Italy.

[100] See below, p. 245.

[101] Boniface VIII, *Reg.*, no. 5348, cols. 853–4.

Granada.[102] But the obvious lands to consider as compensation were those already held by the Angevin crown or by its cadet houses, and of these Achaea and Albania were the most frequently suggested. At the beginning of 1310 negotiations were afoot to cede Frederick the titular right to the Kingdom of Jerusalem, and in 1311–12 he was to get Achaea and Albania, with the rights of conquest covering the rest of *Romania*. Philip of Taranto, suzerain of the Morea, was to be compensated with the sum of 70,000 gold ounces from the Angevin treasury. In spite of his brother's eager commendation of the wealth and standing of Achaea and Albania, Frederick would not accept the offer.[103] But Robert of Naples persisted. In 1316–17 two alternative plans were proposed. Frederick could have either Achaea–Albania or Sardinia. In either case he could also retain the western half of the island of Sicily, which would be surrendered at his death, and if he chose Sardinia he would receive Angevin naval or financial aid to conquer it. James II, in compensation for the loss of his claim to Sardinia, was to receive 100,000 ounces of gold from Robert, together with the confiscated lands and possessions of the Aragonese Templars; if there were obstacles to the second point, Robert would add another 50,000 gold ounces.[104] In 1320 the Angevin–Sicilian truce was broken and these plans were abandoned in favour of renewed fighting.

iii. THE DIVERSION OF CRUSADE RESOURCES

The subordination of the crusade to the Latin East to the crusade in Italy did not simply entail the discouragement of western crusade projects, the postponement of crusade preaching for the Holy Land, and the deferment of planned passages to the East. It found its most frequent, most noticeable, and most unpopular expression in the diversion to Italy of crusaders and crusade money originally intended for the East. The commuta-

---

[102] *Acta arag.* i, no. 87.

[103] Ibid., ii. nos. 440, 443, 445; G. M. Monti, 'L'Albania e la guerra di Sicilia: trattative diplomatiche', in his *Nuovi studi angioini, passim.*

[104] *Acta arag.*, ii, no. 449. Cf. ibid., no. 448. See also *Diplomatari de l'orient català (1301–1409). Collecció de documents per a la història de l'expedició catalana a orient i dels ducats d'Atenes i Neopàtria*, ed. A. Rubió y Lluch, no. 99.

tion of crusade vows, and the use in Italy of clerical tenths, vow redemption money, legacies, and obventions paid or donated for the Holy Land is a characteristic feature of the period 1254–1343. Such measures formed a logical extension of the concept of crusade priorities and were justified as such;[105] but the duplicity which they often involved makes them the aspect of the papal approach most difficult to defend.

Vow commutation for crusades against Christian lay powers probably originated in the crusade against Frederick II.[106] In February 1241 Gregory IX allowed John of Civitella, who was preaching the cross against the Emperor in Hungary, to commute the vows of crusaders who had sworn to fight in the Holy Land, so that they would fight Frederick instead. The justification for this move was the threat which Frederick posed to 'the mother and head of the Faith'.[107] In 1247 and 1248 Innocent IV commuted the vows of Frisian crusaders *en bloc* so that they could help their lord, William of Holland, against the Emperor, and in 1251 he threatened to direct against Ezzelino of Romano and his allies crusaders from Italy and elsewhere, regardless of the reason for which they had taken the cross.[108] In 1255 Henry III's vow was commuted to one of undertaking the conquest of Sicily on behalf of Edmund, and the vows of other English *crucesignati*, and of Norwegians (including King Hakon), were similarly commuted.[109] In May 1264 Simon of Brie was permitted to commute vows in favour of Charles of Anjou, though he was not to exercise this faculty 'without a special mandate from the lord pope'. Unsuccessful attempts were made by Urban IV, Clement IV, and the poet Rutebeuf to persuade

---

[105] See, e.g., Clement IV, *Reg.*, no. 216; Boniface VIII, *Reg.*, no. 2321.

[106] For vow commutation in general, see Riley-Smith, *What were the Crusades?*, p. 47. It is possible that Innocent III commuted the vows of Walter of Brienne and his French followers to engage their services against Markward of Anweiler, but there is no definite proof of commutation. See Strayer, 'Political Crusades', pp. 346–7; D. E. Queller, *The Fourth Crusade. The Conquest of Constantinople 1201–1204*, pp. 20–1.

[107] *MGH, Epist. pont.* i., no. 801.

[108] *MGH, Epist. pont.* ii., no. 113; Innocent IV, *Reg.*, nos. 3779, 4068, 4070. Cf. ibid., no. 4060.

[109] *Foedera*, i, pt. 1, pp. 320–2; Matthew Paris, *Chronica maiora*, v. 519–20; 'Ann. de Burton', p. 349. See also Pope Alexander IV, *Registres*, ed. C. Bourel de la Roncière *et al.*, no. 1253.

Alphonse of Poitiers to commute his vow in this way.[110] This bias in favour of Charles's expedition was to some extent counterbalanced in May 1267, when Clement IV told Simon of Brie that vows made to help the count, and left unfulfilled, could be commuted to vows to crusade in the East, if the *crucesignati* requested it.[111]

During the crusade against the Sicilians and the Aragonese there is no evidence for any commutation of vows. In 1302 Boniface VIII forbad anybody accompanying Charles of Valois's expedition to Sicily to commute for that purpose a vow made to go on crusade in aid of the Holy Land.[112] This was in accordance with general papal policy on the relaxation of vows, which became less compliant in the last third of the thirteenth century.[113] The registers of Pope John XXII also do not, to my knowledge, contain any orders relating to the commutation of crusade vows in favour of the crusades against the Ghibellines, although he did authorize the commutation of pilgrimage vows into subsidies for the Italian crusades.[114] An incident noted in the heresy charges against Matthew Visconti, however, indicates that there may have been some commutation of crusade vows in practice. One of the charges was that 'when many *crucesignati*, more than 300, were gathered at Milan to begin their journey to the Holy Land, and were listening to the preaching of the cross in the convent of the Franciscans at Milan, his troops attacked them, drove them away, harassed them, and violently imprisoned several of them.'[115] Since one

---

[110] Urban IV, *Reg.*, nos. 813–14; Clement IV, *Reg.*, no. 817; Rutebeuf, *Onze poèmes*, p. 51. See also Clement IV, *Reg.*, no. 1677; 'Maius chronicon lemovicense, a Petro Coral et aliis conscriptum', *RHGF*, xxi. 771. Simon of Brie's faculty to commute vows was confirmed in March 1265; it also covered vows of pilgrimage and abstention. See Clement IV, *Reg.*, no. 216; Sternfeld, *Ludwigs des Heiligen Kreuzzug nach Tunis*, p. 319.

[111] Clement IV, *Reg.*, no. 496. See also *Layettes du trésor des chartes. Inventaires et documents publiés par la Direction des Archives*, ed. A. Teulet *et al.*, iv, no. 5339.

[112] Boniface VIII, *Reg.*, no. 4625. Boniface made an interesting distinction between the vow and the cross: 'We do not intend to grant to anybody the benefit of absolution of a vow made to travel, or of a cross taken to travel, in person in aid of the Holy Land.'

[113] See Purcell, *Papal Crusading Policy*, p. 114; J. A. Brundage, *Medieval Canon Law and the Crusader*, p. 133.

[114] See below, p. 141.

[115] 'Pluresque crucesignatos ultra numerum trecentorum dudum congregatos Mediolano ad transfretandum in subsidium terre sancte dum in loco fratrum minorum Mediolano predicationem crucis audirent per suos satellites invasit hostiliter ipsosque fugavit gravavit et aliquos eorum detinuit violenter.' Bibl. Vat., MS Vat. lat. no. 3937, p. lviii. Cf. Michel, 'Le Procès', p. 320.

of the witnesses claimed to have heard the crusaders shouting out 'death to Matthew Visconti, who is trying to prevent the crusade',[116] it is plausible that the friars, acting with or without papal authority, were attempting to persuade the crusaders to commute their vows to participate in the crusade against Matthew Visconti.

Even if John XXII did not authorize the commutation of crusade vows, he was responsible for the outstanding example of the diversion of crusade resources from the East to Italy. The most concrete outcome of the pope's co-operation on the crusade with the French King, Philip V, was the construction and purchase in 1319 of a Franco-papal crusade squadron at Narbonne and Marseilles, using money from the tenth levied at the Council of Vienne. The squadron consisted of ten ships, and was intended to sail to Cyprus under Louis of Clermont and attack ships trading with Egypt, thus enforcing the papal decrees against Christians engaging in commerce with the Muslims.[117] At the end of August 1319 Robert of Naples suggested that 'since the weaponry of these galleys would be a futile waste in those far-off parts because of the rapid approach of winter weather',[118] the ten ships should be assigned to the Angevin fleet for the campaign in progress against the Genoese Ghibellines. Expert naval advice was cited to the effect that the ships would be damaged by a winter spent at anchor in port, 'not without loss to the Holy Land', and Robert promised, under threat of excommunication should he fail to keep his word, to send ten galleys to Marseilles in the following spring together with 20,000 florins for wages and provisions provided by the Pope. John agreed to this and explained the situation to Philip V; the permission of the French King was apparently not asked for, although care was taken to remove the insignia of the French crown from the ships.[119] The galleys were assigned to the Angevins and were lost in a naval battle off Genoa in 1319,

[116] Ibid., pp. 320–1.

[117] See John XXII, *Lettres secrètes*, nos. 784–5, 846–7, 852–3, 887–8, 926; C. Bourel de la Roncière, 'Une Escadre franco-papale (1318–1320)', *Mélanges*, xiii (1893), *passim*.

[118] 'quod ipsarum armatio galearum propter instantiam proximam temporis yemalis esset inutilis et inanis in partibus tam remotis'. ASV, Instr. misc., no. 666.

[119] John XXII, *Lettres secrètes*, nos. 927, 983.

together with fourteen of Robert's own vessels.[120] There is no record of Angevin compensation, and as the crusade failed to materialize because of the English threat, it is fair to suppose that Robert was not called to account.

The diversion to Italy of money originally intended for the Holy Land also began during the crusade against the Staufen. In 1241 Hungarians who had taken the cross to crusade in the East could redeem their vows, provided they paid papal collectors the sum which they would have spent on travelling to the Holy Land, fighting there, and returning home; this money would be used for the purposes of the crusade against Frederick II.[121] A few years later Henry III was granted the contribution of the English clergy towards the twentieth levied at the First Council of Lyons, converted into a tenth and extended to five years, as well as money from the redemption of English and Scottish crusade vows, and legacies and obventions for the Holy Land, to help him undertake the conquest of Sicily.[122]

In so far as it related to clerical tenths, legacies, and obventions, this policy was not officially adopted in the case of Charles of Anjou's expedition; Clement IV specifically denied that any money left for the Latin East would be used for other purposes, an approach no doubt dictated by the need to placate Louis IX.[123] The sincerity of Clement's denial is confirmed in part by a papal letter to the Dean of Paris in July 1266, in which Clement wrote that £100 *Tours* left 'in aid of the Holy Land' by a knight called Simon of Rali could be paid to another knight, Odo of Corpelay, if the latter gave suitable security for his forthcoming journey to the Holy Land and for the restitution of the legacy should he fail to set out. Odo had taken a vow to go to the East previously, but had commuted it to one of supporting Charles of Anjou's expedition, which had rendered him in-

---

[120] Bourel de la Roncière ('Une Escadre', pp. 416–17), believed that the ships were handed over to Robert's officials in the winter of 1319–20 and lost in late August or September 1320. But it is more likely from the letters of John XXII and the account in John of St. Victor's 'Memoriale historiarum, excerpta' (*RHGF*, xx p. 669), that the galleys were handed over and lost in the period late September–December 1319.

[121] *MGH, Epist. pont.* i, no. 801.

[122] *Foedera*, i, pt. 1, p. 322; Matthew Paris, *Chronica maiora*, v. 536; 'Ann. de Burton', p. 350; Lunt, *Financial Relations*, i. 254–6, 266.

[123] *Cal. of Entries*, i. 439.

eligible for Simon's legacy.[124] Abuses seem, however, to have occurred in practice through the excessive zeal of Simon of Brie's collectors. The Archbishop of Tyre, who tried to uphold the interests of the Latin East in the face of Simon of Brie's superior legatine powers, complained in a private letter in November 1265 that money left 'in aid of the Holy Land' was being used to finance Charles of Anjou, against the expressed desire of the testators; he had found this to be the case 'in many places, while travelling around preaching'.[125] Moreover, Clement did permit vows of pilgrimage and abstention to be redeemed, and the money thus collected to go to Charles of Anjou. Ricaut Bonomel, a Templar poet who wrote a lament for the fall of Arsuf and Caesarea, claimed that crusade vows too were being redeemed and the money going to Charles's crusade.[126]

During the War of the Sicilian Vespers the popes gave in completely to the temptation to use for their Italian concerns money which had been raised for Palestine. By May 1284 money given for the Holy Land in the form of oblations and legacies by the inhabitants of the *Regno* was being used to finance the Angevin war effort.[127] Martin IV and Honorius IV granted Philip III the obscure legacies (*legata indistincte relicta*) which traditionally went to the crusade in the East; he was allowed to collect these legacies for the period of time for which the clerical tenth had been granted to him.[128] In 1297 Boniface VIII told his cardinal-nuncios in France to authorize the redemption of crusade vows, the money from which was to be used in the Sicilian war; they were, however, only to permit redemption by people whose military value on crusade would be negligible, such as women, the sick, and the old.[129] These sources were soon complemented by legacies for the Holy Land, £15,000 *Tours* of which helped to finance the construction of an Angevin fleet in Provence. Obscure legacies in Aragon were allocated to James II in June 1299 for two years, and English

---

[124] *Thes. novus*, ii. cols. 384–5. Odo was paid £40 for a horse lost while serving Charles I. See *RCAR*, i, Reg. 2, no. 7.

[125] *Layettes*, iv, no. 5119.

[126] *Poesie prov. storiche*, ii. 224. See also Throop, *Criticism*, pp. 61–2.

[127] *Documenti delle relazioni tra Carlo I d'Angiò e la Toscana*, ed. S. Terlizzi, no. 869.

[128] Honorius IV, *Reg.*, no. 484 (confirming a grant of Martin IV).

[129] Boniface VIII, *Reg.*, nos. 2316, 2321.

obventions and legacies to the Holy Land were collected for the use of the papal *camera* in 1300. In the same year Robert of Artois was made a conditional grant for three years of money raised from the redemption of all vows in his French lands.[130]

More scandalous than the diversion of these comparatively small sums was that of the larger part of the tenth which Gregory X had levied at the Second Council of Lyons in 1274 to finance his planned general passage.[131] As the crusade never took place the money remained with its collectors or in deposit. At the end of 1282 Martin IV asked Philip IV for his permission to use £100,000 *Tours* of the French tenth, which was deposited at the Paris Temple, to fight the Church's war in Romagna. He promised that the money would be repaid in full.[132] Then, after the failure of early attempts to crush the Sicilian revolt, the Pope started drawing on the tenth to finance Charles I until the new Italian tenth could be collected, this time without any guarantee or hint of eventual repayment. In the period April–June 1283 over 15,000 gold ounces were paid to Charles of Salerno from the tenth which had been collected in Hungary, Sicily, Sardinia and Corsica, Provence, Aragon, and the imperial dioceses. In November another 16,000 gold ounces were paid to Charles from the same sources, and in 1284 crusade funds were used which had been collected in Scotland, Denmark, Sweden, Hungary, Poland, and other parts of eastern Europe. Payments continued until the death of Charles I in January 1285.[133] Thereafter there was no need to use the Lyons tenth since the tenth levied for the Aragonese crusade itself was available, and both Honorius IV and Nicholas IV seem to have kept a careful division between the two sums. This division was abandoned by Boniface VIII when military operations escalated again after the treaty of Anagni. Boniface evidently applied his close identification of the Sicilian war with the affairs of the Holy Land to financial as well as diplomatic

---

[130] Ibid., nos. 3067, 3453, 3539, 5492.

[131] For Gregory's crusade plans and the Council of Lyons, see Throop, *Criticism*, pp. 215–76.

[132] Martin IV, *Reg.*, no. 272. Cf. Salimbene, 'Cronica', p. 438; E. Jordan, *De mercatoribus camerae apostolicae saeculo xiii*, pp. 86–7.

[133] See *Reg. pont. rom.* ii, no. 22168; 'Les Décimes ecclésiastiques dans le royaume d'Arles de 1278 à 1283', ed. P. Fabre, *Annales du Midi*, iv (1892), *passim*; Jordan, *De mercatoribus*, pp. 88–96.

matters, and he used the Lyons tenth indiscriminately as payments of, or backing for, his loans and payments to Charles II and James II.[134] By the end of his reign the tenth levied at Lyons had vanished without trace.

This series of events was repeated during the crusades of John XXII. Once again a general council, that held at Vienne in 1311–12, had decreed a general passage to the East. Once again no such passage took place, and the temptation to use the money in Italy was strong. Clement V himself prepared the way for the diversion of the tenth. When it was levied in 1312 its aim was described simply as 'in aid of the Holy Land', but by March 1314 this had been significantly modified to 'aid for the Holy Land, or elsewhere against the unfaithful and the enemies of the Catholic Faith'.[135] Nevertheless, John XXII was at first strict in his use of the tenth: it was to be treated as a loan, which would be paid back in due course. Typical is his letter of 1319 to the Treasurer of the March of Ancona telling him to collect the Vienne tenth in his province and in the neighbouring Duchy of Spoleto, and to give the money to the Rector of the March to pay his troops fighting the rebels. A full account was to be kept of how much was raised and spent, so that it could be repaid when revenue again flowed in from the subdued areas. 'It is our intention that you receive the said money as if it were a loan, which is to be paid back in due course from the revenues of the provinces and lands themselves, to help the Holy Land, for which purpose, as we have said, it was originally levied.'[136] The same criteria applied to the three years of the Vienne tenth which Robert of Naples was allowed to use in 1321 from the money collected in the *Regno*.[137] It too was 'in the form of a loan from us and from the Roman church', and the penalty for not paying it back on time was to be excommunication for Robert

---

[134] Boniface VIII, *Reg.*, nos. 1550, 1691–2, 3001, 1698; Jordan, *De mercatoribus*, pp. 96–102.

[135] Clement V, *Reg.*, nos. 7759, 10298.

[136] 'Nostre intentionis existat quod velut mutuatam vobis pecuniam recipiatis candem restituendam suo tempore de ipsarum provinciarum et terrarum redditibus pro dicte terre sancte subsidio ad quod ut predicitur extitit deputata.' ASV, Reg. Vat. 69, f. 539ʳ⁻ᵛ, no. 174. Cf. ibid., ff. 545ᵛ–546ʳ, no. 195; *Codex dipl.*, i, no. 661; Bock, 'Kaisertum', pp. 184–5.

[137] The other three years' proceeds had been granted to Philip of Taranto in April 1312 to help him to defend the Morea against the Greeks. See Clement V, *Reg.*, no. 7759.

and Charles of Calabria and an interdict on all Robert's lands in France and Italy.[138] In 1322 the Pope wrote that he could not relax these conditions because 'a tenth imposed in aid of the Holy Land is concerned'.[139]

It seems that these good intentions were soon abandoned. At the end of 1323 the loan to Robert of Naples and Charles of Calabria of the proceeds of the Vienne tenth was converted into a subsidy; it is true that the money was sent to Avignon, where it was deducted from the Angevin census arrears, but it was still, probably, lost to the Holy Land.[140] Similarly, in the course of 1323 the coda on the treatment of the Vienne tenth as a loan was dropped in papal letters ordering the consignment of the money to Bertrand du Poujet and the authorities of the March of Ancona.[141] The same was true of later transfers, including the 10,000 florins from the tenth which Gerard of Valle, collector in the *Regno* and Rector of Campagna-Marittima, was told to send to the Treasurer of the March in May 1325, 'for the payment of the troops which the rector needs for the repression of the rebels and the unfaithful in the March'.[142] John XXII also started to employ his predecessor's comprehensive description of the tenth's purpose when instituting or renewing its collection. Thus when collection was set up in Germany at the end of 1329 the appeal to the clergy to pay was couched in terms of 'the necessities of the Holy Land or of the unfortunate Christians overseas', and of 'the defence of the Catholic Faith, which is being cruelly attacked by heretics and rebels against God and the Church'.[143] By March 1332 John was claiming that Clement V had imposed the tenth 'for aid for the Holy Land and for the necessities of the Church', and he besought the

---

[138] 'ex causa et nomine mutui nostri et ecclesie Romane nomine'. ASV, Instr. misc., no. 748.

[139] 'hic de decima imposita pro subsidio terre sancte agitur'. ASV, Reg. Vat. 111, f. 117ʳ, no. 447. Cf. ibid., ff. 116ʳ–117ʳ, nos. 475–6.

[140] ASV, Reg. Vat. 112, ff. 79ʳ–80ʳ, nos. 933–4. Cf. Reg. Vat. 113, ff. 57ᵛ–58ʳ, no. 442; Reg. Vat. 114, f. 161ʳ⁻ᵛ, nos. 1014–15. See also *Die Einnahmen*, pp. 419–21.

[141] ASV, Reg. Vat. 111, f. 377ᵛ, nos. 1570–1, f. 382ᵛ, nos. 1594–5.

[142] 'in solutione stipendariorum quos dictum rectorem pro repressione rebellium et infidelium dicte Marche tenere oportet'. ASV, Reg. Vat. 113, f. 175ᵛ, no. 1035. See also ibid., f. 148ʳ, no. 944.

[143] 'pro dicte terre seu christicolarum in partibus transmarinis degencium necessitatibus defensioneque fidei predicte catholice que ab hereticis et rebellibus dei et ipsius ecclesie crudeliter impetitur'. ASV, Reg. Vat. 115, f. 149ʳ, no. 1862.

clergy of Hungary to pay in order to help the Roman church sustain the struggle against heresy and schism.[144] There could hardly be a clearer admission that the bulk, if not all, of the money would be spent in Italy.

iv. PUBLIC OPINION AND PAPAL CRUSADE POLICY

Rarely can any great power have adhered to a chosen policy as rigidly as the papal Curia clung to its order of priorities on the crusades. It is important not to overestimate the effects of this inflexibility on events in the Latin East. Many other developments, most of them beyond the control or influence of the Holy See, worked towards the disasters which occurred there in this period: the military and economic strength of the Mamluk sultanate, the rise of the Turks in Asia Minor, the instability caused by the weakness of the restored Byzantine empire, chronic Anglo-French hostility, and the reluctance of great secular rulers and their nobles to leave their lands and go on crusade.[145] Some contemporaries thought differently. They believed that the preoccupation of the Holy See with Italy constituted a major element, if not the major element, in the loss of the Holy Places and Christendom's failure to regain them. Typical was Marino Sanudo's comment that 'as you know, so many misfortunes befell Christianity as a result of this Sicilian war . . . that it can be said that Acre and the rest of the Holy Land was lost because of it'.[146] Did public opinion, as has been argued, disapprove of papal crusade policy and blame the Curia for such disasters as the fall of Acre?

A distinction has to be made between the diversion of crusade resources and the broader question of papal policy in general. There can be no doubt that the misappropriation of crusade tenths and the commutation and redemption of crusade vows were extremely unpopular and were vigorously attacked. Suspicions that the popes were diverting crusade funds did not originate with the crusades against Christian rulers. They were rather the inevitable consequence of the procedure used to

---

[144] 'pro succursu terre sancte et eiusdem necessitatibus ecclesie', ASV, Reg. Vat. 116, f. 246ʳ⁻ᵛ, no. 1282.

[145] See Atiya, *Crusade, passim*; Luttrell, 'Crusade', *passim*.

[146] *Gesta Dei*, ii. 305.

transmit money donated to the Holy Land, since it was collected by papal agents and channelled through the *camera*: as early as 1200 fears of Roman greed were aroused when a papal envoy replaced the Hospitallers and Templars as the transmitter to the Holy Land of English crusade funds.[147] But complaints became more vociferous when such fears were confirmed and it became clear that the diversion of crusade funds had indeed become an integral part of papal crusade policy.

Complaints came from many quarters. Those involved in the defence of the Latin East naturally objected strongly to the loss of valuable manpower and money. The Archbishop of Tyre and Ricaut Bonomel both complained in the 1260s about the redemption and commutation of vows in favour of Charles of Anjou.[148] The clergy and Orders became reluctant to pay tenths for the Holy Land because they thought the money would be diverted to Italy. Thus Nicholas III had to rebuke some of the German clergy in January 1278 for displaying reluctance to pay the Lyons tenth because of their suspicion that it had been and would be converted 'into other uses', a suspicion which they expressed again in the reign of Martin IV.[149] One German chronicler complained that 'although the tenth was exacted and collected with care, it is nevertheless not clear what advantage was thereby gained for the Holy Land'.[150] Secular rulers also objected to the duplicity involved. Edward I took umbrage when Martin IV started to use the proceeds from the Lyons tenth on behalf of Charles I, and in May 1282 he took steps to prevent the export of the contribution of the English clergy to the tenth. No doubt Edward thought that he might himself need the money for the Welsh war (he was in 1283 to seize several sacks of it for that purpose), but his fears that the money would be diverted to Italy at least furnished him with a useful excuse for his actions, and only a long struggle could secure even part of the tenth for the papal *camera*.[151] The

---

[147] See W. E. Lunt, *Papal Revenues in the Middle Ages*, i. 120. See also Queller, *Fourth Crusade*, p. 45.

[148] *Layettes*, iv, no. 5119; *Poesie prov. storiche*, ii. 224.

[149] *Actenstücke zur Geschichte des deutschen Reiches unter den Königen Rudolf I. und Albrecht I.*, ed. F. Kaltenbrunner, no. 107; Martin IV, *Reg.*, no. 244. See also Matthew Paris, *Chronica maiora*, v. 536.

[150] 'Annales altahenses', *MGHS*, xvii. 410.

[151] See *Foedera*, i, pt. 2, pp. 608, 631; Lunt, *Financial Relations*, i. 335–46.

parliament of Carlisle, in 1307, complained about the misuse of crusade alms and legacies, and the diversion of the Vienne tenth scandalized contemporaries.[152]

Not surprisingly, the enemies of the Curia gave this theme lavish attention in their attacks on papal crusade policy. In his Sachsenhausen manifesto of 1324 Louis IV declared that this use of money donated to the Holy Land in order to fight Christians in Italy was 'contrary to the Catholic Faith and contrary to all Christ's faithful, who are blessed with the name of Christian, in contempt of God and an open scandal to all Christians'.[153] In the same year Marsilius of Padua added his criticisms in the *Defensor pacis*, and the attack was renewed in the imperial deposition of John XXII in 1328, in which the diversion of the crusade squadron against the Genoese Ghibellines—'to the slaughter of Christians subject to our empire, namely the Genoese'—was also castigated.[154]

On the question of papal crusade policy as a whole, it is much less easy to judge contemporary reactions. Considerable evidence has been adduced in support of the view that public opinion was wholly critical, but it invariably comes from sources representing the enemies of the Curia, or from groups traditionally hostile to the papacy, such as the Provençal troubadours.[155] It is not surprising to find such sources attacking papal policy. But it is also possible to find pro-papal and Angevin commentators who were equally vociferous in their defence of it. Thus the provincial Council of Sens in January 1292 supported the crusade against the Aragonese as a necessary preliminary measure for a crusade to the Holy Land, and declared that if James of Aragon did not submit to the Church then all Christians should participate in it.[156] The same argument was used by Charles II of Naples in his negotiations with the Genoese for naval help against Sicily.

But most importantly it is argued and asserted, that the intention of

---

[152] See *Rotuli parliamentorum; ut et petitiones, et placita in parliamento*, ed. J. Strachey *et al.*, i. 221; *Vita Edwardi secundi monachi cuiusdam Malmesberiensis*, p. 46; Peter Dubois, *De recuperatione*, p. 91; E. Hennig, *Die päpstlichen Zehnten aus Deutschland im Zeitalter des avignonesischen Papsttums und während des Grossen Schismas*, p. 23.

[153] *MGH Const.* v, nos. 909–10.

[154] *Defensor pacis*, Dict. II, Cap. xxvi, 16, p. 511; *MGH, Const.* vi, pt. 1, no. 436.

[155] See, e.g., the very full account in Throop, *Criticism*, pp. 28–68.

[156] Digard, *Philippe le Bel*, ii. 281–2.

the lord King of Sicily is that this fleet, which is to be dispatched by the Commune of Genoa, with God's help, against Sicily, should be considered as aid to the Holy Land, concurring in this with the wishes of Holy Mother Church and the lord King of France and the other faithful Christians. For without the recovery of the said island, which is the inheritance of the said king, the Holy Land cannot be recovered, nor can the necessary aid be sent there, according to the counsel of princes, prelates, and other estates, openly stated and given to the Roman church.[157]

While it is comparatively easy to find comments openly supporting or attacking papal policy, it is more difficult to discover sources which can be quoted as reliable indicators of neutral public opinion. There are two reasons for this. First, as Carlo Merkel demonstrated when comparing contemporary comments on the crusade against Manfred, most chroniclers who left evidence of their feelings on the crusades which the popes were waging in Italy had their judgement of papal policy dictated by the wider repercussions of the events in Italy or at least by *a priori* attitudes towards papal temporal claims.[158] Secondly, those chroniclers whose rulers were not directly or indirectly involved in the Italian crusades left, as a consequence, little indication of their views.

Given these problems, it would be rash to make generalizations about the feelings of neutral public opinion, but some comments might be made. Certainly some people were critical of the papacy's order of priorities on the crusade. These included, at various times, the kings of England and France. Even their criticisms, however, arose as much from political and financial considerations as from genuine concern for the Latin East. Edward I, in the 1280s, was anxious to prevent French expansion across the Pyrenees and to retain for his own use the contribution of the English church towards Gregory X's tenth. Philip V and Charles IV, in the 1320s, wanted to establish French influence in Lombardy and to secure a royal hegemony over the crusading funds paid by the French church and even the Church at large. One is on more secure ground with the

---

[157] 'Annali genovesi di Caffaro e de' suoi continuatori', ed. L. T. Belgrano and C. Imperiale di Sant'Angelo, *Fonti per la storia d'Italia*, v. 157.

[158] C. Merkel, 'L'opinione dei contemporanei sull'impresa italiana di Carlo I d'Angiò', *Atti della R. Accademia dei Lincei*, 4th series, *Classe di Scienze morali, storiche e filologiche*, iv (1888), part i, *passim*.

extensive attacks made on the diversion of crusade resources: but it is far too large a step from this specific and limited criticism to claim that the Holy See was held largely responsible for the disasters in the Latin East or that the crusades in Italy were unpopular for that reason. Moreover, against these attacks must be set the success of recruitment for the Italian crusades,[159] as well as the 'deep acquiescence' which, as Beryl Smalley wrote, still characterized the way contemporaries regarded papal policy and which offset attacks on individual abuses of papal power.[160]

[159] See below, chapter 5.
[160] See her 'Church and State, 1300–77: Theory and Fact', in Hale *et al.* (eds.), *Europe in the Late Middle Ages*, pp. 41–2.

Chapter 4

The Preaching and Organization of the Italian Crusades

The first questions to be settled by the papal Curia in the arrangement of crusade preaching were, naturally enough, over what area the crusade was to be preached and who was to carry out the preaching. Chroniclers often assumed that the crusades against the pope's Christian enemies were preached throughout Europe. Thus the 'Annales placentini Gibellini' asserted that Martin IV 'has arranged and set in motion a great crusade by the Christians, so that a great crusade is being preached generally and everywhere by his nuncios against him (Peter of Aragon) and against the land which he holds, on the pretext that the same Peter of Aragon invaded and occupied the land of Sicily, which lord King Charles held for the Church'.[1] The evidence of the papal registers, however, shows that the preaching was usually quite restricted in area. This policy seems to have been determined partly by the political circumstances behind the crusades, partly by the nature of their justification. A secular power not involved in the Italian wars often disapproved of its subjects going to fight there. For example, in the early years of the War of the Vespers Venice, which enjoyed good relations with Peter of Aragon, refused to allow the crusade against the Aragonese to be preached in Venetian territory. The city was placed under an interdict and it was not until 1289 that the excommunication of the leading Venetians was annulled.[2] In general, as those in the Curia knew, it was simply not worthwhile to create such a prolonged and mutually damaging dispute for the sake of a crusading response which would probably be limited anyway. Once a prince had intervened in Italy on behalf of the papacy or its allies, however,

---

[1] 'Ann. plac. Gib.', p. 579. Cf. Raymond Muntaner, *Chronicle*, i. 181.
[2] See N. Nicolini, 'Sui rapporti diplomatici veneto-napoletani durante i regni di Carlo I e Carlo II d'Angiò', *ASPN*, NS, xxi (1935), 268–9; Yver, *Le Commerce*, pp. 248–9; F. Soldevila, 'L'amistat catalano-veneciana en 1283–1285', in *Miscellanea in onore di Roberto Cessi*, i, *passim*.

preaching was both welcomed by him and, usually, achieved a better response. Thus the crusade against Manfred was preached in various Guelf areas of Italy, in England (in 1255), and in France (in 1264–6).[3] The same approach is found during the struggle for Sicily in the 1280s and 1290s; only for the Guelf regions of Italy, and for France, is there documentary evidence of crusade preaching.

As I have shown, the crusades against the Staufen and the Aragonese were justified largely in terms of their persecution of the Church and the harm which they were doing to the Holy Land. When heresy was involved the Curia had the crusades preached more widely. Thus in 1258 the crusade against Ezzelino of Romano was to be preached in northern Italy and the Kingdom of Germany.[4] It is possible that the crusade against Ezzelino furnished a precedent for John XXII when he considered where to order the preaching of his crusades against Ghibellines who bore a marked resemblance to the great thirteenth-century *signore*. The crusades which John declared at the end of 1321 against Matthew Visconti, the Estensi, the Montefeltro, and the rebel communes of the Papal State were also preached in Italy and the empire. The Pope would have liked to include France, but its exclusion at this stage was dictated by the disapproval with which the French court viewed papal actions in Italy.[5] By the end of 1323 this disapproval had been effectively diminished by the Curia. This enabled it to get the crusades preached in France, and the preaching against the Visconti and the Estensi in 1324 and 1325 reached the widest audience of any of the Italian crusades—Italy, France, Germany, parts of Iberia, England, Hungary, and Poland.[6] The exact geographical limit is very hard to establish; the crusade bull in the relevant papal register is followed not by the usual list of its recipients, but by the unhelpful phrase 'Many

[3] *Thes. novus*, ii, cols. 70–2; 'Ann. de Burton', pp. 350–3.

[4] *Cod. dipl. ecel.*, no. 236.

[5] ASV, Reg. Vat. 111, f. 155^{r-v}, nos. 644–6; John XXII, *Lettres communes*, nos. 16125–7, 16180, 16183, 16189, 16212–13; Franceschini, *I Montefeltro*, p. 213. For France, see above, pp. 84ff.

[6] ASV, Reg. Vat. 112, ff. 122^v–123^r, no. 484; John XXII, *Lettres secrètes*, nos. 2082–3; John XXII, *Lettres communes*, nos. 20578, 23143, 23146, 23148; *MGH, Const.* v, nos. 906–8; *Vat. Akten*, no. 376; *Cal. of Entries*, ii. 459; *Vet. mon. hist. Hung. sacr. ill.*, i, no. 757. The 'Ann. mediolanenses' (col. 701) specified that the crusade against the Visconti was preached in England, France and Italy.

letters of execution of this kind were drawn up and sent to various prelates'.[7]

When the crusade was preached against Louis IV in the early months of 1328 the area covered was again reduced to Italy, specifically to the legatine areas under Bertrand du Poujet and Giovanni Orsini, and the Kingdom of Naples.[8] Even the inclusion of the *Regno* was the result of the efforts of King Robert's friends and agents at Avignon. They reported to the King that they had persuaded the Pope to extend the 'indulgence of the cross' to his lands, and that they were working to secure the extension of crusade preaching to other areas, 'so that the said indulgence be proclaimed both in France and elsewhere . . . as befits the importance of the matter'.[9] In this they were unsuccessful. French interest in the empire had dropped, and the kingdom was faced in the early months of 1328 with the difficulties of the Valois succession, closely followed by the proclamation of the *arrière-ban* for a campaign in Flanders.[10] The crusade against Louis was never allowed to escalate to the proportions of previous papal–imperial conflicts. When preaching against him was renewed, in 1329 and 1337, it was again kept to local levels.[11]

In appointing its preachers the Curia had, for most of Europe, the possibility of three broad choices: specially designated legates and nuncios, the secular clergy (particularly local bishops), and the Orders of friars.[12] All three were used extensively in the period 1254–1343, and there seems to have been no over-all pattern or policy in the way they were chosen: the aim was simply to secure effective preaching by the best possible means. When maximum coverage was required all three groups were told to preach, under the general supervision and co-ordination of a legate. This was the case in France

---

[7] 'Huiusmodi vero executorie multiplicate fuerunt et diversis prelatis directe.' ASV, Reg. Vat. 112, f. 122ᵛ, no. 483. Cf. ibid., f. 123ʳ, no 484, and *MGH, Const.* v, no. 883.

[8] *Thes. novus*, ii, cols. 716–23.

[9] 'quod memorata indulgentia tam in Francia quam alibi puplicetur . . . iuxta negotii qualitatem'. ASN, MS Minieri-Riccio, formerly Reg. Ang. 268, ff. 26ᵛ–27ʳ. Robert's informants included Hélion of Villeneuve, the Master of the Hospitallers.

[10] See Henneman, *Royal Taxation*, pp. 68–70.

[11] *Thes. novus*, ii, cols. 777–82. Benedict XII, *Lettres closes et patentes*, no. 1609.

[12] See Riley-Smith, *What were the Crusades?*, pp. 42–5. For the origins and powers of papal legates, see F. Claeys-Bouvaert, 'Légat du pape', in R. Naz (ed.), *Dictionnaire de droit canonique*, vi. 371 ff.

during the preaching against Manfred, and in Italy and France during that against the Visconti. Just as important as effective coverage, however, was the quality of the preaching. In the second half of the thirteenth century, with popular enthusiasm for crusading perceptibly declining, vigorous crusade preaching was increasingly being seen as a key element in the organization of a crusade, whether against Christians or Muslims. In 1266 or 1267 Humbert of Romans, the great Dominican general, wrote his tract on crusade preaching, *De praedicatione crucis,* which stressed the ability of a well-structured and rousing sermon to overcome apathy in the crusade audience and to counter the arguments of the sceptical.[13] Such ideas seem to have found a favourable reception at the Curia, or at least to have reflected general feeling at the time, for those charged with preaching were invariably told to be careful to appoint preachers with the right qualities for the task. Simon of Brie was told in 1265 'to preach the word of the cross, and to have it preached by those whom you find suitable for it', while the Cardinal-bishop of Albano in 1266 was to have the cross preached 'by yourself, and by other suitable people, both the secular and the religious [clergy]'.[14]

This power of delegation was, of course, particularly important for legates and nuncios. Given responsibility over large areas, and commissions which included preaching as one among many other duties, they could not possibly do all their own preaching. The nuncio Rostand, arriving in England in 1255 to execute 'the business of the cross' against Manfred, appointed Alexander, a canon of Hereford Cathedral, and William of Ros as his deputies in the dioceses of Coventry, Hereford, and Worcester.[15] Similarly, at the end of 1267 Simon of Brie, who had been told to preach the cross against the Muslims now that Charles of Anjou had conquered Sicily, deputed a Franciscan guardian to preach in his place throughout the province of Narbonne, carefully instructing him on the terms which he was to observe.[16] The legatine commissions of

[13] See A. Lecoy de la Marche, 'La Prédication de la Croisade au treizième siècle', *Revue des questions historiques,* xlviii (1890), 19–25 and *passim.* For Humbert's ideas, see also Throop, *Criticism,* pp. 147–213.

[14] *Thes. novus,* ii, col. 198; Clement IV, *Reg.,* no. 297.

[15] 'Ann. de Burton', pp. 353–4.

[16] *Layettes,* iv, no. 5339.

men like Simon of Brie in 1264, Rudolf of Albano in 1266, John Cholet in 1283, Gerard of Sabina in 1282 and 1299, and Bertrand du Poujet in 1320, also included a general authority to use the Orders of friars in their work.[17] Not that this prevented the legates from doing any preaching themselves; Simon of Brie, who is recorded as preaching the cross 'many times, in the king's garden and also elsewhere', in 1266 or 1267, was rebuked by Clement IV in October 1266 for neglecting his other legatine duties because of his love of preaching. 'When we gave you the office of preaching the cross you know that our intention was to attach the preaching to the legation, not the legation to the preaching.'[18]

Simon of Brie commented in 1267 that archbishops and bishops had too much work to do connected with the affairs of their churches to be able to give crusade preaching the attention which it needed.[19] This was probably true, though there are examples of preaching by the secular clergy and their prelates. The Archbishop of Bourges toured his province in 1284 preaching the 'cross of Aragon' and had great success.[20] Guy, Bishop of Auxerre, was specifically requested to take the cross and to participate in the crusade against Manfred, because 'the Lord endowed you with the spirit of wisdom, granted you also a fluent tongue, and has built up your understanding with many years of experience; so you lack none of the graces which can be used in the promotion of this most pious business'.[21] Efforts were also made to make the lesser clergy co-operate with and help in the preaching of the crusades. In 1255 the nuncio Rostand ordered that the deans in England assist those who were being sent out to preach the cross against Manfred, and that they ensure that the crusade was preached frequently in all parish churches. Ten years later Clement IV told Simon of Brie and the French bishops to instruct and, if necessary, compel the rectors of churches to attend crusade preaching against Manfred

[17] Urban IV, *Reg.*, no. 833; Clement IV, *Reg.*, no. 272; Martin IV, *Reg.*, nos. 451d, 451h, 451q, 270t, 270x; Boniface VIII, *Reg.*, no. 3372; John XXII, *Lettres communes*, no. 12121.
[18] *Thes. novus*, ii, col. 416; 'Chronique anonyme des rois de France', *RHGF*, xxi. 85.
[19] *Layettes*, iv, no. 5339.
[20] See Langlois, *Le Règne de Philippe III*, p. 152.
[21] *Thes. novus*, ii, col. 200.

alongside their parishioners, 'devoutly and reverently'.[22]

It was, however, the Orders of friars, particularly the sister Orders of St. Francis and St. Dominic, on which the Curia relied most to preach the crusades.[23] Unlike most of the secular clergy, the friars could spend all their time preaching, and could move from place to place to do so, singly or in groups. Fortunately a remarkable document has survived which illustrates this: the list of daily expenses of one group of itinerant friars, ecclesiastics, and their servants, who moved about northern France in the summer of 1265 preaching the crusade and collecting the crusade hundredth at the order of the Archbishop of Tyre. Although the group was concerned with the crusade to the Holy Land, not with the contemporaneous crusade against Manfred, the differences in the way the cross was preached must have been minimal. The group consisted of about fifty people, and included both Franciscan and Dominican friars. Travelling from Paris to Flanders, they preached the cross regularly, publicizing the event beforehand, and sending out members *en route* to towns and villages not on their itinerary. Like the Archbishop of Bourges in 1284, they sometimes preached in the open air, and occasional expenses were laid out for the construction of a rough platform or pulpit from which to do so.[24]

The Dominicans were particularly noted for their allegiance to the Holy See and for their involvement in preaching crusades against its Christian enemies, sometimes at considerable personal risk. Some friars preachers were abused and attacked when they came to the abbey of St. Etienne at Lille in 1284 to preach the cross against Peter of Aragon: a crusade whose aim, the aggrandisement of the French crown, did not appeal to the Flemings.[25] In 1286 two Dominicans went secretly to Sicily to

---

[22] 'Ann. de Burton', pp. 359–60; Sternfeld, *Ludwigs des Heiligen Kreuzzug nach Tunis*, p. 319. See also John XXII, *Lettres communes*, nos. 20375, 20378–9, 20383, 20397–8.

[23] On the friars and the preaching of the crusades, see J. Moorman, *A History of the Franciscan Order from its Origins to the Year 1517*, pp. 300–1; 'De praedicatione cruciatae saec. xiii per fratres minores', ed. P. F. Delorme, *Archivum franciscanum historicum*, ix (1916), *passim*.

[24] See 'Compte d'une mission de prédication pour secours à la Terre Sainte (1265)', ed. Borrelli de Serres, *Mémoires de la Société de l'histoire de Paris et de l'Ile de France*, xxx (1903), *passim*.

[25] See Langlois, *Le Règne de Philippe III*, p. 152.

attempt to raise an anti-Aragonese revolt there with offers of the plenary indulgence.[26] During the 1320s the association of Ghibellinism with heresy, the extinction of which was one of the fundamental aims of the Dominican Order, made the friars preachers central to the activities of the Curia in Italy, an importance which was heightened by the fact that John XXII could not rely on the friars minor. It has even been suggested that the canonization of Thomas Aquinas in July 1323 was partly intended as a political move and as a compliment to the allegiance of the Order.[27] The importance of the Order's role at this time is reflected in the decrees of the chapter meetings of the Dominican province of Rome. In 1324, for instance, it was decreed that all the priors should ensure that the Pope's crusades be preached.'They must make sure that they themselves, or the brothers who undertake the preaching in the convent, solemnly publish them in the convents when a very large number of the people are present, and expound them, word by word, so that they can be understood by all.'[28] This decree was repeated in 1326 and 1329, and in 1331 and 1332 it was established that the friars should actively preach on behalf of John XXII, 'to counter the slanders and lies of certain people, by which they attempt openly or secretly to detract from his integrity and sanctity'.[29] The 1324 chapter meeting also enjoined those friars permitted to hear confessions 'to excite and induce such suitable persons as approach them for confession, so that they offer aid, in person or through others, against the rebels of the Roman church, relating to them how a great indulgence has been granted for opposing these people.'[30] Dominican zeal appalled and angered the Pope's enemies. Marsilius of Padua attacked the 'false, so-called brothers' who preached the crusade against the Ghibellines. The Visconti

---

[26] Bartholomew of Neocastro, 'Historia sicula', p. 78. See also ibid., pp. 85 ff.

[27] See Bock, in 'Studien zum politischen Inquisitionsprozess', xxvi. 59–60. See also 'Die Beteiligung', *passim.*

[28] *Acta capitulorum provincialium Provinciae romanae (1243–1344)*, ed. T. Kaeppeli and A. Dondaine, p. 230. Cf. the similar decrees of the Dominican Chapter General in 1328 and 1330, in *Acta capitulorum generalium Ordinis Praedicatorum*, ed. B. M. Reichert, ii. 178–9, 201–5.

[29] *Acta cap. prov.*, pp. 236, 246, 255, 270. This was possibly at the request of the Pope himself. See ASV, Reg. Vat. 115, ff. 166ʳ–167ᵛ, nos. 1942, 1948. The Dominicans had performed the same service for Boniface VIII in 1297. See *Acta cap. gen.* i., 284.

[30] *Acta cap. prov.*, p. 231.

forbad synods by both the Franciscans and the Dominicans in their lands, and Louis IV ordered the expulsion from their convents of Dominican friars who published the papal decrees against him.[31]

Many of the various 'limbs of the Church', including the secular clergy, the episcopate, the Orders of friars, and papal nuncios and legates, thus helped to preach the Italian crusades. But the laity also had its part to play. A lay individual could not preach or distribute the cross; he could however 'publish' a crusade in the limited sense of reading out a crusade bull. For example, when Bishop Ranuccio of Volterra sent the crusade bull against Louis IV to the Guelf commune of San Gimignano in June 1328, it was first read out before the assembled people by a notary, Jacopo di Lippo, on the orders of the provost, then expounded by an Augustinian friar.[32] Civil authorities could also transmit crusade bulls and co-ordinate crusade activity. Such secular participation in 'the business of the cross' was widespread by the end of the thirteenth century, reflecting the growing assertiveness and administrative ability of the lay powers. Edward I's exchequer accounts reveal that he paid for the copying and transmission of Nicholas IV's crusade bulls in 1292–3.[33] In the case of the Italian crusades there is documentary evidence of the participation of civil authorities in the publication of the crusades for both the Papal State and the Kingdom of Naples.

In the 1260s normal administration in the Papal State collapsed under Manfred's pressure and the Curia relied largely on cardinals to preach the crusade against him in the Duchy of Spoleto and the March of Ancona.[34] In the 1320s, on the other hand, the normal administration was maintained and the rectors and treasurers co-ordinated crusade preaching not only against the Ghibellines in their own provinces but also against those in Lombardy. Consequently the crusade bulls of

---

[31] See *Defensor pacis*, Dict. II, Cap. xxvi, 16, p. 509; *Chronica et chronicorum excerpta historiam Ordinis Praedicatorum illustrantia*, ed. B. M. Reichert, p. 22.

[32] *Forschungen*, ii, no. 2264.

[33] See B. Beebe, 'Edward I and the Crusades' (Univ. of St. Andrews dissertation), p. 307.

[34] Urban IV, *Reg.*, nos. 633, 860. One of the cardinals, Simon, Cardinal-priest of St. Martin, was also rector of the two provinces. See Waley, *Papal State*, pp. 165–6, 312, 315. On the collapse of provincial government, see Waley, 'Papal Armies', p. 13.

1321 against the rebels in the Papal State were sent to the rectors of all the provinces, as well as to the papal vicar *in spiritualibus* at Rome;[35] the same procedure was followed in the case of the crusades against the Visconti and the Estensi in 1324.[36] On receipt of these bulls the rectors sent copies to the clergy and the civil authorities in their provinces to be preached and proclaimed. If they held their office *in spiritualibus* as well as *in temporalibus* they themselves would preach the cross.[37] The accounts kept by the treasurers of this period record their dispatch of the copies of the bulls. Thus in June 1325 the Treasurer of the Duchy of Spoleto, Peter Maynarde, recorded an expenditure of thirty florins,

for the notification and publication by the towns, estates and villages, and the bishops and prelates of the duchy, of the process drawn up by the lord rector at the order of our lord the pope against Milan and the sons of Lord Matthew Visconti and against the ambassadors of the Duke of Bavaria, the Bishop of Arezzo, and the people of Fermo and Fabriano.[38]

Of course if the crusade was against rebels in his own province it was in the interests of the rector to make sure that it was preached as widely as possible. Under the heading 'crusade' (*crutiata*), one of the account books of the Treasurer of the March recorded money spent in 1322 'to help promote the preaching of the holy cross against the heretics', in the form of travelling and living expenses for messengers carrying the bulls against Recanati and Osimo not only to the corners of the province itself, but also to Rome, Campagna, the Patriarchate of Aquileia, Tuscany and the Marittima, Romagna, the *Regno*, and even Germany. The total amounted to over 630 florins and included payments for infantry and cavalry escorts to defend the preachers, and notaries to make copies of the bulls.[39] Two years later the treasurer noted payments of over 680 florins 'for the expenses of ambassadors, inquisitors of heresy, notaries,

[35] John XXII, *Lettres communes*, nos. 16125–7.
[36] See, e.g., ibid., nos. 20587, 20593.
[37] See, e.g., ibid., nos. 20479, 20597, 20602.
[38] 'I registri', iii. 524.
[39] 'Crutiata. Pecunia data et soluta per supradictum dominum Hugonem Thesaurarium in subsidium et pro favore predicationis sancte crucis contra hereticos.' ASV, I et E, no. 50, ff. 28ʳ–32ʳ.

clerks, and their servants for the matter of preaching the cross against those convicted of heresy and of aiding heretics; some of the ambassadors went to Germany, some to the Kingdom of Naples, some to Tuscany, some to Campagna, and others to various parts of Italy.'[40]

The Angevin civil authorities also played a prominent role in the transmission and publication of the crusade bulls. In March 1328 King Robert received from Avignon the news that John XXII had granted a plenary indulgence to all who fought in the Angevin army against Louis IV. He passed it on immediately to many of the civil authorities in the *Regno* for publication, and in April wrote to his agents in the Roman Campagna, James of Colonna and Francis of Gaeta, who were clerics, to tell them to preach the cross, dividing Campagna up between them.[41] Two years later Robert's justiciars were told to publish the crusade bull recently issued against the Catalan Grand Company.[42] Giordano Russo, the Justiciar of Principato Ultra, designated Pasquale di Guanderisio and Giacomo di Giorgio to make a tour of the villages and towns in one district carrying out the royal commission. Their orders make it clear that in this case the publication of the crusade varied little, if at all, from that of any Angevin royal decree.

We order, under penalty of ten ounces of gold, that as soon as you have received these letters, and when you have summoned a public notary and judge and reliable witnesses, you publicly announce and have announced the content of these papal letters, and the letters themselves, in suitable places and in the usual manner, throughout those estates and places in our jurisdiction and your commission in which it is expedient . . .

This was followed by a list of eighteen towns and villages in

---

[40] 'pro expensis embaxiatorum et inquisitorum heretice pravitatis notatoriorum et scripturarum et famulorum pro negocio predicationis crucie contra dampnatos de eresi et favore hereticorum de quibus embaxiatoribus aliqui iverunt in Alamaniam aliqui in regnum Cicilie citrafarum aliqui in Tusciam aliqui in Campaniam et aliqui per diversas partes Italie'. ASV, I et E, no. 62, f. 141^v.

[41] ASN, MS Minieri-Riccio, formerly Reg. Ang. 268, ff. 26^v–27^r; *Urkunden*, nos. 108–9.

[42] For the crusade against the Catalan Grand Company, which was declared in June 1330 in support of Walter II of Brienne's attempt to rewin the Duchy of Athens, see *Diplomatari*, no. 150; K. M. Setton, 'The Catalans in Greece, 1311–1380', in his *History of the Crusades*, iii. 189–90.

which Pasquale and Giacomo were to proclaim the crusade within twenty-five days of the drawing up of their orders.[43]

In general the crusade bulls of the Avignon popes contain much more detail on the preaching and organization of the crusade than those of their predecessors. This development is particularly noticeable in the case of such aspects as the frequency with which the crusade was to be preached. In 1248 the papal vicar at Rome was told to preach against Frederick II 'publicly . . . and frequently', and the German clergy were told to preach against the Emperor 'at least twice a month',[44] but no such instructions appeared in the bulls against Manfred or the Aragonese and the Sicilians. In 1322, however, Bertrand du Poujet was told to preach against Matthew Visconti and to see that preaching was carried out 'in the churches and public places of your legation and elsewhere, wherever, as often and whenever you think best'.[45] Virtually the same instructions were sent to the Rector of the Duchy of Spoleto with regard to the crusade against Frederick of Montefeltro.[46] The local ecclesiastical authorities were not permitted such freedom of choice; they were to preach with solemnity 'in all the churches and public places of your various towns and dioceses, as you think best, on every Sunday and on other feast days'.[47] Similar formulae characterized the other crusades of the 1320s.

In other respects too the added detail of the Avignon bulls enables us to build up a clearer picture of how the crusade was actually preached. There was, first, the injunction to preach in the vernacular, presumably local dialect speech, 'in order that it can be better and more clearly understood by all'.[48] Secondly, the preachers were to ensure that their sermons had a good attendance. The secular clergy were to preach 'with a large number of the faithful present, when they have assembled for the divine offices', and the rectors of the Papal State and the

[43] *Diplomatari*, no. 152. They were able to cover this itinerary in just twelve days.

[44] Innocent IV, *Reg.*, no. 4681; *Reg. pont. rom.*, ii, no. 12902.

[45] 'quociens et quando tibi videbitur in ecclesiis et locis tue legationis et aliis de quibus expedire credideris'. ASV, Reg. Vat. 111, f. 155ʳ, no. 643. Cf. ibid., f. 155ᵛ, no. 644.

[46] 'Eretici e ribelli', iii. 481.

[47] 'in singulis ecclesiis et locis singularum vestrarum civitatum et diocesium de quibus videritis expedire singulis diebus dominicis et aliis festivis studeatis solenniter publicare', ASV, Reg. Vat. 73, f. 7ᵛ, no. 28. Cf. ibid., f. 9ᵛ, no. 29.

[48] See, e.g., *Thes. novus*, ii, col. 721.

legates were to summon a special assembly for the purpose.[49] The same intention that the crusade should be advertised as widely as possible lay behind the precept that the bulls should be fixed to the doors or walls of churches, starting at Avignon itself.

In order that this indulgence and its remission be made known to all, we have arranged that these letters, containing the said indulgence and sealed with our bull, be fixed or hung to the doors or walls of Avignon Cathedral, so that all the faithful, because of their zeal for the Faith and the Church, may be aroused to attack these evil-doers and to help carry out this business the more promptly and more fervently, for the reward of eternal salvation.[50]

Thirdly, and most importantly, the Curia of John XXII always added to its crusade bulls the postscript that the recipients should send back a notarial act to testify that the crusade had in fact been preached.[51] The fortunate result is that the two great collections of miscellaneous acts in the Vatican Archives, the Instrumenta miscellanea and the Archivum arcis, both contain dozens of acts sent back to Avignon in accordance with the ruling. The great interest and importance of these acts is, as Yves Renouard commented on the Instrumenta miscellanea in general, that 'they allow us to follow an affair, they show us to what degree and in what way the orders emanating from the Curia were carried out'.[52] For the crusade preaching of the 1320s they are valuable in several respects. They throw light on how often and by whom the crusade was preached. In 1325, for instance, the crusade against the

---

[49] 'astante fideli populo dum convenerit ad divina', ASV, Reg. Vat. 112, f. 122ᵛ, no. 483. Cf. ibid., f. 57ʳ, no. 260.

[50] *Codex dipl.*, i, no. 710. This was common procedure for the publication of important decrees and summonses, and was used by both ecclesiastical and secular authorities. See, e.g., Otto, 'Zur italienischen Politik', p. 221; *Diplomatari*, no. 119; Davidsohn, *Geschichte*, iii. 788.

[51] Notarial acts had been drawn up in the past to testify to crusade preaching. See, e.g., *Cod. dipl. ecel.*, no. 237 (preaching against Ezzelino of Romano by the Bishop of Treviso at Venice, 1258). But the number of surviving acts from the 1320s is unprecedented.

[52] Renouard, 'Une Expédition', p. 288. The notarial acts were catalogued by Mollat in the appendices to each year of the *Lettres communes* of John XXII, especially years 6, 8, 9, 10. The acts in Archivum arcis were listed in *Vat. Akten*, pp. 177–9. Some have been published: see *MGH, Const.* v, nos. 907, 977–8; 'Vatikanische Urkunden zur Geschichte Ludwigs des Bayern', ed. C. Erdmann, *Archivalische Zeitschrift*, xli (1932), no. 4.

Visconti was preached at least three times in the city of Naples between June and September, while in the city and diocese of Orleans it was preached at Epiphany and on subsequent Sundays into April. In January 1325 it was preached three times in one day at Paris.[53] Although there is no reason to think that the acts are complete or even that they form a representative sample of those sent back to Avignon (there is, for instance, a preponderance of acts from central Italy and southern France), they do confirm the large role played in the preaching by the Dominicans and, to a lesser extent, by the Franciscan and Augustinian friars. They also reveal that the Orders employed their best preachers, 'specially appointed for this work', including bachelors and doctors of theology. One of the preachers at Paris in January 1325 was Peter de la Palu, a Dominican theologian and canonist of some standing, who preached 'in the new hospital of St. James by St. Denis's gate'.[54]

The acts also yield details on the procedure of the preaching itself. When Amelio of Lautrec, Rector of the March of Ancona, preached against the Visconti at Macerata in June 1324, the notary wrote a very graphic description of the event.

On the 24th day of this month, the feast day of St. John, when the clergy and people of the city of Macerata had been summoned and had congregated in the church of St. John in the city of Macerata, and a large body of the faithful, both clergy and laity, were in attendance at the solemn celebration of the Mass, the said letters . . . were read through and expounded, publicly and loudly, clearly and in the vernacular, and the lord rector himself published them with vigour.[55]

When the mass had ended and the preaching was completed, the bull was pinned up in the town square of Macerata, 'in which audiences are held and legal decisions rendered, openly and publicly, by the judges and officials of the said rector, and many people gather and stand about every day both from the

[53] ASV, Instr. misc., no. 5149; John XXII, *Lettres communes*, nos. 23346, 23357, 23389 (2), 23291, 23301, 23323–4.

[54] ASV, Instr. misc., no. 5149. See also Wilks, *Problem of Sovereignty*, p. 556.

[55] 'convocato et congregato clero et populo civitatis Macerate in ecclesia beati Johannis de civitate Macerate predicta die xxiiii dicti mensis qua die fuit festivitas beati Johannis dicti in missarum celebratione solenni adstante multitudine copiosa fidelium videlicet clericorum et laycorum predictas . . . litteras . . . per seriem alta voce et in publico legi fecit et exponi et claris et vulgaribus vocibus dimilgari et etiam ipse dominus Rector suis viris vocibus publicavit'. ASV, Instr. misc., no. 892.

city and from elsewhere in the province generally'.[56] Here the letters remained for three days, 'so that the rebels cited in them should have no ground for complaint . . . and both they and all others in the said province should know about them'.[57] A vivid picture is also drawn by the report of the preaching at Paris in 1325, which includes an unusual detail on the reaction of the audience: 'they listened diligently and showed wonder and horror at the impieties committed by the said heretics'.[58]

A papal order for the preaching of a crusade could present rather curious problems. How, for instance, could a papal process or a crusade bull be published in a town which lay under an interdict? Faced with this dilemma in 1314, the Bishop of Arezzo, Guido da Petramala, published Clement V's excommunication of the Spiritual Franciscans in Arezzo Cathedral, but without celebrating mass.[59] Taddaeus, the vicar of the Bishop of Jesi, did not go so far when sent the crusade bull against the Visconti in 1324; because Jesi lay under an interdict he called a special outdoor assembly to publish the crusade, using the services of Jesi's town-crier, the *publicus banditor communis*.[60] A different problem confronted the German clergy. Bishop Rudolf of Constance, who in 1324 preached the crusade against the Visconti, as ordered, 'inducing the faithful with exhortation, and with preaching, and with all care and diligence, to acquire the remissions and indulgences', wrote that he was unable to send back a proper notarial act in testimony of this because 'the use of notaries is not possible in Germany'.[61] His complaint was clarified, and a solution suggested, in a letter sent to the Curia by the Provost of St. Severino of Cologne three years later.

[56] 'in qua publica et aperta per iudices et offitiales dicti Rectoris tenentur audientia et iura redduntur et multi cotidie tam de ipsa civitate quam aliunde communiter de ipsa provincia conveniunt et morantur', ibid.

[57] 'ad omnem predictorum rebellium citatorum cavillationis materiam evitandam . . . sed ut tam eis quam omnibus aliis de dicta provincia predicta omnia nota forent', ibid.

[58] 'audientibus diligenter et admirantibus atque horrentibus propter scelera per dictos hereticos perpetrata', ASV, Instr. misc., no. 5149.

[59] *Documenti*, ed. Pasqui, ii, no. 707.

[60] ASV, Instr. misc., no. 901. The Curia eventually evolved a solution to this problem. In 1370 Pope Urban V allowed preachers of the crusade against the mercenary companies and Perugia to suspend the interdict for three days while preaching. See *Codex dipl.* ii, no. 467.

[61] *MGH, Const.* v, no. 907. Cf. ibid., nos. 877–8.

There are few notaries in Germany by apostolic authority, and those who are notaries by imperial authority make difficulties in the drawing up of instruments testifying to the publication of processes. Consequently, if it pleases our lord, it would be expedient if he were to give the Archbishop of Cologne the authority to create two or three notaries by apostolic authority, then he could select persons who were suitable for publishing processes and for travelling to various places.[62]

With the help of the detail in the papal bulls and in these acts we can establish a fairly clear picture of how the *crux cismarina* was preached in the fourteenth century and, more tentatively, in the thirteenth. The first aim was the securing of a large audience. Besides the procedures already described of preaching the cross during mass, and of calling a special assembly of the clergy and laity, the Curia had other means of attracting the faithful. One was to issue indulgences for simply attending crusade sermons, a practice begun by Innocent III.[63] Clement IV granted indulgences ranging from forty days to 400 days to people who attended the preaching of Simon of Brie and Rudolf of Albano against Manfred, or who were present at large-scale gatherings which were connected to the crusade, such as the consecration of new churches and the translation of relics.[64] From Martin IV onwards an indulgence of a year and forty days became the rule for 'solemn preaching', until John XXII permitted Bertrand du Poujet to grant a year and a hundred days.[65] Another popular procedure was the organization of ceremonial processions by the prelates and clergy. Giovanni Villani recorded such processions taking place at Florence when the crusade was preached against Louis IV, 'praying to God that he would give his help to Holy Church for her defence against the Bavarian'.[66] At Paris in June 1329, when the schism and its attacks on the Pope were solemnly denounced by the city's bishop, there was also a long procession and a congregation of clergy and laity assembled which was so large that 'they

---

[62] 'Reise nach Italien im Herbst 1898', ed. J. Schwalm, *Neues Archiv*, xxv (1900), 742.

[63] See Brundage, *Med. Canon Law*, p. 154; Purcell, *Papal Crusading Policy*, pp. 62 ff.; Riley-Smith, *What were the Crusades?*, p. 42.

[64] Clement IV, *Reg.*, nos. 262–5; *Thes. novus*, ii, col. 114.

[65] Martin IV, *Reg.*, nos. 451n, 270m, 472f; Nicholas IV, *Reg.*, no. 2192; Boniface VIII, *Reg.*, no. 3360; John XXII, *Lettres communes*, no. 12147.

[66] *Cronica*, iii. 49. Cf. Matteo Villani, *Cronica*, ii. 70.

could scarcely be held by the church and the great square in front of the church doors, and the surrounding neighbourhood'. A description of the event concluded that 'never has more solemnity been displayed in the publication of decrees or other acts of the Church, at Paris or anywhere else'.[67]

Even the colour and magnificence of this occasion were, however, rivalled if not surpassed by the preaching of Philip Fontana, the Archbishop of Ravenna, against Ezzelino of Romano at Venice in 1256. Philip had the full co-operation of the Venetian state for his legatine commission to organize and lead a crusade against the heretical tyrant. On a chosen Sunday he celebrated mass in St. Mark's, in the presence of the Doge, the Patriarch of Aquileia, the Bishop of Venice, and seven other bishops (the Paris gathering of 1329 could only boast seven bishops in all). After the mass the prelates and the Doge mounted temporary platforms specially erected for the occasion in St. Mark's Square, 'and then my lord the archbishop began to preach the cross'. Philip Fontana's crusade sermon was followed by an impressive speech by the Doge, who praised the legate's bearing, lineage, and importance, expounded the needs of the Church, appealed to the crusading deeds of past Venetians, and promised that the commune would supply all who took the cross with ships, arms, food supplies, and a captain to lead them. The response was immediate and overwhelming: 'When my lord the Doge had finished his discourse, all the great men of Venice took the cross, and after them the whole of the Venetian *popolo*'.[68]

It is clear that the basis for the crusade sermon itself was the crusade bull; indeed, some of the notarial acts of the 1320s, which describe the 'publication' or 'reading out' of the crusade bulls, give the impression that there was very little elaboration. Sometimes it is only the reference to 'remissions' or 'indulgences' which allows the reader to know that the process being published was indeed a crusade, especially since the crusade bulls were dispatched with other bulls, of excommunication or conviction for heresy. and were published at the same time. The Curia did, however, expect both that the

---

[67] *Acta arag.* i, no. 298.

[68] Martino da Canale, 'Cronaca veneta', pp. 424–7. For another description of Philip Fontana's preaching, see below, pp. 167–8.

audiences at crusade sermons should be harangued, and that the haranguing should be based on judicious emphasis on those parts of the bull which seemed to have effect. The preachers against Manfred were to use 'zealous exhortations . . . according to the discretion which God gave you', and 'sedulous admonitions and eager appeals'.[69] Such expressions were dropped from use during the War of the Vespers, but during the crusades against the Visconti, the Estensi, and Louis IV they reappeared, and the clergy and legates were told to 'induce the faithful to acquire these remissions and indulgences by preaching and other means, as it seems most expedient to you'.[70] Here again the similarity to the ideas of Humbert of Romans is striking. In John XXII's advice to the Archbishop of Compostella on how he should appeal to his clergy to grant the Holy See a financial subsidy for the crusades in Italy one can see a clear parallel to, if not the adoption of, Humbert's idea that the preaching should mount to a climax with the offer of the plenary indulgence. The Archbishop was to stress,

the injuries, outrages, insults, and other terrible crimes which the heretics and their allies and supporters have dealt against our Redeemer and the Holy Church his one Bride, and which they continue brazenly to deal them, the various dangers which are likely to threaten the whole of Christianity and the Faith unless these heretics . . . are wiped out from the midst of the faithful, and finally the spiritual gifts granted to those who fight the said heretics . . . or who contribute of their goods as the Highest inspires them.[71]

Anybody who was inspired by appeals such as this to take the cross received certain spiritual and material benefits and, in exchange, incurred certain obligations. The spiritual benefit

---

[69] Urban IV, *Reg.*, no. 778; 'Les Déviations', p. 398.

[70] 'fideles ad acquirendum huiusmodi remissiones et indulgentias per verbum predicationis et aliis solerter perut expediencius fuerit inducturi', ASV, Reg. Vat. 112, f. 122[v], no. 483.

[71] 'iniurias excessus contumelias et alia horrenda scelera per eosdem hereticos ac complices et fautores ipsorum adversus redemptorem nostrum et sacrosanctam ecclesiam unicam sponsam suam commissa nequiter et que committere continue non verentur necnon varia pericula que toti christianitati et eidem fidei nisi predicti heretici . . . extirparentur de medio fidelium proventura probabiliter formidantur et demum dona spiritualia expugnantibus predictos hereticos . . . seu ad hoc de bonis suis congrue ministrantibus perut eis altissimus inspirabit concessa', ASV, Reg. Vat. 112, ff. 57[v]–58[r], no. 814.

was the plenary indulgence for sins committed. Until about 1180 confusion marked papal decrees on the crusades, some of which promised crusaders a full remission of temporal punishment for their sins, while others offered only a dispensation of penance. By 1254, however, this confusion had long been resolved in favour of the former interpretation, and crusade bulls guaranteed a full remission of sins, a promise made possible by the theological concept of the Treasury of Merits, 'an inexhaustible credit-balance of merit stored up by Christ and the saints on which the Church can draw on behalf of a repentant sinner'.[72] This indulgence, which first appeared in crusade bulls concerning the Holy Land, was duplicated in the simplest way for crusades against Christian lay powers. The most popular form in which the indulgence was phrased, throughout the period 1254–1343, originated with Innocent IV, who in 1246 granted to all who took the cross against the Emperor Frederick II 'the same indulgence, for sins of which they are truthfully contrite of heart, and which they have confessed . . . which has been granted generally to those who go to aid the Holy Land'.[73] More picturesque phrasing was occasionally used. John XXII assured those who took the cross for his Italian crusades that 'under the banner of victory you can earn the same indulgence as that enjoyed by those who travel across the sea in the service of the Holy Land'.[74] A description which perhaps conveys more realistically the terms in which the indulgence was explained by the preachers of the crusade was put into the mouth of John Cholet by Bernard Desclot: 'If any man die there, which may God forbid, then will he in shining whiteness ascend into the presence of God, for God will not in any wise permit that his soul be sent to purgatory'.[75]

But although the spiritual benefit conferred by the crusade indulgence had become fixed, the services expected in exchange

---

[72] Riley-Smith, *What were the Crusades?*, p. 58. See also ibid., pp. 59–62; Purcell, *Papal Crusading Policy*, pp. 36 ff. Brundage (*Med. Canon Law*, pp. 147–8), believes that confusion persisted into the thirteenth century.

[73] Innocent IV, *Reg.*, no. 2945.

[74] 'sub vexillo victorie possitis indultam quam merentur ultra mare in terre sancte servicium transfretantes veniam promereri', ASV, Reg. Vat. 112, f. 39ᵛ, no. 176. Cf. ibid., f. 40ᵛ, no. 177.

[75] *Chronicle*, ii. 219. Cf. Raymond Muntaner, *Chronicle*, i. 352, 356–7.

for it varied considerably. The indulgence was an instrument of papal crusading policy and its availability could be extended or retracted according to the military situation in Italy and the financial needs of the pope and his allies.[76] In addition, the authority to fix the exact nature of the service to be performed by the *crucesignatus* was sometimes delegated to the preachers of the crusade. On occasion the indulgence was granted only to those who actually died during a crusade, and who were thus considered to be martyrs. Such an indulgence was granted to the defenders of Aquila in 1256, when Pope Alexander IV wrote that 'to those who perchance die in the service of God and the Church in the defence of the said city, we mercifully grant an indulgence of all their sins for which they are truly contrite and which they have confessed; we also extend this indulgence, in the abundance of our mercy, to the deceased who died for this cause and in this way.'[77] Similarly, in his first two crusade bulls against Peter of Aragon, those of January 1283 and April 1284, Martin IV did not include any reference to an extension of the indulgence beyond those who died on crusade, and in 1296 Boniface VIII granted the indulgence to all who died while fighting against the Sicilians.[78] At the opposite extreme was the very liberal wording which characterized most of the early crusade bulls against Manfred, which granted the indulgence to all who helped 'effectively, in persons or in goods', or to those who fought in person or sent 'suitable fighters'.[79]

In the majority of the crusade bulls, however, the three categories of *crucesignatus* familiar to students of the later crusades to the Latin East were specified. It was accepted that a crusader could fight and pay for himself, fight 'at the expense of others', receiving a wage for the period of his service in the field, or himself provide soldiers without personal attendance. This is true of some stages at least of all the major crusades in Italy— those against Manfred, the Aragonese and the Sicilians, the Colonna, and Louis IV and his Ghibelline supporters.[80]

[76] This could lead to confusion. See Boniface VIII, *Reg.*, no. 2878.

[77] *Antiq. ital. medii aevi*, vi, col. 517.

[78] Martin IV, *Reg.*, nos. 301, 570; Boniface VIII, *Reg.*, no. 1575.

[79] ASV, Reg. Vat. 28, f. 121ᵛ, no. 156; Urban IV, *Reg.*, nos. 633, 778, 860; *Thes. novus*, ii, col. 72; 'Ann. de Burton', p. 353. Cf. 'Les Déviations', pp. 398–9.

[80] See, e.g., Urban IV, *Reg.*, no. 321; *Thes. novus*, ii, cols. 197, 720; Martin IV, *Reg.*, no. 591; 'Eretici e ribelli', iii. 480; Boniface VIII, *Reg.*, no. 2878; *Codex dipl.* i, no. 710.

There were obvious dangers in equating personal service, with its perils and hardships, with the provision of troops, and Clement IV, following the decrees of the Fourth Lateran and First Lyons Councils, made a distinction between those who fought in person and at their own expense, and those who were paid to fight, or who paid others to do so. Not only did the former receive the plenary indulgence, but Clement promised them, 'as a reward for the just, an increase of their eternal salvation'.[81] This distinction was not adopted by Clement's successors; John XXII used the phrase on occasion, but applied it to all three categories of crusader.[82]

There were other contributions to the crusades which were rewarded by the grant of a full, or partial, indulgence. The most important was the simple financial donation, not connected to the provision of soldiers. Such donations were regularly requested for crusades against Christian enemies of the pope—for example, in 1265, 1284, 1299, and throughout the 1320s.[83] It is not clear from the texts whether contributors received a full or a partial indulgence, for the Curia adopted the unclear phraseology employed by Pope Innocent III and the Fourth Lateran Council. This had established that 'we wish and concede that all who minister suitably to the relief of the Holy Land from their goods should participate in this remission, according to the value of their subsidy and the devotion they show.'[84] That a difference existed between this grant of the indulgence and the plenary indulgence is shown by Clement IV's bull of November 1265 against Manfred, in which he used the above phraseology to describe the indulgence offered to all who gave a tenth 'or another part' of their goods to the collectors in France, or who gave the expedition aid or advice, while the full indulgence was granted to those who gave a quarter or more of their income, or who took the cross under any of the three standard categories.[85]

---

[81] ASV, Reg. Vat. 32, f. 64^{r-v}, no. 25; *Thes. novus*, ii, col. 197. See also Purcell, *Papal Crusading Policy*, p. 195. Cf. ibid., p. 199.

[82] See, e.g., *Thes. novus*, ii, col. 720; *Codex dipl.* i, no. 710.

[83] See ASV, Reg. Vat. 49, f. 177^v, no. 192; *Thes. novus*, ii, cols. 197, 720; Martin IV, *Reg.*, no. 591; 'Eretici e ribelli', iii. 481.

[84] See Lunt, *Financial Relations*, i. 423, for text and comments.

[85] See ASV, Reg. Vat. 32, f. 64^{r-v}, no. 25; *Thes. novus*, ii, col. 197. On the other hand, Clement also employed this phraseology to describe the indulgence granted to preachers of the crusade, for which a plenary indulgence was customary.

The crusade indulgence was always available to the clergy as well as the laity, and in some respects the clergy were especially well favoured. If a beneficed cleric took the cross, he could enjoy the fruits of his benefice for three years during his absence on crusade, and sell or mortgage these fruits should the need arise; these rulings were established at the Fourth Lateran Council, if not earlier, and were specifically applied to the Italian crusades by Clement IV in 1265.[86] A cleric could also gain the indulgence by preaching the crusade or by collecting crusade revenues.[87] In the course of the thirteenth century the Curia also came to associate the indulgence with the financing of the crusades by the Church. In 1255 the nuncio Rostand declared that all the English clergy who paid the tenth in full to Henry III for the crusade against Manfred would participate in the crusade indulgence, and ten years later Pope Clement IV offered the indulgence to French clerics who paid the last two years of Charles of Anjou's three-year tenth immediately, giving them in addition permission to mortgage their benefices for up to three years, if necessary, to raise the money.[88] In June 1284 Martin IV repeated Clement's move and offered the indulgence to all the Italian clergy who paid in one year the whole of the three-year tenth levied on the previous day, an offer which also applied to the four-year tenth levied in France in September 1283 and May 1284. Both Clement and Martin were driven to make these concessions by the financial exigencies of the moment. Although Honorius IV renewed his predecessor's grant on 30 April 1286, he told John Cholet in May that he was only to use it if collection should prove very difficult or impossible without it, because 'only two years at the most remain of the time for which the said tenth was conceded . . . and we should not grant such a great indulgence lightly, or without strong cause'.[89]

Clearly the papal Curia was in a quandary. It wanted to employ the attraction of the indulgence to loosen clerical purse-strings, yet to avoid attaching the crusade indulgence to the

[86] *Thes. novus*, ii, col. 198; Purcell, *Papal Crusading Policy*, p. 25; Brundage, *Med. Canon Law*, pp. 177–9; Riley-Smith, *What were the Crusades?*, p. 56.
[87] *Thes. novus*, ii, col. 197; Purcell, *Papal Crusading Policy*, pp. 60–2.
[88] 'Ann. de Burton', pp. 363–4; *Thes. novus*, ii, cols. 243–4.
[89] Martin IV, *Reg.*, no. 591; Honorius IV, *Reg.*, nos. 395, 399.

payment of a compulsory tenth. The problem was solved, in the final decades of the thirteenth century, by the initiative of the leading secular rulers of western Europe, particularly the kings of England and France: by excluding the papacy from the enjoyment of much of the money collected from the clerical tenth, they compelled it to shift the emphasis of its clerical taxation to the voluntary subsidy. Unlike the clerical tenth, such subsidies could be regarded as non-mandatory crusade oblations, to be rewarded by participation in the indulgence, and it is clear that all the clerical subsidies collected on behalf of John XXII's crusades involved the grant of a partial indulgence. Thus it was written of the Church of Nice in 1324 that it had granted the Pope a subsidy, 'desiring to become participants in and sharers of the indulgences which were granted recently by our most holy father and lord, by divine providence Lord Pope John XXII to the truly penitent and confessed who fight the heretics and rebels of the said Church in the regions of Lombardy or make a suitable contribution from their goods.'[90]

The offer of the crusade indulgence in exchange for a subsidy constituted a significant extension of the availability of the indulgence and was a move of some consequence in the development of papal finance. It was undoubtedly a success. Writing to the Archbishop of Compostella in 1324, John XXII claimed that it had already led to 'profuse and welcome subsidies'.[91] It cannot be denied, however, that by attaching even a partial indulgence to the payment of a more-or-less compulsory subsidy 'towards the destruction of heresy and rebellion in Italy', the papacy was taking a step in the direction of divorcing the indulgence from its penitential framework. Nor was this the only such innovation made at this time. In 1297–8 and 1299 Pope Boniface VIII granted the plenary indulgence to all who died while fighting for the Church in the crusades against the Colonna and the Sicilians, whether they were crusaders or not,

---

[90] 'cupientes indulgentiarum olim vere penitentibus et confessis impugnantibus hereticos et rebelles dicte ecclesie partium Lombardie vel de bonis suis congrue ministrantibus per sanctissimum patrem et dominum nostrum dominum Johannem divina providentia papam xxii nuper concessarum fieri participes et consortes', ASV, Instr. misc., no. 917.
[91] 'grata et largia subsidia', ASV, Reg. Vat. 112, ff. 57ᵛ–58ʳ, no. 814.

and possibly in the 1320s, certainly by the 1350s, the Curia was to grant the full crusade indulgence to the populations of whole cities in Italy in exchange for communal contingents of crusaders.[92]

It was accepted by the Curia that the *crucesignatus* would enjoy his indulgence from the moment he took his vow, or at least from the moment he set out to fulfil it. Thus Martin IV wrote in 1284 that a crusader who died during his period of service nevertheless received the indulgence, to which John XXII added the case of crusaders who were unable to complete their period of service because of the premature conclusion of the crusade itself.[93] Great care was taken to ensure that if a crusader did die he had first fulfilled the conditions for the enjoyment of the indulgence, in particular that he had confessed and had been absolved of his sins. Charles of Anjou was absolved of all his sins by the cardinals who were present in Rome in January 1266, before he started his invasion of the *Regno*.[94] Before the battle of Benevento the Bishop of Auxerre, who had been given 'the apostolic power' for the purpose by Clement IV, did the same for the entire crusading army, imposing on it as penance the command that the crusaders should strike Manfred's soldiers with double their normal force.[95] Andrew of Hungary added the picturesque detail that the Dean of Meaux, Charles of Anjou's chancellor, organized a body of friars to hear the confessions of all the soldiers and administer the sacrament to them.[96]

The spiritual benefit of the indulgence was augmented by a wide range of material privileges and exemptions. These were specified in Clement IV's bull of November 1265, from which it is clear that they differed only marginally, if at all, from those

[92] ASV, Reg. Vat. 49, f. 177ᵛ, no. 192; Boniface VIII, *Reg.*, no. 2878 (cf. Waley, 'Papal Armies', p. 26). See also below, pp. 160–1.

[93] Martin IV, *Reg.*, no. 591. See also Purcell, *Papal Crusading Policy*, pp. 44–5. For John XXII's addition, see, e.g., 'Eretici e ribelli', iii. 481.

[94] See Saba Malaspina, 'Rerum sicularum', col. 819.

[95] See William of Nangis, 'Gesta sanctae memoriae Ludovici regis Franciae', RHGF, xx. 424–5; 'Chronique anonyme', p. 88.

[96] Andrew of Hungary, 'Descriptio', p. 572. For John d'Acy, Dean of Meaux, see C. Minieri-Riccio, *Cenni storici intorno i grandi uffizii del Regno di Sicilia durante il regno di Carlo I. d'Angiò*, p. 185; L. Cadier, *Essai sur l'administration du royaume de Sicile sous Charles Ier et Charles II d'Anjou*, p. 237.

granted to men who took the cross to fight in the East.[97] One of the most important privileges was that guaranteeing ecclesiastical protection for a crusader's wife, family, and possessions until his return or the arrival of trustworthy news of his death. In September 1265 the Pope issued a letter assuring Charles of Anjou that his lands, and those of all who took part in his expedition, would enjoy apostolic protection during his campaign against Manfred; anybody who presumed to attack their lands would incur 'the indignation of Almighty God and of his apostles, saints Peter and Paul'.[98] Similarly, one of the charges brought against Peter of Aragon in 1282 was that he had attacked the lands of a crusader, 'signed with the cross in aid of the Holy Land and openly prepared to perform services to God and his Faith'.[99] Fifteen years later Peter's own son, James II of Aragon, was taken under the protection of St. Peter by Pope Boniface VIII.[100] It was expected that secular rulers would supplement his ecclesiastical protection with their own measures. Thus in 1271 Charles I ordered his seneschal in Provence to refund to two Dominicans and some Frisian crusaders returning from the Tunis crusade 300 marks which had been stolen from them at Marseilles.[101]

Privileges such as these were valuable and, notoriously, led to abuses.[102] Some people took the cross in order to benefit from the moratorium on debts which it bestowed. In 1270 the Angevin seneschal in Provence was instructed to separate real *crucesignati* from knights who were claiming to be crusaders 'with the aim of avoiding paying their debts to the Jews'.[103] Others became crusaders in order to enjoy the crusader's privilege of exemption from some of the effects of the interdict. In July 1326 John XXII wrote that the inquisitor of heresy in Romagna was persuading people to take the cross in order to evade the interdict which had been imposed on part of the province. People were taking the cross 'indifferently' and the

---

[97] *Thes. novus,* ii, cols. 197–8. For a good account of these privileges and their place in canon law, see Brundage, *Med. Canon Law,* pp. 159–90.

[98] *Thes. novus,* ii, col. 195 (cf. col. 198).

[99] Martin IV, *Reg.,* no. 276.

[100] Boniface VIII, *Reg.,* no. 2340.

[101] *RCAR,* vi, Reg. 22, no. 1472. See also Brundage, *Med. Canon Law,* pp. 164–5.

[102] Ibid., pp. 188–9.

[103] *RCAR,* iv, Reg. 14, no. 1173.

result was detrimental to the effectiveness of the interdict. The Rector of Romagna was to prevent such crusaders hearing the divine offices unless they clearly intended to execute the 'business of the Faith'.[104]

Just as the crusader who fought in Italy enjoyed the same indulgence and the same privileges as his counterpart elsewhere, so he incurred the same obligations. These obligations arose from his vow and were expressed in his wearing of the cross. Once the vow had been made, only papal absolution could release the crusader from it.[105] The authority to grant such an absolution could, however, be delegated to a legate; thus in 1266 Clement IV authorized Rudolf of Albano to absolve *crucesignati* who had failed to keep their vows to participate in the crusade against Manfred because of physical incapacity, and who wished to redeem their vows.[106] Unfortunately little evidence appears to have survived on the form of the crusade vow for any of the crusades in Italy, or for the ceremony which accompanied it. In the case of Philip of Marerio, an excommunicated Italian noble who agreed to take the cross against Manfred as an act of penance in 1265, Clement IV ordered that the ceremony be performed in the presence of trustworthy witnesses and that a notarial act be drawn up as proof and sent to him.[107] But this was a special case, and had such acts been drawn up for other *crucesignati* it is certain that at least some would have survived. When a secular prince took the cross his action had widespread implications and his vow was usually noted and recorded. The news of James II's crusade vow of 1297, which he made against his own brother Frederick, was triumphantly sent by Robert of Calabria to all the civil authorities in the *Regno*, to be published.[108] The alignment of the Aragonese crown on the side of the Angevins was not popular in Catalonia, and James probably found the obliga-

---

[104] ASV, Reg. Vat. 113, f. 331ʳ, no. 1943. See also Brundage, *Med. Canon Law*, pp. 156–7.

[105] Ibid., p. 133.

[106] Clement IV, *Reg.*, no. 291.

[107] *Thes. novus*, ii, cols. 155–6. See also *Codice diplomatico del regno di Carlo I. e II. d'Angiò*, ed. G. Del Giudice, i. 245–8. Because Philip was a *regnicolo*, possibly from Rieti, the ceremony was to be kept secret and he could be temporarily excused the wearing of his cross in public.

[108] *Codice diplomatico sulmonese*, ed. N. F. Faraglia, no. 97 (also in *Studi storici su' fascicoli angioini*, ed. C. Minieri-Riccio, p. 6).

tions arising from his crusade vow a convenient excuse for continuing to participate in the struggle for Sicily in 1298 and 1299. In November 1298 he assured his mother Constance that he would take her back to Aragon when he had completed the 'matter of Sicily', 'which we are pursuing because of our vow'.[109]

There is more evidence on the visible sign of the crusader's votive obligation—the cross. Like all *crucesignandi*, a man intending to go on crusade in Italy took the cross from the hands of a cleric and displayed it on his shoulder or chest while fulfilling his vow. The French crusaders of 1265–6 'placed the sign of the lifegiving cross on their shoulders with no little devotion',[110] and in 1328 the Archbishop of Capua was to ensure that *crucesignandi*, 'accepting with reverence the sign of the cross and fastening it to their shoulders and hearts, prepare themselves manfully to carry out in this way the cause of God'.[111] Some received the cross from the pope himself. In 1297 James II of Aragon 'took the sign of the cross from the hands of the pope'.[112] Later in the same year, when the crusade was preached against the Colonna cardinals, Boniface VIII announced that 'last Sunday . . . in the Basilica of the Prince of the Apostles in the city, our said brothers [the cardinals] took the sign of the cross humbly and devoutly from us, and a great multitude of the nobility, clergy, and people received the same cross, on the same Sunday and afterwards, both from us and from our said brothers.'[113]

It is typical of Boniface VIII that he should personally have distributed the cross, but even a weak pope like Alexander IV took a personal part in the preaching and distribution of the cross at Naples in 1255.[114] More detail on the ceremony employed emerges from the crusade against Louis IV in 1328.

---

[109] *Acta arag.* i, no. 38.

[110] Andrew of Hungary, 'Descriptio', p. 567.

[111] 'suscipientes cum reverencia signum crucis ipsumque suis humeris et cordibus affigentes ad prosequendum causam dei huiusmodi viriliter se accingant', ASV, Reg. Vat. 114, f. 229ᵛ, no. 1263.

[112] *Cod. dipl. sulm.*, no. 97.

[113] 'cuius crucis signaculum dominica preterita proximo . . . in basilica principis apostolorum de Urbe dicti fratres nostri humiliter et devote receperunt a nobis et magna nobilium cleri et populi multitudo in eadem dominica et post tam a nobis quam a fratribus nostris predictis crucem recepit eandem', ASV, Reg. Vat. 48, f. 384ʳ, no. 76.

[114] 'Ann. de Burton', p. 352.

Charles of Calabria took the cross from the hands of the Archbishop of Capua, 'kneeling in great devotion', as did his father two weeks later, 'having it placed on and fastened to our shoulders'.[115] The chroniclers recorded that the cross worn by the French crusaders of 1265–6 was a mixture of red and white, and was displayed on the left shoulder.[116] The same colours were used for the papal banners during the crusades of John XXII. The Treasurer of the March of Ancona paid a Florentine merchant for a quantity of red and white cloth for 'a great banner showing the arms of the Church, when the cross was preached against the heretics of Recanati and Osimo, which banner was assigned to Fulcher of Calbulo, the general-captain of war'.[117]

The length of time which the crusader was to spend fighting in order to gain his indulgence was subject to great variations, and was sometimes left puzzlingly unspecified. For most of the thirteenth century the Curia was searching for a term which would both merit the full indulgence and also satisfy the exigencies of recruitment. Innocent IV established that at least some of the crusaders who fought against Frederick II were to serve for three years, while in March 1264 Urban IV expected only three months' service from those who took the cross against Manfred.[118] This was evidently considered too short a period,[119] and when a limit was again laid down, by Martin IV in 1284, it was a year.[120] Boniface VIII introduced a disparity by setting a six-month period for his crusade against the Colonna

---

[115] 'flexis genibus devotissime amplexantes signum crucis . . . humeris nostris affigi fecimus et apponi', ASN, MS Minieri-Riccio, formerly Reg. Ang. 271, f. 111ʳ⁻ᵛ.

[116] See 'Maius chron. lemovicense', p. 771 ('unum brachium crucis erat album, et aliud rubeum'); 'Excerpta e chronico Gaufridi de Collone', *RHGF*, xxii. 4 (which distinguishes it from the all-red cross worn by crusaders in the Holy Land); 'Chronique rimée dite de Saint-Magloire', *RHGF*, xxii. 83–4; 'Cronaca di Morea', ed. C. Hopf, in his *Chroniques gréco-romanes inédites ou peu connues*, p. 451.

[117] 'pro uno magno vesillo ad arma ecclesie quando predicata fuit Crus contra hereticos de Racaneto et Ausimano quod vesillum fuit adsignatum Fulcerio de Calbulo Generali Capitaneo guerre', ASV, I et E, no. 50, f. 35ʳ. Cf. ibid., f. 33ʳ, and I et E, no. 77, f. 97ʳ.

[118] Innocent IV, *Reg.*, no. 3886; Urban IV, *Reg.*, no. 778.

[119] Although those who had taken the cross against the Albigensians had only been expected to serve for forty days, the *quarantaine* of normal feudal practice. See Belperron, *La Croisade*, p. 149, and cf. J. L. La Monte, *Feudal Monarchy in the Latin Kingdom of Jerusalem 1100 to 1291*, p. 142.

[120] Martin IV, *Reg.*, no. 591.

and a year for the crusade against the Sicilians, probably on the grounds that the Colonna posed a more immediate threat to the Church than the Sicilian rebellion.[121] The bull of 1299 specified that the crusaders were to serve against Frederick of Aragon and the rebels 'until, with the aid of God, this expedition is completed, or at least for one year, if the expedition should last longer than that, which God forbid'.[122] Boniface was more confident by 1302. Those who served with Charles of Valois were to fight 'until there is a general victory over the rebels'.[123] One year's service was laid down in all of John XXII's crusade bulls, but he added the rider that 'we wish that those who do not labour in the service of God in this manner for the whole of a year, but do so only for part of the year, should participate in the indulgence, according to the amount of work they do and the devotion they show.'[124] John also permitted crusaders to split the year's service into various parts over a period of two years.[125] Some notable examples are missing from this list, including the expedition of Charles of Anjou in 1265–6. It is possible that the crusaders were expected in such cases to remain until the military objective of the crusade had been achieved.[126]

Many of the crusade bulls also included information on how the crusaders were to accomplish their vows. In May 1261 Alexander IV told the Bishop of Alatri, who was to preach the cross against Manfred in the Campagna, to instruct the *crucesignati* to prepare 'arms and the other necessary things', and to be ready to assemble when the order was given.[127] Those who took the cross against Manfred at Rome in 1264 were also to be ready to assemble at the command of Urban IV, while crusaders in the Duchy and the March were to be ready 'to come to our aid and that of the Church without delay'.[128] French crusaders were to march against Manfred with Charles of Anjou or his captain, again 'without delay'.[129] John XXII

---

[121] ASV, Reg. Vat. 49, f. 177ᵛ, no. 192; Boniface VIII, *Reg.*, no. 2878.

[122] 'quousque actore domino huiusmodi expugnatio fuerit terminata vel saltem per unum annum si expugnationem eandem quod absit tantum differri contigerit', ASV, Reg. Vat. 49, f. 177ᵛ, no. 192.

[123] Boniface VIII, *Reg.*, no. 4625.

[124] See, e.g., 'Eretici e ribelli', iii. 480–1. This appears to be a partial indulgence.

[125] Ibid., p. 480.

[126] See below, pp. 154–5.

[127] 'Les Déviations', p. 399.

[128] Urban IV, *Reg.*, nos. 633, 778.

[129] *Thes. novus*, ii, col. 72.

also instructed the crusaders to 'arm themselves well' and then to join a commander specially appointed for each crusade. In the crusades in the Papal State the commanders were the rectors of the Duchy and the March. Bertrand du Poujet and Giovanni Orsini directed the crusade forces in their legatine areas, and Charles of Calabria the *regnicoli* and others who joined the Angevin army as crusaders in 1328.[130]

Under John XXII the Curia arranged that a day should be fixed in advance on which the year's service of each crusader was to begin. The responsibility for setting this date was variously allocated. In the case of the crusade of 1324 against the Estensi, for instance, Bertrand du Poujet was told to choose a day for the crusade to begin and to publicize it widely.[131] In January 1323, on the other hand, it was the Inquisitors of heresy in the province of Lombardy who issued the order to assemble for an assault on the Visconti *signoria*, addressing it both to *crucesignati* and to all who owed feudal service to the Church or the empire. When the crusade against Galeazzo Visconti and his brothers was renewed, in April 1325, the Pope himself chose the assembly date, and in 1330 he wrote that the year's service for Walter of Brienne's crusade against the Catalans in Greece was to start on the day chosen by the Patriarch of Constantinople and the archbishops of Corinth and Patras.[132]

Several of the dates chosen have survived. On 19 May 1322, writing to his suffragan bishops with instructions to preach the cross against Frederick of Montefeltro and the rebel communes of the March of Ancona, the Archbishop of Salzburg told them that Amelio of Lautrec had chosen 29 June as the assembly date for crusaders coming from the archdiocese of Salzburg. Bearing in mind that the rector's messenger had taken several weeks to reach Salzburg, this gave the crusaders barely enough time to make their way south.[133] It was, however, a generous allocation of travelling-time compared with the curious situation in 1325,

---

[130] See ASV, Reg. Vat. 73, ff. 6ʳ–8ʳ, no. 28; *Codex dipl.* i, no. 710; *Urkunden*, nos. 108, 127.
[131] ASV, Reg. Vat. 112, f. 131ᵛ, no. 489.
[132] See ASV, Reg. Vat. 113, f. 175ʳ, no. 1033; *Diplomatari*, no. 150; Otto, 'Zur italienischen Politik', pp. 219–22.
[133] *Acta imperii inedita*, ii, no. 1122.

when the Pope sent a crusade bull against the Visconti to Bertrand du Poujet on 29 April and fixed the year's service to begin on 1 May.[134] The crusade on which we possess the most detail in this respect is that against Louis IV. The Archbishop of Capua was told to choose the assembly date for crusaders who joined Charles of Calabria. Because of the size of the *Regno* and the remoteness of certain areas two dates were chosen. On 16 April King Robert wrote that those who had already taken the cross, or took it before 15 May, were to begin their year's service on that day, or earlier if possible, presenting themselves before Charles of Calabria. All others were to join the prince's forces on St. John the Baptist's Day (24 June).[135]

The essence of the crusade vow was that it was made voluntarily, but service in the Latin East had long been accepted also as suitable enjoined religious penance or as a substitute for a punishment imposed by the civil authorities.[136] Supporters of the Staufen in France were thus to be pardoned in 1267 on condition that they took the cross and went on crusade to the Holy Land or sent soldiers or money, and Charles I sent one of his subjects there as the punishment for murder, while in 1334 criminals in the Kingdom of Naples were spared execution if they went to fight the Turks.[137] This tempting source of extra recruits and money was also exploited for the crusades in Italy. Clement IV's crusade bull of November 1265 gave a long list of crimes for which absolution could be gained by personal service or the donation of money. In the case of the laity the list covered attacks on the secular or religious clergy, incendiarism, sacrilege, the practice of sorcery, illegal trading with the Muslims, helping the Muslims against other Christians, and visits to the Holy Places without papal licence. Clerical crimes were excommunication for keeping a mistress or for refusing to pay a tenth or a twentieth, and attendance at prohibited lectures.[138]

---

[134] ASV, Reg. Vat. 113, f. 175ʳ, no. 1033.

[135] *Urkunden*, no. 108.

[136] See Purcell, *Papal Crusading Policy*, pp. 114–18.

[137] See Clement IV, *Reg.*, no. 493; *RCAR*, x, Reg. 48, no. 552; *Annali*, ii. 397. In 1344 or 1345 Queen Joanna I pardoned a *regnicolo* for his crimes provided that 'he should take the cross and fight the Turks for a year'. See *Notizie storiche tratte da 62 registri angioini dell'Archivio di Stato di Napoli*, ed. C. Minieri-Riccio, p. 16.

[138] ASV, Reg. Vat. 32, ff. 64ᵛ–65ʳ, no. 25; Sternfeld, *Ludwigs des Heiligen Kreuzzug nach Tunis*, pp. 318–19.

Philip of Marerio was an example of a *crucesignatus* who took the cross in 1265 as penance, and nineteen years later Charles I offered a condemned criminal and his accomplices pardons if they joined the Angevin expedition against Sicily, though it is not known if they were to go as crusaders.[139] We have seen that crusade as a form of penance for specified sins played a very large role in the papacy's negotiations with the Aragonese kings in the 1290s;[140] James II even employed the idea that he was performing penance on his father's behalf in order to justify his realignment on the side of the Church: 'Our soul was plunged into doubts and tormented by various worries, because we were informed in public consistory that the soul of our father could not be absolved, unless we returned Sicily to King Charles or to his heirs.'[141]

The tradition of the crusade as penance was also important in the crusades waged in Italy by John XXII. In March 1330 the penalty of sending fifteen cavalry to fight for a year in Italy 'against the rebels, heretics, and schismatics, for the defence of the Church and the Catholic Faith', which had been imposed on a French nobleman, was waived at the request of Philip VI of Valois.[142] John also ordered that vows to make a pilgrimage to Rome or Compostella, in Lombardy, Scandinavia, and Scotland, could be commuted to the payment of a subsidy for the Italian crusades. The amount given was to be equal to the expenses which the pilgrim would have incurred *en route*. In the cases of Scotland and Scandinavia, this also applied to vows taken to go on pilgrimage in the Holy Land, and Scandinavians who had assaulted clerics were to be granted absolution if, as penance, they paid a subsidy equal to the cost of a trip to Avignon and of paying for absolution there.[143] Even the profits of theft and usury, if they could not be returned to the victims, were allocated to the crusade against the Visconti.[144]

---

[139] *Thes. novus*, ii, cols. 155–6; 'Il regno di Carlo I d'Angiò dal 4 gennaio 1284 al 7 gennaio 1285', comp. C. Minieri-Riccio, *Archivio storico italiano*, 4th series, vii (1881), 23.

[140] See above, pp. 92ff.

[141] Nicolaus Speciale, 'Historia sicula', *RIS*, x, col. 1001.

[142] John XXII, *Lettres secrètes*, no. 4123. See also no. 4129.

[143] ASV, Reg. Vat. 111, f. 158ᵛ, no. 655, Reg. Vat. 113, f. 374ʳ, no. 2198, Reg. Vat. 114, f. 159ʳ, no. 1004, Reg. Vat. 115, f. 127ʳ, no. 1738, f. 128ᵛ, no. 1748. See also *Die Einnahmen*, pp. 327, 339.

[144] ASV, Reg. Vat. 111, f. 158ᵛ, no. 656.

The evidence suggests that the popes enjoyed a high degree of success in promoting the preaching of their Italian crusades. This is not surprising, as they controlled an efficient apparatus of command, reward, and censure, and showed that they were determined that the crusades should be widely and effectively preached. In 1322 the Archbishop of Salzburg ordered and exhorted his suffragan bishops to preach the crusade against the rebels in the Papal State with zeal, adding that 'we have information from a friend that our lord has this business at heart and will display severity towards those whom he discovers to have treated it with idleness or rebelliousness'.[145] Clement VI did, indeed, reprimand several bishops who, deterred by the length of the papal process against Louis IV and the regularity with which the Curia wanted it read out at services, treated their responsibility slackly.[146]

Nevertheless, two problems arose with regularity in 'the course of the preaching and caused the Curia some concern. One was opposition to the preaching, in the form of argument or physical violence. In November 1265 Simon of Brie and the French clergy were told to forbid certain grumblers (*questuarii*), who had argued against the crusade preaching, to address people gathered to hear the crusade sermons; if they persisted, they were to be punished with ecclesiastical censures.[147] Similarly, in March 1322 Bertrand du Poujet was ordered to use spiritual and temporal sanctions against people who, 'inspired by the Devil', were obstructing the preaching against Matthew Visconti, and in August 1329 Robert of Naples permitted the six companions of a friar who was preaching the cross against Louis IV in the Kingdom of Naples to carry arms because they had encountered 'various obstacles' and 'grave dangers'.[148]

The extent and motivation of this opposition is impossible to establish with any certainty. Much of it came from secular authorities who disapproved of the crusades because they were directed against themselves or their allies. In 1263 Pope Urban IV accepted that there would be parts of northern Italy in

---

[145] *Acta imperii inedita*, ii, no. 1122.
[146] *Vat. Akten*, no. 2239.
[147] ASV, Reg. Vat. 32, f. 65ʳ, no. 25; Sternfeld, *Ludwigs des Heiligen Kreuzzug nach Tunis*, pp. 319–20.
[148] ASV, Reg. Vat. 111, f. 158ʳ, no. 653; *Urkunden*, no. 291.

which it would not be safe to preach the crusade against Manfred, and Peter of Aragon threatened with the death penalty any cleric who attempted to publish his excommunication and deposition in 1285.[149] The Visconti took active steps to prevent crusade preaching against themselves in those parts of Lombardy over which they had any control, keeping a careful watch on the borders of their *signoria* to prevent papal bulls entering. The envoys of 1322 were forced to strip almost to the skin in the middle of winter so that their clothes could be searched for hidden letters.[150] These problems were at their worst in Germany and the empire in the 1320s and 1330s. It was often impossible for loyal bishops and nuncios to preach the cross against the Ghibellines there after 1323. In September 1324, for example, the Archbishop of Salzburg wrote to the Pope describing in vivid terms the appalling state of his province, in which the interdict was violated, papal authority defamed, and the Pope himself slandered by the clerical supporters of Louis IV. To attempt to carry out papal orders in such circumstances was to invite attack, imprisonment, torture, and even murder.[151] There were similar difficulties in neighbouring Poland.[152] Another source of opposition to the preaching was that of disaffected friars, mainly Franciscans but also some Dominicans: in 1324 the Dominican province of Rome decreed that friars who spoke out against the pope or his crusades should be imprisoned.[153]

The second problem was that of the forging of papal bulls, which weakened popular credibility and made preaching the crusade more difficult. This was a problem which had been growing since the early thirteenth century, especially in the form of the sale of false redemptions from vows.[154] There are signs that it was becoming a serious nuisance by the 1320s. In

---

[149] *Thes. novus*, ii, col. 22; Hillgarth, *Spanish Kingdoms*, p. 256.

[150] See Otto, 'Zur italienischen Politik', pp. 214–15.

[151] *MGH. Const.* v, no. 973. See also ibid., v, nos. 974–5, vi, 1, no. 380; *Acta arag.*, i, no. 271; *Acta cap. gen.*, ii. 160–1; *Kaiser, Volk und Avignon*, nos. 4–19; W. Hofmann, 'Antikuriale Bewegungen in Deutschland in der Zeit Ludwigs des Bayern (1314–1346)', *Forschungen und Fortschritte*, xxxv (1961), *passim*.

[152] See *Vetera monumenta Poloniae et Lithuaniae gentiumque finitimarum historiam illustrantia*, ed. A. Theiner, i, no. 357.

[153] *Acta cap. prov.*, p. 230.

[154] See Stickel, *Der Fall von Akkon*, p. 167; Purcell, *Papal Crusading Policy*, p. 124; Lunt, *Financial Relations*, ii. 477.

June 1322 the rectors and secular clergy of all the provinces in the Papal State were warned by the Curia of a group claiming to be members of the Hospital of St. James of Altopascio, who were selling false indulgences and displaying false relics and forged papal privileges. The activities of this group were hindering recruitment for the crusade against the Visconti.[155] The Rector of the Duchy of Spoleto had caught this party, or one very similar, by October 1322, but the problem re-emerged in Savoy in 1326–7, with a man selling 'great remissions and indulgences', in Germany and Poland in 1326, and in Scandinavia in 1326 and 1330.[156] The situation was aggravated by the confusion caused by the schism.[157] Again, it was renegade Spiritual Franciscans who were causing much of the difficulty. One group of *fraticelli* was issuing false indulgences in southern Italy at the end of 1331, and letters were sent out by the Curia ordering the seizure of 'very many false letters and writings' which one of Peter of Corbara's cardinals, the friar minor Paul of Viterbo, had left behind at Viterbo before fleeing to Germany to join Louis IV.[158]

[155] ASV, Reg. Vat. 111, ff. 107ᵛ–108ʳ, no 438. Cf. ibid., f. 108ʳ⁻ᵛ, no. 439.
[156] ASV, Reg. Vat. 111, 320ᵛ–321ʳ, no. 1288; Reg. Vat. 114, f. 43ᵛ, no. 215; Reg. Vat. 115, ff. 128ᵛ–129ʳ, no. 1750, ff. 130ᵛ–131ʳ, no. 1753, ff. 163ᵛ–164ʳ, no. 1926; *Acta pontificum svecica, I. Acta cameralia*, ed. L. M. Bååth, i, no. 227; *Vet. mon. Pol.*, i, no. 371.
[157] See, e.g., ASV, Reg. Vat. 115, f. 66ʳ, no. 414, f. 46ʳ⁻ᵛ, no. 1258.
[158] ASV, Reg. Vat. 116, ff. 329ᵛ–330ʳ, no. 1647, f. 231ʳ, no. 1195, f. 336ᵛ, nos. 1675–7.

Chapter 5

The Crusade Armies in Italy
and the Crusade Ethos

It is clear that the papal Curia employed a wide range of
arguments to justify the crusades against its Christian enemies
and to persuade people to take the cross to fight in Italy, that it
built up an extensive and efficient apparatus of preaching to
communicate these arguments, and that it strove to organize
the military contributions of those who responded to them. Did
these efforts bear fruit? The only way to answer this question is
to examine the response which the crusade preaching achieved.

i. POPULAR RESPONSE TO THE PREACHING

Documentary evidence on the response to the crusade preaching is disappointingly meagre, especially when it is compared
with that on the organization of the preaching itself. For
example, when the Curia of the 1320s asked for written proof
that the crusades had been preached, it neither expected nor
received any indication of what the response was. Similarly, the
Curia rarely commented in retrospect on the results of its
attempts to rouse the Christian Republic in defence of the
Faith, and on the occasions when it did so its remarks were
inconsistent. In April 1327 John XXII replied to a request from
Charles of Calabria for a crusade to be preached against Louis
IV. The Pope wrote that he had discussed it with the cardinals,
would discuss it again, and would decide what to do for the best.
But he was not optimistic about the result which could be
expected from crusade preaching, adding that 'in similar cases
it has not produced the hoped-for fruit'.[1] On the other hand, in
a process of April 1324 against the Ghibelline communes of
Fermo and Fabriano, on the charge that they had aided the
heretics in the March of Ancona when the crusade was used
against them in 1322, the Curia observed that 'many of the

---

[1] 'in casibus similibus speratum fructum non produxerit'. ASV. Reg. Vat. 114.
f. 157ʳ⁻ᵛ, no. 987.

faithful proceeded manfully against the heretics and idolaters
. . . with the sign of the life-giving cross'.[2] A similar process of
1324 against Raynaldo Bonacolsi of Mantua described 'a multitude of the faithful' making 'the vow of the cross' against
Matthew Visconti in 1322.[3]

There is, of course, not necessarily a contradiction here.
'Many', even 'a multitude' of people, could still be a disappoint-
ment to the Curia. Moreover, none of these comments was
strictly objective. The first was made with the aim of dissuading
the Pope's allies from pressing for a crusade which the Pope was
not yet ready to declare, while the processes of 1324 were
emphasizing the gravity of the crime of aiding convicted heretics.
More persuasive as evidence for the continued efficacy of
crusade preaching is the fact that secular powers like the
Angevin crown were still petitioning for its use, believing that
the preaching of the crusade would bolster the ranks of their
armies. In 1325 Robert of Naples and Charles of Calabria
petitioned John XXII, unsuccessfully, for a plenary indulgence
for their planned expedition to Sicily.[4] In April 1328 Robert
also expressed his hope that when the crusade was preached
against Louis IV in Campagna, 'through this the faithful . . .
will be aroused and rise up the more readily, because they will
know that they are gaining the great indulgence which is described in the process, and when a multitude of armed men has
gathered from all sides the rebels and heretics will be vigorously
driven out and their brazenness confounded.'[5]

The Commune of Florence had no less confidence in the
effectiveness of the crusade than the Angevin kings. In the early
months of 1327 it joined Charles of Calabria in petitioning Pope
John XXII for crusade preaching against Louis IV, who, it was
claimed, had allied himself with the heretics and rebels of
Lombardy 'to offend God, the Church, and the faithful'. A
crusade would greatly facilitate Guelf opposition to Louis, the

---

[2] 'multis fidelibus adversus hereticos et ydolatras . . . viriliter procedentibus cum
vivifice crucis signo', ASV, Reg. Vat. 112, f. 123ᵛ, no. 485.

[3] 'multitudo fidelium contra dictos hereticos assumpsant votum crucis', ASV, AA.,
Arm. C, no. 1030.

[4] ASV, Reg. Vat. 113, f. 59ʳ, no. 453, f. 60ʳ⁻ᵛ, no. 461. Robert probably repeated this
request in 1335. See Benedict XII, *Lettres closes et patentes*, no. 123.

[5] *Urkunden*, no. 109.

Ghibellines, and their supporters.[6] In the following year Florence petitioned Giovanni Orsini for the crusade to be preached against the Ghibelline *signore* Castruccio Castracani on the charge of aiding heresy. The occasion for this request was Castruccio's siege of Pistoia. Florence claimed that the only way to save the city was to employ the crusade to secure a *levée en masse* of the surrounding population. 'Because of it the entire populace will be aroused to act with vigour against the above-named tyrant, and, if the Lord permits it and helps his own cause, the result will be very advantageous for the faithful of the Church and a blow to the unfaithful.'[7] Giovanni Orsini was therefore to use his legatine powers to extend the crusade to include Castruccio, and also to appoint a captain to lead the Florentine crusading forces, 'so that all those who follow the standard in an attack and assault on the said Castruccio will be understood to be following the standard of the Church, according to the tenor of the said papal letters'.[8] Other secular powers within the Guelf ambit attached importance to the crusade. In 1303 James II of Aragon asked Boniface VIII for indulgences for his forthcoming attempt to enforce his claim to Sardinia and Corsica, and in February 1322 the arrival of the crusade bull against Matthew Visconti and his allies (who included the Genoese Ghibellines) was greeted with enthusiasm by the Genoese Guelfs besieged in the city.[9]

Such evidence is, however, inconclusive. The simplest way of finding out how successful crusade preaching was would seem to be to examine the surviving documentary and chronicle references to the crusade armies themselves. But there are two difficulties in doing this. First, the number of crusaders who fought in Italy bore no definite relation to the total number of people who received or participated in the crusade indulgence. The extension of the indulgence to all who granted a financial subsidy to the crusades, let alone vaguer categories such as those who furnished 'aid or counsel', means that there is no reliable way of estimating how many people benefited from the

---

[6] ASV, Reg. Vat. 114, ff. 57ᵛ–58ʳ, no. 314.

[7] *Urkunden*, no. 127.

[8] Ibid.

[9] Salavert y Roca, *Cerdeña*, ii, no. 42; 'Georgii Stellae Annales genuenses', *RIS*, xvii, col. 1047. To secure the indulgence, and fired by their hatred for the Visconti, the Genoese Guelfs sent a contingent of crossbowmen to Bertrand du Poujet.

indulgence, and thus how great its popularity was.[10] More importantly, the crusade armies in Italy had a very heterogeneous character. It is impossible, for example, to draw a clear line of distinction between crusaders and mercenaries.[11] The most obvious distinction, that between paid and unpaid service, does not apply, as it was accepted by the thirteenth century that a crusader could be paid a wage without any effect on his status and privileges. John of Joinville is probably the most famous example of this development for the crusades to the East. He paid the expenses of nine knights and three knights-banneret, and was himself paid by Peter of Courtenay and Louis IX.[12] It is clear that crusaders were also paid throughout the Italian crusades. The most interesting instance of the combination of vow and wage comes from the recruitment in France on behalf of Charles of Anjou. The Chronicle of Limoges reported that in 1265,

Peter of Beaumont, a knight, came to Limoges and promised a wage to all who should take the cross: ten shillings and thirty pounds for preparations to knights, and five shillings and fifteen pounds for preparations to crossbowmen. He gave more to others who were specially commended to him. For this reason, many from the town and diocese of Limoges took crosses . . . He also promised to all who took the wage that he would restore to them any horses, arms, and armour that they lost in the service of the said Charles.[13]

Peter of Beaumont, Chamberlain of the Kingdom of Sicily between 1267 and 1273, was one of Charles's most trusted familiars.[14] There can be no doubt that Charles had sent him to recruit for the expedition, and that the plenary indulgence is here envisaged as a 'bonus', a spiritual addition to Charles's wage. The same was true of the indulgence offered by Martin IV and his successors in the War of the Vespers. When it became clear that Charles I would need extra help in suppressing the revolt, French knights started to arrive in the *Regno*, attracted by the high rates of pay. Typical was a contract

---

[10] Cf. Purcell, *Papal Crusading Policy*, p. 54.

[11] See Waley, 'Papal Armies', p. 25; *Deutsche Ritter und Edelknechte in Italien während des 14. Jahrhunderts*, ed. K. H. Schäfer, ii, p. viii.

[12] See Purcell, *Papal Crusading Policy*, p. 52.

[13] 'Maius chron. lemovicense', p. 771.

[14] See Minieri-Riccio, *Cenni storici*, pp. 162–5.

between Charles and Bertrand 'Artus', drawn up at the end of 1282. The mercenary captain was bringing twenty mounted crossbowmen to the King's service from Carcassone and Toulouse, and Charles agreed to pay them 'the customary wages which are paid to other mercenaries'.[15] Charles recruited most successfully in Provence through his seneschal there, but he also sent Charles of Salerno to recruit men in the rest of France, and wrote to his nephew Robert of Artois, asking him to raise 500 knights. The biggest group of arrivals came to the kingdom in September and November 1282, led by Charles of Salerno, Robert of Artois, and Peter of Alençon, another nephew of Charles I. There were about 1,600 men who received two ounces of gold each (presumably per week).[16] In September 1283 Martin IV even released John Eppes and the French mercenaries serving under him in Romagna, so that they could enlist under Charles of Salerno in the *Regno*.[17]

Given this large influx of French mercenaries, it is not surprising to find that when Martin IV ordered Cardinal Gerard of Sabina to preach the crusade against Peter of Aragon and the Sicilians in January 1283, he included the rider that the indulgence was offered 'to all the faithful of Christ, from whichever parts they come'.[18] The indulgence was, as in the crusade against Manfred, an added incentive to fight for the Angevin cause. A similar procedure was followed in recruiting the armies which fought in Italy for Pope John XXII. The continuator of William of Nangis's chronicle remarked that 'the lord pope, when he had assembled many mercenaries, gave them the plenary indulgence and sent them against the Ghibellines, and in particular against Galeazzo Visconti and his brothers, since

[15] *Actes et lettres de Charles Ier roi de Sicile concernant la France (1257–1284). Extraits des Registres Angevins de Naples*, ed. A. De Boüard, no. 1124.

[16] See 'La *ratio thesaurariorum* della cancelleria angioina', comp. N. Barone, *ASPN*, x (1885), 663, xi (1886), 5; *Actes et lettres*, no. 1122; 'Memorie della guerra di Sicilia negli anni 1282, 1283, 1284', comp. C. Minieri-Riccio, *ASPN*, i (1876), 92, 98–9, 101, 287–8; A. De Saint-Priest, *Histoire de la conquête de Naples par Charles d'Anjou frère de Saint Louis*, iv. 204–5; William of Nangis, 'Gesta Philippi regis Franciae', *RHGF*, xx. 522.

[17] See *Reg. pont. rom.*, ii, no. 22064. This was in response to a request from Charles I in June. See Amari, *La guerra*, i. 337.

[18] 'omnibus Christi fidelibus de quibusvis partibus oriundis', ASV, Reg. Vat. 41, f. 111ʳ, no. 36. The phrase was repeated in 1284 and a slightly modified form was used in 1291. See Martin IV, *Reg.*, no. 570 (cf. no. 591); ASV, Reg. Vat. 46, f. 164ᵛ, no. 13 (cf. Reg. Vat. 46, f. 20ᵛ, no. 107).

their father, Lord Matthew, had died an excommunicate, and against the other people of Milan.'[19]

There is no reason to infer from such quotations that all the mercenaries who fought for the popes or the Angevin kings in Italy also took the cross.[20] It is likely that the crusade armies in Italy throughout the period 1254–1343 were composed of several elements, including simple *stipendiarii*, feudal levies and crusaders who, although they were fighting under vows, were also getting paid for doing so. Such a variety of sources of recruitment was not unusual in this period, in which mercenaries were commonly supplemented by feudal contingents and the *arrière-ban* was still issued. Daniel Waley has shown how diverse was the range of recruits who fought in the non-crusading papal armies of the thirteenth century, and in the forces raised by the Commune of Florence.[21] Nor did the composite and haphazard nature of the armies necessarily lead to military inefficiency, although it has been suggested that the hordes of French peasants who joined the crusade against Aragon in 1285 were a hindrance to the French army.[22] It did, however, result in a very uneven residue of documentary evidence. For whereas the summoning of baronial *auxilium*, and the payment of mercenaries, were recorded in very rich detail in the Angevin registers and the papal cameral account-books, the presence of the crusaders, who needed little administrative attention, went largely undocumented.[23]

Luckily it did not go unnoticed. The spectacle of the armies of the cross marching against Christians in Italy was remarkable enough for chroniclers to record the fact and, although the dividing line between crusaders and mercenaries was obscure, contemporaries realized that two different forces were present.

---

[19] 'Continuatio', pp. 642–3.

[20] Though sworn allegiance to the Roman church and the Guelf party was sometimes required. See D. P. Waley, *'Condotte* and *Condottieri* in the Thirteenth Century', *Proceedings of the British Academy*, lxi (1975), 342, 371.

[21] See Waley, 'Papal Armies', *passim*, and 'The Army of the Florentine Republic from the Twelfth to the Fourteenth Century', in N. Rubinstein (ed.), *Florentine Studies. Politics and Society in Renaissance Florence*, *passim*. Cf. M. Mallett, *Mercenaries and their Masters. Warfare in Renaissance Italy*, p. 15.

[22] Hillgarth, *Spanish Kingdoms*, p. 257. But see Waley, 'Papal Armies', pp. 26, 29.

[23] For papal payments to mercenaries, see *Die Ausgaben*, pp. 348–76; *Deutsche Ritter*, i–ii, *passim*. For summonses to perform feudal service in the crusades, see *RCAR*, xxviii–xxx, *passim*.

Saba Malaspina remarked of the recruitment in France in 1265 that Clement IV 'paid many knights with the tenth to come to the kingdom with Charles, and conceded to others the crusaders' indulgence, which the Church has been accustomed to grant to those travelling overseas . . . Some who were paid by the said tenth, and others who were in truth signed with the cross, prepared themselves to come against the said king [Manfred].'[24] Saba Malaspina also drew a distinction between the Campanians who were fighting for wages in the papal army of 1255, and the Tuscans who, while they received wages, 'so that they should not fight in the service of the Roman church at their own expense', were also crusaders who had taken the cross and assembled under the patronage of the papal legate, the great feudal lord Octavian degli Ubaldini.[25] In the process of 1324 against Raynaldo Bonacolsi for aiding heresy the inquisitors of Lombardy even referred to 'the army of the Church *and* the faithful signed with the character of the cross'.[26] Thanks to this awareness one can use narrative sources to see, if not how many benefited from the indulgence, or what proportion of the crusading forces was actually made up of *crucesignati*, at least whether the crusade preaching seems to have had much effect in terms of the personal presence of crusaders. The crusaders were recruited in two main areas, France and Italy, and these will be discussed in turn.

The Kingdom of France and the remains of the old Carolingian Middle Kingdom which lay along its eastern frontier constituted a vast pool of potential crusading manpower, and the military prowess of the French enjoyed an unrivalled reputation in Italy. As long as the French court permitted preaching in France for the Italian crusades there seems to have been no difficulty in persuading the French nobility to take the cross. All the evidence shows that the preaching of 1264–6 in particular achieved an overwhelming success, even if Pope Clement IV exaggerated when he told Charles of Anjou in July 1265 that 'all France' and 'all

[24] Saba Malaspina, 'Rerum sicularum', col. 813.

[25] Ibid., col. 794.

[26] 'exercitus ecclesie et memorati fideles crucis caratere insigniti', ASV, A.A., Arm. C, no. 1030. See also four lines further on: 'predictos fideles et exercitum ecclesie qui se reduxerant in eundem Burgum'.

Provence' were preparing to join the army.[27] No doubt this success was due partly to the energy of Peter of Beaumont and his agents, whose promised wage made it possible for knights like Reginald 'de Piquignaco' to raise short-term loans from merchants to pay off their debts, using as backing 'the debt which he is owed, so he has asserted, by the illustrious King of Sicily, for the service which he is to perform to the said lord king in overseas parts'.[28] Certainly the rapid expenditure of the clerical tenth by Simon of Brie, in the form of wages to those who took the cross, caused great financial embarrassment to Charles and Clement IV in the autumn and winter of 1265–6.[29]

Charles's own lineage, standing, and reputation in France also contributed to the success of the preaching of 'the cross of Apulia'. In an age of burgeoning nationalism, the conquest of Sicily was regarded as a French triumph and an addition to the glory of the House of Capet, 'a great exaltation of the whole French nation', as Clement IV expressed it in 1267.[30] King Louis encouraged the preaching, pressing the French nobility to aid his brother, and Rutebeuf, one of France's leading poets, composed two remarkable poems aimed at arousing people to take the cross, 'La Chanson de Pouille' and 'Le Dit de Pouille'.[31] The chronicler Gilles le Muisit placed the importance of Charles's leadership second only to the indulgence itself as a stimulus. 'A very great multitude of nobles and of commoners followed him, first because the lord pope and his court had granted great indulgences for doing so, and also because the prince was most renowned and courtly, experienced in war and graced before others with the flowers of the virtues.'[32]

One of the most persuasive pieces of evidence that 'the business of Apulia' was regarded as increasing the reputation and honour of the Capetians comes from an appeal to Philip III, or possibly Philip IV, by an old soldier called Peter Pillart of Le Mesnil-Saint-Denis, who had fought for both Louis IX

[27] *Thes. novus*, ii, col. 153. Cf. Saba Malaspina, 'Rerum sicularum', col. 813.
[28] *Layettes*, v, no. 774.
[29] See below, pp. 224ff.
[30] Clement IV, *Reg.*, no. 595; *Ann. eccles.*, ad ann. 1267, no. 56, xxii. 208.
[31] *Thes. novus*, ii, col. 153; Rutebeuf, *Onze poèmes*, pp. 43–51.
[32] Gilles le Muisit, *Chronique et annales*, p. 7.

and Charles of Anjou, and was claiming justice over a stolen horse. 'I have served you and your ancestors', he wrote, 'in the year when they went to Damietta, and to Sicily, and at the siege of Marseilles, and that of Tunis.'[33] Equally evocative of the depth of France's commitment to the expedition of 1265–6 is one of the Limoges chronicle entries for 1266.

In the year of our Lord 1266, on the Saturday after the Octaves of Easter, the dean sent word to us, and to our prior, at St. Martial's, about the time of Vespers, that we should descend into the town to hear the reports of the victory of Lord Charles; and when we had gone down, and heard the reports, the dean said that we should join them in a procession next day.[34]

Charles I himself considered that the battles of Benevento and Tagliacozzo had been won by French prowess, despite the fact that there had been Tuscan and Lombard Guelf contingents there. This is shown very clearly in his foundation of the *ex voto* monasteries which he had built near the battle-sites, S. Maria de Real Valle and S. Maria della Vittoria. He insisted that French and Provençal Cistercian monks be brought to the *Regno* for the new monasteries,

because it is acknowledged to be both fitting and decent that men of the said nations should serve God in this monastery, since it was from those nations that the athletes sprang, who liberated the Kingdom of Sicily from the hands of her persecutors, for the honour of God and of Holy Mother Church, with great toil and labour, and with the effusion of much blood.[35]

He remembered the crusaders of 1266 with lasting gratitude, exempting French and Provençal knights resident in the *Regno* from the taxation of his justiciars, 'because they followed us, with great loss to their goods and danger to their persons, when we arrived in the kingdom'.[36]

The composition of the armies of 1265–6 and 1268 is fairly well known. The original expedition was joined by many of the

[33] See 'Requête adressée au roi de France par un vétéran des armées de Saint Louis et de Charles d'Anjou', ed. É. Berger, in *Études d'histoire du Moyen Âge dédiées à G. Monod*, p. 349 and *passim*.

[34] 'Maius chron. lemovicense', pp. 772–3.

[35] P. Egidi, 'Carlo I d'Angiò e l'abbazia di S. Maria della Vittoria presso Scurcola', *ASPN*, xxxv (1910), 161–2. Cf. ibid., pp. 125–6.

[36] *RCAR*, xx, Reg. 86, no. 156.

most important French nobles, including the Marshal of France, Hugh of Mirepoix, the Constable, Giles le Brun, and the Count of Vendôme.[37] As an army it was dominated by two regional contingents: the Provençals, led by the De Baux brothers and the Bishop of Auxerre, Guy of Mello (who was able to contribute to the victory at Benevento without breaking the ruling on clerical participation in fighting),[38] and the north French and Flemings, led by Robert, the heir to the County of Flanders, and Giles le Brun, who was sent to look after him because he had not yet come of age. Recruitment in Flanders was particularly successful because Robert was Charles of Anjou's son-in-law. The thirteenth-century song, 'Le Garçon et l'aveugle', refers to Charles's recruitment in the region of Tournai. The Flanders contingent maintained a very strong sense of regional identity, refusing to allow itself to be subjected to Charles's discipline.[39] Prominent French crusaders also played a part in the campaigns. Érard of Saint-Valéry, returning from the Latin East, offered Charles his help and drew up the successful battle-plan of Tagliacozzo.[40] William of Villehardouin crossed from the Morea with 1,100 knights and helped his new lord at Tagliacozzo, and Geoffrey of Sergines, the son of Louis IX's seneschal at Acre, was paid £500 by the Church for his participation at Benevento.[41]

After the defeat and death of Manfred Charles I faced a problem which had been encountered by Simon of Montfort in Languedoc, and, on many occasions, by the Franks in Syria: he was unable to retain the services of the crusaders to defend his newly won lands.[42] In May 1266 Clement IV wrote to the

---

[37] See. e.g.. William of Nangis. 'Gesta sanct. mem. Ludovici', pp. 420–1; Andrew of Hungary. 'Descriptio'. p. 567; 'Chronique anonyme'. p. 87.

[38] See 'Ex continuatione gestorum episcoporum Autissiodorensium', *MGHS*, xxvi. 586. Barral de Baux had commuted his vow from one of accompanying Alphonse of Poitiers to the Holy Land. See Clement IV, *Reg.*, no. 1677.

[39] See Gilles le Muisit. *Chronique*. pp. 8, 10–12; *Le Garçon et l'aveugle. Jeu du xiiie siècle*, ed. M. Roques. pp. iii–iv. 5. See also below. p. 165.

[40] See A. Busson, 'Die Schlacht bei Alba zwischen Konradin und Karl von Anjou, 1268'. *Deutsche Zeitschrift für Geschichtswissenschaft*, iv. pt. 2 (1890). pp. 309 ff.; William of Nangis. 'Gesta sanct. mem. Ludovici'. pp. 403–1.

[41] See 'Compte d'une mission'. pp. 254–9, 264; 'Cronaca di Morea'. p. 454.

[42] For shortage of manpower in Languedoc and Latin Syria, see Belperron, *La Croisade*, pp. 179–80; J. Prawer, *The Latin Kingdom of Jerusalem. European Colonialism in the Middle Ages*, pp. 29–30, 68, 280–1. See also below, note 46.

victorious king that 'as the business (*negotium*) has, by the grace
of God, been successfully accomplished, we declare that you
have implemented the conditions agreed upon . . .'.[43] The end
of the *negotium* presumably also meant the fulfilment of the vows
of the French *crucesignati*.[44] The Pope advised Charles not to
allow them to return to France yet, as the *regnicoli* (inhabitants
of the *Regno*) were not to be trusted; but Charles could not let
them go for a simpler reason: he could not pay them the wages
they had been promised.[45] Consequently many of the crusaders
fought for Charles in Tuscany in 1267–8. They were still present
when Conradin invaded Italy and were able to save the new
dynasty at the battle of Tagliacozzo in 1268. After Tagliacozzo,
however, it became more difficult to retain the French. Infuriated by the support which the native nobility had offered
Conradin, Charles adopted a policy of enfeoffing as many of the
crusaders as he could persuade to stay in the kingdom. His
efforts at persuasion were not generally successful; even when
they were, the feudatories preferred to reside in France, and
laws were necessary threatening the confiscation of the fiefs of
vassals who absented themselves from the country for more
than a year and a day.[46]

Largely as a result of this failure to colonize the *Regno*, the
Angevin crown was placed in peril in 1282 by a critical lack of
reliable manpower with which to put down the Sicilian rebellion. In May Charles I wrote of his 'very great need to have a
large number of good men-at-arms'.[47] It was natural to turn
once again to France. The crusade preaching of 1283–4 can
thus be seen as an attempt to rekindle the remarkable crusade
atmosphere of the years 1264–6 by the man who had, as papal
legate in France at the time, helped to create it. In this Martin
IV was successful, for the Vespers was seen as an insult to the
French nation and its king.[48] Men who had fought for Charles

[43] Clement IV, *Reg.*, no. 416.
[44] Cf. Gilles le Muisit, *Chronique*, p. 12.
[45] See below, p. 228.
[46] See P. Durrieu, 'Études sur la dynastie angevine de Naples. Le liber donationum Caroli primi', *Mélanges*, vi (1886), 213–15 and *passim*; id., *Les Gascons en Italie*, pp. 7–8; Cadier, *Essai*, pp. 18–19. La Monte (*Feudal Monarchy*, pp. xxiv-xxv) believed that this legislation may have been modelled on similar laws in the Kingdom of Jerusalem.
[47] De Saint-Priest, *Histoire*, iv. 204.
[48] See, e.g., William of Nangis, 'Gesta Philippi', pp. 521–2.

of Anjou in 1266 returned to fight for him in 1282–5. Typical was the career of Jourdain IV of l'Isle Jourdain, a Gascon vassal of Alphonse of Poitiers. Jourdain fought with a following of knights and crossbowmen in 1266, receiving the warm praise of Pope Clement IV for his services against 'the enemies of God, the Church, and the king'. He was enfeoffed in Principato and then Calabria, but he soon returned to Gascony. Disregarding the threats of Charles I that his fief would be confiscated by the crown, he did not come back until October 1282, when he brought a contingent of soldiers with him. He took part in Philip III's crusade against Aragon in 1285, and died three years later.[49] Though not prepared to live in the *Regno,* many French nobles would fight to help the Angevin dynasty to retain it. The outstanding example of this attitude was Robert, Count of Artois, the nephew of Charles I. He was active in the *Regno* between 1273 and 1276, holding the regency in 1275–6, then returning to France and forfeiting his lands in his absence. Recruited by Charles of Salerno in 1282, he helped Cardinal Gerard of Sabina to administer the Kingdom of Sicily during Charles of Salerno's imprisonment, but in 1292 he returned again to his French lands.[50] The defence of the Angevin monarchy of Sicily united even those divided by the war in Flanders. One of Robert's lieutenants in the Kingdom of Sicily was Philip of Flanders, who joined the Flemings shortly after Robert fell at Courtrai on the French side.[51]

Some Frenchmen also took the cross to fight in John XXII's crusades in Italy. In 1324 Philip of Valois's chancellor, John of Vienna, took a vow to go on crusade in Italy, and the Pope allowed him, at Philip's request, to delay his departure to fulfil the vow. John, who was a papal chaplain and Dean of Le Mans, was evidently a man of some standing; he led a contingent of forty-one men-at-arms, himself paying the wages of ten. He

---

[49] See *Thes. novus,* ii, cols. 561–2; *RCAR,* i, Reg. 2, nos. 58, 187, iii, Reg. 12, no. 415; Durrieu, *Les Gascons en Italie,* pp. 3–12. Jourdain's son-in-law, Amauri of Narbonne, continued this tradition by leading the Angevin and Florentine troops at the battle of Campaldino in 1289. See Waley, 'The Army of the Florentine Republic', pp. 87–8.

[50] See 'Una legge suntuaria inedita del 1290', ed. G. Del Giudice, *Atti dell'Accademia pontaniana,* xvi, pt. 2 (1886), pp. 44–58. For a eulogy of Robert's regency, see William of Nangis, 'Gesta Philippi', pp. 526–7.

[51] See B. Croce, 'Filippo di Fiandra, conte di Chieti e di Loreto', *ASPN, NS,* xvi (1930), 26–7 and *passim.*

eventually returned to France in March 1326 with the bene-
diction and praise of the Pope.[52] Letters of safe conduct and
thanks were addressed to other French nobles and ecclesiastics,
possibly *crucesignati*, in 1323, 1324, and 1328. These included the
Bishop of Liège, who in 1324 offered to come 'to the service
of holy Roman church against her enemies and rebels in
Lombardy' with 100 knights.[53] Despite the persistent attempts
of John XXII and Robert of Naples to interest the French court
in the Guelf cause, it is very doubtful that recruitment in France
at this time was at all comparable to that of the thirteenth
century. There was some compensation in the successful
preaching which took place in Germany and the empire.
Giovanni Villani remarked that 1,500 German cavalry joined
Henry of Austria at Brescia as crusaders in 1322, and in April
1323 the Doge of Venice was asked to permit and help crusaders
to pass through the city on the way to Lombardy to help the
Church 'against its enemies and the unfaithful'.[54]

The evidence afforded by narrative sources on Italian participation in the crusades is subject to important regional
variations. It is difficult to know whether this is a true reflection
of differing responses to crusade preaching, and thus of a difference between the religious temper of one area and that of
another, or is simply the result of the varying degree of detail in
the chronicles themselves. For the *Regno*, for instance, many of
the sources are disappointingly summary or derivative. During
the War of the Vespers the provenance of the crusaders is left
extremely vague. Thus, in a passage in Bartholomew of Neocastro's history of the war, in which a captured Dominican friar
is interrogated by Roger of Lluria in 1287, Bartholomew makes
him claim that 'the Count of Artois and the legate of the Church
have an innumerable army of fighters of lords, barons, knights,
cavalry, foot-soldiers, and crusaders from all parts of
Christendom'.[55] Surviving documents from the Angevin

[52] John XXII, *Lettres secrètes*, nos. 2179–80, 2735; *Die Ausgaben*, p. 354.

[53] *Lettres de Jean XXII (1316–1334)*, ed. A. Fayen, no. 1312; ASV, Reg. Vat. 111, ff. 363ᵛ–364ʳ, no. 1503, Reg. Vat. 112, f. 84ʳ, no. 389; John XXII, *Lettres secrètes*, no. 3629.

[54] See John XXII, *Lettres secrètes*, no. 1661 (Coulon related this letter to the crusade to the East, but it is clear that it refers to the crusade in Lombardy); Giovanni Villani, *Cronica*, ii. 240. See also ASV, Reg. Vat. 113, ff. 108ᵛ–109ʳ, no. 774; *Vat. Akten*, no. 468; 'Cronaca senese attribuita ad Agnolo di Tura del Grasso detta la Cronaca maggiore', *RISNS*, xv⁶. 392.

[55] Bartholomew of Neocastro, 'Historia sicula', p. 93.

registers attest that the Angevin authorities did indeed search far and wide for recruits in the War of the Vespers. Their armies contained Muslims from Lucera, Guelf contingents from Tuscany and Lombardy, Aragonese and French mercenaries, even almogavars, the tough guerrilla fighters responsible for many of the early Aragonese successes, who had been won over by bribery to the Angevin side.[56] But did the *regnicoli* themselves take the cross on behalf of their papal or Angevin lords?

The sources suggest that at least some did so. In 1255 Pope Alexander IV claimed that 'very many' people took the cross against Manfred when it was preached by himself at Naples, and that 'innumerable' others had followed suit. Bartholomew of Neocastro described crusaders from southern Italy as being present in the campaign of 1287 against the Sicilians.[57] In 1328 Robert of Naples claimed that there was a good response to crusade preaching against Louis IV, and that besides himself and Charles of Calabria, 'the counts of Montescaglioso, Andria, and Squillace and many other barons and nobles of our realm there present, in a copious number', had taken the cross.[58] The best example of successful crusade preaching within the kingdom is the relief of Gaeta in the summer of 1289. In June 1289 Robert of Artois besieged the castle of Catanzaro in Calabria. James II and Roger of Lluria attempted to relieve the castle, failed, and sailed north to Gaeta in July to compel the Angevin army to raise the siege by threatening Gaeta. This port, as Pope Nicholas IV remarked, was essential for the defence of the *Regno*.[59] Unable to pay in full even the soldiers in Calabria, in desperation Charles II called on the towns and villages of Terra di Lavoro to supply troops.[60] It was to help deal with this crisis that Nicholas IV declared the crusade

---

[56] See, e.g., *Codice diplomatico dei Saraceni di Lucera*, ed. P. Egidi, nos. 20, 87, 189, 191, 220b; *Documenti*, ed. Terlizzi, nos. 865–8, 871, 873–5, 880; D. Tomacelli, *Storia de' reami di Napoli e di Sicilia dal 1250 al 1303*, ii. 433; *Gli atti perduti della cancelleria angioina transuntati da Carlo de Lellis. Parte I: Il regno di Carlo I*, ed. B. Mazzoleni, i, pp. 492–3, 504–5, 558, 577, 609; *Cod. dipl. sal.*, ii. nos. 272–3, 276, 312.

[57] 'Ann. de Burton', p. 352; Bartholomew of Neocastro, 'Historia sicula', pp. 97–8.

[58] 'Montis Caveosi Andrie et Squillacii comites pluresque alii barones et nobiles regni nostri in numero copioso ibi presentes.' ASN, MS Minieri-Riccio, formerly Reg. Ang. 271, f. 111^{r-v}.

[59] See ASV, Reg. Vat. 45, f. 63^{r}, no. 328. Cf. Léonard, *Les Angevins de Naples*, p. 175.

[60] *RCAR*, xxx, Reg. 8, nos. 159, 267–72, 281–6, 302–3.

afresh. A nondescript army of papal mercenaries and crusaders, both *regnicoli* and Guelfs, relieved Gaeta in August. According to Bartholomew of Neocastro, who was in James II's retinue, and wrote a vivid if fanciful description of these events, the crusade preaching was immensely successful.[61] The numbers were an embarrassment for Charles II, who on 20 August ordered Peter of Brayda to find and transport food supplies for the 'innumerable multitude of people' in the Angevin camp.[62]

In northern and central Italy the sources are richer and the evidence of successful crusade preaching in Guelf cities and areas more widespread. In parts of northern Italy an *ad hoc* army could be raised on every occasion when the crusade was preached. Particularly impressive was the response to the crusade preaching against Alberich and Ezzelino of Romano in Venice, Ferrara, and the Guelf communes of north-east Italy.[63] This response was repeated, on a lesser scale, only a few years later when Geoffrey of Beaumont preached the crusade on behalf of Charles of Anjou. Bologna, Ferrara, Mantua, and other cities in Lombardy, Romagna, and the March of Treviso all sent troops.[64] Similarly, the preaching against Matthew Visconti in 1322 provided Raymond of Cardona with 'innumerable crusading foot-soldiers'.[65] The same favourable response could be relied upon in central Italy. On the two most important occasions when the crusade was preached in the Papal State, in 1264 and 1322, the Guelf communes contributed large crusade contingents. Giovanni Villani remarked of the preaching of 1264 that 'many of the faithful took the cross, and formed an army to oppose them'.[66] The Tuscan Guelfs were also prepared to send crusaders to aid the pope or the Angevin kings. Saba Malaspina remarked of the crusade army assembled

---

[61] Bartholomew of Neocastro, 'Historia sicula', pp. 109–11. Other accounts of the siege of Gaeta and the crusade are in Giovanni Villani, *Cronica*, i. 464–6; 'Cronicon suessanum', p. 59.

[62] See *RCAR*, xxx, Reg. 8, no. 324.

[63] See Rolandino Patavino, 'Chronica', pp. 107–8; Salimbene, 'Cronica', p. 366; Canz, *Philipp Fontana*, pp. 59–75.

[64] See Andrew of Hungary, 'Descriptio', p. 568; 'Annales mantuani', *MGHS*, xix. 24; Salimbene, 'Cronica', pp. 435–6.

[65] Giovanni Villani, *Cronica*, ii. 240.

[66] Ibid., i. 312. See also Saba Malaspina, 'Rerum sicularum', col. 810; Thierry de Vaucouleurs, 'Vita Urbani IV', *RIS*, iii², col. 418.

by Cardinal Octavian degli Ubaldini at Foggia in 1255 that, although Campanian mercenaries were also present, 'the larger and better part' of the army was said to have been composed of Tuscan crusaders.[67] In 1328 the cross was preached in defence of Florence and the Tuscan Guelfs against Castruccio Castracani, and Giovanni Villani gave a vivid description of the Guelf army drawn up in Piazza S. Croce and receiving the cross and the banner of the Church from Giovanni Orsini.[68]

The success which was usually achieved by preachers of the Italian crusades in Guelf cities in northern and central Italy was undoubtedly due in part to the encouragement and aid which they received from the communal authorities, often at the instigation of the *parte guelfa*. Very often a city's crusade contingent was organized, paid, and supplied with a banner and a leader so that it represented the commune as a whole. This was a tradition which reached back at least to the Fifth Crusade, when the papal legate, Cardinal-bishop Ugolino of Ostia, toured the cities of Tuscany and Lombardy raising crusade contributions in the form of men or money, which were granted by each commune 'for the reverence of God and the remission of our sins'.[69] It is probable that Philip Fontana's crusade preaching against Ezzelino of Romano in 1256 owed a great deal of its effectiveness to the active backing of the Venetian authorities.[70] Giovanni Villani wrote of Florence's contribution to the crusade against the Colonna that 'the Commune of Florence sent there to the service of the pope six hundred crusaders, crossbowmen and heavy infantry, wearing the insignia of the Commune of Florence'.[71] In such circumstances chains of command became complicated. In the crusade army of 1256 against Ezzelino of Romano the Venetian contingent was commanded by a captain, Tommasino Giustiniano, who was appointed by the Doge. Tommasino was under the authority of 'the lord and master of the whole host', Marco Badoero, who was in turn subject to the orders of the legate,

---

[67] Saba Malaspina, 'Rerum sicularum', col. 794.

[68] *Cronica*, iii. 78. See also ibid., ii. 238 for Florentine crusaders in 1322.

[69] *Registri dei cardinali Ugolino d'Ostia e Ottaviano degli Ubaldini*, ed. G. Levi, pp. 7, 11–12, 19–24.

[70] See above, p. 126, below, pp. 162–3.

[71] *Cronica*, ii. 27.

Philip Fontana. Even the Paduan exiles elected their own leader.[72]

In the 1320s, too, the Guelf communes played an active organizational role. A Sienese chronicle recorded that the Bishop of Rimini arrived in Siena in April 1322 with a papal commission to preach the cross against Frederick of Montefeltro and his supporters.[73] Many people took the cross in Siena, Florence, and other cities, and

The Commune of Siena and the Nine had a standard made bearing the arms of the Commune of Siena, which was carried by the Sienese crusaders with the above-named bishop together with other banners showing the arms of the pope, the Church, and the Rector of the March, and they went with the said bishop to the March against Recanati and the other places where the Rector of the March was fighting for the Church.[74]

The account-books of the Commune of Siena recorded payments of £75.10s. for five such standards.[75] In such cases as this, unfortunately, it is never clear if the crusade indulgence was believed to extend to the whole commune or simply to its officials. A letter of John XXII to the Commune of Bologna asking for the cavalry which the commune had promised talked in vague terms of 'the spiritual gifts conceded to you and to others of the faithful fighting the said heretics and rebels'.[76]

Given the limited sources available, many of the most interesting questions surrounding the crusade armies which fought for the Guelf cause in Italy must remain unanswered. It is not possible, for example, to say what proportion of the armies consisted of actual *crucesignati*, which region of France or Italy provided the greatest or most consistent crusade response, or

---

[72] See Martino da Canale, 'Cronaca veneta', pp. 426–9. Cf. Rolandino Patavino, 'Chronica', p. 108; Hyde, *Padua*, p. 202.

[73] For the Bishop of Rimini, see Franceschini, *I Montefeltro*, pp. 213–14, and the hostile description by Ferrarius de Apilia in *Acta arag.* i, no. 326.

[74] 'Cronaca senese', p. 391.

[75] Ibid.

[76] 'dona spiritualia vobis et aliis fidelibus impugnantibus dictos hereticos et rebelles concessa', ASV, Reg. Vat. 112, f. 71ᵛ, no. 335. In July 1357 it was agreed between the Bishop of Narni and the Commune of Florence that any contrite Florentine who confessed within three months would receive the crusade indulgence in return for the dispatch of a communal contingent of crusaders for the crusade against the Grand Company. See Matteo Villani, *Cronica*, ii. 72–3. But this may not have been the procedure followed in the 1320s.

whether other areas of Christendom in which the crusades were preached, such as England, Iberia, or eastern Europe, were represented by crusaders. From the information which we possess, however, two things are clear. First, the crusaders who fought in Italy were of very varied geographical and social origins. There were French and German nobles and mercenaries who crossed the Alps for the honour of France, to pay off their debts, or in search of regular employment or plunder; crusade contingents sent by the Guelf communes in answer to papal or Angevin requests; disorganized but enthusiastic groups of peasants responding to an appeal issued in an emergency by the Curia.[77] Secondly, it is clear that crusade preaching was, if not always, at least very often effective, and that Pierre Toubert was wrong to call the crusade against the political enemies of the Church 'a business above all financial and political', with the implication that the crusades did not have either as their aim or as their result the recruitment of actual crusade armies.[78] The response to the preaching shows that the crusade was an important means of swelling the ranks of the papal and Angevin armies, and that the care taken by the Curia to justify and preach the crusades was well rewarded.

ii. THE CRUSADE ETHOS AND THE ITALIAN CRUSADES

When the Doge of Venice, Rainieri Zeno, appealed to the Venetians to take the cross against Ezzelino of Romano in 1256 he was reported as beseeching them 'that through you Holy Church should be aided, in the way that you are accustomed to help her, and that deeds should be performed like those you did at Ferrara, and those your ancestors did at Tyre, and throughout Syria, and as they did at Constantinople, always in the service of Holy Church.'[79] When he again appealed to the Venetians to take the cross against Ezzelino, in 1258 or 1259,

---

[77] Cf. Riley-Smith, *What were the Crusades?*, pp. 62–4.

[78] 'Les Déviations', pp. 393–4. This is not to deny that the declaration of a crusade facilitated and justified the exploitation of new sources of revenue, or that this consideration influenced papal policy. See below, chapter 6, and p. 256.

[79] Martino da Canale, 'Cronaca veneta', pp. 426–7. The Venetians helped to capture Ferrara from the supporters of Frederick II in 1240, and played a leading role in the capture of Tyre in 1124 and Constantinople in 1204.

the Doge was reported as adding the capture of Padua, the outstanding success of the earlier crusade, to this list.[80] Similarly, in 1309 the Venetian ambassadors sent to the Curia to protest against the sanctions directed against the republic were to remind Pope Clement V that Venice 'was always a faithful and constant defender of the honour and of the glory of the Roman church, whether it be in Palestine against the Saracens and the other barbarians, or in Italy against Frederick II, against Ezzelino of Romano and many other persecutors of the Church'.[81] As has been shown, the French knight Peter Pillart equated his crusading service in Italy with that in Egypt and Tunis, an equation apparent too in the epitaph in a church at Laon of John Eppes, seneschal of Charles I and rector of Martin IV in Romagna:

> He was in Apulia, and at Tunis;
> He performed many feats of arms in Calabria,
> And suffered much pain for the love of God
> In Abruzzi and in Romagna.[82]

There could be no clearer indication that for the supporters of the Italian crusades they were directly equivalent in their purpose and character to crusades against the Muslims. Such men accepted the papal view that all crusades were linked by the unique authority of the pope to grant the plenary indulgence and by the fact that they were all waged in defence of the Church and the Christian Faith. This equivalence is a striking aspect of descriptions of the Italian crusades by contemporary Guelf chroniclers. It has long been accepted that the crusade armies in the Holy Land enjoyed from the start an ethos which characterized them and distinguished them from ordinary armies. Descriptions of the great expeditions to the East used phrases and analogies from the Bible, patristic writings, Church liturgy, and a wide variety of other sources to establish the sanctity of the crusade forces and their purpose. Underpinning these descriptions was the belief that the crusaders formed the armies of Christ, setting out to fight in his

---

[80] Ibid., pp. 438–9.

[81] Soranzo, *La guerra*, pp. 133–4.

[82] See Jordan, *Les Origines*, p. 404–5. Cf., for the fourteenth century, Schäfer's comment in *Deutsche Ritter*, i. 148.

cause and under his divine protection.[83] This ethos was to a great extent shared by the crusades in Italy.

It was, of course, very difficult to represent the Italian crusades as pilgrimages, which was common practice in the case of the crusades to the East. The War of the Sicilian Vespers, and John XXII's wars against the Ghibellines and Louis IV, had no geographical goal which could bear comparison with Jerusalem, no strategic aim at all analogous to the defence or recovery of the Holy Places. The exception to this rule was Charles of Anjou's expedition of 1265–6. Although his crusade's ultimate aim was the conquest of the Kingdom of Sicily, it was also intended to free the Papal State from Manfred's supporters and allies, 'to recover the lands of St. Peter', as the Chronicle of the Morea expressed it.[84] Charles's expedition was thus occasionally described as a pilgrimage. Guy of Mello, Bishop of Auxerre, was thanked by Clement IV for offering to take the cross against Manfred and was given the necessary permission to go on pilgrimage; he was described as 'going to Rome in aid of Charles, inspired by the devout zeal of pilgrimage'.[85] In 'Le Dit de Pouille' Rutebeuf compared the crusade to a pilgrimage to Rome to seek absolution.[86]

It was much easier to describe the crusade forces in Italy as armies engaged in a holy war. 'The cause is God's, the battle his.'[87] Such statements were commonplace in French and Guelf chronicles, while papal letters, especially those of John XXII in the 1320s, were full of asseverations that the Guelf party and its army were doing 'the work of the Lord'.[88] Phrases like 'the soldiers of Christ', 'the soldiers of God', 'the athletes of Christ', were continually used by Guelf or pro-papal chroniclers.[89] Particularly interesting is a passage in Andrew of Hungary's chronicle of the battle of Benevento in which, after the cele-

---

[83] See P. Rousset, *Les Origines et les caractères de la première croisade*, pp. 68–109.

[84] 'Cronaca di Morea', p. 451. The Kingdom of Sicily was also part of the *patrimonium beati Petri*, but it seems to be the Papal State which is referred to here.

[85] See 'Ex continuatione', p. 586; *Thes. novus*, ii, col. 200.

[86] Rutebeuf, *Onze poèmes*, p. 51.

[87] Andrew of Hungary, 'Descriptio', p. 573.

[88] See, e.g., the interesting letters of May 1322 in which John XXII asked the Guelfs to support the intervention of Henry of Austria. ASV, Reg. Vat. 111, ff. 186ʳ–187ʳ, nos. 778–81.

[89] The old Gregorian formula *milites sancti Petri* was still occasionally used. See, e.g., Rolandino Patavino, 'Chronica', pp. 107, 133.

bration of mass which preceded the battle, Charles of Anjou addresses his troops as 'the soldiers of Christ, joined today to Christ by the communion of his most precious body and blood'.[90]

As God's soldiers, the crusaders considered themselves to be under divine protection. In his life of St. Louis William of Nangis recounted how Giles le Brun told Charles of Anjou that the contingent of crusaders from Flanders intended to engage Manfred's forces as soon as possible, 'because they had hope that our Lord, in whose service they were and whose Church they defended, would give them the victory'.[91] On several occasions God was indeed represented as actively intervening on behalf of Charles and his soldiers. For example, when Charles sailed to Rome in 1265 he not only survived a storm at sea, but evaded Manfred's scouting fleet. 'Our Lord Jesus Christ, the king of kings, who wanted to save his champion and his defender of Holy Church, a man also destined to be king, guarded him so well that amongst all his enemies he passed over the sea and came to Rome at ease, a feat which was held to be a great miracle.'[92] Charles's army, passing through northern Italy in the depths of winter, was aided by abnormal weather conditions. 'A great miracle occurred, for in the year in which they came there was no cold, no freezing, no snow, no mud, and no rain. The road was in perfect condition, secure and pleasant, just as if it were May. And this was the Lord's work, because they came in aid of the Church to exterminate that accursed Manfred.'[93] Similarly, the army was able to negotiate the difficult pass at Ceprano without loss. 'Truly whoever is led by God goes everywhere without danger. So that because King Charles was going in Christ's name and fighting for God's Church, to redeem the lands of the said Church, he negotiated the pass with his army without encountering any obstacle.' The same explanation was advanced in the case of the comparative ease with which the crusaders captured the castle at San Germano.[94]

[90] Andrew of Hungary, 'Descriptio', pp. 573–4.
[91] 'Gesta sanct. mem. Ludovici', p. 423. Cf. Giovanni Villani, *Cronica*, i. 329.
[92] William of Nangis, 'Gesta sanct. mem. Ludovici', p. 421. Cf. Andrew of Hungary, 'Descriptio', p. 564.
[93] Salimbene, 'Cronica', p. 470.
[94] 'Annali genovesi', iv. 86.

Charles's speech to his army before the battle of Benevento was an ideal opportunity for chroniclers to stress the sanctity of the Angevin cause, and one they rarely missed. William of Nangis included a speech which, with its appeals to French patriotism and the crusading spirit, closely followed by a ruthlessly disparaging assessment of Manfred's army, has an authentic ring about it.

O sires and knights and people of France, of whom so many deeds are told and have been told, you do not fight for me, but for the cause of Holy Church, by whose authority you are absolved of all your sins. Regard and look upon your enemies, who despise God and his Holy Church, who are excommunicated, which is a mark of bad Christians and the beginning of eternal death, and who are assembled here from various lands, so that they are weaker and will be the more easily and rapidly cut down.[95]

In a similar vein was a speech attributed to Charles at the battle of Tagliacozzo, in an attempt to rally his troops at the crisis-point of the struggle.

Now we have the greatest reason to fight manfully against the enemies of the Church, in order that, following in the footsteps of our noble ancestors, who went through grave dangers in defence of Christianity, we should earn praise and glory for our nation. And if, by chance, it should be the Lord's will that we die in this battle, we must not be sad, like those who have no hope, because we shall win the kingdom of heaven as our reward.[96]

A belief in astrology was widely attributed to the Ghibellines after Frederick II and, as we have seen, played a part in the papal accusations of heresy in the 1320s. For the Guelf chroniclers this belief constituted useful colour in their depiction of the war between the crusaders and the pope's enemies as that between the forces of good and evil. Thus Andrew of Hungary included speeches by both Charles of Anjou and Manfred in his account of the battle of Benevento. Charles's speech, full of piety and sound scriptural references, was contrasted with a speech by Manfred which relied on a prediction in books of astrology.[97] Similarly, the Annals of St.

---

[95] 'Gesta sanct. mem. Ludovici', p. 425.
[96] 'Annales sanctae Justinae patavini', *MGHS*, xix. 191.
[97] Andrew of Hungary, 'Descriptio', pp. 572–4.

Just saw the fall of Padua to the crusaders of 1256 as proof that 'Ezzelino's astrology and magical prophesies were completely empty'.[98]

It was not only Charles of Anjou's expedition which, in the eyes of pro-papal and Guelf chroniclers, enjoyed divine protection. It was claimed that the Virgin Mary saved the French crusaders of 1285 from an Aragonese ambush on the feast day of her Assumption: 'The most pious virgin Mary, who never deserts her people in times of need, did not suffer her Franks, who had on that day solemnly celebrated her Assumption, to be ambushed on the same day by the blasphemous enemies of God's Holy Church.'[99] The same belief in the protection exercised by Mary was put into the mouth of a French knight, Mahy de Roye, by William of Nangis: 'It is the eve of the Assumption of the sweet virgin maid Mary, who will aid us today. Be of good cheer; for they are excommunicated and cut off from the Faith of the Holy Church. We do not need to go overseas to save our souls, for we can save them here.'[100]

The Italian crusade which most insistently reminds one of the crusades in the Holy Land, both in the enthusiasm with which it was greeted and followed and in the atmosphere of religiosity which enveloped it, was that organized by Pope Alexander IV against Ezzelino and Alberich of Romano between 1255 and 1260.[101] The most vivid descriptions of the crusade were written by Salimbene de Adam and Rolandino Patavino; there is some compensation for their pronounced Guelf bias in the fact that they were present at, or very near, the events which they described. In the early months of 1256 Philip Fontana, Alexander's legate, preached the cross against Ezzelino at Ferrara and at Venice. His preaching was recorded by Salimbene in a moving description which also forms one of the few first-hand accounts of preaching for the Italian crusades.

---

[98] 'Ann. sanct. Just. pat.', p. 167.

[99] 'Chronicon Girardi de Fracheto et anonyma eiusdem operis continuatio', *RHGF*, xxi. 6.

[100] 'Gesta Philippi', p. 535. For French reliance on the aid of the Blessed Virgin Mary, see also 'Ann. sanct. Just. pat.', p. 191.

[101] Preaching against Ezzelino was organized at the end of 1255. See *Cod. dipl. ecel.*, no. 225. Preaching against Alberich was begun in 1258 or 1259. See Salimbene, 'Cronica', pp. 364–6.

Standing in the porch of the Lord's house, the legate began to say his words in a loud voice, and preached briefly . . . He told us that he had been made legate by the lord pope against Ezzelino of Romano, and that he wanted to create a crusading army [*crucesignare exercitum*] to recover the city of Padua . . . Whoever wanted to join his army in that expedition would have an indulgence and a remission and absolution of all his sins . . . And the legate added 'I say to you, for the honour and praise of Almighty God and his blessed apostles Peter and Paul, and of St. Anthony, whose body is venerated in Padua, that if I had in my army only orphans, waifs, widows, and other people who have been tormented by Ezzelino, I would hope to win the victory over that limb of the Devil and son of iniquity'.[102]

People flocked to take the cross and in June the crusading army, consisting of contingents from Venice, Padua, Treviso, Ferrara, and Vicenza, marched on Padua, singing the great hymn 'Vexilla regis prodeunt' 'in honour of the venerable and holy cross', and recruiting more crusaders *en route*.[103] 'Now the Christian people is on the march and advancing in ranks, indeed, to speak truly, now the people of Israel is advancing against the Philistines.'[104] The efforts of Ezzelino's *podestà* at Padua to prepare the city's defence by digging ditches and diverting canals were dismissed as futile, since 'the fortification of sites and the banking-up of water could not oppose the venerable sign of the cross'.[105] Indeed, the 'athletes of Christ and soldiers of St. Peter' took the city rapidly and without difficulty. 'Nobody should attribute the capture of such a very strong city to human strength, but only to God, who is glorious in his perfect works, and by the aid of whose power the starving defeated the well-fed, the unarmed crushed the armed.'[106] In July and August the crusaders moved on to attack another Ezzelinian city, Vicenza. Once again the legate's advance took an almost processional form: 'He rode in Christ's name, with a silver cross preceding him in the usual way and the banner of the cross raised above him.'[107] The army was harassed by

[102] Ibid., pp. 394–5.
[103] See Martino da Canale. 'Cronaca veneta', pp. 428–9; Rolandino Patavino, pp. 103–8.
[104] Rolandino Patavino, 'Chronica', p. 108.
[105] Ibid., p. 103.
[106] 'Ann. sanct. Just. pat.', p. 167.
[107] Rolandino Patavino, 'Chronica', p. 116.

Ezzelino's troops and the crusaders were unable to take Vicenza. There were no more successes comparable to the capture of Padua, and in 1258 Philip Fontana was captured. But the crusade had initiated the downfall of Ezzelino. Preaching against him was continued by the Bishop of Treviso and a new legate, the Archbishop of Embrun, and in 1259 he was captured and killed.[108]

The crusade against Ezzelino of Romano was an expression of popular will, the result of the horror aroused by his cruelty and arbitrary exercise of power. An even more striking example of this is the crusade against his brother Alberich. According to a picturesque account in Salimbene's chronicle, the crusade against Alberich was preached as a direct result of his excesses at Treviso, the centre of his *signoria*. Thirty noble women were compelled to witness the torture and execution of their husbands, sons, and fathers, and were then expelled from the city. They made their way to Venice, where the Pope's legate,[109] after listening to their story, called an assembly of all the Venetians to St. Mark's Square. There he recounted what had occurred and, in a splendid *coup de théâtre*, exhibited the women to the crowd in the same 'dishonoured and unclothed' state in which they had been expelled from Treviso. Aroused to indignation and fury, the Venetians called for a crusade against the perpetrator of such crimes. A crusade was preached on the spot, 'by the authority of Almighty God and of his blessed apostles Peter and Paul and also by the legatine commission which he had from the Holy See', and set in motion a chain of events which led to Alberich's death in 1260.[110]

While the crusade against the Romano brothers was probably unique in the extraordinary religious fervour which it enjoyed,[111] all those who fought for the Church or for the

---

[108] Henry of Embrun was told to stop preaching the crusade in December 1259; but he was not to make people who had taken the cross against Ezzelino redeem their vows, which suggests that these crusaders were to fight Alberich. See *MGH, Epist. pont.* iii, no. 503.

[109] Salimbene calls him Octavian, presumably meaning Octavian degli Ubaldini. At this time, however, the legate was the great canonist Henry of Susa, Archbishop of Embrun. See Martino da Canale, 'Cronaca veneta', pp. 436–9.

[110] Salimbene, 'Cronica', pp. 364–7.

[111] Cf. Jordan's comment that 'jamais peut-être, dans les luttes des partis italiens, la religion n'avait tenu une si grande place'. Jordan also compared the crusade to that against the Albigensians. See *Les Origines*, pp. 93, 98.

Angevin kings between 1254 and 1343 were bolstered by the belief that their cause was that of God. During some of the crusades this identification was also a blow to the morale of the enemies of the Curia. James of Aragon forbad open manifestations of joy after the defeat of the Angevin army at Agosta in 1287 in case it should be interpreted as rejoicing at the frustration of God's cause.[112] The religious implications of the declaration of a crusade could be damaging in a more direct sense: in 1309 Venice was unable to raise mercenaries to fight against the papal army because of the spiritual sanctions involved, and the city had to organize an *ad hoc* citizen army to fight at Ferrara.[113] As the fourteenth century progressed such a reaction became less common. In the 1320s, when Ghibelline opposition to Pope John XXII was very closely associated with the denial of papal power, or at least with the rejection of John's own authority, the crusade indulgence could inspire not fear but derision and contempt. Marsilius of Padua and Louis IV called the crusaders murderers and declared that they would gain not heaven but hell as their reward.[114] When the Genoese Guelfs displayed the crusade bull against Matthew Visconti outside the walls of the city in 1322, the besieging Ghibellines simply shot arrows and threw stones at it.[115]

That the Ghibellines ceased to fear or believe in the crusade indulgence was comparatively unimportant. What mattered was that people continued to take the cross and that the declaration of a crusade transformed the struggle in Italy into a holy war. But to enjoy the benefits of this transformation the Curia had also to suffer the serious religious repercussions of military defeat. Just as the failure of the crusades in Syria led to demoralization in Europe, so the Curia found it hard to explain how God could desert his own cause in Italy, which he did disturbingly frequently. The Annals of St. Just recorded the dismay which followed the loss of Brescia and the capture of Philip Fontana in 1258.

---

[112] Bartholomew of Neocastro, 'Historia sicula', p. 98. Paradoxically, services of thanksgiving were permitted.

[113] See Soranzo, *La guerra*, p. 149.

[114] *Defensor pacis*, Dict. II, Cap. xxvi, 16, pp. 509–10; *MGH, Const.* vi, pt. 1, no. 436.

[115] 'Georgii Stellae Ann. gen.', col. 1047. For later Ghibelline reactions to the crusade, see Larner, *Lords of Romagna*, p. 92.

In addition, some people were thrown into very great confusion by the sudden loss of Brescia and by the capture of the legate, who was a most resolute man and one filled with fervour for the Faith, who worked assiduously from his youth to his old age for the defence of the liberty of the Church against the raging of the tyrants, exposing himself to various dangers. They began to complain vehemently and to wonder at it, that divine providence permits the Church to be afflicted in this way over such a period of time and allows the impious to prosper and grow strong.[116]

There were of course traditional solutions to this old problem. Rolandino Patavino's comment on the capture of Philip Fontana was that 'up to this point fortune blessed with success the Catholic people fighting against the enemies of the Faith in the March of Treviso. But it is appointed by the Lord, that in the affairs of this world there should be but little prosperity, which is not in the end afflicted by adverse events.'[117] Giovanni Villani drew a similar moral from the defeat of the crusading army at Milan in 1323. 'And so it is to be noted, that we can place no firm hope in any human force, since such a powerful and victorious army as that of the Church abandoned the siege of Milan in such a short time because of these events.'[118]

Some people interpreted the facts differently. They clung to the idea that God's favour should express itself in worldly success, and saw the defeat of the crusaders as proof that they had not really been fighting for the cause of God. Thus the continuator of William of Nangis's 'Chronicon' commented that the defeat of a crusading force in Italy in 1326 led to criticism of the Pope's use of the temporal sword, particularly since he had not consulted the cardinals first.[119] Such discontent was fuelled by Ghibelline propaganda. In 1321 Frederick of Sicily wrote that the success of his island kingdom in defeating the attacks of its great and powerful neighbours showed that it enjoyed the protection of God, while the history of the past century proved that the enemies of the pope were not God's enemies.[120] Bartholomew of Neocastro described the despair of Apulian

---

[116] 'Ann. sanct. Just. pat.', p. 171.
[117] Rolandino Patavino, 'Chronica', p. 130.
[118] *Cronica*, ii, p. 277.
[119] 'Continuatio', p. 643. According to the 'Chron. Girardi de Fracheto' (p. 68), this criticism was made *in curia*. It may not therefore have been a widespread reaction.
[120] *Acta arag.* iii, no. 452.

crusaders at the disastrous siege of Agosta in 1287 turning to anger against the Dominicans who had preached the crusade. 'Take away your crosses, which we have worn against the Sicilians, the vile price of our souls, which you gave to us for the shedding of Christian blood.'[121]

The papal Curia knew that its every defeat in Italy benefited its enemies in more than just the material sense. In November 1323 John XXII wrote to Raymond of Cardona to rebuke him for the negligent generalship which had contributed to the defeat of the Guelf army in the summer and autumn. Not only had the cause of God and the Church suffered a setback and the rebels in Lombardy been encouraged in their pride and malignancy, but the crusading zeal of the faithful had been diminished.[122] In the first half of the fourteenth century the crusade was still an effective weapon, and crusade preaching capable of rousing the spirits of Christians; but for this very reason its failure, and therefore its use, was fraught with dangers for the Church.

---

[121] Bartholomew of Neocastro, 'Historia sicula', pp. 97–8.
[122] ASV, Reg. Vat. 112, f. 48^r, no. 212.

Chapter 6

The Financing of the Italian Crusades (1)

It would be unrealistic to attempt to draw a rigid distinction between money collected for the crusades in Italy and that collected for other items of papal expenditure. Careful written accounts were kept both by individual collectors and by the papal chamberlain which divided the money collected into its various sources,[1] but once paid into the *camera apostolica* the money was treated as one sum. Thus, although efforts were made by popes such as John XXII to ensure that money raised for the Holy Land was kept separate from other sources of revenue, they seem to have been exceptional and, as we have seen, usually failed in practice.[2] The history of the financing of the crusades in Italy is therefore, at its widest, the history of papal finance generally in the thirteenth and fourteenth centuries.[3]

On the other hand, certain types of revenue can be clearly associated with the financial needs arising from the Italian crusades. As Baethgen showed in the case of Boniface VIII, what might be termed 'ordinary' sources of revenue—service and visitation taxes, census payments, taxes on bulls, procurations and the revenue from the Papal State and the Comtat Venaissin—were barely enough to cover day-to-day papal expenditure: the running of the Curia, charitable acts, and minor military expenses. For 'extraordinary' expenditure, of which the Italian wars were usually the chief and often the sole item, extra sources of revenue were needed.[4] It is thus quite

---

[1] See, e.g., ASV, Reg. Vat. 112, f. 102^{r–v}, no. 454; *Acta pontificum danica. Pavelige aktstykker vedrørende Danmark 1316–1536*, ed. L. Moltesen *et al.*, i, no. 247.

[2] Cf. Lunt, *Papal Revenues*, i. 121.

[3] The only comprehensive survey of papal finances in the later Middle Ages is Lunt, *Papal Revenues, passim*. Y. Renouard, *Les Relations des papes d'Avignon et des compagnies commerciales et bancaires de 1316 à 1378*, is fundamental for the Avignon period. For the financing of the crusades, see Riley-Smith, *What were the Crusades?*, pp. 45–9.

[4] F. Baethgen, 'Quellen und Untersuchungen zur Geschichte der päpstlichen Hof-u. Finanzverwaltung unter Bonifaz VIII.' *QFIAB*, xx (1928–9), 172–3. For revenue from the Papal State, see Waley, *Papal State*, pp. 252–75; C. Reydellet-Guttinger, *L'Administration pontificale dans le duché de Spolète (1305–1352)*, pp. 85–7; Renouard, *Les Relations*, pp. 24–5.

easy to associate certain sources of revenue, in particular clerical tenths, caritative subsidies, annates, and lay subsidies, with the Italian crusades. Two other considerations help. First, the bulls dealing with these sources of revenue usually specify that the money is needed because of the extra expenses of the Italian wars: 'for the matter of the Kingdom of Sicily', 'for the matter of the Kingdom of Aragon', or 'for the destruction of the heretics and rebels of the Holy See in Lombardy'. Secondly, there is a definite correlation between the mounting expenses of the Curia in Italy and the intensification of taxation or the levying of new taxes. Boniface VIII's conduct of the War of the Vespers was accompanied by an unprecedented series of clerical tenths in Italy and the imperial dioceses on France's eastern borders, while John XXII's wars in central and northern Italy led to continual demands for caritative subsidies and to the systematization of annates as a form of taxation.[5] It is my intention in this chapter first to look at these sources of revenue, and secondly to describe the problems encountered by the popes in levying their taxes for the crusades.

i. THE SOURCES OF REVENUE

(a) *The Clerical Tenth*

The clerical tenth was an income tax levied on the revenues of the Church. The precise nature of the connection between the tenth and the crusade is hard to pin down. Both in its origins in the twelfth century and in its regularization as a form of clerical taxation in 1199 and 1215, it was clearly associated with the needs of the Latin East. This specific association was soon lost. In 1228 Pope Gregory IX introduced a clerical tenth for his struggle with Frederick II, a war which had not yet acquired the status of a crusade and was only marginally connected with the Holy Land.[6] But while the Curia had, with extraordinary rapidity, converted a tax levied for the needs of Christians in the East into a tax levied for an ordinary military campaign in the West, the association of the tenth with the crusade in general

---

[5] Cf. Renouard, *The Avignon Papacy*, p. 102.

[6] Gregory IX, *Reg.*, no. 251. For the significance of the tenth and its reception in England, see W. E. Lunt in *The Valuation of Norwich*, pp. 19–27; id., *Financial Relations*, i. 247–9.

persisted for some time. This was partly because the presentation of the papacy's financial exigencies in the form of a holy war continued to make it easier to justify and collect the tenth; as we have seen, Clement IV and Martin IV even attached the crusade indulgence to its payment.[7] It was not until the last decade of the thirteenth century, with the increasing concessions of tenths to secular rulers for purposes totally unconnected with the crusade, that this association was weakened.

Both the crusade against Manfred and that against the Aragonese and the Sicilians were financed chiefly by the proceeds of the clerical tenth. The contribution of the English clergy to the three-year twentieth levied at the First Council of Lyons in 1245 was converted, in two stages, into a five-year tenth and granted to Henry III in connection with his undertaking to conquer the *Regno* on behalf of his son Edmund. In practice, this money went to pay the mercenaries employed, fruitlessly, by Alexander IV and Urban IV.[8] A three-year tenth levied on the Church in France, Provence, and the imperial dioceses was a feature of the agreement between the Pope and Charles of Anjou in 1263–4.[9] The tenth was decreed by Urban IV in May 1264 and covered the Kingdom of France, Provence, and the provinces of Lyons, Vienne, Embrun, Tarentaise, and Besançon. The tenth was also collected in those parts of the dioceses of Cambrai and Tournai which were ruled by or held of the Countess of Flanders, and Clement IV extended its collection to include part of the County of Hainault, the Venaissin, and the valley of Aosta.[10]

Thanks to the decisive victories of 1266 and 1268, this tenth was the only one needed to establish and maintain Angevin rule in the Kingdom of Sicily. Between 1283 and 1302, on the other hand, the Curia taxed with rigour and frequency a broad sweep of Christendom stretching from the British Isles to Greece, in an unsuccessful attempt to re-establish that rule. Some of these

---

[7] See above, pp. 131–2.

[8] See Lunt, *Financial Relations*, i. 250–90.

[9] *Thes. novus*, ii, cols. 21–2. The negotiations of 1253 between Innocent IV and Charles of Anjou had envisaged 'a subsidy, which the lord Pope will procure from the churches and prelates of the Kingdom of France or Provence'. See Innocent IV, *Reg.*, no. 6819.

[10] Urban IV, *Reg.*, no. 804; *Thes. novus*, ii, cols. 120–2, 255. For the Comtat Venaissin, see also *Acta imperii inedita*, ii, no. 1050.

tenths were ceded to the French crown to pay for its help, while the others financed the Angevin and, after 1295, the Aragonese endeavours to regain the island of Sicily. In September 1283 Martin IV levied a three-year tenth on the French church in support of Philip III's expedition against Aragon on behalf of Charles of Valois. He converted this into a four-year tenth in May 1284 and included in it the provinces of Besançon, Vienne, Tarentaise, Embrun, and Lyons, and the dioceses of Liège, Toul, Metz, and Verdun.[11] In June 1284 he also levied a three-year tenth on the clergy of the *Regno* and Provence. The proceeds of this were to go to Charles I, and the contribution of the *regnicolo* clergy was to include the two-year tenth which they had already granted their king voluntarily. Before his death in March 1285 Martin also levied a three-year tenth on all the provinces of northern and central Italy,[12] and granted a three-year tenth in Majorca to King James of Majorca, who had declared himself an ally of Philip III of France.[13]

Almost as soon as these tenths had been collected, Pope Nicholas IV ordered a series of renewals. In September 1288 he granted a three-year tenth to Philip IV, who had undertaken to continue the Aragonese crusade; the collection of the tenth began in June 1289. In 1289 Nicholas also levied a three-year tenth in Italy and those areas of the imperial dioceses not ruled by Philip IV, on behalf of Charles II.[14] Celestine V, who owed his election largely to Charles II, granted him a four-year tenth in France and the imperial dioceses, and a year's tenth in England.[15] This concession was revoked by Boniface VIII, who between July and October 1295 levied his own three-year tenth throughout Italy, Frankish Greece, and the imperial dioceses, excluding from the latter the Comtat Venaissin and lands over which Philip IV exercised sovereignty.[16] A three-year tenth was again levied in Italy, Provence, and the imperial dioceses in

[11] Martin IV, *Reg.*, nos. 457–8, 583–6.
[12] For the dioceses of Latium, details of this and subsequent tenths were compiled by Giulio Battelli. See *Rat. dec. Italiae. Latium*, ed. G. Battelli, pp. x-xviii.
[13] Martin IV, *Reg.*, nos. 587–90, 549; Honorius IV, *Reg.*, no. 12 (referring to the levy of a tenth by Martin IV).
[14] Nicholas IV, *Reg.*, nos. 613, 615, 991–1004, 1142–52. The tenth in Italy was only extended to imperial Tuscany in 1290. See Nicholas IV, *Reg.*, nos. 2136–7.
[15] *Ann. eccles.*, ad ann. 1294, no. 15, xxiii, pp. 139–40.
[16] Boniface VIII, *Reg.*, nos. 369–70, 497.

October 1298, and in Italy, Sardinia and Corsica, and the Frankish church in Greece and Crete in August 1301.[17] Boniface also levied a three-year tenth on the English and Irish churches in February 1301, ceding a half of the collected money to Edward I. In October 1308 Clement V ordered an inquiry into the collection of a tenth levied by Boniface in the provinces of Cologne and Trier for the crusade against the Sicilians, but there is no trace of this tenth in Boniface's own registers.[18]

Boniface VIII also granted tenths to his allies outside the Italian peninsula for their services against the Sicilians. To pay for James II's campaigns against his brother Frederick the clergy of the kingdoms of Aragon and Valencia were taxed for a tenth for four years in February 1297 and for two years in April 1300.[19] Boniface's plans for Charles of Valois involved the French prince in Sicilian affairs and he was granted a one-year tenth in France and the provinces of Lyons, Vienne, Besançon, and Tarentaise in November 1300. This was followed in September 1301 by a three-year tenth in the imperial dioceses, but after the débâcle of 1302 this tenth was converted into a tax 'for the burdens and necessities of the Roman church', and its proceeds went to the papal *camera*.[20] In February 1300 Robert of Artois, whom Boniface was hoping to persuade to return to Italy, was offered a three-year tenth in all his lands in the County of Artois and the dioceses of Arras, Cambrai, Amiens, Le Mans, and Thérouanne.[21]

Nor did this series of tenths end with the treaty of Caltabellotta; the diplomatic and financial complications of the war led to the levying of several more tenths in the reigns of Benedict XI and Clement V. Because of their agreements with Boniface VIII, the Curia felt obliged to grant several tenths to James II of Aragon and Charles of Valois for their plans to conquer Sardinia and Constantinople.[22] The war also left the Curia with a substantial financial deficit.[23] In an attempt to restore solvency to the *camera* Clement V appealed for voluntary

[17] Ibid., nos. 2888, 4127, 5079.
[18] Ibid., no. 4482; Clement V, *Reg.*, no. 3611; Lunt, *Financial Relations*, i. 366 ff.
[19] Boniface VIII, *Reg.*, nos. 1679, 3569.
[20] Ibid., nos. 3917–18, 4395; Pope Benedict XI, *Registres*, ed. C. Grandjean, no. 181.
[21] Boniface VIII, *Reg.*, no. 3455.
[22] See below, p. 202. See also Clement V, *Reg.*, nos. 244–6.
[23] Cf. *Rat. dec. Italiae. Apulia-Lucania-Calabria*, p. 363.

tenths. In 1310 he asked the clergy of the *Regno* for a double tenth, and, also in 1310, the clergy in the provinces of Tarentaise, Embrun, Vienne, and Besançon granted the Pope a three-year tenth.[24] In 1311 the Bishop of Silves, acting through his proctors, promised to pay the Pope two tenths.[25]

The clerical tenth played a less important role in the Italian crusades of John XXII than it had done in the crusades of his predecessors, but it continued to be levied on a rigorous and extensive scale. Between 1317 and 1320 John XXII granted Robert of Naples a two-year tenth in aid of his imperial vicariate in Lombardy and Tuscany.[26] This was followed by a three-year tenth in June and July 1321; it was to cover all of Italy, Sardinia and Corsica, Frankish Greece and Cyprus, Provence, the Kingdom of Arles, and the other imperial dioceses.[27] In 1323 he asked Edward II of England for a quarter of the two-year tenth which he had recently granted him, and in March 1328 conceded to Robert of Naples a three-year tenth in the *Regno* and a year's tenth in Provence, 'so that he should be strong enough to hold back the invaders of the said kingdom and land'.[28] In April 1329 a three-year tenth was levied in Scotland and a two-year tenth in the province of Nicosia in Cyprus.[29] In 1330 there was another arrangement with the King of England, by which a four-year tenth in England, Wales, and Ireland was divided equally between *camera* and exchequer.[30] The clergy in the Papal State faced the heaviest burden: they had to pay a one-year tenth in 1328 and a two-year tenth in 1331 and 1333.[31]

Pope Benedict XII, whose expenses in Italy were slight, did

[24] See Clement V, *Reg.*, nos. 7461-2, 7591-4, 8762.

[25] Ibid., no. 10498.

[26] See ASV, Reg. Vat. 111, f. 117ʳ, no. 477; Bock, 'Kaisertum', pp. 216-17.

[27] John XXII, *Lettres communes*, nos. 14289-90, 14294-307, 16138; John XXII, *Lettres secrètes*, nos. 1263-76. Collection of the tenth was suspended in the Kingdom of Naples until 1326, and in Cyprus until 1328. See ASV, Reg. Vat. 113, f. 259ᵛ, no. 1534, Reg. Vat. 114, ff. 279ᵛ-280ʳ, no. 1589.

[28] *Cal. of Entries*, ii. 456; John XXII, *Lettres communes*, nos. 40797-801.

[29] ASV, Reg. Vat. 115, ff. 71ʳ-72ʳ, nos. 429-32; *Cal. of Entries*, ii. 490.

[30] *Das deutsch-englische Bündnis von 1335-1342. I. Quellen*, ed. F. Bock, no. 57. Cf. *Cal. of Entries*, ii. 494-5.

[31] ASV, Reg. Vat. 114, ff. 254ʳ-255ʳ, nos. 1391-2, Reg. Vat. 116, ff. 162ᵛ-163ʳ, nos. 801-3, Reg. Vat. 117, f. 48ʳ⁻ᵛ, nos. 276-7. Reydellet-Guttinger (*L'Administration pontificale*, p. 42), discovered four quittances for the collection of a twenty-fifth of clerical revenues in the Duchy of Spoleto by Bertrand du Poujet and Giovanni Orsini in 1324, 1326, 1327, and 1330. I have not succeeded in finding any other references to this tax.

not levy any tenths for the Curia, but he did grant tenths to secular allies who were carrying on the struggle against Louis IV. The justification for the grant of a two-year tenth to Philip VI in March 1338 was that the French king numbered Louis, heretic, schismatic, and 'manifest enemy of God and the sacrosanct Roman church', amongst his enemies.[32] Philip made considerable propaganda use of Louis's heresy, as well as of the idea that the Anglo-French conflict stood in the way of his planned crusade.[33] In 1339 Benedict granted a two-year tenth to Robert of Naples in the *Regno*, Provence, and Piedmont, in order to reconquer Sicily and, if the need should arise, defend the Kingdom of Naples against an invasion by Louis IV.[34]

(b) *Caritative Subsidies*

In theory, caritative subsidies were donations to the pope by the clergy which were made voluntarily, on behalf of a cause which affected the whole Church. In practice the clergy rarely felt free to refuse a request, though it is difficult to be sure how much pressure was applied. Both Mollat and Renouard considered that the clergy were compelled to give something, but that the amount given and the nature of the gift were left to the donor to decide.[35] There were certainly varying degrees of compulsion. In August 1288 Nicholas IV asked the clergy and Orders of the *Regno* to give up a year's tenth to the defence of the realm; if they did not do this voluntarily they would be compelled to do so.[36] This was clearly only a step away from the tenth. Similarly, the Bishop of Vicenza, who collected Boniface VIII's subsidy from the French church in 1298–9, was told that if persuasion failed, clerics were to be suspended and summoned to appear before the Pope.[37] Even when the subsidy itself was granted voluntarily, the full range of ecclesiastical penalties was threatened

---

[32] Pope Benedict XII, *Lettres closes, patentes et curiales se rapportant à la France*, ed. G. Daumet, no. 420.

[33] See Henneman, *Royal Taxation*, pp. 114, 129.

[34] ASV, Reg. Vat. 127, ff. 139ᵛ–141ᵛ, no. 199.

[35] See C. Samaran and G. Mollat, *La Fiscalité pontificale en France au xivᵉ siècle (période d'Avignon et Grand Schisme d'Occident)*, p. 56; Renouard, *Les Relations*, p. 28. Cf. Lunt, *Papal Revenues*, i. 80–1.

[36] Nicholas IV, *Reg.*, nos. 617–18.

[37] Boniface VIII, *Reg.*, no. 2887.

and employed to ensure its payment.[38] Moreover, John XXII in particular demanded payment as quickly as possible. In the autumn and winter of 1325–6 he wrote several times to the archbishops of Saragossa and Tarragona urging them to put forward the collection dates of the subsidies which their clergy had promised.[39]

The first appeals for subsidies for the Italian crusades after 1254 came from Urban IV. In January 1262 he sent Leonard, Precentor of Messina, to England to exact a subsidy for the needs of the Church, 'and especially for the matter of the Kingdom of Sicily'. England was chosen because, technically, Henry III was still involved in the Sicilian issue.[40] In June 1264, as Manfred launched his most determined attack on the Papal State, a similar but more dramatic appeal for aid was issued to dioceses throughout Spain, Portugal, and southern France.[41] Urban's appeals were the last until Boniface VIII, who asked for a subsidy from the French church in October 1298 to help pay the heavy and simultaneous expenses of the Colonna crusade and James II's fleet against Sicily.[42] This appeal brought substantial returns. The provincial Council of Auch and others granted Boniface a year's tenth, and in April 1300 he made a conditional grant of a half of the proceeds to Charles of Valois.[43] In 1296 Boniface also permitted Charles II to ask for a subsidy from his clergy to pay for his campaigns 'against his enemies and those of the Roman church', permission which he reiterated in 1302 when asked by Charles to allow him to levy a clerical subsidy in Provence.[44]

It was not until the reign of John XXII, however, that the caritative subsidy became a major source of revenue for the Italian crusades.[45] From April 1324 until the end of his reign

[38] See, e.g., ASV, Reg. Vat. 113, f. 222ᵛ, no. 1307, f. 225ᵛ, no. 1326, Reg. Vat. 115, f. 159ʳ, no. 920, f. 20ʳ, no. 1106.

[39] ASV, Reg. Vat. 113, f. 234ᵛ, no. 1373, f. 236ʳ, no 1382, f. 237ʳ, no. 1388, f. 237ᵛ, no. 1391, f. 238ʳ⁻ᵛ, nos. 1396–7, ff. 283ᵛ–284ʳ, no. 1673.

[40] Urban IV, *Reg. Cam.*, nos. 124–5; Lunt, *Financial Relations*, i. 227–8. The grant of the Kingdom of Sicily to Edmund was not formally revoked until July 1263.

[41] Urban IV, *Reg. Cam.*, nos. 463–4, 468–70. The area to be covered consisted of the kingdoms of Castile, León, Portugal, Navarre and Aragon, Catalonia and Gascony, and the provinces of Bordeaux and Narbonne.

[42] Boniface VIII, *Reg.*, nos. 2886.

[43] Ibid., nos. 3471, 3650.

[44] Ibid., nos. 1467, 4612.

[45] For subsidies collected by Clement V, see his *Reg.*, nos. 10538–9.

John appealed to the whole of the Church for subsidies with which to fight the Italian heretics and rebels. His most urgent appeals were addressed to the English, French, and Scandinavian clergy in 1326 in response to a serious financial crisis.[46] The French church alone contributed 300,000 florins between June 1324 and January 1333, and the 'Liber de diversis', together with the papal letters of thanks, tell of constant payments from all over Christendom.[47] That these subsidies were compulsory is undeniable, and the determination and severity with which they were demanded led many contemporaries to see them as a new form of taxation, rather than as the refinement of an old one. Michael Stephani, a proctor of Frederick of Sicily at Avignon, waxed indignant at what he thought was a radical innovation: 'This is certainly a new form of subsidy, because it is unheard of, that a pope should impose a subsidy. It is accepted that he reserves the fruits of vacant benefices, or concedes tenths to princes for the conquest of the lands of the enemies of Christ, but a subsidy has never been imposed by the pope.'[48]

The form of the subsidy varied considerably, from the two-year tenth offered by the lesser clergy of the province of Narbonne to the many individual contributions from prelates—1,000 florins from the Archbishop of York; 1,500 from the Bishop of Bologna; 2,000 from the Bishop-elect of Arras; 3,000 from the Bishop of Paris and the Bishop-elect of Toul; 4,000 from the Bishop of Strasburg; 6,000 from the bishops of Salisbury and Amiens.[49] In 1326 John, Bishop of Lisbon, promised to pay to the *camera* all his episcopal revenues from the time of his provision to the see, in February, to St. John the Baptist's Day.[50] In 1328–9 the archbishops of Tarragona,

---

[46] See 'Continuatio', p. 643.

[47] See John XXII, *Lettres secrètes*, nos. 2006, 2354, 2904–20, 3154–68, 3244–8, 3276–82, 3295, 3303, 3800, 3896; *Acta pont. svecica*, i. 225, 235 ff., 251, 315; *Die Einnahmen*, pp. 103*–6*, 414–15, 422 ff., 488–9, 500 ff.; *Die Ausgaben*, pp. 358–9; P. Gasnault, 'La Perception dans le royaume de France du subside sollicité par Jean XXII "contra haereticos et rebelles partium Italiae"', *Mélanges*, lxix (1957), *passim*.

[48] *Acta arag.* i, no. 273.

[49] John XXII, *Lettres secrètes*, nos. 3545, 4172, 4728, 4470, 5015, 5194, 5467 (cf. nos. 2995, 3253–5, 3348, 3614, 3104); *Codex dipl.*, i, no. 758; Lunt, *Financial Relations*, i, p. 239; Gasnault, 'La Perception', p. 291.

[50] ASV, Reg. Vat. 113, f. 123ʳ, no. 1311. For his provision, see *Hierarchia catholica medii aevi sive summorum pontificum, S.R.E. cardinalium, ecclesiarum antistitum series ab anno 1198 usque ad annum 1431 perducta*, comp. C. Eubel, p. 506.

Saragossa, and Toledo granted the Pope the proceeds of procurations arising from visitations in their provinces for the
period of a year, and Gundisalvus, Archbishop of Braga, ceded
procurations and provincial subsidies.[51] John XXII himself set
an example to the rest of the Church: enormous sums from the
Pope's private treasury were sent to Bertrand du Poujet in
Lombardy.[52]

The monastic and religious Orders furnished large subsidies
for the crusades in Italy. Boniface VIII called on the Templars
for a subsidy of 6,000 gold ounces in 1297. In the following year
the expenses of the Colonna crusade drove the Pope to demand
subsidies of 12,000 florins each from the Templars and the
Hospitallers, and 1,000 marks from the Teutonic knights.[53]
Cluny gave 10,000 florins, while in response to Boniface's
appeal of October the French Cistercians gave 7,000 florins, the
Premonstratensians 6,000.[54] John XXII renewed Boniface's
demands. He asked Cluny and its dependencies for a subsidy
'for the Italian wars' in 1326.[55] They granted two tenths, but
proved slow to pay them: in April 1330 the Pope asked that
provision for the payment of the money, which was urgently
needed, be made at the General Chapter.[56] A comparatively
small sum was paid into the *camera* by the Order's proctor on 26
May.[57] In 1327 the Cistercians voted the Pope a subsidy 'for the
destruction of the heretics and of the enemies of the sacrosanct
Church'. The abbeys in France gave 10,000 florins, those outside it a tenth. Sums which had been paid already by individual
abbots in response to earlier papal appeals were to be deducted
from their contribution.[58] In the following year the Cistercian
abbots were again asked, when about to meet in General

[51] ASV, Reg. Vat. 115, ff. 160ᵛ–161ʳ, nos. 933–4, ff. 163ᵛ–164ʳ, no. 946, ff. 165ᵛ–166ʳ,
no. 958, ff. 85ᵛ–86ʳ, no. 1460, ff. 197ᵛ–198ʳ, no. 2049.

[52] See E. Göller, 'Aus der Camera apostolica', *RQ.* xvi., 181–5; P. D. Partner,
'Camera papae: Problems of Papal Finance in the Later Middle Ages', *Journal of
Ecclesiastical History*, iv (1953), 59.

[53] Boniface VIII, *Reg.*, nos. 2318, 2323 (in which *florenorum* should read *unciarum*),
2324, 2426–30.

[54] Boniface VIII, *Reg.*, nos. 2803, 3682.

[55] John XXII, *Lettres secrètes*, nos. 2753–4, 2757–66, 2795–822.

[56] John XXII, *Lettres secrètes*, no. 4175. See also *Die päpstlichen Kollektorien in
Deutschland während des xiv. Jahrhunderts*, ed. J. P. Kirsch, pp. 115, 118.

[57] *Die Einnahmen*, p. 553.

[58] *Statuta capitulorum generalium Ordinis Cisterciensis ab anno 1116 usque ad annum 1786*,
ed. J-M. Canivez, iii. 375–6.

Chapter, 'that they should do what will be pleasing to God, and pray to God for the pope'.[59] Their response to this thinly-veiled appeal for money was similar to that of 1327—a block sum of 6,000 florins from the French abbeys, a twentieth from abbeys outside France.[60] The Hospitallers also gave subsidies to John XXII.[61]

(c) *Annates and Intercalary Fruits*

The reservation of annates (a portion of the first year's income of a new incumbent of a benefice) and the associated taxation of intercalary fruits (the revenue accruing to the benefice during the vacancy) together formed the second major benefice tax imposed by the Curia. Like the clerical tenth, annates and intercalary fruits began as an 'extraordinary' form of taxation but, even more quickly than in the case of the tenth, they became a regularized and indispensable source of papal revenue. Annates were associated from the start with the expenses of the Italian crusades. The first significant reservation, that of Clement V in the British Isles in 1306, was occasioned by the financial deficit left by the Sicilian war, while John XXII was to adopt and develop his predecessor's innovation to meet the rising costs of his crusades against the Ghibellines.[62]

It is true that John's Italian expenses played no part in his great three-year reservation of December 1316, 'Si gratanter advertitis', which covered, technically, all Christendom.[63] But they became prominent in the series of reservations which followed. John XXII never again levied a reservation of annates on all benefices which fell vacant. From 1323, however,

[59] John XXII, *Lettres secrètes*, no. 3651.

[60] See *Stat. cap. gen.* iii. 383, 389; John XXII, *Lettres secrètes*, nos. 3764, 3803, 3920, 3995; *Lettres de Jean XXII*, nos. 2370, 2551; Lunt, *Financial Relations*, i. 239.

[61] *Die päpstlichen Kollektorien*, pp. 115, 118; *Die Einnahmen*, p. 523.

[62] For the institution of the reservation of annates, see W. E. Lunt, 'The First Levy of Papal Annates', *American Historical Review*, xviii (1912–13), *passim*; id., *Financial Relations*, i. 486–502.

[63] Text in *Vet. mon. hist. Hung. sacr. ill.* i, no. 682. See also ASV, Reg. Vat. 111, ff. 234ʳ–235ʳ, no. 961, f. 241ʳ⁻ᵛ, no. 979; John XXII, *Lettres communes*, nos. 4934 ff. The reservation arose from the financial chaos caused by Clement V's extraordinary will. See F. Ehrle, 'Der Nachlass Clemens' V. und der in Betreff desselben von Johann XXII. (1318–1321) geführte Process', *Archiv für Literatur-und Kirchengeschichte des Mittelalters*, v (1889), *passim*; Partner, 'Camera papae', pp. 55–6.

he adopted the practice of imposing reservations covering limited areas of Europe, which he continued until his death. In 1323 there was a three-year reservation of annates in Cyprus, and a one-year reservation in northern Italy and the Papal State. Both were needed to meet the costs of the war in Italy, and the collectors of the annates in northern Italy were told to transfer them to Bertrand du Poujet as soon as they were collected, so that he could use the money to pay his troops.[64] In August 1324 the archdioceses of the Kingdom of Arles (Arles, Aix, and Embrun) were covered by a one-year reservation.[65] From 1325 onwards such limited reservations became steadily more frequent. Just as Italy and the imperial dioceses had been taxed most heavily for the tenth by Boniface VIII, so they suffered the most from the new form of taxation. Annates were reserved in northern Italy and the Papal State for over a decade, 1325–36, and the Kingdom of Arles, together with the province of Vienne, was taxed annually from 1326 to 1334, the reservation usually taking place in April.[66] Annates were reserved annually in the other imperial dioceses from 1329 to 1333.[67] The clergy of the Kingdom of Naples seem to have been taxed for only a year, from the end of 1332.[68].

In other areas of Europe taxation of annates was more intermittent. England and Ireland were taxed for four years from August 1329.[69] Annates were reserved for two years in the Scandinavian kingdoms in 1326, for a year in Poland in 1325, and for a year in Spain in 1329.[70] Cyprus was taxed for two years from 1326, and this reservation was prolonged for another two years in 1327. The Kingdom of Hungary was taxed for

[64] ASV, Reg. Vat. 111, ff. 280ʳ–281ᵛ, nos. 1157–8, Reg. Vat. 112, ff. 65ᵛ–66ʳ, nos. 306–7.

[65] John XXII, *Lettres secrètes*, nos. 2171–7.

[66] ASV, Reg. Vat. 113, ff. 142ʳ–143ᵛ, nos. 913–16, 919–20, ff. 156ʳ–157ʳ, nos. 962–3, ff. 301ʳ–302ᵛ, nos. 1747–51, Reg. Vat. 115, ff. 66ʳ–67ʳ, nos. 415–16, Reg. Vat. 116, ff. 163ʳ–164ʳ, nos. 804–5, Reg. Vat. 117, ff. 47ʳ–48ʳ, nos. 274–5; Benedict XII, *Lettres closes et patentes*, nos. 125–30 (northern Italy and the Papal State); John XXII, *Lettres secrètes*, nos. 2779–82, 3548–52, 3826–7, 4142–3, 4521–8, 5130–1, 5452–3 (the Arlelate).

[67] John XXII, *Lettres secrètes*, nos. 3983, 4299, 4312, 4992–3, 5296–7; *Vat. Akten*, nos. 1205–6, 1392, 1627; *Die päpstlichen Kollektorien*, pp. 119–37.

[68] ASV, Reg. Vat. 117, ff. 129ᵛ–134ʳ, nos. 665–6, 673.

[69] ASV, Reg. Vat. 115, ff. 70ᵛ–71ʳ, nos. 427–8, ff. 132ᵛ–133ᵛ, nos. 1757–8.

[70] ASV, Reg. Vat. 113, ff. 302ᵛ–303ʳ, nos. 1752–3, Reg. Vat. 115, ff. 67ʳ–68ᵛ, nos. 417–18, ff. 84ᵛ–85ʳ, nos. 1452–53ᵃ; *Vet. mon. Pol.* i, nos. 345–6.

three years from 1331.[71] In 1327 there was a three-year reservation in the provinces of Mainz and Magdeburg, and in November 1329 a three-year reservation in the province of Cologne, which was subsequently abandoned.[72] Besides these limited reservations, John XXII annually reserved the annates and intercalary fruits of all benefices whose provision belonged to the Holy See, from 1326 to the end of his reign.[73]

Benedict XII seems to have imposed only one levy of annates: in the Papal State for a year in 1335. He did, however, insist on the collection in full of the arrears of the annates reserved by John, as of his tenths and subsidies.[74]

(d) *Other Sources of Crusade Revenue*

Although clerical tenths, subsidies, annates, and intercalary fruits formed the chief sources of papal revenue for the Italian crusades, both the clergy and the laity made contributions in a number of other ways.

First, there were the block subsidies voted by, or imposed upon, the inhabitants of lands subject to the Holy See. These subsidies were in addition to the ordinary forms of taxation associated with papal rule and they were often granted to the pope as spiritual rather than temporal lord, for the defence of the Faith. Thus extraordinary parliaments were held in the Duchy of Spoleto in 1327 and 1328 to raise money with which to fight Louis IV, and in 1326 the people of the Comtat Venaissin, 'both nobles and commoners', contributed a subsidy 'for the destruction of the heretics and rebels of the Roman church in Lombardy'.[75] In 1329 even the abbots of the Roman monasteries were expected to make a contribution to Giovanni Orsini's advance against Viterbo, a matter which 'is known to be of foremost importance to the Roman church and the defence of the Catholic Faith'.[76]

[71] ASV, Reg. Vat. 113, f. 302ʳ, no. 1748, Reg. Vat. 114, ff. 89ʳ–90ʳ, nos. 512–14, Reg. Vat. 116, ff. 164ʳ–165ᵛ, nos. 806–7.

[72] ASV, Reg. Vat. 114, ff. 287ᵛ–288ʳ, no. 1639, Reg. Vat. 115, f. 148ʳ⁻ᵛ, no. 1859; *Vat. Akten*, nos. 1227, 1229, 1336; *Lettres de Jean XXII*, no. 2575.

[73] See Lunt, *Papal Revenues*, i. 95, 100.

[74] Benedict XII, *Lettres closes et patentes*, nos. 125–30, 289–316.

[75] See *Die Einnahmen*, p. 502; Reydellet-Guttinger, *L'Administration pontificale*, pp. 34–5.

[76] 'Romanam ecclesiam deffensionemque fidei catholice dinoscitur principaliter tangere', ASV, Reg. Vat. 115, f. 5ʳ, no. 32.

As individuals, the laity gave money as an act of enjoined or spontaneous penance. Just as criminals were pardoned on condition that they participated in the Italian crusades, so punishment, both civil and ecclesiastical, could be commuted into a financial donation to the crusades. Subjects of Robert of Artois who had been convicted of usury or robbery were to receive absolution in 1300 provided they gave the proceeds of their crimes to Robert or his proctors to subsidize the count's projected expedition in aid of Charles II.[77] A constant source of revenue for the *camera* between 1325 and 1334 was made up of the small sums paid as enjoined penance by merchants, clerics, and others who had passed through cities and regions under ecclesiastical interdict, particularly Ferrara.[78] Similarly, clerics who held benefices uncanonically were permitted by John XXII to keep the profits they had received provided they donated money to the struggle against heresy and rebellion in Lombardy.[79] Communities as well as individuals could contribute money as penance. In 1284 John Cholet imposed a fine of £4,000 *Paris* on the aldermen of Lille because of an attack which had been made on some Dominican friars who came to Lille to preach against Peter of Aragon; the money was to be used to finance the crusade.[80] In 1331 and 1332 the consuls and citizens of Magdeburg were paying to the *camera* a fine of 9,000 florins because of their involvement in the murder of the Archbishop of Magdeburg, Burchard, in 1325. The money 'is to be converted into a subsidy towards the destruction of heretics and of the rebels of the Roman church'.[81]

A particularly apt arrangement, in view of the connection which the Curia made between the Italian wars and the needs of the Latin East, was that concerning men and women who traded, or financed trade, in forbidden items with the Muslims contrary to papal decree.[82] In April 1297 the bishops of Barcelona and Tortosa were given the authority to absolve

---

[77] Boniface VIII, *Reg.*, no. 3454. This was only to be done if the victims of the crimes could not be found first by public announcement. Cf. Brundage, *Med. Canon Law*, p. 186.
[78] *Die Einnahmen*, pp. 327, 329–36, 338, 343, 348, 349, 372, 374.
[79] Ibid., pp. 324, 334, 339, 339–40, 344, 356, 358, 365; Lunt, *Papal Revenues*, ii. 383–4.
[80] Langlois, *Le Règne de Philippe III*, p. 152.
[81] See *Die Einnahmen*, p. 524.
[82] See Atiya, *Crusade*, pp. 17–19, 35, 114 ff.; Luttrell, 'Crusade', pp. 129–30.

those involved in this commerce in Aragon, on condition that the men gave a fifth, the women a quarter, of their profits to the Church, and that the men served for four months in James II's crusade against Sicily, or at least sent suitable substitutes. The financial proceeds of this were to be given to James II.[83] This concession was renewed in 1298 and confirmed in 1299, and Clement V renewed it at James's request in 1305 to subsidize his conquest of Sardinia.[84] In 1329 John XXII told his nuncios in Cyprus to absolve those guilty of trading with Alexandria after receiving from them a subsidy for the defence of the Catholic Faith in Italy. The size of the contribution was to depend on 'the condition of the person and the quality of the offence'.[85] In Spain too those guilty of trading with the Muslims 'contrary to the wording of the decrees and prohibitions of the Apostolic See' were to be absolved by John's nuncio provided they gave a half of the profits to the struggle against heresy and schism in Italy.[86] The ruling on Egypt also applied to the Muslim Kingdom of Granada. In 1327 a Majorcan merchant guilty of trading with Granada did penance by paying a subsidy towards the crusade in Lombardy.[87]

Besides subsidies granted in order to obtain absolution for specific sins, the laity and the clergy also gave money in order to participate in the crusade indulgence. Thus on 16 June 1325 Durandus Mercatoris, a cameral notary and collector, paid into the *camera* sums donated *ex causa devotionis* to the crusade against the Ghibellines by people 'wishing to participate in the indulgences conceded by our lord . . . to those driving out the said rebels and heretics'. He appended a list of the donors, some of whom gave money on behalf of others, particularly near-relatives, as well as for themselves.[88] The proceeds from the 'sale' of the indulgence are recorded in the accounts of Bertrand du Poujet and the Treasurer of the March of Ancona in the

---

[83] Boniface VIII, *Reg.*, nos. 2338–9.

[84] Ibid., nos. 2397, 3109; Salavert y Roca, *Cerdeña*, ii, no. 128.

[85] 'iuxta conditionem persone cuiuslibet et qualitatem delicti', ASV, Reg. Vat. 115, f. 61ᵛ, no. 391. See also Reg. Vat. 115, f. 62ᵛ, no. 395.

[86] 'contra tenores constitutionum et prohibitionum sedis apostolice', ASV, Reg. Vat. 115, ff. 164ᵛ–165ʳ, no. 952. The amount to be given was originally fixed at two-thirds of the proceeds.

[87] *Die Einnahmen*, p. 336. See also ibid., pp. 285–364, *passim*; Lunt, *Papal Revenues*, i. 131–2.

[88] *Die Einnahmen*, p. 325.

1320s,[89] but curiously little evidence survives for the whole period on how great an indulgence was offered and what procedure was followed for its administration.[90]

In striking contrast is the rich detail on the collection of lesser contributions granted by the faithful 'as the Lord inspires them', in return for partial indulgences. Since the twelfth century the laity had donated money to the crusades in the Holy Land by placing it in chests in cathedral and parish churches.[91] There is no evidence for the use of such chests for the crusades in Italy before 1320. But Pope John XXII seems to have favoured the chests as a means of raising money, and he decreed their use for the benefit of such diverse projects as the Armenian crusade and the repair of St. Peter's in Rome, as well as for his crusades against the Ghibellines. From 1321 onwards crusade bulls against the Ghibellines often included a postscript ordering the placing of the chests in churches where the crusade was preached. The higher clergy were expected to pay for the chests, although in 1325 John XXII allowed the prelates of the Kingdom of Portugal to share the expense with the lesser clergy of their dioceses. The chests were equipped with three locks, the keys for which were distributed between the secular clergy, the Orders of friars, and trustworthy local laymen.[92] In 1328 Robert of Naples wrote that the chests were to be large enough to receive gifts of clothing 'and other articles' offered by those without any money, and that registers were to be compiled containing the names and describing the oblations of donors.[93] Robert's demand seems to have been exceptional; the papal letters do not suggest that such administration was called for.

There were other traditional sources of crusade revenue which the Curia also extended to its crusades in Italy. Obscure

[89] See ASV, I et E, no. 62, ff. 90ʳ–91ʳ, no. 49, f. 4ʳ⁻ᵛ, 6ʳ; *Les Archives*, p. 20. Cf., for a later period, ASV, I et E, no. 276, ff. 31ʳ–35ᵛ.

[90] Matteo Villani (*Cronica*, i. 478–9, ii. 72–3), has details on the sale of the indulgence for the crusades of the 1350s.

[91] See Lunt, *Papal Revenues*, i. 115–16. See also 'La Décime de 1274–1280 dans l'Italie septentrionale', ed. M. H. Laurent, in *Miscellanea Pio Paschini. Studi di storia ecclesiastica*, i. 381–91.

[92] See ASV, Reg. Vat. 113, f. 129ʳ, no. 861, Reg. Vat. 115, f. 158ᵛ, no. 918; *Sacr. conc. coll.* xxv, cols. 596–7; John XXII, *Lettres communes*, nos. 16128, 16181–2, 16213, 20381; *Septem dioeceses aprutienses medii aevi in Vaticano tabulario*, ed. F. Savini, pp. 444–6; *Thes. novus*, ii, col. 721; *Vat. Akten*, no. 363; *Vet. mon. hist. Hung. sacr. ill.* i, no. 757.

[93] *Urkunden*, no. 108.

legacies, such as money left 'for pious uses', were allocated to the Italian wars during the crusade against the Sicilians.[94] Some obventions and legacies were given and bequeathed specifically for the waging of crusades against Christian rulers. The proceeds of these were granted to William of Holland in 1249.[95] In 1292 John Cholet, the legate who accompanied the army of Philip III in 1285, left £6,000 *Tours* to 'the matter of Aragon, on condition that Lord Charles, the King of Aragon, sets out with a suitable army into the said realm'. If Charles failed to do so, the money was to be distributed to the poor.[96] In the 1320s and early 1330s there was a flow of such legacies, usually 'for the needs of the Roman church', or 'for the suppression of heresy in Italy'.[97] Money raised from the redemption of vows to take part in the crusades against Frederick II and Manfred was assigned to William of Holland and Charles of Anjou.[98]

The *camera* also received various sums of money which were the direct result of the struggle in Italy. One source for such money was the confiscation of the goods of rebels and heretics, whose property was collected and converted into cash to be sent to the Curia; difficult but financially rewarding inquiries into the possessions of convicted heretics and rebels were made in the Duchy of Spoleto, Lombardy, and Tuscany throughout the 1320s.[99] The Curia also derived considerable income from fines imposed on communes and *signori* when they submitted to the Church. In July 1266 Clement IV ordered the repayment of debts contracted by himself with Francesco Guidi and his partners 'from fines or other revenue of the March of Ancona'.[100] Similarly, in May 1323 the Treasurer of the March

---

[94] Boniface VIII, *Reg.*, nos. 3067, 3453, 5492.

[95] *MGH, Epist. pont.* ii, no. 631.

[96] L. Delisle, 'Mémoire sur les opérations financières des Templiers', *Mémoires de l'Institut national de France. Académie des inscriptions et belles-lettres*, xxxiii, pt. 2, pp. 161–2. For the date of John Cholet's death, see *Hierarchia*, p. 10.

[97] See, e.g., ASV, Reg. Vat. 115, ff. 152ᵛ–153ʳ, no. 1873, Reg. Vat. 116, f. 330ʳ⁻ᵛ, no. 1649, Reg. Vat. 117, f. 36ʳ⁻ᵛ, no. 209; John XXII, *Lettres secrètes*, nos. 3286, 4111, 5525; *Vet. mon. Pol.* i, no. 333; *Die Einnahmen*, pp. 115*–116*.

[98] *MGH, Epist. pont.* ii, no. 631; *Thes. novus*, ii, col. 22.

[99] ASV, Reg. Vat. 115, f. 20ᵛ, no. 1109, Reg. Vat. 116, f. 332ʳ, no. 1657; Reydellet-Guttinger. *L'Administration pontificale*, pp. 76–7. See also Otto, 'Zur italienischen Politik', pp. 220–1.

[100] Clement IV, *Reg.*, no. 788.

was told to use fines to pay troops engaged against Fermo,
Fabriano, and other rebels of the Church, and an Estensi
payment of 15,000 florins was assigned to Bertrand du Poujet
for the war in Lombardy in June 1330.[101]

ii. THE PROBLEMS OF CRUSADE TAXATION

The picture of papal crusade finance presented in the preceding
pages is that of a powerful Curia drawing skilfully and with ease
on the financial resources of both clergy and laity in all areas of
Christendom. From the administrative point of view this is a
realistic portrayal. Throughout the period 1254–1343 the papal
monarchy was becoming a more efficient institution; its central
organs of government and supervision, including the *camera*,
were made more sophisticated, and its control over the Church
was growing.[102] These developments were reflected in crusade
taxation: the introduction of regular taxation to areas of
Christendom which had previously been exempt from all taxes
except those decreed at the great crusade councils, and the
levying of new taxes, such as annates, intercalary fruits and the
more or less compulsory subsidies, would not have been possible
without them. But there were grave attendant problems. First,
the Curia had to deal with clerical resistance to crusade taxation, at national or provincial level. Secondly, it had to face the
demands or the opposition of the secular authorities of
Christendom, at a time when these authorities were increasingly prepared to incur and defy the strictures of the Holy
See. Thirdly, and most importantly, there was the dual problem
made up of rising military costs and the steady diminution of
the revenue which could be collected from the areas most
frequently taxed by the Curia.

Clerical resistance often left documentary evidence of its
existence, either in the form of the lists of complaints (*gravamina*)
presented by the clergy, or in that of the papal response. It is
well charted in particular for the French and English churches.
The French church seems to have put up its fiercest resistance
to the tenth of 1264. This followed a period of heavy taxation,

---

[101] *Codex dipl.* i, nos. 703, 758.
[102] See, e.g., Ullmann, *Short History*, pp. 245–50; Lunt, *Papal Revenues*, i. 10 ff. These
remarks apply particularly to the Avignon period. See, e.g., Guillemain, *La Cour
pontificale*, pp. 277–356 and *passim*.

with a tenth for Louis IX's first crusade, and a series of subsidies for the papal struggle with Frederick II. Innocent IV's
policy of granting French benefices to his Italian supporters
had further embittered relations between the Curia and the
French church, and created a sense of national opposition to
what were seen as increasingly assertive papal demands.[103]

Urban IV must have expected opposition to the 1264 tenth,
since an attempt to raise a hundredth in 1262 in aid of the Holy
Land and the Latin Empire of Constantinople had met with
resistance in France. Several reasons were put forward against
paying the subsidy, including the poor harvests, the truce in the
Holy Land, the obvious fact that no crusade was being planned
and, above all, the numerous financial burdens which the
French church had had to bear on behalf of the Latin East in the
recent past.[104] The hundredth was nevertheless levied in the
following year, 'without the consent of the prelates'.[105] The levy
of the three-year tenth in 1264 naturally led to an even stronger
reaction. With the backing of Louis IX and 'after we had
diligently expounded to them the needs of the Roman and
universal Church and the dangers to the Christian Faith',
Simon of Brie was able to secure the assent of the leading clergy
at councils held at Paris, Clermont, and Lyons in August and
September 1264.[106] Early in the new year, however, archbishops, bishops, and abbots started appealing to the Holy See,
claiming that they had not granted their assent, and arguing
that Simon of Brie's legatine powers had expired at the death of
Urban IV. If they hoped that Clement might annul or modify
the tenth, they were rapidly disillusioned. He confirmed
Simon's powers and told him that he was determined to carry
on with his predecessor's policy.[107]

Nevertheless, collection was held up by the scale of the
resistance, and in July 1265 the Pope had to reply to an appeal
against the tenth from the provinces of Rheims and Lyons. He
pleaded that it was sheer necessity which dictated the actions of
the Holy See, and that the tenth must be collected.

[103] See Berger, *Saint Louis et Innocent IV*, pp. 267–98.
[104] See Eude Rigaud, *Regestrum visitationum archiepiscopi Rothomagensis*, pp. 440–2.
[105] 'Maius chron. lemovicense', p. 770.
[106] Ibid., p. 771; *Acta imperii inedita*, ii, no. 1050. See also Eude Rigaud, *Regestrum*, p. 495; 'Ex annalibus normannicis', *MGHS*, xxvi, 515.
[107] Clement IV, *Reg.*, no. 217; *Thes. novus*, ii, col. 121.

We do not want to skin you or to feast on your flesh, but we cannot and will not break off a matter undertaken for God. We are urged on by love of Christ, by zeal for the Faith, and by the salvation of the Christian people; and since our strength will not suffice for all things, we accept material help from the limbs [of the Church], from whom we do not demand greater compassion than we ourselves have for them, as the searcher of hearts knows.[108]

A note of anger revealed the hopelessness of further appeals. 'So pay the tenth quietly, and pay the hundredth as well, all subterfuge, all exceptions, all objections and appeals placed to one side.'[109] Appeals against the tenth did indeed cease, but its collection met wholesale resistance. Many of the clergy were excommunicated for refusing to pay, and the Pope complained that their obstinacy was slowing down collection.[110] In his recruiting song for the crusade, 'Le Dit de Pouille', Rutebeuf attacked the avarice of the clergy, but in practice their resistance sprang more from lack of funds than from lack of generosity, as the Pope himself acknowledged in his private letters.[111] The situation was aggravated by the procedure adopted by Simon of Brie for collection. There were reports that he was taxing clerics who had taken the cross, that he was demanding the tenth from benefices with less than the minimum stipulated income, £15 *Tours*, and that he was allowing people with no local knowledge to make ludicrously high assessments of income, which were then used for the collection of the tenth. Liberal use was made of excommunication and the secular arm to enforce payment. 'Jesus knows if it was well done', wrote the chronicler of Limoges, 'and although the cardinal was French by birth and had been a chancellor of the King of France and a treasurer of Tours, he had learnt well the Roman art of gnawing at purses. It is impossible to describe the exactions, extortions, and compulsions which were made for that tenth and for his procurations.'[112]

Consequently when, in 1267, Louis IX asked the Pope to grant him a new three-year tenth for his crusade, there was

[108] *Thes. novus*, ii, col. 159.

[109] Ibid., cols. 157–60.

[110] *Thes. novus*, ii, col. 241; Clement IV, *Reg.*, no. 180. See also Andrew of Hungary, 'Descriptio', pp. 563–4; Eude Rigaud, *Regestrum*, p. 536.

[111] Rutebeuf, *Onze poèmes*, p. 51; *Thes. novus*, ii, col. 313.

[112] 'Maius chron. lemovicense', p. 770. See also *Layettes*, iv, no. 5119.

substantial resistance from the French church. Proctors of the cathedral churches convened at Paris and an appeal against the tenth was made to Simon of Brie. When he rejected the appeal, the deans, chapters, and suffragan bishops of the northern French provinces, Rheims, Sens, and Rouen, sent proctors to Clement IV with a list of *gravamina*. They complained about the frequency of taxation, the excommunication and suspension of clerics genuinely unable to pay, and the harsh methods of collection which were used. The French church was being taxed more than any other. The history of the Jews, moreover, taught that the levying of tenths was unpleasing to God; indeed, it was through such exactions that Rome had lost the allegiance of the eastern Church. These written arguments were supplemented by the proctors, who had been commissioned to tell Clement that if the tenth was none the less granted, the chapters would prefer excommunication to payment, as this seemed to be the only way to stop the papal demands.[113]

Under pressure from, or at least with the backing of, Louis IX, Clement IV treated the proctors 'with great severity' and 'hard words'. He had already granted the tenth and had no intention of revoking it;[114] the threat of resistance he regarded as insolence and blasphemy. It would be countered by the full temporal and spiritual powers of the Pope. On 14 September he wrote to the deans and chapters of Sens and Rheims, correcting their history on the causes of the schism between east and west, and reminding them that the conquest of the Kingdom of Sicily, which had obviously enjoyed God's favour, had been largely paid for from the tenth.[115] He also wrote to Simon of Brie that he was to proceed with the collection of the tenth, using if need be the full range of ecclesiastical censures against 'rebels of the Church', whatever their condition or dignity.[116] Behind these fulminations, however, Clement harboured some sympathy towards the suffering of his former colleagues. In August 1267 he promised the province of Auch, which had paid a five-year tenth to Henry III and a three-year tenth to Charles of Anjou,

---

[113] See 'E chronico Normanniae ab anno 1169 ad annum 1259, sive potius 1272', *RHGF*, xxiii. 219–20; *Thes. novus*, ii, col. 522.

[114] The tenth was granted on 5 May, to start as soon as the three-year tenth levied for Charles of Anjou had expired. See Clement IV, *Reg.*, nos. 463–5.

[115] See ibid., no. 595; *Ann. eccles.*, ad ann. 1267, nos. 55–9, xxii, pp. 208–10.

[116] *Thes. novus*, ii, cols. 522–3.

and was now faced with another three-year tenth for Louis IX, that it would not be taxed again for a decade, unless specifically included in a papal bull.[117]

The experiences of the French church in the years 1263–7 were not very different from those of the English clergy in the late 1250s, when the severe taxation of the period of the papal struggle with Frederick II was followed by the five-year tenth which was supposed to finance the conquest of Sicily by Henry III, but was in fact absorbed by the papal *camera*. Heavy taxation accompanied by disingenuousness left a double legacy of distrust which long affected the relations between the English church and the papacy.[118] In 1274 envoys were sent to Lyons to oppose the levy of any tax, which the English suspected would end up financing the Pope's wars in Italy, 'especially since its collectors and receivers are to be appointed by the Apostolic See'.[119] Even John XXII's appeal of 1326 for a subsidy did not win favour at a council held to discuss it. The council decided to reject it, citing as its reasons the internal and external threats to the realm and the burdens by which the English church was already oppressed. The papal appeal had to be reissued in the form of letters to individual bishops.[120]

The organized and coherent opposition to crusade taxation which was manifested by both the French and English churches was exceptional. In most other areas heavily taxed by the Curia, notably Italy and the imperial dioceses, little evidence exists testifying to opposition at regional or provincial level.[121] Fortunately there is one detailed exception in the case of the Kingdom of Sicily. The clergy in the *Regno* and Provence were particularly hard-pressed to pay for the wars of their Angevin rulers, especially during the long and expensive struggle for Sicily. In 1302 both Boniface VIII and Charles II acknowledged that the Church in Provence had borne and was bearing

---

[117] Clement IV, *Reg.*, no. 508.

[118] See Lunt, *Financial Relations*, i. 255–90, 311.

[119] *Documents illustrative of English History in the Thirteenth and Fourteenth Centuries, Selected from the Records of the Department of the Queen's Remembrancer of the Exchequer*, ed. H. Cole, p. 358.

[120] Lunt, *Financial Relations*, i. 238–9.

[121] This silence is particularly surprising when compared to the vociferous complaints received from the Spanish church, which was not even a profitable source of revenue for the papacy. See P. Linehan, 'The *Gravamina* of the Castilian Church in 1262–3', *EHR*, lxxxv (1970), *passim*.

heavy burdens because of the war, though these did not save it from a new subsidy.[122] In the 1290s Boniface had to annul, in the case of the *Regno*, the minimum tax threshold of £7 *Tours* established for the payment of the clerical tenth; such was the poverty of many of the benefices in southern Italy that, while this threshold applied, 'more are exempt from paying this tenth than pay it'.[123]

It is not surprising that the opposition to taxation for which we have evidence came soon after the end of the War of the Vespers. In 1309 Pope Clement V appealed to the clergy in the Kingdom of Naples and in Sicily for a voluntary subsidy for the Hospitaller crusade and the war against Venice.[124] Clement's collectors, William of Balaeto and Bernard Regis, toured the provinces of the *Regno* in the early months of 1310 and recorded in detail the response of several of the provincial councils which they summoned to consider the papal request.[125] A payment of two tenths was asked for. Conza, Acerenza, and Siponto were the only provinces which granted the tenths without objections. Bari, Trani, and Taranto pleaded poverty. The mainstay of the Church's economy in these Adriatic provinces was commerce with Venice, whose merchants rented houses, paid port dues, and bought at a good price the produce which the Church received as tithes. But the merchants, taking fright at the papal decrees against the property and persons of Venetians, had abandoned their Apulian colonies and fled to Venice. Trani would pay only a half of one tenth, and some of the bishops in the province of Bari would only pay one, though others promised two. Taranto and Otranto complained that they were still suffering from the destruction caused by the War of the Vespers, but they granted two tenths when the collectors promised to try to get payment of the second postponed. The province of Brindisi granted both tenths, except for the Bishop of Monopoli, who claimed to be weighed down with debts and could only pay one. Finally, the secular clergy of Benevento promised to pay in full, but the exempt abbots refused, 'because

---

[122] Boniface VIII, *Reg*, no. 4612.
[123] Ibid., no. 5589. In 1301 Boniface reiterated the exemption of benefices in the *Regno* from the clause on minimum earnings. See his *Reg.*, no. 4127.
[124] *Rat. dec. Italiae. Apulia-Lucania-Calabria*, pp. 360–4.
[125] Ibid., pp. 359–60, 364–74. Cf. Clement V, *Reg.*, no. 10462.

there was no mention of the exempt [Orders] in the said apostolic letters . . . and thus they offered nothing and would not promise to give anything, until the exempt were covered by our lord in other letters'.[126]

Clement V's response throws some light on the nature of a 'voluntary' subsidy. The Pope told his collectors to begin collecting the subsidy on 27 May 1310. At this point there was little hint of compulsion; the subsidy was to be collected from those who had promised to pay, 'and those who should promise to pay in future', as well as from the clergy of the province of Benevento, including the exempt abbots.[127] This was followed five days later by a letter ordering that a part at least of the subsidy of two tenths was to be paid by all.[128] In November, on the pretext of resistance from clerics who had earlier promised to pay the subsidy, Clement converted it into a compulsory two-year tenth covering the clergy throughout southern Italy and Sicily. He also asked Robert of Naples and Frederick of Sicily to help the collectors in their work.[129] Thus had resistance proved vain and the promises of the collectors useless. All the clergy could do was to follow the lead of Bishop Philip of Capaccio, who was excommunicated for refusing to pay the tenth.[130] Many did so, and resistance to paying the tenth, by archbishops, abbots, and other ecclesiastics, was still causing Bernard Regis problems in 1313.[131] Fresh difficulties were created by the heavy taxation of John XXII; in 1333, for example, there was a substantial revolt against papal taxes in the province of Benevento.[132]

Unless they had the determined backing of the secular authorities, clerics throughout Christendom were in as weak a position in opposing papal taxation as the bishops of southern Italy. Not only were there very adequate justifications and precedents for the Curia to tax the Church as a whole for a cause which it believed to be of importance to the Church and the

---

[126] *Rat. dec. Italiae. Apulia-Lucania-Calabria*, p. 367.

[127] Clement V, *Reg.*, nos. 6310–11.

[128] Ibid., nos. 6381–2.

[129] Ibid., nos. 6370–1.

[130] ASV, Instr. misc., no. 637. See also *Rationes decimarum Italiae. Campania*, ed. M. Inguanez *et al.*, p. 457.

[131] Clement V, *Reg.*, no. 10532.

[132] ASV, Reg. Vat. 116, f. 235ʳ, no. 1217.

Faith, but there was no real ideological or material platform on which the clergy could oppose the decrees of the Apostolic See or its rigorous and extensive sanctions. Clerical opposition *per se* was not therefore, in most cases, a serious problem; it did not prevent taxes being levied, although it could delay or prolong their collection. Much more serious than the opposition itself was the cumulative effect of the taxation. There can be no doubt that the heavy taxation necessitated by the waging of the Italian crusades had very bad effects on the relations between the papacy and the Church.[133] The terms of clerical *gravamina* show that the clergy increasingly regarded the Curia not as its protector against the secular powers, but as another threat to its revenues. As early as 1267, as we have seen, the French church was threatening a withdrawal of obedience, a move which the Pope could only counter with the crudest threats.[134] In such circumstances there was little or no incentive for an alliance between episcopate and papacy in the face of secular demands for a share of the revenues of the Church. The Curia found this out in its disputes with the secular authorities on clerical taxation. These disputes were of two kinds, both reflecting the growing tendency of lay rulers to regard the revenues of the Church as a national asset. The Angevin, the French, and, during the War of the Vespers, the Aragonese kings all expected the financial support of their clergy when engaged in crusades against the enemies of the Church. On the other hand, princes who were not allies of the Curia in Italy objected to their clergy being taxed to pay for the wars there.

The French crown is the outstanding example of both aspects of the problem. If Philip III embarked on the Aragonese crusade because of his ambitions for his younger son and his admiration for his uncle, Philip IV almost certainly maintained French participation in the crusade after 1285 simply in order to collect the financial reward of the tenth to pay for other projects.[135] In September 1288, when the first tenth had been collected, nuncios of the King approached Pope Nicholas IV at

---

[133] See, e.g., Mollat, *Popes at Avignon*, pp. 329–34; R. Fawtier, *The Capetian Kings of France. Monarchy and Nation (987–1328)*, pp. 214–15.

[134] Clement IV, *Reg.*, no. 595; *Ann. eccles.*, ad ann. 1267, nos. 55–9, xxii, pp. 208–10.

[135] See Digard, *Phillippe le Bel*, i. 26–8, ii. 218–23, for Philip IV's demands of February 1286. See also *RHGF*, xxi. 529–31, for his comments on the cost of the crusades of his father and grandfather and the losses which they had entailed for the French crown.

Rieti for a renewal. The Pope was suspicious of Philip's motives and very conscious of the fact that the French church had been oppressed for 'many years' by the exaction of tenths and by the procurations of papal nuncios and legates, which it had borne with 'laudable patience'. In addition, the grant of a new tenth would prejudice the negotiations in progress for the release of Charles of Salerno. He granted a two-year tenth, but hedged it about with restrictions. The tenth was to be collected by clerics appointed by Nicholas, in a manner laid down by the Pope; the rules of exemption established in the collection of previous tenths were to be strictly observed; the Curia was to dictate how the money would be spent, and if peace was reached while the tenth was being collected, the proceeds were to be at the disposal of the Pope; no tenth was to be levied until Philip agreed in writing to these proposals. Not content with these terms, Philip's nuncios pressed for more concessions, and just two weeks later a new bull was drawn up. A year was added to the tenth and the imperial provinces taxed in 1284 were included in the area from which it was to be collected. But £200,000 *Tours* of the tenth was to be assigned in prearranged stages to the *camera* for 'the burdens and necessities' of the Roman church.[136]

Three years later, in December 1291, Philip asked for a new tenth, together with a renewal of crusade preaching against Aragon in France, but this time his requests were refused outright. Nicholas IV gave a variety of reasons for this. He was anxious not to offend crusaders like Edward I, who would be dismayed at the Pope adding fuel to the war in Italy at a time of crisis in the Latin East; he had hopes that the war might be ended by a settlement soon; he did not wish to burden the French church, which was already complaining about the 'grave injustices' which it had suffered and was suffering daily at the hands of the royal officials.[137] But in addition to these reasons there must have been an awareness of how little the French king had done since 1285 in prosecuting the crusade against Aragon, as well as annoyance at his dilatoriness in paying the £200,000, £37,000 of which was still not paid in

136 Nicholas IV, *Reg.*, nos. 613, 615. See also Digard, *Philippe le Bel*, i. 58–62.
137 Nicholas IV, *Reg.*, no. 6849.

1297.[138] In his diplomatic negotiations with Charles II, Philip IV tried to get the Angevin to persuade the Pope to remit the £200,000, or to grant Philip another tenth to cover it. As late as February 1293 he was hoping to receive another tenth on the basis of French participation in the crusade against the Aragonese.[139] But the subsidies which Philip was to exact from the French clergy in the 1290s were to have other justifications, notably 'the defence of the realm'.[140]

The Curia was not again able to involve the French kings in the Italian crusades. Not only did Philip IV and his successors fail to respond to the frequent appeals for aid from the Curia and from their Angevin cousins, they also resented the taxation of the French church for the crusades in Italy. Philip IV succeeded in establishing a royal hegemony over the tenth supplied by the French clergy in the last decade of the thirteenth century. He and his sons secured the bulk, if not the whole, of the French contribution to the Vienne tenth, and this was followed by a series of tenths liberally granted by the popes for the crusade plans of the French court or simply for 'the needs of the realm'.[141] In Charles IV's reign the proceeds of the clerical tenth normally accounted for more than 20% of the annual income of the French treasury.[142] After the failure of 'Clericis laicos' the Curia accepted the loss of the French tenth, but clashes continued over other sources of crusade revenue which the Pope tried to export to Italy. This was particularly serious during the crisis of 1296–7, when the King forbad the export of precious metals, jewels, and all forms of negotiable currency and documents, a move intended to hamstring papal–Aragonese negotiations.[143] In September 1296 James II of Aragon complained that the £15,000 *Tours* which Boniface VIII was paying him could not be transferred from Montpellier by the bankers because of Philip IV's decree. The personal

---

[138] See Boniface VIII, *Reg.*, nos. 2318, 2327.

[139] Digard, *Philippe le Bel*, i. 109–10, ii. 275–8, 279–80, 285–6.

[140] See J. R. Strayer, 'Defense of the Realm and Royal Power in France', in his *Medieval Statecraft, passim*; J. R. Strayer and C. H. Taylor, *Studies in Early French Taxation*, pp. 8, 25 ff.

[141] See Samaran and Mollat, *La Fiscalité pontificale*, pp. 13–16. Their view that papal policy was one of complete surrender to the demands of the French crown was modified by Tabacco, in *La casa di Francia*, pp. 139–51.

[142] See Henneman, *Royal Taxation*, p. 37.

[143] See Boase, *Boniface VIII*, pp. 139 ff.; Digard, *Philippe le Bel*, i. 271–2.

intervention of Charles II was needed to persuade Philip to release legacies for the Holy Land, and means had to be thought of to avoid the opposition of the King's officials to the transport of sums from France to Provence.[144] As late as December 1297 the Francisi were still using royal opposition as the excuse for their failure to obey a papal order to pay £2,262 to Charles II.[145]

Another clash occurred in 1326 when John XXII appealed to the French church for a subsidy. In October Charles IV wrote to his seneschal at Beaucaire, and to all other royal seneschals and baillis, forbidding its collection and ordering the restitution of what had been collected so far. The appeal, he claimed, was unprecedented and impossible to meet. All the spare revenue of the Church was needed for the defence of the realm against the English.

We have several wars at the moment in many places, and it is essential that not only the nobility, but also the clergy, respond to necessity, and that they make large contributions and undertake heavy expenses for the defence of our lands, and theirs, and of the common good. This they will not be able to endure at the same time as providing the said subsidy.[146]

The Pope expressed his amazement at the King's opposition to a subsidy which had been requested 'for the defence of the Catholic Faith and the destruction of heretics and heresy'. In the past, he wrote, subsidies had frequently been levied in France for this purpose on the French laity as well as the Church, and there had been no complaints. Long-drawn-out negotiations ensued. In March 1327 Charles rescinded his order and the Pope was allowed to collect the subsidy..[147] The price of royal permission was high. The Pope accepted the monopoly of the French crown in collecting tenths in France, undertook to continue granting such tenths, and in return was allowed to collect subsidies for his own needs. It was the clergy who suffered. The Benedictine monk of St. Denis who continued the chronicle of William of Nangis complained that the

---

[144] *Acta arag.* i, no. 22; *Forschungen*, iii, nos. 279, 283; Boniface VIII, *Reg.*, no. 5492.
[145] Ibid., nos. 5494–5.
[146] 'Dagli *Instrumenta miscellanea* dell'Archivio segreto Vaticano', ed. A. Mercati, *QFIAB*, xxvii (1936–7), 141.
[147] Ibid., pp. 153–5; Gasnault, 'La Perception', pp. 277–83; id., 'Le Subside caritatif de 1326. Note additionnelle', *Mélanges*, lxxviii (1966), *passim*.

agreement of 1327, which he described as a cynical division of spoils, was the downfall of the French church. 'And so while one of them is shearing the wretched Church, the other skins it.'[148] Pope and King were not, however, equal partners, and the setbacks which the papacy had suffered over the previous half century were reflected in the fact that papal collectors were frequently harassed by royal officials.[149]

The Pope's loss of the French tenth was, as so often, mirrored by events in England. The débâcle of Henry III's Sicilian adventure was the last occasion on which a pope was able to extract a complete tenth from the English clergy for the waging of crusades in Italy. Edward I was almost completely successful in his financial negotiations with the Curia. He secured the bulk of the 1274 tenth in the face of papal attempts to export it for the war in Sicily. He also, by a series of very dexterous and unscrupulous moves, secured more than two-thirds of Boniface VIII's tenth of 1301.[150] It is true that the situation in England was not as serious as it was across the Channel; the Pope was still able to levy tenths and demand annates in England, but a half or three-quarters of these had to be ceded to the exchequer.[151]

Most tortuous of all the papacy's financial dealings with secular authorities in connection with the Italian crusades were those with James II of Aragon. In February 1297 Boniface VIII granted the King a four-year tenth to cover the expenses of his fleet and soldiers. In September James petitioned for the inclusion of Majorca in the tenth, the taxation of the military Orders, and the exemption of the Kingdom of Aragon from the provisions laid down in 'Clericis laicos'. He was basing such demands on Boniface's recent concessions to Philip IV, but his petitions were rejected and the inadequacy of the tenth was

---

[148] 'Continuatio', p. 643. Cf. 'Chron. Girardi de Fracheto', p. 68.

[149] See 'Compte d'un subside fourni par le diocèse de Bourges au pape Jean XXII', ed. M. De Laugardière, *Mémoires de la Société des antiquaires du Centre*, xxxiii (1910), 104–5; *Les Collectories pontificales dans les anciens diocèses de Cambrai, Thérouanne et Tournai au xive siècle*, ed. U. Berlière, p. 19; Mollat, *Popes at Avignon*, p. 331.

[150] See 'The Account of a Papal Collector in England in 1304', ed. W. E. Lunt, *EHR*, xxviii (1913), *passim*; W. E. Lunt, 'Papal Taxation in England in the Reign of Edward I', *EHR*, xxx (1915), *passim*; id., *Financial Relations*, i. 311–46, 366–81.

[151] See Lunt, *Financial Relations*, i. 411–18, ii. 75–88; id., 'Clerical Tenths levied in England by Papal Authority during the Reign of Edward II', in C. H. Taylor (ed.), *Anniversary Essays in Medieval History by Students of Charles Homer Haskins, passim*.

used by James to plead poverty as the excuse for his poor performance in the military activities of the next two years.[152] Payment of the tenth was, moreover, suspended when James failed to appear in the theatre of war in 1297, and was renewed at the end of 1297 on condition that James promised in writing to use the money only for the purposes of the Sicilian war.[153] Nevertheless, negotiations were begun during the last year of the tenth (1300–1) for its renewal by the Pope. Boniface was ready to grant a three-year tenth when news reached him of the decision of the court at Barcelona not to stop Catalans setting out to help Frederick of Sicily or to trade with Alexandria. In anger the Pope reduced the tenth to two years.[154]

No sooner had the Sicilian war ended than James II started pressing the Curia to grant him a tenth in his lands 'for a suitable period of time' to help him to undertake the conquest of Sardinia and Corsica.[155] A three-year tenth was granted by Boniface VIII in April 1303 and, despite the opposition of the Aragonese clergy, was confirmed by Benedict XI.[156] In October 1305 Clement V, under pressure from James, granted him another tenth, of four years, for the conquest of Sardinia. Like Boniface VIII, Clement related this to the reconquest of the Holy Land, though he failed to expound the association in detail.[157] John XXII was less susceptible to the obligations of a twenty-year-old treaty, the terms of which James himself could hardly be said to have fulfilled. In 1323 he refused to grant James II the contribution of the Aragonese clergy to the Vienne tenth, citing the scandal which would be caused by the Holy See subsidizing a war between Christians with money raised for the Holy Land.[158] He granted James a tenth in 1324, but refused him again in 1328 because the clergy of Aragon were already being heavily taxed for the defence of the Faith in Italy.[159]

[152] Boniface VIII, *Reg.*, nos. 1679, 2384; *Acta arag.* i, no. 30. James also tried to secure exemption from 'Clericis laicos' in 1300. See *Acta arag.* i, no. 59.

[153] Boniface VIII, *Reg.*, no. 2385.

[154] Ibid., no. 3569; *Acta arag.* i, no. 56. See also ibid., i, nos. 58–9.

[155] Salavert y Roca, *Cerdeña*, ii, no. 42.

[156] Ibid., nos. 48–9; *Acta arag.* i, no. 113. See also ibid., i, no. 122.

[157] Salavert y Roca, *Cerdeña*, ii, nos. 128–30.

[158] *Acta arag.* ii, no. 500. John added that he was prepared to grant the tenth for an expedition 'against the enemies of the Faith'.

[159] ASV, Reg. Vat. 113, f. 112^{r-v}, no. 792, Reg. Vat. 115, ff. 169^v–170^r, no. 975.

The intricacies of the papacy's financial relations with the Angevin kings will be described in the next chapter, but it is worth noting here that the popes did not accede to every Angevin request for clerical subsidies. In May 1322 John XXII refused Charles of Calabria a new tenth, allowing him only more favourable terms for the repayment of the three years of the Vienne tenth which the Angevin monarchy had been granted as a loan. In the same year a subsidy from the clergy was denied to the Angevin prince, John of Gravina, and Philip of Taranto's requests for tenths and subsidies were consistently refused because of the priority of the Italian wars.[160] In February 1340 Benedict XII refused to grant Robert of Naples a tenth in Tuscany, because he had recently granted him a tenth in the *Regno* and Provence, and the granting of a Tuscan tenth would encourage other Catholic kings to press their claims.[161] When tenths were conceded, they were not always granted willingly or at the first request. An Aragonese proctor reported that Boniface VIII used 'many harsh, virulent, and abusive words' against Charles II before conceding him the tenth of 1301.[162]

In its relations with other princes, and with prelates of the Church, the Curia was even less willing to accede to financial requests which conflicted with its own needs. The complaints of the German king, Rudolf of Habsburg, about the taxation of the imperial dioceses in aid of Philip III and Philip IV were countered in 1285 and 1290 with comments on the expensiveness, sanctity, and universal importance of the cause which the French kings had taken up.[163] Philip of Valois and Otto of Burgundy were denied the financial support of the clergy in France in the 1320s because they were already being heavily taxed by both Pope and King.[164] In March 1330 Archbishop Peter of Saragossa was refused papal permission to exact a subsidy from his provincial clergy for his forthcoming expenses in the Granada crusade because the clergy were paying sub-

---

[160] ASV, Reg. Vat. 111, f. 117^{r–v}, no. 477, ff. 260^v–261^r, no. 1088, Reg. Vat. 113, f. 59^r, no. 454, f. 264^v, no. 1565, Reg. Vat. 115, f. 148^r, no. 876.
[161] Benedict XII, *Lettres closes et patentes*, no. 2693.
[162] *Acta arag.* i, no. 71.
[163] Honorius IV, *Reg.*, no. 476; Nicholas IV, *Reg.*, no. 4312.
[164] John XXII, *Lettres secrètes*, nos. 2435, 3296, 3916.

sidies both for the Pope's wars in Italy and for King Alfonso's own crusade expenses.[165]

Clearly the response of the Pope to the demands and objections of the secular authorities was regulated by the strength of the petitioner and the extent to which the Curia had need of his services. If the Curia found its negotiating position *vis-à-vis* the French and English kings weakening, it was still able to engage in and win diplomatic skirmishes with the kings of Germany, Aragon, and Naples. The increasingly successful attempts made by the French and English kings from the end of the thirteenth century to tax the Church have been interpreted as a reaction to the fact that the papacy was itself taxing the Church to pay for crusades against Christian rulers.[166] This is an erroneous interpretation, if only because such a reaction would have been shared by rulers who were notably less successful in their taxation policies. The French and English monarchies were able to achieve what others could not because of their own strength, which they were driven to employ with skill and ruthlessness by their soaring military expenses. They were aided in this by the disaffection and demoralization of the clergy which was caused by heavy papal taxation, but this was only a secondary factor. It was the growing power and prestige of monarchy which led to the subjugation of the clerical estate to the crown, not the actions of the papacy.

The Curia continued to extract large sums of money from the clergy of both France and England for the Italian wars. The French clergy contributed at least 300,000 florins in caritative subsidies to John XXII, while revenue carried from the British Isles to Avignon by cameral bankers between 1317 and 1342 totalled 438,388 florins and 6,000 marks sterling.[167] This compares favourably with the 55,750 florins carried by the bankers from Cyprus, one of the most heavily taxed of the churches which John XXII succeeded in bringing within the sphere of regular crusade taxation, between 1328 (the first recorded entry) and 1343.[168] But when the situation of 1343 is compared with that of a century earlier the diminution of

[165] ASV, Reg. Vat. 115, f. 193ʳ, no. 2018.
[166] See above, p. 7
[167] See *Die Einnahmen*, p. 104*; Renouard, *Les Relations*, pp. 131–4.
[168] See ibid., pp. 164–5.

revenue from France and England is striking. The loss of the
French tenth was exceptionally severe. Including the imperial
dioceses, it was worth about £260,000 *Tours* a year. The whole
of Boniface VIII's tenth of 1301–4, which extended to the
imperial dioceses, Italy, Provence, and Achaea, only resulted
in about £130,000 *Tours* (266,000 florins).[169]

These developments in France and England were particularly serious because the Curia was already having difficulties
in meeting its financial needs when they began. As early as 1265
Pope Clement IV lamented that the existing sources of papal
revenue were too few.

No treasure lies concealed here, nor do we intend to create one in the
ways suggested by many men. Look around you at the regions of the
world in turmoil, and you will discern the reasons for our poverty.
England resists us, Germany scarcely obeys us, France sighs and
complains, Spain is not sufficient for her own needs, Italy does not
help, but demands help, and where can the Roman pontiff, if he fears
God and has respect for men, find help in soldiers or in money for
himself or for others?[170]

Clement's successors found themselves in an even more serious
plight. The financial pressure under which John XXII worked
throughout virtually the whole of his long pontificate can be
gauged from a letter written to Charles of Calabria in 1322,
denying him additional financial aid. The *camera*, John wrote,
was so hard pressed by the burdens of the conflicts in
Lombardy, the March of Ancona, and the Duchy of Spoleto,
'not to mention Ferrara', that 'when we look around us, we do
not know where to find the money to sustain them any
longer'.[171]

This impecuniosity was created by rising military costs and
declining revenue. Warfare was becoming more expensive
largely because of increasing reliance on mercenaries, a trend
occurring all over western Europe but particularly noticeable in
Italy, seed-bed and battleground of long, destructive wars. In
the Papal State and the Kingdom of Sicily, as elsewhere, feudal

---

[169] See Clement V, *Reg.*, nos. 1151–2, 2271. For the value of the French tenth, see
RHGF, xxi. 545–57; Boase, *Boniface VIII*, p. 141.

[170] *Thes. novus*, ii, col. 174. Cf. ibid., col. 313.

[171] 'oculos levantes in circuitu non videmus unde ista sustinere diutius valeamus',
ASV, Reg. Vat. 111, f. 117ʳ, no. 477.

military service was giving way to the use of paid troops, with serious financial consequences for those in authority. The actual cost of hiring mercenaries seems to have fallen steadily throughout the period, but this was more than offset by the fact that conflicts lasted longer and often continued during the winter months.[172] At the same time, many of the papacy's traditional sources of revenue, notably Italy, the Kingdom of Arles, and the other imperial dioceses, were yielding diminishing returns. This was partly due to the continual taxation to which they were subjected, which was in the long run self-defeating.[173] More important were the poor harvests, trade contraction, and warfare which marked the end of the thirteenth century and the beginning of the fourteenth. The areas which suffered most were those without strong civil authorities, and it was these which, for political reasons, were taxed most heavily by the Curia. The collectors' accounts for northern Italy and the Rhineland reveal that clerical revenues were severely affected by economic stagnation and civil disorder.[174]

The introduction of new forms of taxation, and the attempts made to tax new areas of Christendom, were thus innovations forced on the Curia by diminishing resources and rising expenses.[175] But the levying of the taxes, and the reconcilement to these taxes of the clergy and their secular lords, constituted only the first stages in the lengthy process of financing the Italian crusades. The money had still to be collected, transported to the *camera* and to Italy, and employed there to pay the Angevin and papal crusading forces.

---

[172] See *Deutsche Ritter*, i. 123–5; Mallett, *Mercenaries and their Masters*, pp. 15–24; Waley, *Papal State*, pp. 287–90; Waley, 'Papal Armies', pp. 1, 15, 19, 21.

[173] See Reydellet-Guttinger, *L'Administration pontificale*, p. 75.

[174] See, e.g., *Rationes decimarum Italiae. Tuscia ii. Le decime degli anni 1295–1304*, ed. M. Giusti and P. Guidi, *passim*; *Rationes decimarum Italiae. Aemilia. Le decime dei secoli xiii–xiv*, ed. A. Mercati *et al.*, pp. 43–54, 213–20, 225–68, 356–91; *Rationes decimarum Italiae. Venetiae-Histria-Dalmatia*, ed. P. Sella and G. Vale, pp. 73–102, 215–66, 267–96, 403–9; 'La decima pontificia del 1301–1304 in Toscana. Un nuovo codice', ed. M. H. Laurent, *Rivista di storia della Chiesa in Italia*, iii (1949), 60–1, 64; 'La Décime de 1274–1280', p. 397; *Die päpstlichen Kollektorien*, pp. 5–27, 115–18. For declining ecclesiastical revenues in northern Italy, see also C. M. Cipolla, 'Une Crise ignorée. Comment c'est perdue la propriété ecclésiastique dans l'Italie du nord entre le xie et le xve siècle', *Annales*, ii (1947), 318–22.

[175] Cf. Lunt, *Papal Revenues*, i. 10–12.

Chapter 7

The Financing of the Italian Crusades (2)

i. THE COLLECTION OF CRUSADE REVENUE

Most of the period 1254–1343 falls between two important developments in the procedure of the collection of crusade revenue. In 1274 Gregory X placed the collection of the clerical tenth on a regular basis by dividing all Christendom into twenty-six collectorates and establishing rules for the assessment of income and for the exemption of certain religious foundations and certain types of revenue. In the mid-fourteenth century Clement VI started to set up permanent 'apostolic collectors' in the successors to Gregory's collectorates, thus establishing the centralized machinery which endured until the Reformation.[1] The period between these two developments was a transitional one, when the need for a more systematic taxation of the Church was making itself felt but the machinery for that taxation had not yet been conceived or applied.

Even the best scholars of papal finance have hesitated to depict the machinery for the collection of revenue as methodical or systematic.[2] In the case of the collectors, for example, it is not possible to see either clear continuity or development in the personnel used before Clement VI's innovations. As in the preaching of the crusade, the Curia tended to use all its available resources of manpower. In some cases cardinal-legates or nuncios were sent out to collect, or those already on the spot were told to organize or supervise collection. In 1264 the French clergy were ordered to obey the instructions of Simon of Brie on the payment of the tenth for Charles of Anjou, and the same procedure was employed in 1283, when John Cholet was legate and a tenth was levied in France for the crusade against the Aragonese. Similarly, Cardinal Gerard of Sabina supervised the collection of the tenth in the *Regno* in 1284, and Boniface

---

[1] See *Rationes decimarum Italiae. Tuscia i. La decima degli anni 1274–1280*, ed. P. Guidi, pp. xiii–xvii; Samaran and Mollat, *La Fiscalité pontificale*, pp. 69–75; Lunt, *Papal Revenues*, i. 40–4.

[2] See, e.g., Lunt, *Papal Revenues*, i. 41–2.

VIII sent a cardinal-legate to the *Regno* to collect his tenth of
1295.[3] Bertrand du Poujet organized the collection of the 1321
tenth in the dioceses of Pavia and Piacenza, and throughout the
period of his Italian legation he supervised and occasionally
took over the collection of crusade revenue in the area under his
authority, although the actual collection was normally done by
nuncios sent out from Avignon.[4]

In other instances, such as Nicholas IV's French tenth of
1288, and Boniface VIII's tenth in Italy in 1301, the Curia
picked its collectors from amongst the resident episcopate.[5]
Other popes preferred to appoint or send relatively low-ranking
clerics, such as canons. In April and July 1324 John XXII
appointed a canon of Saintes, a rector of Saintes, and a canon of
Agen to collect his subsidy from the French clergy.[6] The
resultant heterogeneity is best illustrated by the collection of the
tenth which Martin IV levied in Italy for the crusade against
the Sicilians. Hugh of Tours, titular Bishop of Bethlehem and a
familiar of Charles I, was assigned the eastern half of the Papal
State, centring on the March of Ancona and the province of
Ravenna. The Duchy of Spoleto and the Patrimony of St. Peter
in Tuscany were given to the Archdeacon of Florence,
Campagna-Marittima and adjacent dioceses to the Bishop of
Ferentino, Tuscany and the Maremma to a canon of Lichfield,
Simon of Lucca. All of northern Italy was assigned to
Christopher Tolomei, Prior of Sarteano, in the diocese of Siena,
and the Archbishop of Arborea was appointed to collect in
Sardinia and Corsica.[7]

It is extremely difficult to judge the efficiency of such collectors, but the difficulties which led to Clement VI's replace-
ment of this ramshackle procedure by a system of permanent
collectors were making themselves felt by the turn of the century, if not earlier. The wide range of revenues which had to be
collected continually from Clement V's reign onwards—tenths,
arrears of tenths, annates, and older forms of revenue such as

---

[3] Urban IV, *Reg.*, no. 804; Martin IV, *Reg.*, nos. 457–8, 587–8; Boniface VIII, *Reg.*,
no. 370. But see below, p. 211.

[4] John XXII, *Lettres communes*, nos. 14306–7. See also ASV, Reg. Vat. 113, f. 169ᵛ,
nos. 1007–8, Reg. Vat. 114, f. 47ʳ, no. 232.

[5] Nicholas IV, *Reg.*, nos. 991–1003; Boniface VIII, *Reg.*, no. 4127.

[6] John XXII, *Lettres secrètes*, nos. 2006, 2139. See also *Die Einnahmen*, p. 488.

[7] Honorius IV, *Reg.*, nos. 12, 333, 335.

census payments and Peter's pence—impressed upon the Curia the need for the wider establishment of the sort of permanent machinery of collection which had existed in England since the early thirteenth century.[8] Moreover, John XXII's preference for sending out nuncios does seem to indicate a growing dissatisfaction with the performance of the local high-ranking clergy as collectors.[9] The failure of the local clergy in this respect is vividly illustrated by a series of events in the Kingdom of Naples in the early fourteenth century. In 1301 Boniface VIII appointed Archbishop John of Capua collector of the new tenth there.[10] In March 1302 the Pope already suspected the Archbishop of collusion with the clergy, to the detriment of Charles II; provision was made for the appointment of clerics by the Angevin court to supervise the operation of John's sub-collectors and safeguard royal interests.[11] Like Edward I of England, the Archbishop evidently decided to profit from the chaos which followed the Anagni *attentat*, and in January 1304, shortly before his death, he was dismissed 'for certain reasons' and replaced by the Archbishop-elect of Salerno, while the Bishop of Aversa was told to cite him peremptorily to appear at the papal Curia to present his accounts.[12] The collection of the tenth was, however, handled no more satisfactorily by the new collector, and he in turn was replaced towards the end of 1308 by William of Balaeto, a nuncio, canon of St. Astier in the diocese of Périgueux and an experienced curial official.[13] William found the collection of the tenth to be in total confusion, 'for many churches, monasteries, and ecclesiastical persons in the kingdom, both religious and secular, have not yet paid the tenths from their income and must be made to pay them'.[14] In May 1309 he cited John of Rogerio, the new Arch-

[8] See Lunt, *Papal Revenues*, i. 42–4. For the widening range of revenue with which the collector had to deal see, e.g., *Acta pont. danica*, i. nos. 67–9, 81; *Vet. mon. Pol.* i. nos. 317, 322, 327, 333. See also Gasnault, 'La Perception', p. 294.

[9] Cf. Lunt, *Papal Revenues*, i. 40.

[10] Boniface VIII, *Reg.*, no. 4127.

[11] Ibid., no. 4484.

[12] Benedict XI, *Reg.*, nos. 240, 1152.

[13] For William's commission, see Clement V, *Reg.*, no. 5284. In October 1308 he was still actively working in northern Italy, but he was in the *Regno* before the end of the year. See ibid., nos. 10408, 10415, 10418.

[14] 'multa quoque ecclesie monasteria et persone ecclesiastice tam religiose quam seculares regni de suis proventibus decimas ipsas . . . nondum solverunt adhuc solvere teneantur', ASV, Instr. misc., no. 462.

bishop-elect of Salerno, to appear before Clement V, under pain of excommunication; not only had collection of the tenth been badly handled by William's predecessors, but John had celebrated the divine offices under interdict and had imprisoned the nuncio's messengers.[15]

It would be wrong to take the example of the clergy of the Kingdom of Naples as typical; in the early fourteenth century they were exceptionally corrupt and demoralized.[16] Nevertheless, the idea that John XXII in particular suspected the local clergy of incompetence or corruption as collectors is supported by his actions in the Papal State. There the Pope took collection out of the hands of the local bishops and gave it to the treasurers of the various provinces, thereby giving their role in provincial administration much more importance than before.[17] For collection in the Kingdom of Naples John relied on the Rector of Campagna-Marittima, who was expected to act as papal representative in the *Regno*. In 1318 William of Balaeto was appointed rector while he was still collecting revenue in the *Regno*, while in 1323 Gerard of Valle was given simultaneously the posts of Rector of Campagna-Marittima and collector in the kingdom.[18] This dual responsibility proved impossible to carry out satisfactorily, and during the crisis of 1328 Gerard was replaced as rector in order that he could concentrate on the collection of revenue in the *Regno* and his duties as vice-rector of the papal city of Benevento.[19]

The Curia usually made clear its desire to keep the collection of crusade revenue in the hands of its own officials and to avoid secular interference; even in the case of obdurate refusal to pay,

---

[15] Ibid. See also Clement V, *Reg.*, nos. 10408, 10422, 10430, 10446, 10481, 10494, 10532; *Rat. dec. Italiae. Campania*, pp. 181, 383. The election of John of Rogerio was disputed and annulled by Clement V in 1310. See his *Reg.*, nos. 5445, 5675; *Hierarchia*, p. 429.

[16] See Caggese, *Roberto d'Angiò*, i. 248–73. Perhaps too bleak a survey, as it relies almost exclusively on the Angevin registers.

[17] See Reydellet-Guttinger, *L'Administration pontificale*, p. 74. See also ibid., pp. 23, 59–61.

[18] ASV, Reg. Vat. 111, f. 310ʳ, no. 1233, ff. 312ʳ–314ᵛ, nos. 1247–9, 1251, 1254–5, 1258; John XXII, *Lettres communes*, no. 8327. See also ASV, Reg. Vat. 112, f. 18ᵛ, no. 82, where Gerard of Valle's appointment is defined as 'exercising the office of rector in Campagna-Marittima and dealing with other matters concerning ourselves and the Roman church both there and in the Kingdom of Sicily'.

[19] ASV. Reg. Vat. 114, ff. 344ᵛ–345ʳ, no. 2005. See also f. 265ᵛ, no. 1479, f. 266ᵛ, no. 1490.

the 'secular arm' was to be invoked as the last resort.[20] By the later thirteenth century, however, it was impossible to exclude the frequent intervention of royal officials. In England and France this could amount to the control or wholesale usurpation of the machinery of collection, as is shown by the conditions which Nicholas IV attached to the grant of a tenth to Philip IV in 1288.[21] Martin IV, indeed, appears to have allowed the secular powers to collect the tenth in France and the *Regno*: his bulls established no machinery of ecclesiastical collection.[22] In June 1284 Gerard of Sabina gave permission for Angevin officials to collect the subsidy which had been voted to the crown by the clergy at the synod of Melfi, and in 1328 King Robert intervened in the collection of the tenth which John XXII had granted him, telling the collectors to assign one and a half years' payments to the treasury by January 1329.[23]

It has been written that the office of collector was regarded as a desirable one.[24] This obviously depended on the rank of the collector and the nature of his collectorate. In 1256 Lawrence of Sumercote wrote that he would rather go to prison than return to Ireland to collect the tenth for Henry III, or, as he put it, 'to be crucified any longer for the business of the cross'.[25] The complaint of one papal agent that he had been robbed and imprisoned for forty-eight days by a nobleman while passing through the pope's own province of Campagna-Marittima in 1332–3 would have sounded familiar to many papal collectors of the period, as well as to their predecessors of the thirteenth century.[26] Two deputy collectors of the tenth were nearly killed by hostile clerics and laymen at Sorrento in 1310.[27] But while collectors could face imprisonment and attack in areas under papal or Angevin rule, they were especially threatened when the secular powers were hostile, as in Germany in the 1320s and

---

[20] See, e.g., Nicholas IV, *Reg.*, no. 1008; Boniface VIII, *Reg.*, no. 3455.

[21] See above, p. 198. See also 'Account of a Papal Collector', p. 314.

[22] Martin IV, *Reg.*, nos. 457–8, 587–8. The powers of Martin's cardinal-legates in France and the *Regno* were limited to exhorting and compelling the clergy to pay the tenth, presumably to royal officials.

[23] See 'Il regno di Carlo I', p. 19; *Urkunden*, no. 201.

[24] Lunt, *Papal Revenues*, i. 49.

[25] *Royal and other Historical Letters illustrative of the Reign of Henry III*, ed. W. W. Shirley, ii, no. 509.

[26] ASV, Reg. Vat. 117, ff. 48ᵛ–49ʳ, no. 278.

[27] Caggese, *Roberto d'Angiò*, i. 264.

1330s.[28] It is true that there were lucrative rewards. The collector received the crusade indulgence and pay for his services; on one occasion in 1281 Martin IV increased the pay of one collector because of the rising cost of living.[29] If he held a benefice in his collectorate he was granted exemption from the tenth, and in at least one case a deputy collector was permitted to retain an actual percentage of the money which he collected.[30] But, like most aspects of papal financial administration, these valuable privileges were at the mercy of individual popes. For example, Nicholas IV did not allow any expenses to the Archbishop of Rouen and the Bishop of Auxerre, who were to collect the tenth in France in 1289, nor did he exclude their benefices from taxation.[31]

The procedure of collection itself is well documented. On the arrival of the collector, or of the bull itself in those cases where the local clergy were to collect, the papal commission would be publicized by being read out aloud, deputy collectors would be chosen, instructed, and sworn in, and the tenth would be collected in two annual instalments, usually at Christmas and on St. John the Baptist's Day.[32] It was then stored in churches and monasteries and, in England and France, in the London and Paris Temples. By the early fourteenth century the collectors were sending regular reports to the Curia on the progress of the collection, often sad accounts of clerical resistance and non-co-operation by the secular powers.[33] The collection of the tenth was based on the assessment of the annual income of a benefice or religious house, and this assessment was later also

---

[28] See, e.g., the stories of attack, robbery, and imprisonment in *Römische Quellen zur konstanzer Bistumsgeschichte zur Zeit der Päpste in Avignon, 1305–1378*, ed. K. Rieder, no. 627; *Die päpstlichen Kollektorien*, p. 114.

[29] Martin IV, *Reg.*, no. 28. The collector, the Bishop of Rieti, was collecting the six-year tenth levied at the Council of Lyons.

[30] *Codice diplomatico barese*, ed. a cura della Commissione provinciale di Archeologia e Storia patria, xvi, no. 16.

[31] Nicholas IV, *Reg.*, no. 991. The Pope wrote that he was establishing these conditions so that their heavenly reward would be the greater.

[32] See, e.g., 'Ann. de Burton', pp. 350–60 (Rostand in England, 1255); *Cod. dipl. barese*, xvi, no. 16 (the archbishops of Naples and Brindisi in the *Regno*, 1312); *Rat. dec. Italiae. Apulia-Lucania-Calabria*, pp. 130–1 (deputy collectors of Gerard of Valle at Taranto, 1324).

[33] See, e.g., 'Lettere di collettori pontifici nel secolo xiv', ed. U. Mannucci, *RQ*, xxvii (1913), *passim*; 'Account of a Papal Collector', *passim*.

used for the purposes of annates and intercalary fruits.[34] Such assessments failed to take account of variations in revenue, and in the War of the Vespers and afterwards, as many benefices and monastic endowments fell dramatically in value, the Curia increasingly granted its collectors the authority to 'compound', or work out a valuation based on the current year's income, as agreed between collector and incumbent.[35]

It is accepted that the majority of collectors were reliable and honest, but the comprehensive powers allocated to them, including those of excommunication, interdict, suspension, and the invocation of the secular arm, led to abuses, and it is these which recur in the papal registers and attract one's attention. Few collectors reached the depths of iniquity plumbed by John Bernier, a canon of Chalon-sur-Saône, who collected annates in France in the late 1320s and early 1330s. His extensive and methodical misuse of his powers, which included excommunicating the dead so that their family and friends could not bury them without buying absolution, enabled him to build up a fortune of more than £10,000 *Tours* by 1334.[36] He was found out, but it is impossible to know how many were not. In 1324 the embezzlement of more than 6,000 florins from the tenth by a Lucchese called Lasarus de Fombra was only discovered because he confessed to it in his will, 'wishing to satisfy his conscience and provide for his soul's salvation'.[37] Nor were the regular clergy immune from temptation. In February 1330 a deposed Cistercian abbot was accused of failing to present his accounts for the collection in Italy of part of the subsidy voted by his Order, of failing to pay a subsidy of 400 florins which he had promised himself, and of neglecting to pay his service tax of 150 florins.[38] Several high-ranking prelates, such as the Patriarch of Alexandria, the Archbishop of Besançon, and the

---

[34] See Lunt, *Financial Relations*, i. 491–3, 496–7.

[35] See, e.g., ASV, Reg. Vat. 113, f. 100ʳ⁻ᵛ, no. 713, f. 129ʳ⁻ᵛ, no. 863, f. 283ʳ, no. 1668, ff. 335ᵛ–336ʳ, no. 1970, f. 345ᵛ, no. 2034; Honorius IV, *Registres*, nos. 190, 266, 498, 541; Nicholas IV, *Reg.*, nos. 8–10, 1882–3, 1950–1.

[36] G. Mollat, 'Procès d'un collecteur pontifical sous Jean XXII et Benoît XII', *Vierteljahrschrift für Social-u. Wirtschaftsgeschichte*, vi (1908), *passim*. Cf. the similar example in Lunt, *Papal Revenues*, i. 48–9.

[37] 'sue volens satisfacere conscientie et saluti anime providere', ASV, Reg. Vat. 112, ff. 67ᵛ–68ʳ, no. 318. For corrupt collection in the Kingdom of Naples, see Benedict XII, *Lettres closes et patentes*, no. 2634.

[38] ASV, Reg. Vat. 115, f. 74ʳ, no. 1400.

bishops of Bologna and S. Agata dei Goti, had to be ordered to present their accounts as collectors, or to send the money which they had collected to the *camera*.[39] When a bishop died while collecting papal revenue, there was often a lengthy and acrimonious exchange of letters, such as that with the Bishop of Paphos in 1329, in which the Curia tried to compel his successor to surrender the money.[40]

In 1274 Gregory X laid down the rules for the exemption from the tenth of hospitals, lazar-houses, and the poorer monasteries. These instructions were adopted by both Honorius IV and Nicholas IV for the tenths levied in aid of the crusade against the Sicilians, and they were finally incorporated into canon law by Boniface VIII.[41] Many hospitals and poor monasteries insured themselves more fully against taxation by securing specific letters of exemption, and they despatched a stream of petitions to this effect to Honorius IV, Nicholas IV, and Boniface VIII. These letters were regularly renewed; thus the Poor Clares were granted bulls of exemption in 1289, 1295, and 1304, the Hospital of St. James at Alto Passo in 1286, 1290, 1296, 1302, and 1314.[42]

The most intractable and recurrent problem facing popes and collectors was that of the military Orders and the Cistercians. In general it was accepted by the Curia that the Hospitallers, the Templars, and the other military Orders were exempt from the tenths and annates levied for the Italian crusades because of their activities in Latin Syria, Cyprus, Rhodes, and Spain. They were fighting 'against the enemies of the Catholic Faith, and because of this have to undergo frequent and various financial burdens'.[43] The problem was that this exemption was based on the privileges granted to the

---

[39] ASV, Reg. Vat. 112, ff. 53ᵛ–54ʳ, no. 245, Reg. Vat. 113, f. 99ʳ⁻ᵛ, no. 704, f. 163ᵛ, no. 990, Reg. Vat. 116, f. 234ᵛ, no. 1215; John XXII, *Lettres secrètes*, no. 3802.

[40] ASV, Reg. Vat. 115, f. 61ʳ⁻ᵛ, no. 389, f. 63ʳ⁻ᵛ, no. 400. See also *Chypre sous les Lusignans*, p. 34; ASV, Reg. Vat. 115, f. 215ʳ, no. 2147.

[41] Pope Gregory X, *Registres*, ed. J. Guiraud, no. 571; Honorius IV, *Reg.*, no. 60; Nicholas IV, *Reg.*, no. 1009; Boniface VIII, *Reg.*, no. 4131. See also Lunt, *Financial Relations*, i. 314–17.

[42] See, e.g., Honorius IV, *Reg.*, nos. 242, 246, 749; Nicholas IV, *Reg.*, nos. 798, 1989, 2607–10, 2759, 5208; Boniface VIII, *Reg.*, nos. 574, 1201, 898, 928, 4708; Benedict XI, *Reg.*, no. 997; Clement V, *Reg.*, nos. 7009, 8334, 10298.

[43] *Vet. mon. hist. Hung. sacr. ill.* i, no. 836. Cf. Clement V, *Reg.*, no. 5284; John XXII, *Lettres communes*, no. 40797.

Orders by individual popes in the first half of the thirteenth century; it was not treated by Gregory X and thus did not pass into canon law. Later popes could and did overrule their predecessors under pressure from secular rulers or from their own financial needs. The wealth of the Orders made taxation tempting. In 1297 James II of Aragon claimed that the loss of their contribution would reduce the value of the Aragonese tenth by more than a third, and that if Boniface VIII did not wish to include them he should add another two years to the tenth.[44] In 1305 James submitted an unsuccessful petition to Clement V for a grant of a third of the revenues of the Templars and Hospitallers in Aragon over a four-year period.[45].

Papal policy towards the problem of whether to tax the military Orders was thus changeable. They were specifically included by Martin IV in his tenths of 1283–5, and in 1291 Nicholas IV spared them payment of the tenth on their responsions, but not on the other two-thirds of their income.[46] Boniface VIII exempted the Hospitallers completely in 1295, the Teutonic Knights in 1296, the Templars and the Hospitallers in 1297. As we have seen, however, the Orders made a substantial contribution to Boniface's expenses in the form of subsidies.[47] The Pope himself recognized this; in May 1297 he wrote to the bishops of Dol and Thérouanne asking them to plead with Philip IV that the Orders should be taxed lightly for the new French tenth, because they had already been heavily burdened for the Sicilian war.[48] Exempted from the Aragonese tenths of 1300 and 1303, the Orders were not exempted from the French tenth of 1300, nor from that in Italy in 1301.[49] Even when the Orders were consistently exempted, as in the reigns of

[44] *Acta arag.* i, no. 30.

[45] Salavert y Roca, *Cerdeña*, ii, no. 128.

[46] Martin IV, *Reg.*, nos 457–8, 583–90; Nicholas IV, *Reg.*, nos. 4204–6. Responsions were a tax on revenues and produce which provincial officers of the Hospitallers and the Templars sent annually to their central governments in the East. See J. S. C. Riley-Smith, *The Knights of St. John in Jerusalem and Cyprus c.1050–1310*, pp. 45, 51.

[47] See Boniface VIII, *Reg.*, nos. 477, 974, 2059; *Elenco cronologico delle antiche pergamene pertinenti alla Real chiesa della Magione*, ed. V. Mortillaro, no. 272. See also above, p. 182.

[48] Boniface VIII, *Reg.*, nos. 1830–1.

[49] See ibid., nos. 3569, 3917, 4127, 4395, 5202. For examples of the Templars paying a tenth in the Kingdom of Sicily in 1300, and both the Templars and the Hospitallers paying a subsidy in 1302, see *Syll. mem.*, iii. 3, 72. See also A. J. Forey, *The Templars in the 'Corona de Aragón'*, pp. 164–5, 175–6, for the Templars and taxation in Aragon.

Clement V and John XXII, they were occasionally subjected to the demands of over-zealous collectors. In November 1331 John XXII had to issue letters to all his collectors of annates telling them not to tax Hospitaller priories, houses, and preceptories and to return any money collected. The persistent demands of the collectors were preventing the despatch of responsions to Rhodes and hindered the forthcoming crusade.[50]

The Cistercians presented a similar problem. Nicholas IV wrote in 1289 that he was reluctant to tax them for a full tenth 'lest the observance of their rule, which is known to be flourishing in a praiseworthy manner in their Order, be disturbed, and their services to God, which they perform with eagerness and care, suffer a reduction and loss'.[51] Usually, therefore, they were allowed to pay a sum smaller than a complete tenth. This was still a considerable amount: their contribution to the 1283 tenth in France was about £81,000 *Tours*, and they paid £60,750 *Tours* towards the tenth levied in 1289. This bears comparison with the contribution of the entire French clergy to the 1289 tenth, which was between £700,000 and £770,000 *Tours*.[52]

The most dramatic controversy on the taxable status of the military Orders and the Cistercians occurred during the collection of the 1264 tenth for Charles of Anjou. When the tenth was levied the Cistercian Chapter General appointed two abbots to go to the Curia, 'if the necessity arises', and plead the case for the Order's exemption, citing its 'necessities and poverty'. Early in 1265 the Cardinal-bishop of Porto, the Order's protector, reminded Clement IV that it had always been exempted from the tenth, even that levied for Louis IX's first crusade, 'by the special grace of the Apostolic See'.[53] On 15 March the Pope wrote to Simon of Brie granting the Cistercians temporary exemption, until he could establish a definitive ruling on the matter. The same was to apply to the Templars and Hospitallers, 'and certain other religious', who were producing papal letters of exemption when the legate attempted to tax them.[54] On 30

---

[50] ASV. Reg. Vat. 116. ff. 346ᵛ–347ʳ. no. 1728.
[51] Nicholas IV. *Reg.*, no. 991.
[52] See *RHGF*, xxi. 531–2, 545–57.
[53] *Stat. cap. gen.*, iii. 18 (cf. p. 33); Clement IV. *Reg.*, no. 6.
[54] Clement IV, *Reg.*, no. 6; *Thes. novus*, ii, col. 111. Cf. Clement IV, *Reg.*, no. 217.

March, however, Clement wrote to his legate telling him to
ignore his previous letters if they should stand in the way of
Charles of Anjou's plans or 'scandalize' the count.[55].

This confusion prevailed until November, when Clement
adopted a solution which placed the burden of decision on the
shoulders of Simon of Brie. All the Orders were to pay unless
they could show him a papal privilege exempting them. But the
judgement of the validity of these exemptions, which was the
real point at issue, was left to Simon. It was clear that the
obstacle to total exemption was Charles of Anjou, who was
insisting on the full value of the tenth. Thus Simon was to 'keep
diligent watch in these matters, so that the King of Sicily does
not have reason to complain'.[56] Clement also told his legate that
he himself would issue no exemptions and that any already
issued should be treated as nullified. In January 1266 he again
told him to base his decisions on the privileges shown him.[57]
Meanwhile Simon of Brie had summoned the Abbot of Cîteaux
and the four leading abbots to appear for consultation at Paris
on 1 March 1266. He then ordered a meeting of all the
Cistercian abbots in April at Bourges, at which they were to
present all their privileges to him. Under enormous pressure
from Charles's proctors and nuncios, as he himself complained,
Simon was already forcing individual houses to pay the tenth.
In March 1266 even the personal friendship of the Pope could
not secure for the Hospitaller Prior of S. Gilles, Ferrand de
Barras, the exemption of his province from the tenth, although
Clement did write to Simon of Brie telling him to relax any
sentences which he had imposed upon the knights for refusing
to pay.[58]

The successful outcome of the battle of Benevento gave
Clement IV fresh hope that he could persuade Charles I to
agree to the exemption from the tenth of at least the Cistercians.
He wrote to Simon in April telling him to postpone collection
from the Cistercians until June. Meanwhile a strongly worded

---

[55] *Thes. novus*, ii, col. 118.
[56] Ibid., cols. 244–5.
[57] Ibid., col. 246; Clement IV, *Reg.*, no. 195.
[58] *Codex dunensis sive diplomatum et chartarum medii aevi amplissima collectio*, ed. J. Kervyn
de Lettenhove, nos. 203–4; *Thes. novus*, ii, cols. 297–8. For Ferrand de Barras, see
Riley-Smith, *Knights of St. John*, pp. 280–2. The Hospitallers in Provence had still not
paid the tenth in January 1270. See *RCAR*, iii, Reg. 13, no. 624.

letter was sent to Charles 'warning and exhorting' him to give his consent to the exemption of the Order on the grounds of its religious and social functions. But Charles was determined, as Clement bitterly remarked, not to lose a single penny of the tenth. When Louis IX asked for the exemption of two Dominican houses patronized by the French crown Clement was compelled to adopt the humiliating expedient of paying the equivalent amount from the *camera*, without letting the French king know.[59]

It was now settled that the Cistercians should pay a block sum of £30,000 *Tours*, which Charles I appointed two proctors to collect. In 1268 the Chapter General ordered all abbots whose monasteries lay within Simon of Brie's legation to deposit their contributions at Paris, and at least one abbot was severely punished for not doing so.[60] But payment was slow. In July 1269 Charles I complained about the dilatoriness of the Order; he wrote to the papal legate in France, now Cardinal Rudolf of Albano, to ask him to force the Cistercians to pay the money, as well as the interest and expenses on the loan which it was intended to repay. He also asked the college of cardinals to apply pressure on the Cistercians and on the Hospitallers and other Orders, which were proving equally obstinate.[61] Still the money remained unpaid. At the beginning of 1273 Charles appointed proctors to petition the new pope, Gregory X, to compel the Cistercians to pay the £30,000. The Abbot of Cîteaux and the four leading abbots travelled to the Curia and to the Angevin court to negotiate, and in 1273 a final settlement was reached, almost a decade after the tenth was levied.[62]

Jordan commented that the Cistercian resistance to paying the 1264 tenth showed the defensive ability of a great medieval religious corporation.[63] But many of the secular clergy showed a similar obstinacy in the face of the collectors' threats, long after the lists of *gravamina* submitted by their superiors had been

---

[59] *Thes. novus*, ii, cols. 304–5, 412–13; Clement IV, *Reg.*, no. 840.

[60] *Stat. cap. gen.*, iii. 60, 72–3; *RCAR*, ii, Reg. 8, no. 46. See also Clement IV, *Reg.*, no. 811.

[61] *RCAR*, ii, Reg. 8, nos. 424, 555.

[62] *RCAR*, ix, Reg. 45, no. 185; *Stat. cap. gen.*, iii. 107, 116. For payments in 1274–6 by the Hospitallers, the Templars, and Cluny, see *RCAR*, x, Reg. 50, nos. 52–4, xi, Reg. 60, no. 111.

[63] *Les Origines*, p. 541.

rejected and collection instituted. Refusal to pay crusade taxes was endemic and widespread throughout the period 1254–1343, as individual clerics and religious houses dug their heels in and placed their hope in the death of the Pope and the election of a more amenable successor.

Many reasons were put forward to avoid or postpone payment. In frontier areas, especially those where borders were uncertain, clerics pleaded exclusion from the tax on the basis of being outside the relevant area. In 1325 the Bishop of Rieti and some of his clergy told Gerard of Valle that they could not pay him the tenth because the lands from which their revenues were derived lay outside the *Regno*, and they were accustomed to pay the tenth 'to collectors of the tenth appointed for the empire'.[64] Similarly, Cistercian abbots in the Veneto and the March of Treviso claimed to be outside the collectorate established 'in the regions of Lombardy' for the collection of the subsidy of 1328.[65] Sometimes this tactic proved successful. In June 1267 Pope Clement IV confirmed the exclusion from the French tenth of five monasteries which, although they lay within the diocese of Cambrai, were situated in the empire, not in the Kingdom of France or the lands of the Countess of Flanders.[66] On other occasions it failed. In 1328 prelates and clerics whose revenues derived from places outside the counties of Provence and Forcalquier claimed exemption from the tenth which had been granted to Robert of Naples; John XXII responded by extending the tenth to all lands between the Rhône and the Alps over which Robert exercised any jurisdiction, whether they were in the counties or not.[67] A second popular excuse was to give a false assessment of the value of the benefice in order to claim the exclusion granted to those holding benefices worth less than £15 *Tours* a year (or £7 in some cases). In November 1265 Simon of Brie was told to deprive of their benefices all whom he found guilty of this deception.[68] Ignorance was pleaded on occasion. The Archbishop of Salzburg claimed that he had not received letters about the Vienne tenth, and in 1330

---

[64] 'collectoribus decime in Imperio constitutis', ASV, Reg. Vat. 113, f. 79^r, no. 582.
[65] ASV, Reg. Vat. 115, f. 29^r, no. 185. See also *Stat. cap. gen.*, iii. 389.
[66] Clement IV, *Reg.*, no. 479.
[67] John XXII, *Lettres secrètes*, no. 3741.
[68] *Thes. novus*, ii, col. 245.

new incumbents in Spain used a similar excuse to try to explain their failure to send intercalary fruits to the *camera*.[69] Some prelates claimed that they were not liable to pay a tenth or subsidy to which they had not given their assent; the Archbishop of Amalfi was trying this escape route in 1313.[70]

To the Curia such were 'frivolous excuses'.[71] There was only one legitimate excuse for not paying the taxes imposed for the defence of the Faith, and this was poverty. In cases in which genuine hardship already existed, or would be created by the payment of a crusade tax, the pope was usually willing to abandon or, more frequently, postpone collection. Thus in 1326 Pope John XXII instructed Bertrand du Poujet to find a 'suitable and convenient procedure' for the payment of tenths which Pagano della Torre, Patriarch of Aquileia and a leading Guelf, was unable to pay the *camera* 'because of other burdens weighing him down', and in 1329 a monastery administered by the Archbishop of Pisa was exempted from the payment of a tenth because of damage caused to its lands by flooding.[72] In 1334 the Pope suspended collection in Frankish Greece while he had the problems of the Church there investigated, and in 1329 he abandoned completely the collection of annates in the province of Cologne when petitioned by the archbishop.[73] It is difficult to know whether the extension of crusade taxation to new areas which took place from the 1290s onwards caused real hardship there. A collector's report from Riga in the early fourteenth century recorded the dismay of the clergy of the province at the Pope's attempt to tax them, pointing out that they were accustomed to receiving crusade indulgences themselves, not to paying for crusades elsewhere.[74] The Curia had to send out a stream of letters dealing with resistance to taxation in areas which were being taxed seriously for the first time for the Italian crusades, such as Greece, Cyprus, Hungary, Poland, and

---

[69] ASV, Reg. Vat. 115, f. 175^r, no. 1980; 'Lettere di collettori pontifici', p. 197*.

[70] ASV, Instr. misc., no. 627.

[71] 'excusationes frivolas'. ASV. Reg. Vat. 113, f. 141^v, no 910. Cf. ASV, Reg. Vat 116, f. 65^r, no. 314; Clement V, *Reg.*, no. 6370.

[72] ASV, Reg. Vat. 114, f. 41^v, no. 204, Reg. Vat. 115, f. 20^v, no. 139.

[73] ASV. Reg. Vat. 117. f. 265^r. no. 1374. For Cologne, see above, p. 185.

[74] 'Lettere di collettori pontifici', p. *198.

Scandinavia.[75] But such resistance could have been due to the novelty of taxation as much as to the hardship which it caused.

ii. THE EMPLOYMENT OF CRUSADE REVENUE: PAPAL CREDIT AND THE CAMERAL BANKERS.

Once collection was instituted with vigour and determination, and with the active co-operation of the secular powers, resistance became very difficult to sustain. The policy adopted by the papacy, of severe punishment for refusal to pay, and absolution as soon as payment was begun or promised, was an effective one. This was largely because the instruments used to implement it, notably suspension, excommunication, and citation to appear at the Curia, were still powerful weapons.[76] But the outstanding flaw in the system used by the Curia to collect crusade revenue was its slowness. In 1311 Clement V wrote of a Benedictine priory at Cuchet, in the diocese of Lyons, which had sustained for more than twenty years a sentence of excommunication and interdict because of its refusal to pay tenths for the crusade against the Sicilians.[77] Even when comparatively little resistance was encountered, the collection of crusade revenue could span decades. John XXII's tenth of 1321 was still being collected in the reign of Benedict XII, as was the six-year tenth of Clement V.[78] Yet the nature of crusade taxation was such that the money was urgently needed in Italy as soon as the tax was levied; the decision to tax was often a response to already desperate needs. Like many contemporary rulers, the popes controlled considerable resources which could not be harnessed to meet their military requirements without using credit facilities.[79] Also like many contemporaries, they

[75] See, e.g., ASV, Reg. Vat. 113, f. 141ᵛ, no. 910, ff. 271ᵛ–272ʳ, no. 1607, Reg. Vat. 116, ff. 64ᵛ–65ʳ, no. 314, f. 246ʳ⁻ᵛ, nos. 1281–2, Reg. Vat. 117, f. 121ᵛ, no. 617; *Vet. mon. Pol.* i, no. 481.

[76] For papal policy towards clerical resistance to taxation, see, e.g., Clement IV, *Reg.*, no. 180. An incident in the 'Maius chron. lemovicense' (p. 777), graphically illustrates the ramifications of papal sanctions.

[77] Clement V, *Reg.*, no. 7135.

[78] See Benedict XII, *Lettres closes, patentes et curiales*, no. 234; id., *Lettres closes et patentes*, nos. 570, 958, 1215, 1653, 2128, 3043. See also Gasnault, 'La Perception', p. 289.

[79] See E. B. and M. M. Fryde, 'Public Credit, with Special Reference to North-Western Europe', in M. M. Postan *et al.* (eds.), *The Cambridge Economic History of Europe*, iii. 431–3 and *passim*; R. W. Kaeuper, *Bankers to the Crown. The Riccardi of Lucca and Edward I*, pp. 75–6.

turned to Italian, and particularly Tuscan, banking houses to provide such facilities. The role of the bankers was twofold. First, they were able to employ their own agents and system of communications to transfer crusade revenue from the collectors or the place of deposit to the *camera* or to the agents and allies of the papacy. Secondly, they could lend or advance money to the Curia and its allies with the crusade revenue as security.[80] In itself this procedure was reliable and mutually beneficial; the unpredictable factor was the amount of money which the bankers were called upon to supply on credit in Italy or elsewhere. An exact balance between crusade revenue held and money advanced was never possible. But when the disparity between the two became too great, and the ability of the papacy and its secular allies to repay their debts was called into question, the whole structure of credit was imperilled. Both during the crusade against Manfred and in the War of the Vespers the seemingly endless papal and Angevin demands threatened to bring bankruptcy to the *camera* and to its bankers.

(a) *The Crusades against Manfred and Conradin*

For the first ten years of the struggle with Manfred the popes continued to use the financial resources which they had employed against Frederick II and Conrad. Ordinary papal revenue was supplemented by occasional appeals for caritative subsidies and, during the reign of Alexander IV, by large sums extracted by the Savoyard Bishop of Hereford from the English church. But Manfred's activities forced the pace, militarily and financially. Urban IV had to undertake very large expenses, which he himself estimated in July 1264 at £200,000, in defending the Papal State.[81] His dramatic appeal for a subsidy in 1264 was an attempt to meet these costs. Nevertheless, Clement IV inherited an empty treasury at the end of 1264, and papal credit with the cameral bankers was not high after the years of expen-

---

[80] See Jordan, *De mercatoribus, passim;* G. Schneider, *Die finanziellen Beziehungen der florentinischen Bankiers zur Kirche von 1285 bis 1304, passim;* Renouard, *Les Relations, passim;* Renouard, *Recherches sur les compagnies commerciales et bancaires utilisées par les papes d'Avignon avant le Grand Schisme, passim.* Brief account in English in Lunt, *Papal Revenues,* i. 51–6.

[81] See *Thes. novus,* ii, col. 85; A. Gottlob, 'Päpstliche Darlehenschulden des 13. Jahrhunderts', *Historisches Jahrbuch,* xx (1899), 677–81.

sive and fruitless struggle.[82] It was at this inauspicious point that a large sum was needed to organize and pay Charles of Anjou's army. The first year's revenue from the French tenth would not be available until the summer of 1265. A full-scale financial crisis was virtually inevitable.

At first Clement IV hoped that the French tenth would be sufficient to pay both for an Angevin advance guard at Rome and for soldiers for the main army assembling in France. In February 1265 he began writing letters to Simon of Brie telling him to repay debts which he had contracted on behalf of Charles's vicar at Rome, James Gantelme, and his nuncio, Tancred 'de Scharlino'. The threat to Rome made him anxious for the arrival of more Angevin troops, as well as the appearance of Charles in person.[83] Meanwhile he was having to use all his influence with the cameral bankers at Perugia to get loans for James Gantelme, since Charles's credit was very poor at Rome. By the end of April these loans already totalled about £20,000 *Tours*, and in May Clement wrote a concerned letter to his legate. Papal credit too was getting low, he told him. 'Finding money here has become exceptionally difficult, very nearly impossible'. The bankers were worried about their losses in Germany and England, about the difficulties of communicating with France, and about the fact that money already lent had not yet been repaid. It was essential to satisfy these creditors as soon as possible from the proceeds of the tenth.[84]

Charles's arrival in Rome in May 1265 only aggravated the situation. He had spent the available revenue from his French possessions on the fleet for the crossing, and had come without money or horses. He immediately needed a loan of £20,000 *Tours*, negotiated on his behalf by the Pope. Simon of Brie was told to repay this from the tenth which had been collected in the provinces of Sens, Rheims, Rouen, and Tours.[85] By July none of these debts had been repaid, and Clement declared that he did not intend to prejudice papal credit any further by raising loans for Charles. In future the tenth alone would be used as security.

[82] *Thes. novus*, ii, cols. 108, 174–5.

[83] Ibid., cols. 103–4, 107–8, 122, 123–4, 125–6, 127, 128. See also ibid., cols. 118–19; Jordan, *Les Origines*, pp. 522–3.

[84] *Thes. novus*, ii, cols. 132–3.

[85] Ibid., cols. 138–9, 139–40.

Once the debts had been repaid the tenth was therefore to be assigned to Charles's own proctors in France.[86] But the bankers were not prepared to lend with the tenth as security. They simply did not believe that they would be repaid in France. Charles could raise nothing in Provence and neither Louis IX nor Alphonse of Poitiers responded to fervid appeals to lend their brother money.[87] Moreover, in July Manfred led a raid to the neighbourhood of Tivoli, and a Sienese army threatened Perugia.[88] In these circumstances Clement unwillingly accepted the plan proposed by Charles, that many of the churches in Rome, together with their lands and rents, should be used as security to raise a loan of £100,000 *Provence* from the city's bankers. The tenth would then be used to repay the debts before the church property could actually be seized.[89]

Many cardinals distrusted Charles of Anjou and opposed the scheme in a last-ditch attempt to subvert the papal policy of French intervention. At this difficult moment, on 29 July, a letter arrived from Simon of Brie with appalling news. The legate wrote that, contrary to Clement's instructions, he had adopted the practice of using the tenth to pay mercenaries in advance for the main army. When the debts contracted by Charles in Provence had been repaid, nothing would be left to send to Charles at Rome. In cold fury Clement outlined the consequences of Simon's folly. He was paying mercenaries when the basic logistics of the expedition, including its horses, food, and route through Lombardy, had not been settled. Meanwhile Charles was spending £1,000 *Provence* every day at Rome. Worst of all, it now seemed impossible that the Roman loan could be repaid in time to prevent the occupation of the churches.[90]

Stalemate was reached on the Roman loan in consistory and Clement, perplexed, asked the cardinals at Rome for their help and advice. Though he still backed the plan, the Pope himself was pessimistic about its chances of success, and irritated by

[86] Ibid., cols. 149–50, 151.
[87] Ibid., cols. 165–6.
[88] See Waley, *Papal State*, p. 173.
[89] *Thes. novus*, ii, cols. 178–80. On this plan, see F. Schneider, 'Zur älteren päpstlichen Finanzgeschichte', *QFIAB*, ix (1906), 15–37.
[90] *Thes. novus*, ii, cols. 178–80.

Charles's assumption that the Church could and should make these sacrifices. When he was approached by Charles's nuncios for more money and told them that it was impossible to raise it, they replied 'the affair will collapse, if you do not do so'. His answer to this, he told Charles, was that the Church herself would collapse, if he agreed to their proposals.[91] He wrote angry letters complaining about his poverty, and told the Cardinal-priest of St. Martin, who was organizing the struggle against Manfred's troops in the March of Ancona, that the inhabitants of the province would have to provide for their own defence, rather than relying, as they always had done, on the Pope.[92] However, when Simon of Brie wrote again confirming that he could forward no money, the Pope agreed, 'not without bitterness of heart', to Charles's plan. He sent instructions for the use of church property as security and on 4 September appointed his agents, Bérenger of Séguret, a cleric of the *camera*, and Claudius, a papal chaplain, to confirm Charles's loans.[93]

Unfortunately the project was not as successful as Clement had hoped that it would be. Despite the visible security of the churches of Rome and their massive possessions in the city, the merchants there were slow to lend and imposed heavy rates of interest. By mid-November only £30,000 *Tours* had been lent. The offer was formally closed on 17 November but loans against the security of the churches and their lands and rents continued to be made as late as April 1266, bringing the total to just over £62,000.[94] Charles's financial situation remained critical. The cameral bankers refused to lend without a letter from Louis IX guaranteeing repayment in France. Again the Pope asked Simon of Brie to forward money as soon as possible, and made frequent appeals to Louis IX and Alphonse of Poitiers to lend money and accept the tenth as repayment. The King would lend nothing, but Alphonse finally offered a short-term loan of 4,000 silver marks and £5,000 *Tours*.[95] Meanwhile other problems added to Clement IV's worries. There was acrimony between Charles and Simon of Brie, who claimed that his policy

[91] Ibid., cols. 176–7, 186.
[92] Ibid., cols. 182, 186–7.
[93] Ibid., cols. 176–7, 186; *RCAR*, i, Reg. 1, nos. 20, 27.
[94] *Thes. novus*, ii, cols. 189–90, 241–3; *RCAR*, i, Reg. 1, nos. 27–37; Schneider, 'Zur älteren päpstlichen Finanzgeschichte', pp. 21–5.
[95] *Thes. novus*, ii, cols. 187–9, 189–90, 219, 241–3.

of paying mercenaries had been ordered by Charles himself. Charles's expenses at Rome rose to £1,200 a day and he could borrow nothing there, thanks to Manfred's bribery of the bankers and Simon of Brie's slowness in repaying earlier debts. Most serious of all, the whole of the first year of the French tenth had been spent, 'either badly paid by the churches, or exacted with insufficient diligence by the collectors, or spent on other purposes than those intended'.[96]

In October and November 1265 Clement IV's anguish, faithfully recorded in his letters, reached its height. There were two grave difficulties. One was the continual struggle to maintain Charles's force at Rome. The Curia was still raising some money, a trickle of relatively small amounts which Simon of Brie was told to repay, but these were inadequate.[97] Rejecting his legate's suggestions of levying a new tenth or raising a loan in England, Clement saw the only hope as the contracting of loans in France on the basis of the next two years of the tenth: 'Ask the king, ask his brother, ask the prelates, ask the Orders, ask the burgesses, ask the usurers, ask everybody, even if they refuse you ten times over'.[98] On 29 November a Tolomei banker at Troyes wrote home that Simon of Brie was working as hard as possible to collect the tenth; the rate of exchange for florins had risen and that for coins of *Provins* was expected to rise in February.[99] Then there was the problem of paying the army assembling in France. If it did not set out, Rome would be lost, but if it did arrive in Italy, it could not be paid. This would present appalling difficulties if Manfred succeeded in avoiding confrontation.[100]

But at the end of November, and in December, the situation gradually improved. Bonaventura Bernardini and his partners, a branch of the powerful Buonsignori of Siena and cameral bankers of long standing, provided the money necessary to pay for Charles's force at Rome while the army made its descent into Italy. They lent £10,000 on 30 November, £500 on 30

---

[96] Ibid., cols. 213–15, 241–3.

[97] Ibid., cols. 152, 168–9, 177–8, 201–2, 208.

[98] Ibid., col. 243. See also ibid., col. 214.

[99] See *Lettere volgari del secolo xiii scritte da senesi*, ed. C. Paoli and E. Piccolomini, pp. 55–7. Cf. M. Bloch, 'The Problem of Gold in the Middle Ages', in his *Land and Work in Mediaeval Europe. Selected Papers*, p. 190.

[100] *Thes. novus*, ii, cols. 219–20.

December, and £50,000 on 31 December, the last sum with the Pope's personal treasure as security.[101] Clement's letters took on a new tone of intense relief. He praised the faithfulness of the Buonsignori, 'who have always proved liberal to ourselves and to the said king in this affair and in our other needs'. Part of the praise was also due to Simon of Brie, who had restored credit by paying back earlier loans from the Buonsignori, and perhaps most praise of all was due to the Angevin army, which had re-established Guelf confidence and credit by successfully negotiating the passage through Lombardy, and which entered Rome in mid-January.[102]

At the end of December Clement felt sure enough of the approach of the crusading forces to discuss with Charles the strategy of the forthcoming campaign. His views were dominated by the need to finance the army. If Charles first 'terrorized' Tuscany, he wrote, he would acquire not only a much easier flow of loans, but also a series of enforced subsidies from the Ghibelline cities. An immediate invasion of the *Regno*, on the other hand, could also prove profitable, since 'it is believed that its subsequent conquest will bring with it a flow of treasure'.[103] Pressed by his financial needs, Charles chose the latter course, defeated and killed Manfred in one battle, and captured intact the Staufen treasure.[104]

The worst of the crisis was past, but the papal *camera*, the Pope's treasure, and the possessions of many of the Roman churches were still in pawn to the Roman and cameral bankers. On 22 March 1266 Clement urged Simon of Brie to pay all these debts before assigning the tenth to Charles's proctors in France. Simon was to reflect that Charles's salvation was at stake, since the King was technically responsible, under pain of excommunication and the interdict, for the repayment of the debts. The Buonsignori were to be paid first, then the Romans, and finally the other bankers. If the tenth again proved insufficient, he was to borrow from the French prelates.[105] 'We want you to know', Clement wrote, '. . . that we can find absolutely no way

---

[101] Ibid., cols. 248–9, 258–9, 260–1, 262–3. 'C'était sa dernière carte que jouait le Saint-Siège' (Jordan, *Les Origines*, p. 555).

[102] *Thes. novus*, ii, cols. 262–3.

[103] Ibid., cols. 254–5.

[104] Saba Malaspina, 'Rerum sicularum', cols. 819, 828.

[105] *Thes. novus*, ii, cols. 295–7. See also ibid., cols. 269–70, 289–90.

of avoiding the ruin of many churches, unless the means are supplied, prudently and effectively, by your industry'.[106] When the scheme of using the churches as security was first proposed, the cardinals who had opposed it had envisaged what would happen if the debts were not repaid in time: the scandal of empty churches, the need to provide for clerics and monks deprived of their revenues.[107] Now this danger loomed large. Simon of Brie was able to repay the Buonsignori debts of November and December, but was not able to meet the deadline of midsummer for the Roman bankers. It was, in fact, the Buonsignori who again saved the day by advancing the legate the necessary sums.[108]

The collection and expenditure of the French tenth now settled into a regular pattern. Simon of Brie was meant to repay all the debts for which the *camera* had been used as security before he handed over the tenth to Charles I's proctors. Charles claimed in March 1267 that these debts had all been repaid, and from October 1266 he was sending orders to his proctors to use the tenth both to repay his own debts and to pay the wages of soldiers and of members of the Angevin court. In this gradual process of paying for the crusade the tenth was one of several items of Angevin income used, including gabelles and harbour dues from Provence and revenue from Anjou.[109] Charles was dissatisfied with the progress of the tenth's collection. In February 1267 he complained to Simon of Brie that he had ordered the wages of many of his soldiers to be paid from the proceeds of the tenth, only to be told that they were not yet sufficient. He needed £60,000 *Tours* for this purpose immediately, and asked Simon to deposit this sum with William Estendard, his seneschal in Provence.[110] There were also clashes between royal and legatine authority. In March 1267 Charles rebuked Simon of Brie for obstructing the payment of

---

[106] Ibid., col. 297.

[107] Ibid., cols. 176–7.

[108] Schneider, 'Zur älteren päpstlichen Finanzgeschichte', pp. 27–9. See also Clement IV, *Reg.*, no. 788.

[109] See *RCAR*, i. Reg. 1, no. 19. Reg. 2, nos. 2, 5, 58. For payments using the tenth, see *RCAR*, i, Reg. 2, nos. 1, 28–34, 55, 58, 187. Reg. 5, nos. 78, 83–4, 87, 90, 92–6, 118, 120, 127 (payment of wages); *RCAR*, i, Reg. 2, nos. 7, 9, 41–2 (*restor* payments); *RCAR*, i, Reg. 2, nos. 12–13, 20–2. Reg. 5, nos. 77, 82, 98 (repayment of debts).

[110] *RCAR*, i, Reg. 2, no. 56.

£1,141. 9s. 4d. to Jourdain of l'Isle Jourdain from the tenth of Narbonne. Not only had the legate failed to obey a papal order to pay Jourdain the money, he had also demanded the restitution of £420 of Toulouse which the Provost of Toulouse, Jourdain's brother, had secured for him from the collectors of the tenth in the diocese of Toulouse.[111]

Such clashes, which reflected the deteriorating relations between Clement IV and Charles I, ended with the arrival in Italy of Conradin in the autumn of 1267. The threat which he posed forced Charles once again to use the clerical tenth as the security for his loans. Between February and October 1268 loans of sums ranging from £1,000 *Tours* to £30,000 were raised with the tenth as security, in particular the amounts still owed by the Cistercians and the military Orders.[112] Clement IV also arranged loans for the King, pawning once again the *camera* and goods of the Holy See, as well as, for one loan, the lands of the Templars in France.[113] In October 1268 Rudolf of Albano was told to satisfy the Pope's Florentine, Sienese, and Roman creditors with money exacted from the Cistercians and the military Orders. Charles agreed that the £30,000 which the Cistercians had consented to pay towards the tenth should go towards repaying the debts of the Pope. He claimed that all such debts had been repaid by September 1269.[114]

In the years after 1266 Charles I's orders to the individuals whom he appointed as 'collectors of the tenth in France' were numerous enough to form a sub-section of their own in the Angevin registers; these officials were active until at least March 1274, when Charles confirmed their authority to exact the remains of the tenth.[115] Their role is confused, since they sometimes handled other forms of Angevin revenue, but it is clear that Charles long continued to use money from the tenth to pay expenses from the campaigns of 1266 and 1268. Not only did his proctors pay the wages of soldiers engaged against Conradin and debts contracted by Charles in 1268, they also

---

[111] *RCAR*, i, Reg. 2, no. 58.

[112] *RCAR*, i, Reg. 5, nos. 268–9, 272–331.

[113] *RCAR*, i, Reg. 5, nos. 284, 286–9; *Thes. novus*, ii, col. 534.

[114] Clement IV, *Reg.*, no. 811; *RCAR*, v, Reg. 16, no. 298, ii, Reg. 8, no. 46.

[115] *RCAR*, xi, Reg. 59, no. 237. Cf. *RCAR*, xii, Reg. 61, no. 18. See also Mazzoleni, *Fonti documentarie*, pp. 34–5.

used the tenth for purposes unconnected with the crusade, such as £200 in compensation for a knight who had been robbed in the *Regno*.[116] The bulk of the tenth was, however, used to repay debts, which built up considerable interest as they lingered from year to year: in September 1273 £2,995 from a total of £9,217 owed to the Buonsignori consisted of interest on a loan of £27,303.[117]

Despite the fact that debts from 1265–6 and 1268 were not paid until 1274, it seems clear that the tenth levied in 1264, when collected in its entirety, was sufficient to pay them all, as well as other expenses connected with the Angevin conquest of the *Regno*. It is noteworthy that Charles I never complained that the fully collected tenth did not cover all his needs. He himself made little financial contribution to the crusades against Manfred and Conradin. The terms agreed on at the enfeoffment of Charles in November 1265 stipulated that he was to pay at least 40,000 marks to the Church, of which 10,000 marks were to be paid within six months of the conquest, and the rest at intervals of six months. By August 1266, however, Charles was denying that he had agreed to pay the money; he never paid it, and his grandson was absolved of the debt by Clement V in 1309.[118] Clearly, the root cause of the crisis of 1265–6 was not the amount of money which could be raised from the tenth, but the fact that it could not be made instantly available, because of the slowness of collection and the very low credit enjoyed by the various members of the Guelf alliance. The situation was saved by Manfred's dilatoriness, by the unpredictable collapse of Ghibelline opposition in Lombardy, and by the last-minute rally of the Buonsignori, but the danger facing the Church in the autumn and winter of 1265–6 was as serious as it ever had been in the long struggle with the Staufen. The risks and expenses which it had necessitated on the part of the papacy were immense and, Clement IV assured Charles I in 1268,

---

[116] See *RCAR*, ii, Reg. 8, nos. 779–809, iii, Reg. 12, nos. 412, 415, Reg. 13, nos. 624, 632. 656. 662. 676. v. Reg. 20. nos. 144. 176. vi. Reg. 22. nos. 1463–4. 1615 (payment of wages); *RCAR*. ii. Reg. 8. nos. 425. 495. iii. Reg. 12. nos. 413. 442. Reg. 13. no. 635. v. Reg. 20, nos. 4, 91, x, Reg. 50, no. 30 (repayment of debts); *RCAR*, vi, Reg. 22, no. 1480 (robbed knight).

[117] *RCAR*, x, Reg. 50, no. 30.

[118] *Thes. novus*, ii, cols. 231, 396; Clement V, *Reg.*, no. 4764.

would not be repeated even if the *Regno* fell again into the hands of the enemies of the Church.[119]

(b) *The Crusade against the Sicilians and the Aragonese*

At first there seemed to be no prospect of such a crisis recurring in 1282, as Charles I now had substantial resources of his own in the Kingdom of Sicily. But Charles's finances had been under strain for years as a result of his Greek and Italian activities, and the failure of the siege of Messina and the continuing expenses of the war soon made his own revenues, curtailed by the loss of Sicily, inadequate. By October 1282 the Angevin treasury had already sent out at least 32,000 gold ounces (160,000 florins) to the Angevin army fighting the rebels, and Charles was forced to look elsewhere for support, in particular to France. The financial situation soon reached crisis point, and by July 1283 the royal treasure was being pawned for a loan.[120]

'As the health or sickness of the head affects the limbs', Charles I wrote to Martin IV, 'so the status and disposition of the Church is involved in my affairs.'[121] Martin was ready to acknowledge that the King was fighting the Church's war;[122] but he was spending heavily in Romagna and the Duchy of Spoleto, and had limited resources available.[123] The only short-term solution, which he soon adopted, was to use the proceeds of the sexennial tenth levied for the Holy Land at the Second Council of Lyons, and Tuscan bankers, especially the Baccusi of Lucca, started to assign the collected tenth to Charles, or to lend him money with the tenth allotted as repayment.[124] In July 1283 Charles I wrote to Charles of Salerno to give him special powers to negotiate a loan of up to 100,000 gold ounces from the Pope on the basis of the tenth.[125] Angevin loans from the Curia already totalled 35,000 gold ounces, 'of the money from tenths from various provinces, which was deposited . . .

---

[119] *Ann. eccles.*, ad ann. 1268, no. 3, xxii, p. 219.
[120] 'Memorie', pp. 94, 98; *Gli atti perduti*, i. 560; Amari, *La guerra*, ii, pt. 1, pp. 278–80.
[121] Ibid., i. 337.
[122] See Amiani, *Memorie istoriche*, ii, pp. lxiv–lxv.
[123] See *Acta imperii, Angliae et Franciae ab anno 1267 ad annum 1313. Dokumente vornehmlich zur Geschichte der auswärtigen Beziehungen Deutschlands*, ed. F. Kern, no. 38; Waley, *Papal State*, pp. 203 ff.
[124] See Jordan, *De mercatoribus*, pp. 83 ff.; *Documenti*, ed. Terlizzi, no. 844.
[125] See 'Memorie', p. 289.

with the Baccusi society'.[126] In November 1283 proctors were
sent to Martin IV to collect part of the 100,000 ounce loan, and
the money was spent on the wages of the mercenaries who were
arriving from France.[127] The military situation deteriorated
and in 1284 Charles I continued to contract large loans.
Edward I of England lent him 20,000 silver marks and
ambassadors were even sent to Tunis to raise money.[128] Tuscan
bankers lent large amounts and there were subsidies from the
north Italian Guelfs, but the majority of the money continued to
come from the Pope. There were papal loans of 4,000 ounces of
gold in December 1283, 88,393 in February 1284, and 15,608 in
April. Some of these loans formed part of the 100,000 ounce loan
contracted in 1283, but others were new.[129] Charles also
received assignments of the Lyons tenth direct from the bankers
with whom it was deposited, or from the collectors themselves.
Treasury accounts of May 1284 reveal that payments from the
tenth constituted nearly half of the total revenue of 36,706
ounces of gold for the period September 1283 to February
1284.[130] In June 1284 Charles sent Odo of Poilechien and the
Bishop of Troia to the Roman Curia and to the Guelf cities of
Tuscany and Lombardy to negotiate a loan of up to 50,000 gold
ounces, using the possessions of the Angevin crown as security.
The summer witnessed the King's last military expedition
against the rebels, and this was the last major loan he attempted
to raise.[131]

The tenth which Martin IV levied in Italy in 1284–5 enabled
his successors to put the financing of the war on a more secure
footing. Honorius IV instructed the collectors to deposit the
money with a wide range of Tuscan bankers, notably the
Lambertuzzi, Frescobaldi, Abbati, and Bacarelli of Florence,
the Buonsignori of Siena, the Ammanati of Pistoia, and the

---

[126] *Documenti*, ed. Terlizzi, no. 834.

[127] See 'Memorie', p. 296; *Documenti*, ed. Terlizzi, no. 842. See also *Gli atti perduti*, i.
531, 561.

[128] See 'Memorie', p. 306; 'Il regno di Carlo I', p. 10.

[129] See *Actes et lettres*, no. 1129; 'Memorie', pp. 309–10; *Documenti*, ed. Terlizzi, no.
864; Amari, *La guerra*, i. 320. For the subsidies from the Guelfs, see Salimbene,
'Cronica', p. 527.

[130] *Documenti*, ed. Terlizzi, no. 869.

[131] See Testa, *De vita*, pp. 229–30.

Riccardi of Lucca.[132] From 1288 onwards this money was used to repay loans which the same bankers had made to the Angevin crown in the period 1285–8. Thus in May 1288 Nicholas IV ordered the repayment to various Florentine, Sienese, and Lucchese cameral bankers of sums totalling 11,332 gold ounces, which they had lent to the proctors of Gerard of Sabina and Robert of Artois. In August 1288 receipts totalling 4,000 gold ounces were issued for loans made to the baillis 'for the necessary and imminent defence of the realm'. These were to be repaid from the tenth levied for the Sicilian war, or from the revenue of the Kingdom of Sicily itself. The tenth for the Holy Land could be used as security but not as the actual repayment of the debt.[133] A series of similar receipts followed in February 1289 for loans of 6,000 gold ounces, and in May for £5,000 *Tours*. In October Florentine bankers who lent 333 ounces to Charles II were directed to deduct this from the tenth collected in the imperial dioceses.[134] Meanwhile loans continued from other sources. In 1288, 10,000 marks were borrowed from Edward I, and in 1289 Nicholas IV sent 2,000 gold ounces to the Archbishop of Naples to pay troops fighting in Principato and Calabria. In 1293 Philip IV lent £8,000 *Tours* for the reconquest of Sicily. The Curia also allowed Charles II to postpone his census payments for the years 1287–90, a total of 32,000 gold ounces.[135]

It was loans such as these, based for the most part on income from the clerical tenth and the credit of the cameral bankers, which ensured the survival of the Angevin monarchy in the critical period 1285–8. Documentary evidence for these years is slight,[136] but the revenue from the kingdom itself certainly could not have paid all the expenses of the war. Large parts of the *Regno* were occupied by the enemy and others had suffered

---

[132] Honorius IV, *Reg.*, nos. 126, 186, 192–3, 332, 520, 553, 609, 621. See also Nicholas IV. *Reg.*, nos. 96–100.

[133] Nicholas IV, *Reg.*, nos. 101–5, 7108–12. The proceeds of the tenth in Provence were also used to pay for sixteen galleys hired there by Charles I. See Nicholas IV, *Reg.*, nos. 583, 601–3.

[134] Nicholas IV, *Reg.*, nos. 7215–19, 7232–3; *Forschungen*, iii, no. 137.

[135] See *Annali*, ii. 12; *Saggio di codice diplomatico formato sulle antiche scritture dell'Archivio di Stato di Napoli*, ed. C. Minieri-Riccio, supplement, i, no. 112; *Cod. dipl. sal.*, ii, no. 231; Nicholas IV, *Reg.*, no. 4307.

[136] See the comments by Mazzoleni in *RCAR*, xxviii, pp. xiii–xiv.

severely from their attacks. In 1289, for instance, Robert of
Artois told the Pope that he was reluctant to permit the export
of oxen because the stock in Calabria and most of Basilicata had
been so depleted by the war that it was doubtful whether crops
could be sown without bringing in teams from Apulia. Robert's
own sumptuary law of 1290 is an indication of the serious
financial deficit in the kingdom.[137] Nor did the return of
Charles and the realignment of the Aragonese lead to an im-
provement in the Angevin financial situation. The ravages of
the war in the western provinces led to the exemption of dozens
of villages and towns from royal taxation in the years 1291–
1300.[138] James II's alignment of the Aragonese crown on the
Angevin side led to additional expenses, in particular the dowry
of 100,000 marks which he was promised when he married
Charles II's daughter Blanche. In spite of the reconquest of
Calabria and the organizational genius of Bartholomew of
Capua, papal aid, in the form of loans from the pope and
advances from bankers based on the clerical tenth, was still a
sine qua non of the Angevin war effort in the period 1295–1302, as
Boniface VIII recognized by continually renewing the Sicilian
tenth. These years therefore witnessed probably the most prolonged and complicated attempt yet made by the Curia to
marshal large funds and use them to fight its wars in Italy. The
operation of the credit system on which this attempt was based
is best approached in two ways: first by describing the manner
in which it functioned, and secondly by analysing the tensions
and difficulties to which it led.

Boniface VIII used fewer banking houses than his predecessors and, despite his outburst against the 'usurers' of
Florence in 1301, showed a marked preference for Florentine
companies.[139] Not only did the bankers of Florence lend very
heavily to Charles II and James II, they also played a large part
in organizing and supplying the allies' forces. The Bardi in
particular purchased arms and supplies for Charles II, and

---

[137] See Nicholas IV, *Reg.*, nos. 7003, 7222; 'Una legge suntuaria', *passim*. See also
ASN, MS Fusco, formerly Reg. Ang. 51, f. 4ʳ.
[138] See *Cod. dipl. sal.*, ii, nos. 180, 224, 230, 249, 255, 262, 292, 293, 298, 306, 308, 310,
314, 316, 319, 321, 409, 410, 454, 482, 488, 505, 572, 577.
[139] For Boniface's outburst of 1301, see *Aus den Tagen Bonifaz VIII.*, p. xxv.

acted as his representatives in collecting the tenth in Achaea.[140] It is still not clear whether the bankers followed or directed the policy of the Commune of Florence, but this first phase of the Florentine penetration of the economy of the *Regno* certainly coincided with a very close political alliance between Charles II and the city.[141] It was an alliance inaugurated by his reception in the city on his release from captivity in 1289, and was quickly given the seal of success when Angevin troops fought for Florence at the battle of Campaldino. Charles II was able to rely on a steady flow of subsidies from the Tuscan communes and the Florentine *parte guelfa*.[142] The *camera* did not, however, rely exclusively on Florentine bankers. One of the largest papal loans to Charles II, a sum of 43,000 gold ounces (over 200,000 florins), was entrusted to the Clarenti of Pistoia in February 1297. The money was urgently needed to pay for the fleet which Boniface VIII hoped would sail against Sicily in the summer; if the loan could not be raised the result would be 'not just damage and serious injury, but indeed shame and ruin' for the Guelf cause. The constitution of the loan is especially interesting because of the wide variety of sources of revenue called on. The Clarenti were to make up the loan from sums to be assigned to them by Boniface's nuncios in France, the cardinal-bishops of Albano and Palestrina. These sums included money raised from the redemption of crusade vows, the £37,000 *Tours* still owed to the Pope by Philip IV from the 1289 tenth, £9,500 owed by the Abbot of Citeaux, a further £9,500 already paid by the Cistercians to the Mozzi, Spini, and Clarenti, £20,000 held by the Francisi, a 6,000 gold ounce subsidy from the Templars, money due to the Pope from the bishop and diocese of Toulouse, and money from English procurations held by the Clarenti. If these sums did not make up 43,000 gold ounces, the Clarenti were to supply the rest themselves, 'by all possible ways and means', even if it entailed arranging loans at interest.[143]

---

[140] See *Forschungen*, iii, nos. 264, 274, 379, 405. The Acciaiuoli were also prominent in some of these transactions.

[141] See, e.g., Yver, *Le Commerce*, pp. 294–7.

[142] See *Forschungen*, iii, nos. 295, 297, 328, 337, 359, 403; W. M. Bowsky, 'Italian Diplomatic History: a Case for the Smaller Commune', in W. C. Jordan *et al.* (eds.), *Order and Innovation in the Middle Ages: Essays in Honor of Joseph R. Strayer*, pp. 70, 443.

[143] Boniface VIII, *Reg.*, nos. 2317–20, 2322–9.

By employing the facilities of the cameral bankers the Curia also enjoyed a high degree of control over how the tenth was spent. Its aim was to permit as little of the money as possible to flow directly from the collectors into the treasuries of its secular allies.[144] In Aragon this was precluded by the control which James II exercised over the Church, but in March 1300 Charles II claimed that very little of the clerical tenth had reached the Angevin treasury by direct consignment, in his reign or in that of his father.[145] Even in Provence Charles's seneschal received the proceeds of the tenth only after it had been assigned to the bankers. This led to complications in 1296, when the Mozzi, Spini, and Clarenti refused to hand over to the seneschal money which the papal collector, the Bishop of Marseilles, had given to them to be consigned to the *camera*. As a reprisal the seneschal confiscated three cargoes of cloth at Marseilles belonging to the first two companies.[146] In 1298 Boniface VIII told his collectors in the diocese of Toulouse to hand over the tenth collected there to an official of Charles II, Philip of Roccamaura, but this was a temporary measure, probably brought about by Philip IV's decrees against the export of currency; Charles was able to persuade his cousin to waive the ruling in the case of money which was destined for the Angevin treasury.[147] Boniface's determination to retain at least some control over the tenths levied for the crusade against the Sicilians is shown by his testy reaction to Charles II's use of the tenth as security for a loan of 4,000 ounces of gold which he contracted with the Clarenti in 1302, without consulting the Pope. Boniface wrote that 'the obligation made in this way by the king is not enough, since he has not been given the requisite authority by us'.[148]

In the loans made to the allies of the pope it is payments to Naples which predominate. Although loans made to Charles II with the tenth as repayment or as security (which in most cases must have meant the same thing) form neither the only source of Angevin revenue for the period 1295–1302, nor the only loans contracted, they do reflect the great expenses involved in the

[144] See, e.g., the instructions in ibid., no. 4489.
[145] See Egidi, 'La colonia saracena', xxxix. 707.
[146] Boniface VIII, *Reg.*, nos. 5468–9; *Forschungen*, iii, no. 266.
[147] *Cod. dipl. sal.* ii, no. 444.
[148] Boniface VIII, *Reg.*, nos. 4485–6.

war's last phase. In 1295 little could be borrowed on the strength of the tenth, as it had only recently been levied. A Frescobaldi loan of 1,000 gold ounces in July had as its security the remains of Nicholas IV's tenth as well as the proceeds of the new tenth and the Angevin possessions generally.[149] At Boniface VIII's request the Clarenti forwarded Charles II the 25,000 marks needed to pay the first instalment of James II's dowry, and in November Boniface himself lent Charles II £7,000 for the liberation of his hostages in Aragon.[150]

In 1296 more loans were contracted using the new tenth, a total of 50,000 florins from the Francisi, Spini, Mozzi, and Clarenti for the defence of the realm and the construction of a fleet, and £7,000 from the new tenth in Provence was given to the seneschal there for the building of ships.[151] In 1297 preparations were made for the joint expedition of 1298, and the total sums borrowed rose to the highest for the war, about 380,000 florins. The Clarenti, who held half of the 1295 tenth, contributed 43,000 gold ounces and 25,000 marks towards this, besides giving Charles II smaller sums for his expenses in France.[152] The Francisi lent 5,300 gold ounces in January, and £10,000 and 31,586 florins in September. The Pope lent 4,000 ounces of gold and £21,000. The Fenestri gave £1,000 *Tours* to James II, the Clarenti £1,000 *Tours* and £1,458 'in grossis argenteis'. Charles II's proctor in France collected £15,000 in legacies for the Holy Land, and £5,000 owed to the Pope by the diocese of Toulouse.[153] But all this was not enough, and at the end of the year Angevin agents, John Pipino and Henry of Guérard, were sent out to raise extra loans of £40,000.[154]

From 1298 onwards it was the Bardi, the Spini, and the Clarenti who received the tenth from the collectors and assumed the bulk of the lending to the Angevins. In 1298 about 50,000 florins were lent, £2,000 by the Peruzzi, 10,000 gold ounces by the Bardi.[155] The biggest transaction of the following year

[149] *Forschungen*, iii, no. 233.
[150] Boniface VIII, *Reg.*, no. 217; *Saggio*, supplement, i, no. 97.
[151] Boniface VIII, *Reg.*, nos. 1578–9, 5460–1, 5465–7, 5468–9.
[152] Ibid., nos. 1691, 2314, 2317–20, 2322–9.
[153] Ibid., nos. 1495, 1515, 1692, 1698, 5477, 5492–3, 5494–7; *Forschungen*, iii, nos. 274, 283.
[154] Egidi, 'La colonia saracena', xxxix. 701.
[155] *Forschungen*, iii, nos. 291, 304.

arose from Boniface VIII's purchase of the Angevin crown for
100,000 florins.[156] The Spini, besides handling the purchase of
the crown, lent 15,000 florins themselves, and the Clarenti paid
James II 32,000 florins towards the Angevin dowry.[157] The
Bardi lent 1,000 gold ounces on the security of the Provence
tenth, but most of their loans for 1299, which totalled 23,000
gold ounces for the period September–October alone, were
made on the basis of trade concessions by Charles II.[158] The
Pope lent 23,000 florins and 3,300 ounces of gold in September
and October 1299.[159] The year 1300 was dominated by papal
loans, totalling over 34,000 ounces of gold, much of it the profit
from the Jubilee. The Spini also lent 30,000 florins and 4,000
ounces of gold in February and March.[160] In 1301 the Bardi
lent Charles II 6,000 gold ounces, and in 1302 the Clarenti lent
him 4,000 gold ounces, the Bardi 30,000 florins.[161] In 1301–2
Charles of Valois also required loans; the Spini lent him 84,000
florins, the Bardi 31,000. An Aragonese cleric at the Curia
reported that he also received 120,000 florins directly from the
papal *camera* in 1302.[162]

Depending on the exchange rates and the meaning of certain
loans, the total lent to the allies of the pope which was repaid
from the proceeds of the clerical tenth and the subsidy came to
about a million florins.[163] In a system which involved such large
and continual loans, the repayment of which depended on the
pope's ability to tax the Church in the face of clerical and
sometimes secular opposition, tensions and difficulties were
inevitable. The strain which the papal demand for credit imposed on the cameral bankers was immense. The burdens of the

---

[156] Boniface VIII, *Reg.*, nos. 3057, 3116, 3219. See also *Forschungen*, iii, no. 318; Egidi,
'La colonia saracena', xxxix. 708.

[157] Boniface VIII, *Reg.*, nos. 3001, 3220.

[158] See Egidi, 'La colonia saracena', xxxix. 714; Amari, *La guerra*, i. 534.

[159] See Egidi, 'La colonia saracena', xxxix. 714. See also *Annali*, ii. 60.

[160] See Boniface VIII, *Reg.*, nos. 3468–9; Egidi, 'La colonia saracena', xxxix. 714,
721; *Cod. dipl. sal.* ii, no. 568; Amari, *La guerra*, i. 575; Tomacelli, *Storia*, ii. 441.

[161] Boniface VIII, *Reg.*, nos. 4128–30, 4485–6, 4487–9.

[162] Ibid., nos. 4817, 5266, 4489; *Aus den Tagen Bonifaz VIII.*, p. xlvi. For Boniface's
financial relations with Charles of Valois, see also *Aus den Tagen Bonifaz VIII.*, p. xxxi;
Boase, *Boniface VIII*, p. 270.

[163] Baethgen ('Quellen und Untersuchungen', pp. 185–90), reached a total of
1,225,000 florins, but he included loans and subsidies for which there is no evidence
that crusade revenue was used.

Sicilian war coincided with increasing demands for loans from the kings of England and France.[164] Even before the outbreak of war between them the wealth and vulnerability of the bankers made them a tempting source for plunder. In 1291 Philip IV imprisoned several cameral bankers and Nicholas IV had to petition him for their release and for the restitution of their goods.[165] The Anglo-French war brought increased borrowing and savage and unpredictable action against houses which lent to the other side. Boniface VIII, like Nicholas IV, took the view that the bankers were forwarding the cause of the crusade to regain the Holy Land, a cause to which the Anglo-French conflict was in any case a serious obstacle. In June 1299 he begged Edward I not to insist on a large loan from the Spini, 'as they are at present weighed down by similar burdens both across the Alps and in Italy, and in particular at the Holy See'.[166]

The coincidence of papal, French, and English demands, together with the general decline of trade at the close of the thirteenth century, led to falling credit and the collapse in swift succession of several leading banking houses, including the Buonsignori of Siena, the Ammanati of Pistoia, the Riccardi of Lucca, and the Mozzi of Florence.[167] In the case of the Riccardi, it was the pressure of the papal–Angevin loans which brought about the collapse. They had already suffered heavy losses in France and England when, in the autumn of 1295, Boniface VIII called on them to pay 40,000 florins from their holdings of the tenth towards the Angevin dowry. An appeal to the Pope by the Riccardi representative, Labro Volpelli, led him to lessen his demands for a time, but papal insistence on payment from 1298 onwards led to the collapse of the company

---

[164] See, e.g., M. C. Prestwich, *War, Politics and Finance under Edward I*, pp. 205–19; Kaeuper, *Bankers to the Crown, passim.*

[165] Nicholas IV, *Reg.*, nos. 7326, 7384, 7393; E. Re, 'La compagnia dei Riccardi in Inghilterra e il suo fallimento alla fine del secolo xiii', *Archivio della R. Società romana di storia patria*, xxxvii (1914), 99–100. Philip IV's excuse for this action, and for similar measures taken in 1303–4 and 1309–10, was that the Italians were guilty of usury. See Strayer and Taylor, *Studies in Early French Taxation*, pp. 17–18.

[166] Boniface VIII, *Reg.*, no. 3065.

[167] See A. Fliniaux, 'La Faillite des Ammanati de Pistoie et le Saint-Siège (début du xive siècle)', *Revue historique de droit français et étranger*, 4th series, iii (1924), *passim*; E. Jordan, 'La Faillite des Buonsignori', in *Mélanges Paul Fabre, passim*; Re, 'La compagnia dei Riccardi', *passim*; Jordan, *De mercatoribus*, pp. 37–44.

in 1300.[168] The Ammanati too fell because of the activities of Boniface VIII, but in their case it was his interference in Tuscan politics which was responsible. At the beginning of 1302 Charles of Valois, Boniface's 'pacifier of Tuscany', ordered the seizure of the goods of all Pistoians because of the control of the Commune of Pistoia by the White Guelfs. The Ammanati representatives at the Curia were unable to get the exemption granted to their rivals, the Clarenti. They fled overnight and Boniface took vigorous action against the defaulting company.[169] The Buonsignori, 'the Rothschilds of the thirteenth century', had stopped handling cameral business in 1292, but at their collapse in 1298 they still held 80,000 florins of crusade revenue. The Curia did not pursue the Buonsignori as actively as it did the Riccardi and the Ammanati. An investigation of their holdings was ordered by Clement V in 1307, but it was not until 1344 that Clement VI began a determined attempt to recover the money.[170]

The result of such events, and of the unfavourable credit situation generally, was that other houses became unwilling to allow their loans to the Angevins to exceed their holdings of papal revenue. Thus in December 1296 the Spini, Mozzi, and Clarenti objected to handing over £7,000 of the Provence tenth to Charles II's seneschal partly because this sum was already exceeded by papal debts to themselves. Similarly, the Clarenti were not prepared to assign papal money to a nuncio of James II in October 1298 until they had a specific order to do so from Boniface VIII.[171] The solution adopted by the Pope was to cut down the number of cameral bankers and to ensure that loans were more directly linked to sums available from the tenth. After 1299 the bulk of the loans were advanced by the Bardi, Spini, Circuli, and Clarenti, and the repayment of these loans was divided between collectors of the tenth. For instance, when the Bardi lent 6,000 gold ounces to Charles II in September 1301, they received 2,500 from the Bishop of Siena, 2,500 from

---

[168] Re, 'La compagnia dei Riccardi', *passim*; Kaeuper, *Bankers to the Crown*, pp. 209–48. See also Clement V, *Reg.*, nos. 2294–6; ASV, Instr. misc., no. 311 (tr. Lunt in *Papal Revenues*, i, no. 170).

[169] Boniface VIII, *Reg.*, nos. 5000, 5002, 4639, 5331. See also Benedict XI, *Reg.*, nos. 882–7, 1151; Fliniaux, 'La Faillite des Ammanati', *passim*.

[170] Clement V, *Reg.*, no. 2296; Jordan, 'La Faillite des Buonsignori', *passim*.

[171] Boniface VIII, *Reg.*, nos. 5468–9; *Acta arag.* i, no. 37.

the Archbishop of Capua, and 1,000 from the Archbishop of Patras.[172] This was not a new system, nor was it rigidly adhered to, but it ensured that when Clement V closed the papal accounts with the Bardi and the Spini in October 1306, the firms actually owed the *camera* money, despite Spini payments of 84,000 florins to Charles of Valois, and Bardi payments of 83,000 florins to Charles of Valois and Charles II.[173]

Another major problem which arose from the enormous payments and complex credit arrangements of these years was the strain which they imposed on the relations of the Curia with James II and Charles II. The Aragonese proctors have left us with vivid accounts of Boniface's fury and dissatisfaction with the two kings, and the chief cause of these was financial. James II encountered great opposition in Aragon to his new political alignment and undoubtedly found his financial burden a convenient excuse for ending it, but there does seem to have been a genuine failure by Boniface VIII to keep his ally paid.[174] In order to set sail at all in 1297, James was meant to receive loans in anticipation of the tenth, which was only levied in February. Its collection was in any case held up by problems arising from 'Clericis laicos'. He ascribed his failure to arrive in Italy to the fact that he had not received enough money. Charles II responded by sending loans, notably 11,000 gold ounces by way of his seneschal in Provence.[175] James brought his fleet to Italy in late summer 1298 and blockaded Syracuse in October, but soon renewed his complaints. On 25 October 1298 he asked the Pope to tell the Clarenti to pay the 10,000 marks still due from the dowry, explaining that because of its non-payment estates which he had used as a guarantee for the repayment of his debts could not be redeemed and would soon be lost to the royal demesne.[176] At the end of June 1299 he sent a letter to the consul of the Catalans at Naples, to be given to Charles II, asking him to press Boniface VIII to pay at once the 10,000

---

[172] Boniface VIII, *Reg.*, nos. 4128–30. Cf. his *Reg.*, nos. 3116, 3219, 4485–6 (an arrangement involving payments by six different collectors); *Rat. dec. Italiae. Latium*, pp. 434, 435.

[173] Clement V, *Reg.*, nos. 1151–2.

[174] For a different interpretation, see Boase, *Boniface VIII*, pp. 213–14.

[175] *Acta arag.* i, nos. 27, 30; Digard, *Philippe le Bel*, ii. 303–4; Egidi, 'La colonia saracena', xxxix. 700–1.

[176] *Acta arag.* i, no. 37. See also ibid., no. 38.

florins still owed him; the dowry was not in fact fully paid until April 1300.[177] The Pope was also failing to keep his promise to reimburse some of James's expenses from the 1298 campaign. Charles II, anxious to keep James's fleet in operation, acknowledged this and undertook to pay the expenses himself, 20,489 gold ounces. He granted James substantial export dues from the *Regno*, to be paid annually until James's death. Nevertheless, James withdrew his fleet in August 1299, protesting at the failure of his allies to pay him.[178]

In February or March 1300 James again offered his help, but his terms were high. He was to get an immediate subsidy of 2,000 gold ounces, a tenth in Aragon, and an annual revenue of 2,000 gold ounces from Provence and Forcalquier. Of the latter, 8,000 ounces were to be raised in advance from bankers to pay the Aragonese mercenaries and sailors who had taken part in the campaign of 1298–9. Otherwise, he wrote, there was little hope of persuading them to come again. He was, however, ready to permit and aid (though not to pay for) the preparation and despatch of six ships if a letter arrived granting him simply the tenth.[179] Boniface VIII did grant a new tenth, but there was no more Aragonese help. Angevin payments for the services which James had performed continued long after the war ended. In 1304 Charles II paid him 10,000 gold ounces from various sources, including 4,000 from Provence and 1,000 from Robert of Calabria's own income, 'for the voyage to Sicily'.[180] Four years later James was paid a further 2,500 ounces of gold 'in part payment of the debt of 10,000 ounces which we owe to the said king, by reason of the composition and agreement which we entered into and concluded with the king's proctors for the expenses of his voyage to Sicily with his following of cavalry and foot'.[181]

It was, however, papal–Angevin relations which suffered most in the war. In order to pay his expenses, Charles II needed

[177] Ibid., no. 42; *Cartulaire général*, nos. 4490, 4498.
[178] Testa, *De vita*, pp. 253–4, 256–7 (summaries in Egidi, 'La colonia saracena', xxxix. 706, 712). See also *Cod. dipl. sal.* ii, no. 559. For James's protests, see *Acta arag.* i, no. 48.
[179] *Acta arag.* i, nos. 54, 57.
[180] Ibid., no. 98.
[181] *Il regno di Sicilia negli ultimi anni di vita di Carlo II. d'Angiò*, ed. A. Cutolo, no. xxi. See also *Studii storici fatti sopra 84 registri angioini dell'Archivio di Stato di Napoli*, ed. C. Minieri-Riccio, p. 99; *Il regno di Sicilia*, no. xxix.

both frequent loans from the Pope and advances on the tenth. Between 1295 and 1298 both were forthcoming, and Boniface also regularly postponed the census payments to Rome. But in 1299 papal credit was getting low. Boniface made it clear that he wanted Charles to depend less on papal loans, and in January or early February he sent three cardinals to Naples to make an exact calculation of Angevin arrears in paying the census since the start of the war in order that Charles might start paying them. The result was a crisis in Angevin finances. For several months in 1299 Charles II had to grant valuable trade concessions in order to raise loans.[182] For some time Boniface remained unresponsive to the pleas of his vassal; at the beginning of October a proctor of James II at the Curia reported that 'the King of Sicily begs both in and out of season for money . . . in order to send help to the lord duke [Robert of Calabria] and his troops; so far he has not got anything, although the pope has granted some money, which has not yet been despatched, after the greatest difficulty'.[183] The crisis continued into 1300, its climax being the destruction of Lucera, which was almost certainly a last desperate measure to gain a financial respite.[184] Boniface then started lending again, and in 1301 renewed the tenth, but the Aragonese at the Curia reported the deterioration of the papal–Angevin alliance, which in 1301 and 1302 was only held together by the mediation of Charles of Valois.[185]

The difference between the Guelf financial crises of 1265 and 1299–1300 lies in the contrasting reactions of Clement IV and Boniface VIII to Angevin demands for help. Boniface was not prepared, as Clement had been, to throw everything into the struggle to finance his Angevin vassal; on the contrary, it is possible that Boniface even contemplated abandoning the war at this time. Papal–Angevin relations had undergone a dramatic change. Instead of Charles I rescuing the Church from Manfred, the Church was saving the Angevin dynasty

[182] See Egidi, 'La colonia saracena', xxxix. 706–7, 714; *Cod. dipl. sal.*, ii. 605. See also ASN, MS Ferraro, no. 38, ff. 41–2, formerly Reg. Ang. 96, f. 9ʳ; 'Carlo II e i debiti angioini', p. 118; Yver, *Le Commerce*, p. 296.

[183] *Acta arag.* i, no. 49. Cf. *Aus den Tagen Bonifaz VIII.*, p. xv.

[184] See Egidi, 'La colonia saracena', xxxix. 697, 727–32.

[185] See, e.g., *Aus den Tagen Bonifaz VIII.*, pp. xlv–xlvi; Boase, *Boniface VIII*, pp. 289–90.

from the Aragonese. Moreover, Boniface was disgusted at the series of negotiations, cancelled treaties, concessions, and half-hearted military expeditions which had constituted the Angevin war effort since 1285.[186] The Curia had sunk much money and prestige in a war which it had lost. Consequently it was not prepared, as in the case of the crusade against Manfred, to absorb the cost itself. In 1306–8 Angevin lands which were mortgaged for the repayment of various debts owed to the Church were slowly redeemed.[187] In the summer of 1307 Charles II and his representatives, including Bartholomew of Capua, argued with Clement V at Poitiers on who was to pay for the war. Two detailed sets of proposals were made. The undated 'form for the remission of debts', which was drawn up by Bartholomew of Capua, evidently came first. It proposed that all debts, including the arrears of the annual census payments, were to be cancelled in return for the service of twenty galleys for six months at the next general passage to the Holy Land. This optimistic plan was based on three main arguments, which were expounded in consistory by Peter, Archbishop of Arles. First, it was claimed that the war was the cause of the Church and that its cost should be borne by the Church. Secondly, the devastation which the war had brought about in the mainland provinces of the *Regno*, as well as the loss of Sicily and the alienation of the County of Anjou by treaty to Charles of Valois, precluded the possibility of repaying in full the debts incurred by Charles II and his father. Lastly, it was argued that although the proceeds of the tenths levied by Martin IV, Nicholas IV, and Boniface VIII to finance the war had been promised to the Angevins, most of the money had been spent by the Curia; this money should therefore be considered as the repayment of papal loans to Charles I and Charles II.[188]

The Angevin deputation was plainly trying to deceive Clement V. While it is true that the bulls which levied the tenths did give the impression that the money was to be given to the Angevins as a subsidy, Charles II must have expected to

---

[186] This was particularly true of the truce of Gaeta, which Charles II had insisted on concluding in active opposition to the wishes of the Curia. See Boniface VIII, *Reg.*, no. 3425; Boase, *Boniface VIII*, p. 19.

[187] *Forschungen*, iii. nos. 509, 503; *Syll. mem.*, iii. 164; *Il regno di Sicilia*, no. xxix.

[188] See 'Carlo II e i debiti angioini', pp. 123–9, and the summary by Monti, ibid., pp. 121–3.

have to return the money eventually. In the reign of Nicholas IV he had undertaken to pay the Holy See the revenue from the reconquered island of Sicily as the repayment of the debts contracted by his father and himself. The pope was to keep a representative in Sicily specifically for the purpose of collecting the revenue, once the costs of actual administration had been deducted. When the debts had been repaid the revenues of the island were to be returned to Charles II.[189] Obviously, since the island had not been regained, this plan could not be implemented, but Clement did not intend to remit all the debts. On 20 July, in the presence of the King and 'with his willing and special consent', he issued a privilege confuting the 'error' that the Church was legally responsible for the debts of Charles II and his father. While it was undeniable that the Kingdom of Sicily was held of the pope as a fief, this did not constitute an obligation on the Church to pay or relinquish the debts of its vassals for the past war or for any future conflict or rebellion.[190]

On the same day Clement produced a detailed reply to Bartholomew's document. This was a set of proposals which, although formally 'proposed' by Charles II, bears clearly the imprint of Clement's own projects and hopes. As we have seen, this document also envisaged the repayment of the debts, which were estimated at 366,000 gold ounces (1,830,000 florins), in terms partly of Angevin aid to the Holy Land, though the aid was to be greater than that proposed by Bartholomew of Capua.[191] Charles II provided a formal written acceptance of this plan, as well as of Clement's proposals for the repayment of the arrears of the census, 93,340 gold ounces, in varying annual amounts.[192] Clearly, however, the part of the plan relating to the Holy Land was never carried out, and Giovanni Villani believed that Clement acquitted Robert of Naples of the entire debt in 1309[193].

---

[189] See R. Fawtier, 'Documents négligés sur l'activité de la chancellerie apostolique à la fin du xiiie siècle. Le registre 46A et les comptes de la chambre sous Boniface VIII', *Mélanges*, lii (1935), 249. Boniface VIII also intended all payments to Naples to be loans rather than subsidies. See, e.g., *Aus den Tagen Bonifaz VIII.*, p. xlvi.

[190] *Acta pontificum*, ed. G. Battelli, no. 18. In brief in Clement V, *Reg.*, no. 10583.

[191] Ibid., no. 2269. See also above, pp. 95–6.

[192] Clement V, *Reg.*, nos. 2270, 10584–6.

[193] *Cronica*, ii. 140.

(c) *The Crusades against the Ghibellines, 1320–1334*

When the Curia was again faced by the necessity of fighting a prolonged war in Italy, in the 1320s, its problems had changed. The financial innovations of Clement V and John XXII effectively ended, at least for the period considered here, the need to rely heavily on the credit facilities of the Italian bankers. In its place there was the problem of actually transferring the money to Italy from Avignon. This difficulty was complicated by the fact that the struggle with the Ghibelline revival had to be waged on several fronts at once. In Lombardy and Romagna Bertrand du Poujet was engaged in warfare with the Visconti and their allies throughout the period 1321–34.[194] In the Duchy of Spoleto and the March of Ancona the papal authorities had heavy costs to meet from 1321 until about 1330.[195] In Tuscany Giovanni Orsini was fighting Castruccio Castracani from 1326 to 1328 and Louis IV in 1328–9. The soldiers of Robert of Naples participated on all these fronts to some degree. Supplying each area of conflict with money called for an exacting effort of organization.

With so many *stipendiarii* directly dependent on papal revenue, King Robert was unable to secure financial backing on the scale which his father and grandfather had come to expect. The *camera* continued to give valuable support to the Angevin war effort. Apart from the tenths of 1328 and 1339, Robert was granted half of the proceeds of the Vienne tenth from the clergy of the *Regno*.[196] He also received some loans towards the cost of fulfilling his office of imperial vicar in Lombardy and Tuscany, 25,000 florins in 1319, 25,000 in 1320, and 6,500 in 1321.[197] John XXII was generous in granting census postponements and gave Robert occasional subsidies, such as 900 gold ounces from the spoils of the Archbishop of Cosenza in 1322 and half those of the Archbishop of Naples in 1323.[198] It was, however, the papal legates and the rectors in the Papal State who absorbed the bulk of crusade revenue between 1321 and 1334.

[194] For Bertrand du Poujet's expenditure, see *Die Ausgaben*, pp. 348–76, 381–544.

[195] See *Les Archives*, pp. 27–8; *Deutsche Ritter*, i. 13, ii. 118 ff.

[196] See above, pp. 104–5, 178–9.

[197] John XXII, *Lettres communes*, nos. 12292–4, 14392–3, 14403–4; *Die Ausgaben*, pp. 816–17; Bock, 'Kaisertum', pp. 185, 216–19.

[198] ASV, Reg. Vat. 111, f. 314^{r-v}, nos. 1258, 1260–1, Reg. Vat. 112, f. 17^{r-v}, no. 75; John XXII, *Lettres communes*, nos. 2017, 4847, 5499, 5619, 6162, 8378, 10043, 10358, 20591, 44617–18, 46310, 48898, 50805, 50811.

Throughout this period Lombardy and the March of Ancona remained the areas of highest expenditure. Renouard estimated that Bertrand du Poujet received a total of 2,480,000 florins from Avignon in the period of his legation, while the March absorbed another 125,000 florins between 1323 and 1330.[199] Curiously, there are no records for the transfer of money to Giovanni Orsini, who was, presumably, heavily dependent on Angevin and Florentine troops. Of the money transported to Bertrand du Poujet, 1,200,000 was carried by bankers, 1,280,000 by nuncios and other clerics. Thus, although their credit facilities were much less important, the banking houses continued to play a leading role in the transfer of crusade revenue.[200]

Besides authorizing the transfer of these enormous sums of money from Avignon, John XXII also made skilful use of crusade funds raised in Italy itself. Naturally this source was less important quantitatively than Avignon. Papal accounts for Bertrand du Poujet's legation, for the period from 8 July 1324 to 1 July 1327, record that out of 1,164,363 florins spent by the legate on mercenaries, only 42,650 had come from tenths and annates raised in Italy; the equivalent figures for the period between 1 July 1327 and 1 February 1331 were 724,624 florins and 51,066.[201] But the importance of revenue raised in Italy cannot be measured in figures alone. Communication with Avignon took time, messengers could be waylaid and money stolen *en route*: over 28,000 florins were stolen by the Ghibellines between 1327 and 1331.[202] The relative speed and security with which money collected in Italy could be transferred gave it great importance in an emergency.

There were several ways in which crusade revenue raised in Italy could be employed without the money first going to Avignon. In the Papal State John XXII often gave the authorities of a province permission to use the revenue which they were collecting on the spot. Thus in January 1322 the Rector and Treasurer of the March were told to approach the bishops and their sub-collectors in the province for the proceeds of the 1321 tenth, and to use them to pay the wages of the 200 cavalry

[199] See *Les Relations*, pp. 169–80. Cf. *Die Ausgaben*, pp. 13*–14*, 31*.
[200] See Renouard, *Les Relations*, pp. 121–96 and *passim*.
[201] ASV, Reg. Vat. 115, f. 85ᵛ, no. 1459, Reg. Vat. 116, ff. 302ʳ–303ᵛ, no. 1561.
[202] ASV, Reg. Vat. 116, ff. 302ʳ–303ᵛ, no. 1561.

which they had sent to support the Malatesta of Rimini against Urbino.[203] Similarly, in October 1322 and May 1323 the Treasurer of the Duchy of Spoleto, John Amiel, was told to use such sums of the 1321 tenth as had been collected so far in the Duchy to pay the wages of Perugian mercenaries employed against Spoleto, and the Treasurer of the March was given orders to employ both the tenth and annates from his province in the struggle with Fermo and Fabriano.[204] From 1323 onwards the treasurers in both provinces were able to rely on the tenths and annates which were regularly renewed there as a substantial addition to their ordinary sources of revenue.[205]

Outside the Papal State collectors of crusade taxes and subsidies were frequently ordered to transfer their money directly to papal representatives engaged in the struggle against the Ghibellines. As in the dispatch of money from Avignon itself, it was Bertrand du Poujet and the authorities in the March of Ancona who benefited most from this arrangement; from 1323 onwards they received a regular supply of money from all the Italian collectorates, usually the proceeds of tenths and annates.[206] Although the sums involved were fairly small, failure on the part of the collectors to comply with a papal order to transfer money could lead to serious results. In May 1323 John XXII wrote to the Archbishop of Ravenna and his suffragans ordering them for the second time to assign all the proceeds of the 1321 tenth collected by themselves in the province of Romagna to the Rector and Treasurer of the March of Ancona. Their delay in obeying had led to 'much damage' to the cause of the Church in the March.[207] Papal legates and the authorities of the Papal State were also occasionally told to transfer money to another papal representative whose needs were more immediate. Typical is an order of January 1322 to

[203] ASV, Reg. Vat. 111, f. 104^{r-v}, no. 420.

[204] ASV, Reg. Vat. 111, f. 305^{r-v}, nos. 1211–12, f. 320^{r-v}, nos. 1286–7, ff. 323^v–324^r, nos. 1301–2.

[205] See 'I registri', vi. 249–50; *Codex dipl.* 1, no. 703; Reydellet-Guttinger, *L'Administration pontificale*, p. 75.

[206] ASV, Reg. Vat. 111, ff. 355^v–356^r, nos. 1466–7, Reg. Vat. 112, ff. 65^v–66^r, nos. 306–7, Reg. Vat. 113, f. 99^r, no. 703, f. 335^r, no. 1967, Reg. Vat. 115, f. 22^v, nos. 1119–20, f. 26^r, nos. 1137–8, Reg. Vat. 117, ff. 15^v–16^r, no. 69 (to Bertrand du Poujet); ASV, Reg. Vat. 114, ff. 17^v–19^r, nos. 48–9, 51–2, 58, f. 47^r, no. 232, ff. 257^r–258^r, nos. 1406, 1414, f. 265^r, no. 1475, Reg. Vat. 115, ff. 24^r–25^r, nos. 149, 155, f. 27^v, no. 172, f. 29^{r-v}, no. 188, f. 69^v, no. 1368 (to March of Ancona).

[207] ASV, Reg. Vat. 111, ff. 342^v–343^r, no. 1405.

the Rector of Romagna telling him to send money from the 1321 tenth to his colleagues in the March.[208] The Rector of the March in particular received financial, and sometimes military, help from all the other rectors.[209] Sometimes Bertrand du Poujet exerted his over-all authority as director of papal affairs in northern Italy to make financial demands on the provincial administration without consulting Avignon.[210]

This constant transfer of money between papal officials and representatives did not exist in isolation; it has to be seen against the broader background of the Guelf alliance and its operation. Unfortunately very little is known about the financial mechanism of the alliance, which centred on the armies periodically raised by the Guelf leagues, the *tallie*.[211] Certainly there was regular transfer of money between the leading centres of Guelfism, and the accounts of the rectors of the Papal State reveal that they were in close touch with Naples, Florence, and Bologna.[212] The best-documented years in this respect are those of 1327–30, crisis years for the Church, the Angevin kingdom, and Guelfism generally. The arrival of Louis IV, the occupation of Rome, the threat to Naples, and the added impetus which Louis's presence gave to the struggle in the March of Ancona, decisively shifted the focus of the Guelf–Ghibelline conflict from northern to central Italy. The bulk of crusade revenue, on the other hand, remained at Bologna with Bertrand du Poujet. Consequently there are many examples during these years of the rapid transfer of crusade funds to build up defences against the Ghibelline offensive. Bertrand du Poujet was told to send money to the March and the Patrimony of St. Peter in Tuscany, and he also dispatched soldiers and money to Florence and Naples.[213] The two areas most threatened were the March and Campagna-Marittima. At the end of the 1327 and early in 1328 the authorities of

---

[208] ASV, Reg. Vat. 111, ff. 104ᵛ–105ʳ, no. 421.

[209] See, e.g., ASV, I et E, no. 68, ff. 15ʳ–19ʳ, ASV, Reg. Vat. 113, ff. 111ʳ–112ʳ, nos. 788–91, f. 175ʳ⁻ᵛ, nos. 1034–5; 'I registri', iii. 540–1, 547, vi. 42. See also *Rat. dec. Italiae. Latium*, pp. 438–40.

[210] See, e.g., ASV, Reg. Vat. 115, f. 71ᵛ, no. 1386.

[211] See Waley, 'The Army of the Florentine Republic', pp. 81–2; Bowsky, 'Italian Diplomatic History', pp. 64–7.

[212] See, e.g., ASV, I et E, no. 77, ff. 42ᵛ–43ᵛ, 93ʳ–95ʳ; 'I registri', iii. 544, vi. 43, 58.

[213] ASV, Reg. Vat. 114, f. 210ʳ, no. 1143, f. 217ʳ⁻ᵛ, no. 1172, ff. 218ᵛ–219ʳ, nos. 1186–7, f. 221ʳ, no. 1211; 'I registri', iii. 544; *Urkunden*, nos. 101, 147–8.

Romagna, the Duchy, and Campagna-Marittima were told to send all their available money to the March.[214] In February 1328 the Rector of Campagna-Marittima was directed not to send money to the March but to keep it for the defence of his own province.[215] King Robert meanwhile was asked to send 20,000 florins to Campagna-Marittima. But he had enough financial problems of his own in defending the *Regno*, and did not respond even when the sum requested was lowered to 15,000 florins in June.[216] Louis struck north and abandoned Rome, but papal appeals continued for the beleaguered March. In March 1329 Robert was asked to send 25,000 florins for the province 'in money or in grain'. Gerard of Valle was asked to send 10,000, the Treasurer of Campagna-Marittima 4,000, Bertrand du Poujet 5,000, the Treasurer of the Duchy all he could raise.[217] Such appeals continued into 1330, but the centre of the Guelf–Ghibelline stuggle had shifted once again to Lombardy and Romagna and in John XXII's last years it was Bertrand du Poujet who needed extra revenue.[218]

iii. CONCLUSION

The reign of John XXII showed that the Curia had successfully solved the problems of raising money and of getting it to its agents in Italy without an excessive reliance on the credit facilities of the bankers. The relations of the Curia with its bankers were noticeably more formal than those of Boniface VIII and his predecessors had been. The result was that when the major banking houses collapsed in the early 1340s the papacy suffered much less damage than it had done in the 1290s.[219] The *camera* prized its independence and accountability even at the cost of extra bureaucracy. Thus, although nearly two-thirds of John XXII's revenue was spent on his

---

[214] ASV, Reg. Vat. 114, f. 258ʳ, no. 1414, ff. 260ᵛ–261ʳ, no. 1442; John XXII, *Lettres communes*, nos. 42404, 42410.

[215] ASV, Reg. Vat. 114, f. 267ᵛ, no. 1500.

[216] ASV, Reg. Vat. 114, f. 266ᵛ, no. 1487, f. 340ᵛ, no. 1976, f. 342ᵛ, no. 1983, f. 345ʳ, no. 2006. See also Reg. Vat. 114, ff. 342ᵛ–343ʳ, nos. 1985–6.

[217] ASV, Reg. Vat. 115, ff. 34ᵛ–35ᵛ, nos. 217–19, 223–5, f. 43ᵛ, no. 281, f. 44ʳ, no. 284, ff. 47ᵛ–48ʳ, no. 308, ff. 141ᵛ–142ʳ, no. 834, f. 143ʳ, nos. 840–1, f. 145ʳ⁻ᵛ, nos. 857, 859, f. 147ʳ, no. 869, f. 40ᵛ, no. 1205. See also ASV, Reg. Vat. 115, f. 25ʳ, no. 156, f. 137ʳ, nos. 818, 820, f. 147ᵛ, no. 871.

[218] ASV, Reg. Vat. 115, f. 139ʳ⁻ᵛ, nos. 1795–7, f. 140ʳ, nos. 1803–4, Reg. Vat. 117, ff. 15ᵛ–16ʳ, nos. 69–72, ff. 22ᵛ–23ʳ, nos. 123–4.

[219] See Renouard, *Les Relations*, pp. 125–6.

Italian wars, over 170,000 florins of the money raised in Italy was still sent to Avignon.[220] There remained problems. John XXII did not win his wars in Italy and his failure has to be attributed at least partly to inadequate funds. The soldiers of Bertrand du Poujet mutinied at a critical point in 1323 because they had not been paid for some months.[221] But the 1320s and 1330s did not witness a crisis of credit comparable to that of 1265 or 1299–1300.

For a short time the Avignon popes achieved a financial solvency denied to their predecessors; the *camera* held 750,000 florins at the death of John XXII, 1,117,000 at that of Benedict XII.[222] The later Avignon popes were unable to maintain this credit balance, but it was still a remarkable achievement, made possible, albeit at considerable cost to the popularity of the Holy See, by increasing taxation and a proliferating bureaucracy. Such developments have long been recognized as distinctive features of the Avignon papacy;[223] what has not been fully recognized is that the financial system created at Avignon was the product of the crises experienced by the popes of the thirteenth century in fighting their enemies in Italy.[224] The Curia had learnt by its mistakes. It has been suggested that the decision of Pope Gregory X to build up a large crusade treasure, which resulted in the sexennial tenth of 1274 and the innovations made to collect it, was the result of the harrowing experience of Clement IV.[225] Certainly Clement V's aim of financial independence, which manifested itself in the introduction of annates and the dismissal of the cameral bankers in 1306–7, was motivated by a desire not to repeat the experiences of Boniface VIII.[226] To a very considerable extent the fiscal policies which were the distinctive hallmark of the Avignon papacy were the offspring of the Italian crusades.

[220] Ibid., pp. 151–60. This may, of course, have been simple inefficiency.

[221] Schäfer (*Deutsche Ritter*, i. 8), believed that the mutiny and desertion of the German mercenaries in 1323 was caused by political rather than financial considerations.

[222] Renouard, *Les Relations*, p. 36. But see Partner, 'Camera papae', p. 68, for a salutary warning against taking such figures too seriously.

[223] See, e.g., Renouard, *The Avignon Papacy*, pp. 96 ff.

[224] Though see Partner, *Lands of St Peter*, p. 280.

[225] See 'La Décime de 1274–1280', p. 349.

[226] Renouard (*Les Relations*, pp. 94–8), stressed other factors as contributing to Clement's new policy, but admitted that the fall of the bankers played a large part.

General Conclusion

An attempt can now be made to assess the validity of the prevailing attitude of historians towards the crusades against Christian lay powers. The easiest criticism to answer is the assertion that the crusades aroused popular hostility and that they were attacked as the principal reason for the failure of the crusades in the Latin East. As has been shown, there was substantial though largely ineffective diplomatic pressure on the popes to abandon their conflicts in Italy in order to concentrate on the threat posed by the Mamluks, the Mongols, and the Turks in the East; the popes were also heavily criticized by contemporaries for diverting to Italy resources originally intended for the Levant. But it has yet to be proved that these attacks on the papacy and its allies for standing in the way of a crusade to the East represented European public opinion generally. There are signs, moreover, that the arguments deployed by the Curia to justify the crusades in Italy were greeted with sympathy by all who were not predisposed to be critical of papal policies. Above all, the popular response to preaching for the crusades against Christian enemies of the papacy was consistently favourable; indeed, contemporaries of Guelf persuasion regarded them as corresponding in the justice and sanctity of their purpose to the crusades against the Muslims.

Once one accepts the fact that most contemporaries did not view the Italian crusades with indignation as perversions and diversions of the crusade ideal, the claim that they contributed in large measure to the decline of the crusade movement becomes much less convincing. There is, in fact, very little evidence that contemporaries lost their belief in the value of the indulgence as a result of its use against Christians. An analysis of the 453 crusaders travelling East as passengers on the *St. Victor* in 1250 has shown that 'several dozens' came from the empire, where the cross was being preached against Frederick

II and Conrad.[1] Obviously such crusaders did not believe that the indulgence was worthless because it was also being offered to all who fought against their own emperor and his son. Similarly, it is questionable whether people stopped taking the cross because they thought that papal policy in Italy made the fulfilment of their vow impossible. It may be, of course, that some who would have crusaded in Syria fought in the Italian crusades instead because, like Mahy de Roye in 1285, they saw no point in travelling across the sea when they could earn the same indulgence by fighting so much nearer home.[2] But such considerations must have been outweighed for many by the strong religious attraction of the Holy Land, which the Italian crusades, with the possible exception of Charles of Anjou's expedition of 1265–6, could not hope to match.

The most difficult criticism to answer is the assertion that the crusades in Italy damaged the papacy's spiritual authority and its role as arbiter of Christendom. Certainly there is no proof that the consistent propaganda of the pope's enemies, who attacked the crusades as a misuse of the power of the Keys, convinced anybody who was previously of a neutral disposition. Neither is there a clear causal connection between the levying of clerical taxes for the Italian crusades and the growth of secular control over the Church in the leading western monarchies.[3] On the other hand, the prestige of the popes does appear to have been diminished, not by the crusades in themselves, but by their recurrent failure to establish and maintain papal authority in Italy.[4] The ability of the popes to act as the arbiters of Europe generally was, as the Curia itself realized, all too closely connected with their ability to influence events in lands over which they held some form of sovereignty, notably the Papal State and the *Regno*.[5] Thus Peter Dubois's plans for French domination of the Papal State hinged on the pope's own inability to rule there because of the 'poisonous plots' of the Romans and Lombards,

[1] See B. Z. Kedar, 'The Passenger List of a Crusader Ship, 1250: towards the History of the Popular Element on the Seventh Crusade', *Studi medievali*, 3rd series, xiii (1972), pp. 278–9.

[2] See above. p. 167; Stickel, *Der Fall von Akkon*, p. 185; Runciman, *History of the Crusades*, iii. 339.

[3] See above. p. 204.

[4] Cf. Runciman, *History of the Crusades*, iii. 428.

[5] See above, p. 45.

despite his employment of the formidable spiritual armoury which lay at his disposal.[6] Had the crusades in Italy succeeded, the decline in papal authority which characterized the late thirteenth and fourteenth centuries might have been less steep.

The true interest and significance of the Italian crusades does not, however, lie in their detrimental effects, but in their positive contributions to the history of Italy and to that of the crusade movement. The military efforts of crusaders and the employment of crusade revenue undoubtedly helped to shape the course of events in Italy in the period 1254–1343, though the precise extent to which they did so must remain conjectural. The crusades also made an important contribution to the development of Guelfism. The ideological background to the Guelf–Ghibelline alignment has long puzzled historians.[7] In general they have hesitated to ascribe any religious character to the *pars ecclesie* or to the operation of the Guelf alliance;[8] Daniel Waley has probably gone furthest in this direction by remarking that the papacy employed its spiritual weapons in aid of the Guelf cause and adding that 'possibly it conferred also a certain spiritual prestige, though of a rather worn and battered quality'.[9] In fact the use of the papacy's greatest spiritual weapon, the crusade, seems to have had a more pervasive influence than this would suggest. First, the assertion that the cause of the Church was that of God gave considerable credence to the Guelf claim to be fighting a war which was pre-eminently just. In October 1329 Pope John XXII reminded Bertrand of Baux, 'captain-at-arms of the soldiers of the Roman church in the regions of Lombardy', that 'the war whose conduct you have undertaken, against the heretics and rebels of your mother the Church and

[6] See *De recuperatione*, pp. 25, 98–9; *Summaria brevis*, pp. 12–13.

[7] The best recent attempts to explain Guelfism and Ghibellinism are J. K. Hyde, 'Contemporary Views on Faction and Civil Strife in Thirteenth and Fourteenth Century Italy', in L. Martines (ed.), *Violence and Civil Disorder in Italian Cities, 1200–1500*, pp. 293–300; Hyde, *Society and Politics*, pp. 132–41; D. P. Waley, *The Italian City-Republics*, pp. 115–26. There is a short but interesting discussion by Partner, in 'Florence and the Papacy', pp. 76–81.

[8] The great historian Edouard Jordan, for example, believed that 'le sentiment religieux italien, du reste très vivant . . . ne pouvait devenir l'âme d'un parti catholique, dont le pape aurait gardé la direction'. See *Les Origines*, p. cli.

[9] *The Italian City-Republics*, p. 118. See also Heers, *Parties and Political Life*, pp. 261 ff., esp. p. 265: 'spiritual weapons which could move hearts and minds and set into motion vast currents of public opinion, collective reactions of passion'. This passage is curiously at variance with views expressed elsewhere in the book.

the enemies of our most dear son in Christ, Robert, illustrious King of Sicily, is for the justice of God and the just cause of his Church'.[10] When trying to persuade representatives of the towns and communes of the *Regno* to grant King Robert a subsidy against Frederick of Sicily in 1316, Bartholomew of Capua evinced as proof of the justice of his lord's cause the fact that:

Our Mother the church of Rome herself declared war against the same Lord Frederick and the Sicilians and their supporters, excommunicating them, placing the whole land under ecclesiastical interdict, offering their possessions to all the faithful who should attack them, and granting to those killed by the same Lord Frederick, the Sicilians and their supporters the indulgence which has been granted to those travelling overseas in aid of the Holy Land. Because of which it seems manifest that our lord the king is fighting a just war, because it was declared by the Roman pontiff, and Lord Frederick and the Sicilians are fighting an unjust war, because it was against them that he declared it.[11]

But the struggle with the Ghibellines was not only just; it was also holy. The association of Guelf allegiance with the true Faith and of Ghibellinism with heresy enabled the Guelfs, as we have seen, to harness popular religiosity in the form of the Guelf confraternities.[12] Guelfism was also able to reap a rich harvest of ideas and even of vocabulary from the use of the crusade in its favour. Typical is Robert of Naples's appeal to Florence for money in 1328, with its repeated assertion that the Guelf party was the party of God.[13] It was of course inevitable that those who benefited from Guelf unity should emphasize its sanctity; but this religious tone also helped to hold the alliance together. Giovanni Tabacco has suggested that one of the reasons why Guelfism did not disintegrate in the political confusion of the 1330s was that its ideological hold on the powers involved was strong enough to overcome the temporary disorientation caused by John of Bohemia's intervention in Lombardy.[14] An

---

[10] 'susceptum per te contra hereticos et rebelles ecclesie matris tue ac hostes carissimi in Christo filii nostri Roberti Regis Sicilie illustris belli negotium sit pro dei iusticia et iusta ecclesie sue causa', ASV, Reg. Vat. 115, ff. 39ᵛ–40ʳ, no. 1195.

[11] 'Die Reden des Logotheten Bartholomäus von Capua', p. 271.

[12] See above, pp. 56–7.

[13] *Urkunden*, no. 96.

[14] Tabacco, 'La tradizione guelfa', p. 100. Cf. Giovanni Villani, *Cronica*, ii. 187–8.

alliance of the traditional defenders of the Church with men who had for long been condemned as its enemies could not last long. Thus, while the roots of Guelfism were undoubtedly the common political and economic interests of its chief partners, the religious complexion which it derived from the crusades helped to create a form of Guelf mythology which continued to influence the approaches of traditional Guelf powers after those common interests had largely ceased to exist.[15]

The most important contribution which the Italian crusades made to the development of the crusade movement lay in the efforts which the popes had to make in order to finance them. A recent historian of the crusades has remarked that:

While plenary indulgences and crusader vows sprang from, and were a integral part of, the notion of crusade . . . the papal arrangements for financing crusade were part of a system which went far beyond the limits of crusade, and whose service to that movement ended rather by absorbing crusade into the system, and shaping it from outside, not from within.[16]

An examination of the financing of the Italian crusades suggests that this attempt to divorce crusade finance from other aspects of the crusade is fundamentally misguided. It was the exigencies of the Italian crusades, in particular the needs of the *camera* and the Angevin crown, which led to many of the notable advances made in papal finance in the period 1254–1343: the organization of collectorates, the increasing reliance on credit, the subsequent attempt to avoid this reliance by the institution of new taxes and the taxation of new areas of Christendom. Moreover, the fact that such measures were necessitated by the waging of a just and holy war in defence of the Faith furnished the required justification for the papacy to extend its financial grip on the Church. Just as Innocent III's introduction of the first extraordinary benefice tax, the tenth, arose from the needs of the crusade in Latin Syria, so the Italian crusades called forth and facilitated the innovations of his successors.

With the exception of the sphere of finance, the papacy made no radical changes to the institutions of the crusade movement

---

[15] This was most noticeable in the case of Florence. See Brucker, *Florentine Politics*, pp. 74, 346 and *passim*; Bowsky, 'Italian Diplomatic History', p. 65.

[16] Purcell, *Papal Crusading Policy*, p. 137.

in order to incorporate within it the crusades which it waged in Italy. Indeed, the most striking and most significant aspect of the Italian crusades is that, apart from their justification, they differed very little in essential respects from those fought in the East or elsewhere. All the evidence shows that the crusades in Italy and Syria were preached and organized in the same manner, that the *crucesignati* received the same privileges and undertook the same obligations, and that a very similar ethos surrounded the wars in Italy and those in the East. Moreover, it is clear that most contemporaries accepted the interpretation of the crusade which underpinned this homogeneity: that the crusade was a holy war fought against the enemies of the Faith, whoever and wherever they might be. The implications of this are wide-ranging. In the thirteenth and fourteenth centuries men were fighting in defence of the Faith, at papal direction, not only on the borders of Christendom, in Syria and the Levant, in Spain and north-eastern Germany, but also within the heart of Christendom itself. It has long been accepted that the crusades cannot simply be considered as a series of expeditions to Syria or other parts of the East; it should also be accepted that the popes were able to organize, preach, and wage crusades against the internal enemies of the Christian Republic without misusing the crusade indulgence or being castigated by public opinion for doing so. Only when this fact wins general acceptance will the full range, complexity, and richness of the crusading movement be appreciated.

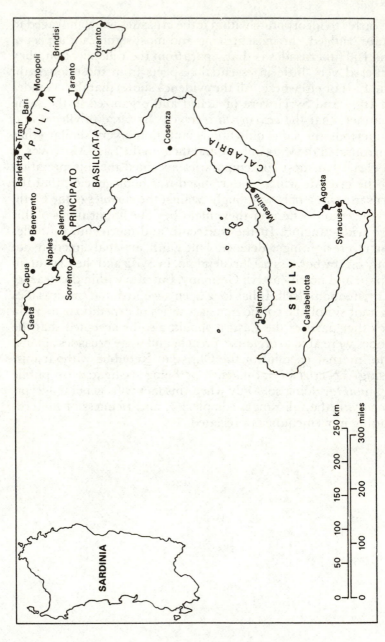

Southern Italy and Sicily in the thirteenth and fourteenth Centuries

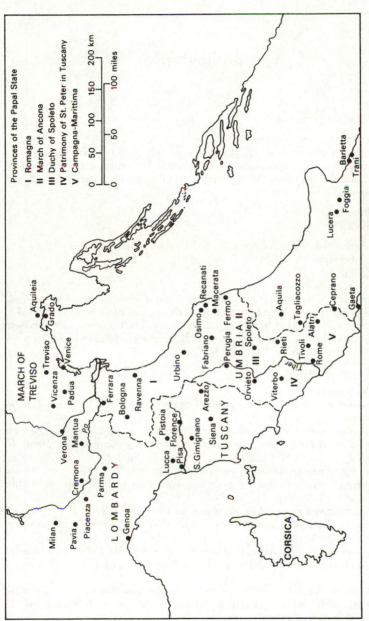

Northern and Central Italy in the thirteenth and fourteenth Centuries

Provinces of the Papal State
I   Romagna
II   March of Ancona
III Duchy of Spoleto
IV   Patrimony of St. Peter in Tuscany
V   Campagna-Marittima

MARCH OF TREVISO

LOMBARDY

Milan
Pavia
Piacenza
Cremona
Parma
Mantua
Verona
Vicenza
Padua
Treviso
Venice
Aquileia
Grado
Genoa
Ferrara
Bologna
Ravenna
Urbino
Pistoia
Lucca
Florence
Pisa
S. Gimignano
Siena
Arezzo
Osimo
Recanati
Macerata
Fabriano
Fermo
Perugia
Spoleto
Aquila
Tagliacozzo
Rieti
Ceprano
Tivoli
Alatri
Rome
Gaeta
Viterbo
Orvieto
Lucera
Foggia
Barletta
Trani

TUSCANY
UMBRIA

Tiber
Po

CORSICA

Bibliography

1. Manuscript Sources

i. Archivio segreto Vaticano

Registra Vaticana, nos. 28, 32, 41, 45, 46, 48, 49, 69, 73, 86, 109–17, 127. Introitus et exitus, nos. 49, 50, 62, 68, 77, 276. Instrumenta miscellanea, nos. 340, 462, 627, 637, 666, 748, 892, 901, 917, 5149. Archivum arcis, Armadio C, no. 1030.

ii. Biblioteca Vaticana

MS Vat. lat. no. 3937.

iii. Archivio di Stato, Naples. Ufficio della Ricostruzione angioina

MSS Ferraro.
MSS Fusco.
MSS Minieri-Riccio.

These are collections containing transcriptions from the Angevin registers. The transcriptions have been arranged in folders (*buste*) which correspond in content and sequence to the original registers. The documents are therefore cited according to their location in the registers, e.g. ASN, MS Ferraro, no. 38, ff. 41–2, formerly Reg. Ang. 96, f. 9^r.

2. Printed Sources

i. Documentary Sources

'The Account of a Papal Collector in England in 1304', ed. W. E. Lunt, *EHR*, xxviii (1913), 313–21.

Acta aragonensia. Quellen zur deutschen, italienischen, französischen, spanischen, zur Kirchen- und Kulturgeschichte aus der diplomatischen Korrespondenz Jaymes II. (1291–1327), ed. H. Finke. 3 vols. (Leipzig–Berlin, 1908–22).

Acta capitulorum generalium Ordinis Praedicatorum, ed. B. M. Reichert. Monumenta Ordinis Fratrum Praedicatorum historica, iii, iv, viii–xiv. 9 vols. (Rome, 1898–1904).

Acta capitulorum provincialium Provinciae romanae (1243–1344), ed. T. Kaeppeli and A. Dondaine. Monumenta Ordinis Fratrum Praedicatorum historica, xx (Rome, 1941).

Acta imperii, Angliae et Franciae ab anno 1267 ad annum 1313. Dokumente vornehmlich zur Geschichte der auswärtigen Beziehungen Deutschlands, ed. F. Kern (Tübingen, 1911).

Acta imperii inedita seculi xiii. et xiv. Urkunden und Briefe zur Geschichte des Kaiserreichs und des Königreichs Sicilien in den Jahren 1198–1400, ed. E. Winkelmann. 2 vols. (Innsbruck, 1880–5).

Acta pontificum, ed. G. Battelli. Exempla scripturarum edita consilio et opera procuratorum Bibliothecae et Tabularii Vaticani, fasc. iii (Rome, 1933).

Acta pontificum danica. Pavelige aktstykker vedrørende Danmark 1316–1536, ed.
L. Moltesen *et al.* 7 vols. (Copenhagen, 1904–43).

Acta pontificum svecica, I. Acta cameralia, ed. L. M. Bååth. Diplomatarium
svecanum. Appendix. 2 vols. (Holmiae, 1936–57).

*Actenstücke zur Geschichte des deutschen Reiches unter den Königen Rudolf I. und
Albrecht I.*, ed. F. Kaltenbrunner. Mittheilungen aus dem Vaticanischen
Archive, i (Vienna, 1889).

Actes et lettres de Charles Ier roi de Sicile concernant la France (1257–1284). Extraits des
Registres Angevins de Naples, ed. A. De Boüard (Paris, 1926).

Pope Alexander IV, *Registres*, ed. C. Bourel de la Roncière *et al.* Bibliothèque
des Écoles françaises d'Athènes et de Rome, 2nd series. 3 vols. incl. tables
(Paris, 1895–1959).

Annales ecclesiastici, ed. C. Baronio *et al.* 37 vols. (Paris–Freiburg–Bar le Duc,
1864–87).

*Annali delle Due Sicilie dall'origine e fondazione della monarchia fino a tutto il regno
dell'augusto sovrano Carlo III. Borbone*, comp. M. Camera. 2 vols. (Naples,
1841–60).

*Antiquitates italicae medii aevi, sive dissertationes de moribus, ritibus . . . italici populi
post declinationem romani imperii ad annum usque MD*, ed. L. A. Muratori. 25
vols. and index (Milan, 1723–1896).

Les Archives de la Chambre apostolique au xive siècle, ed. J. De Loye. Bibliothèque
des Écoles françaises d'Athènes et de Rome, fasc. lxxx (Paris, 1899).

*Gli atti perduti della cancelleria angioina transuntati da Carlo de Lellis. Parte I: Il regno
di Carlo I*, ed. B. Mazzoleni. R. Istituto storico italiano per il medio evo.
Regesta Chartarum Italiae, xxv, xxxi. 2 vols. (Rome, 1939, 1943).

Aus den Tagen Bonifaz VIII. Funde und Forschungen, ed. H. Finke. Vorreformationsgeschichtliche Forschungen, ii (Münster i. W., 1902).

*Die Ausgaben der apostolischen Kammer unter Johann XXII. nebst den Jahresbilanzen
von 1316–1375*, ed. K. H. Schäfer. Vatikanische Quellen zur Geschichte der
päpstlichen Hof-u. Finanzverwaltung, 1316–1378, ii (Paderborn, 1911).

Pope Benedict XI, *Registres*, ed. C. Grandjean. Bibliothèque des Écoles
françaises d'Athènes et de Rome, 2nd series. 1 vol. incl. tables (Paris,
1883–1905).

Pope Benedict XII, *Lettres closes, patentes et curiales se rapportant à la France*, ed.
G. Daumet. Bibliothèque des Écoles françaises d'Athènes et de Rome, 3rd
series. 1 vol. incl. tables (Paris, 1899–1920).

——— *Lettres closes et patentes intéressant les pays autres que la France*, ed. J. M. Vidal.
Bibliothèque des Écoles françaises d'Athènes et de Rome, 3rd series. 1 vol.
incl. tables (Paris, 1913–50).

'Die Beteiligung der Dominikaner an den Inquisitionsprozessen unter Johann
XXII.', ed. F. Bock, *Archivum Fratrum Praedicatorum*, vi·(1936), 312–33.

Pope Boniface VIII, *Registres*, ed. G. Digard *et al.* Bibliothèque des Écoles
françaises d'Athènes et de Rome, 2nd series. 4 vols. incl. tables (Paris,
1884–1935).

*Calendar of Entries in the Papal Registers relating to Great Britain and Ireland. Papal
Letters 1198–1342*, ed. W. H. Bliss. 2 vols. (London, 1893–5).

Calendar of State Papers and Manuscripts relating to English Affairs existing in the

Archives and Collections of Venice and in other Libraries of Northern Italy (1202–1558), ed. R. Brown. 6 vols. in 8 parts (London, 1864–84).

'Carlo II e i debiti angioini verso la Santa Sede', ed. G. M. Monti, in his *Da Carlo I a Roberto di Angiò. Ricerche e documenti* (Trani, 1936), 117–32.

Cartulaire général de l'Ordre des Hospitaliers de S. Jean de Jérusalem (1100–1310), ed. J. Delaville le Roulx. 4 vols. (Paris, 1894–1906).

Chypre sous les Lusignans. Documents chypriotes des archives du Vatican (xive et xve siècles), ed. J. Richard. Institut français d'Archéologie de Beyrouth, Bibliothèque archéologique et historique, lxxiii (Paris, 1962).

Pope Clement IV, *Registres*, ed. E. Jordan. Bibliothèque des Écoles françaises d'Athènes et de Rome, 2nd series. 1 vol. incl. tables (Paris, 1893–1945).

Pope Clement V, *Regestum*, ed. cura et studio monachorum Ordinis S. Benedicti. 8 vols. (Rome, 1885–92).

Codex diplomaticus dominii temporalis Sanctae Sedis, ed. A. Theiner. 2 vols. (Rome, 1861–2).

Codex dunensis sive diplomatum et chartarum medii aevi amplissima collectio, ed. J. Kervyn de Lettenhove (Brussels, 1875).

Codex Italiae diplomaticus, ed. J. C. Lünig. 4 vols. (Frankfurt-Leipzig, 1725–35).

Codice diplomatico barese, ed. a cura della Commissione provinciale di Archeologia e Storia patria. 19 vols. (Bari–Trani, 1897–1971).

Codice diplomatico eceliniano, ed. G. Verci, in his *Storia degli Ecelini*, iii. (Bassano, 1779).

Codice diplomatico dei Saraceni di Lucera, ed. P. Egidi (Naples, 1917).

Codice diplomatico del regno di Carlo I. e II. d'Angiò, ed. G. Del Giudice. 2 vols. in 3 parts (Naples, 1863–1902).

Codice diplomatico salernitano del secolo xiii, ed. C. Carucci. 3 vols. (Subiaco, 1931–46).

Codice diplomatico sulmonese, ed. N. F. Faraglia (Lanciano, 1888).

Les Collectories pontificales dans les anciens diocèses de Cambrai, Thérouanne et Tournai au xive siècle, ed. U. Berlière. Analecta Vaticano-Belgica, series 1, x (Rome, 1929).

'Compte d'une mission de prédication pour secours à la Terre Sainte (1265)', ed. Borrelli de Serres, *Mémoires de la Société de l'histoire de Paris et de l'Ile de France*, xxx (1903), 243–80.

'Compte d'un subside fourni par le diocèse de Bourges au pape Jean XXII', ed. M. De Laugardière, *Mémoires de la Société des antiquaires du Centre*, xxxiii (1910), 99–190.

Constitutiones et acta publica imperatorum et regum, ed. L. Weiland *et al.*, *MGH*, *Legum sectio iv*. 7 vols. so far (Hanover–Leipzig, 1893–).

'Dagli *Instrumenta miscellanea* dell'Archivio segreto Vaticano', ed. A. Mercati, *QFIAB*, xxvii (1936–7), 135–77.

'De praedicatione cruciatae saec. xiii per fratres minores', ed. P. F. Delorme, *Archivum franciscanum historicum*, ix (1916), 99–117.

'La decima pontificia del 1301–1304 in Toscana. Un nuovo codice', ed. M. H. Laurent, *Rivista di storia della Chiesa in Italia*, iii (1949), 55–66.

'La Décime de 1274–1280 dans l'Italie septentrionale', ed. M. H. Laurent, in *Miscellanea Pio Paschini. Studi di storia ecclesiastica*, i (Rome, 1948), 349–404.

'Les Décimes ecclésiastiques dans le royaume d'Arles de 1278 à 1283', ed.

P. Fabre, *Annales du Midi*, iv (1892), 371–80.

Das deutsch-englische Bündnis von 1335–1342. I. Quellen, ed. F. Bock. Quellen und Erörterungen zur bayerischen Geschichte, NS, xii (Munich, 1956).

Deutsche Ritter und Edelknechte in Italien während des 14. Jahrhunderts, ed. K. H. Schäfer. Quellen und Forschungen aus dem Gebiete der Geschichte, xv-xvi. 3 vols. (Paderborn, 1911–14).

'Les Déviations de la Croisade au milieu du xiiie siècle: Alexandre IV contre Manfred', ed. P. Toubert, *Le Moyen Age*, lxix (1963), 391–9.

Diplomatari de l'orient català (1301–1409). *Collecció de documents per a la història de l'expedició catalana a orient i dels ducats d'Atenes i Neopàtria*, ed. A. Rubió y Lluch (Barcelona, 1947).

Documenti delle relazioni tra Carlo I d'Angiò e la Toscana, ed. S. Terlizzi. Documenti di storia italiana, xii (Florence, 1950).

Documenti per la storia della città di Arezzo nel medio evo, ed. U. Pasqui. Documenti di storia italiana, xi, xiii, xiv (Florence, 1899–1937).

'Documenti sulle relazioni tra la corte angioina di Napoli, papa Bonifacio VIII e i Colonna', ed. F. Scandone, *ASPN*, new series, xli (1962), 221–36.

'Documents from the Angevin Registers of Naples: Charles I', ed. E. M. Jamison, *Papers of the British School at Rome*, xvii (1949), 87–180.

Documents illustrative of English History in the Thirteenth and Fourteenth Centuries, Selected from the Records of the Department of the Queen's Remembrancer of the Exchequer, ed. H. Cole (London, 1844).

Die Einnahmen der apostolischen Kammer unter Johann XXII., ed. E. Göller. Vatikanische Quellen zur Geschichte der päpstlichen Hof-u. Finanzverwaltung, 1316–1378, i (Paderborn, 1910).

Elenco cronologico delle antiche pergamene pertinenti alla Real chiesa della Magione, ed. V. Mortillaro (Palermo, 1858).

Epistolae saeculi xiii e regestis pontificum romanorum, ed. C. Rodenberg. *MGH*. 3 vols. (Berlin, 1883–94).

'Eretici e ribelli nell'Umbria dal 1320 al 1330 studiati su documenti inediti dell'Archivio segreto Vaticano', ed. L. Fumi, *BDSPU*, iii (1897), 257–85, 429–89, iv (1898), 221–301, 437–86, v (1899), 1–46, 205–425.

'Der Este-Prozess von 1321', ed. F. Bock, *Archivum Fratrum Praedicatorum*, vii (1937), 41–111.

Foedera, conventiones, litterae, et cuiuscunque generis acta publica, inter reges Angliae et alios quosvis imperatores, reges, pontifices, principes vel communitates, ed. T. Rymer *et al*. 4 vols. in 7 parts (London, 1816–69).

Forschungen zur älteren Geschichte von Florenz, ed. R. Davidsohn. 4 vols. (Berlin, 1896–1908).

Pope Gregory IX, *Registres*, ed. L. Auvray. Bibliothèque des Écoles françaises d'Athènes et de Rome, 2nd series. 3 vols. and tables (Paris, 1890–1955).

Pope Gregory X, *Registres*, ed. J. Guiraud. Bibliothèque des Écoles françaises d'Athènes et de Rome, 2nd series. 1 vol. incl. tables (Paris, 1892–1906).

Pope Gregory XI, *Lettres secrètes et curiales intéressant les pays autres que la France*, ed. G. Mollat. Bibliothèque des Écoles françaises d'Athènes et de Rome, 3rd series. 1 vol. incl. tables (Paris, 1962–5).

—— *Lettres secrètes et curiales relatives à la France*, ed. L. Mirot *et al*. Bibliothèque des Écoles françaises d'Athènes et de Rome, 3rd series. 1 vol. incl. tables.

(Paris, 1935–57).

Hierarchia catholica medii aevi sive summorum pontificum, S.R.E. cardinalium, ecclesiarum antistitum series ab anno 1198 usque ad annum 1431 perducta, comp. C. Eubel (Münster, 1913).

Historia diplomatica Friderici secundi, ed. J.L.A. Huillard-Bréholles. 6 parts in 12 vols. (Paris, 1852–61).

Pope Honorius·IV, *Registres*, ed. M. Prou. Bibliothèque des Écoles françaises d'Athènes et de Rome, 2nd series. 1 vol. incl. tables (Paris, 1888).

Pope Innocent IV, *Registres*, ed. É. Berger. Bibliothèque des Écoles françaises d'Athènes et de Rome, 2nd series. 3 vols. and tables (Paris, 1884–1921).

Italienische Analekten zur Reichsgeschichte des 14. Jahrhunderts (1310–1378), ed. T. Mommsen and W. Hagemann. Schriften der MGH (Deutsches Institut für Erforschung des Mittelalters), 11 (Stuttgart, 1952).

Pope John XXII, *Lettres communes*, ed. G. Mollat. Bibliothèque des Écoles françaises d'Athènes et de Rome, 3rd series. 13 vols. and tables (Paris, 1904–47).

—— *Lettres secrètes et curiales relatives à la France*, ed. A. Coulon and S. Clémencet. Bibliothèque des Écoles françaises d'Athènes et de Rome, 3rd series. 4 vols. (Paris, 1906–72).

Kaiser, Volk und Avignon. Ausgewählte Quellen zur antikurialen Bewegung in Deutschland in der ersten Hälfte des 14. Jahrhunderts, ed. O. Berthold *et al.* Leipziger Übersetzungen und Abhandlungen zum Mittelalter, Reihe A, iii (Berlin, 1960).

Layettes du trésor des chartes. Inventaires et documents publiés par la Direction des Archives, ed. A. Teulet *et al.* 5 vols. (Paris, 1863–1909).

'Una legge suntuaria inedita del 1290', ed. G. Del Giudice, *Atti dell'Accademia pontaniana*, xvi, pt. 2 (1886).

'Lettere di collettori pontifici nel secolo xiv', ed. U. Mannucci, *RQ*, xxvii (1913), *190–201*.

Lettere volgari del secolo xiii scritte da senesi, ed. C. Paoli and E. Piccolomini. Scelta di curiosità letterarie inedite o rare dal secolo xiii al xix, cxvi (Bologna, 1871).

Lettres de Jean XXII (1316–1334), ed. A. Fayen. Analecta Vaticano-Belgica, series 1, ii–iii. 2 vols. (Rome, 1908–12).

'Lettres inédites et mémoires de Marino Sanudo l'ancien (1334–1337)', ed. C. De la Roncière and L. Dorez, *Bibliothèque de l'École des chartes*, lvi (1895), 21–44.

I libri commemoriali della republica di Venezia Regesti, ed. R. Predelli. Monumenti storici publicati dalla Deputazione veneta di storia patria. 1st series. Documenti, i, iii, vii, viii, x, xi, xiii, xvii. 8 vols. (Venice, 1876–1914).

Pope Martin IV, *Registres*, ed. F. Olivier-Martin *et al.* Bibliothèque des Écoles françaises d'Athènes et de Rome, 2nd series. 1 vol. incl. tables (Paris, 1901–35).

'Memorie della guerra di Sicilia negli anni 1282, 1283, 1284', comp. C. Minieri-Riccio, *ASPN*, i (1876), 85–105, 275–315, 499–530.

Pope Nicholas IV, *Registres*, ed. E. Langlois. Bibliothèque des Écoles françaises d'Athènes et de Rome, 2nd series. 2 vols. incl. tables (Paris, 1886–93).

'Notizie storiche tratte dai documenti conosciuti col nome di *Arche in carta bambagina'*, ed. R. Bevere, *ASPN*, xxv (1900), 241–75, 389–407.

Notizie storiche tratte da 62 registri angioini dell Archivio di Stato di Napoli, ed. C. Minieri-Riccio (Naples, 1877).

'Nuove lettere di Marino Sanudo il vecchio', ed. A. Cerlini, *La Bibliofilia*, xlii (1940), 321–59.

'An Offer of the Suzerainty and Escheat of Cyprus to Alphonso III of Aragon by Hugh de Brienne in 1289', ed. E. Lourie, *EHR*, lxxxiv (1969), 101–8.

Die päpstlichen Kollektorien in Deutschland während des xiv. Jahrhunderts, ed. J. P. Kirsch. Quellen und Forschungen aus dem Gebiete der Geschichte, iii (Paderborn, 1894).

Papsttum und Untergang des Templerordens, ed. H. Finke. Vorreformationsgeschichtliche Forschungen, iv–v. 2 vols. (Münster i. W., 1907).

Patrologiae cursus completus. Series latina, comp. J. P. Migne. 221 vols. (Paris, 1841–64).

'La *ratio thesaurariorum* della cancelleria angioina', comp. N. Barone, *ASPN*, x (1885), 413–34, 653–64, xi (1886), 5–20, 175–97, 415–32, 577–96.

Rationes decimarum Italiae. Aprutium-Molisium. Le decime dei secoli xiii–xiv, ed. P. Sella. *Studi e testi*, 69 (Rome, 1936).

Rationes decimarum Italiae. Aemilia. Le decime dei secoli xiii–xiv, ed. A. Mercati *et al. Studi e testi*, 60 (Rome, 1933).

—— *Apulia-Lucania-Calabria*, ed. D. Vendola. *Studi e testi*, 84 (Rome, 1939).

—— *Campania*, ed. M. Inguanez *et al. Studi e testi*, 97 (Rome, 1942).

—— *Latium*, ed. G. Battelli. *Studi e testi*, 128 (Rome, 1946).

—— *Marchia*, ed. P. Sella. *Studi e testi*, 148 (Rome, 1950).

—— *Sardinia*, ed. P. Sella. *Studi e testi*, 113 (Rome, 1945).

—— *Sicilia*, ed. P. Sella. *Studi e testi*, 112 (Rome, 1944).

—— *Tuscia i. La decima degli anni 1274–1280*, ed. P. Guidi. *Studi e testi*, 58 (Rome, 1932).

—— *Tuscia ii. Le decime degli anni 1295–1304*, ed. M. Giusti and P. Guidi. *Studi e testi*, 98 (Rome, 1942).

—— *Umbria*, ed. P. Sella. *Studi e testi*, 161–2. 2 vols. (Rome, 1952).

—— *Venetiae-Histria-Dalmatia*, ed. P. Sella and G. Vale. *Studi e testi*, 96 (Rome, 1941).

'Die Reden des Logotheten Bartholomäus von Capua', ed. A. Nitschke, *QFIAB*, xxxv (1955), 226–74.

Regesta chartarum. Regesto delle pergamene dell'Archivio Caetani, ed. G. Caetani. Documenti dell'Archivio Caetani. 6 vols. (Perugia–Sancasciano Val di Pesa, 1922–32).

Regesta pontificum romanorum inde ab anno post Christum natum 1198 ad annum 1304, ed. A. Potthast. 2 vols. (Berlin, 1874–5).

Registri dei cardinali Ugolino d'Ostia e Ottaviano degli Ubaldini, ed. G. Levi. Fonti per la storia d'Italia (Rome, 1890).

'I registri del ducato di Spoleto', ed. L. Fumi, *BDSPU*, iii (1897), 491–548, iv (1898), 137–56, v (1899), 127–63, vi (1900), 37–68, 231–77, vii (1901), 57–123, 285–314.

I registri della cancelleria angioina ricostruiti, ed. R. Filangieri di Candida *et al.* Testi e documenti di storia napoletana pubblicati dall'Accademia pontaniana. 28 vols. so far (Naples, 1950–).

'Il regno di Carlo I d'Angiò dal 4 gennaio 1284 al 7 gennaio 1285', comp. C. Minieri-Riccio, *Archivio storico italiano*, 4th series, vii (1881), 3–24, 304–12.

Il regno di Sicilia negli ultimi anni di vita di Carlo II. d'Angiò, ed. A. Cutolo (Milan–Rome–Naples, 1924).

'Reise nach Italien im Herbst 1898', ed. J. Schwalm, *Neues Archiv*, xxv (1900), 719–66, xxvi (1901), 709–41.

'Requête adressée au roi de France par un vétéran des armées de Saint Louis et de Charles d'Anjou', ed. É. Berger, in *Études d'histoire du Moyen Âge dédiées à G. Monod* (Paris, 1896), 343–9.

Römische Quellen zur konstanzer Bistumsgeschichte zur Zeit der Päpste in Avignon, 1305–1378, ed. K. Rieder. Monumenta Vaticana historiam episcopatus constantiensis in Germania illustrantia (Innsbruck, 1908).

Rotuli parliamentorum; ut et petitiones, et placita in parliamento, ed. J. Strachey *et al.* 6 vols. (London, 1767).

Royal and other Historical Letters illustrative of the Reign of Henry III, ed. W. W. Shirley. Rolls Series, xxvii. 2 vols. (London, 1862–6).

Sacrorum conciliorum nova et amplissima collectio, ed. G. D. Mansi *et al.* 31 vols. (Florence–Venice, 1759–98).

Saggio di codice diplomatico formato sulle antiche scritture dell'Archivio di Stato di Napoli, ed. C. Minieri-Riccio. 2 vols. and supplement, in 5 parts (Naples, 1878–83).

Septem dioeceses aprutienses medii aevi in Vaticano tabulario, ed. F. Savini (Rome, 1912).

'La signoria di Firenze tenuta da Carlo figlio di re Roberto negli anni 1326 e 1327', ed. R. Bevere, *ASPN*, xxxiii (1908), 439–65, 639–62, xxxiv (1909), 3–18, 197–221, 403–31, 599–639, xxxv (1910), 3–46, 205–72, 425–58, 607–36, xxxvi (1911), 3–34, 254–85, 407–33.

Statuta capitulorum generalium Ordinis Cisterciensis ab anno 1116 usque ad annum 1786, ed. J-M. Canivez. Bibliothèque de la Revue d'histoire ecclésiastique, fasc. 9–14B. 8 vols. (Louvain, 1933–41).

Statuta communis Parmae digesta anno MCCLV. Monumenta historica ad provincias parmensem et placentinam pertinentia (Parma, 1855).

Studi storici su' fascicoli angioini, ed. C. Minieri-Riccio (Naples, 1863).

'Studien über Marino Sanudo den älteren mit einem Anhange seiner ungedruckten Briefe', ed. F. Kunstmann, *Abhandlungen der historischen Classe der Königlich bayerischen Akademie der Wissenschaften*, vii (1855), 697–819.

'Studien zum politischen Inquisitionsprozess Johanns XXII.', ed. F. Bock, *QFIAB*, xxvi (1935–6), 21–142, xxvii (1936–7), 109–34.

Studii storici fatti sopra 84 registri angioini dell'Archivio di Stato di Napoli, ed. C. Minieri-Riccio (Naples, 1876).

Syllabus membranarum ad regiae Siclae archivum pertinentium, ed. A. A. Scotti *et al.* 2 vols. in 3 parts (Naples, 1824–45).

Thesaurus novus anecdotorum, ed. E. Martène and U. Durand. 5 vols. (Paris, 1717).

Pope Urban IV, *Regestum Camerale*, ed. J. Guiraud. Bibliothèque des Écoles françaises d'Athènes et de Rome, 2nd series. 1 vol. (Paris, 1899).

—— *Registres*, ed. J. Guiraud. Bibliothèque des Écoles françaises d'Athènes et de Rome, 2nd series. 4 vols. incl. tables (Paris, 1899–1958).

Urkunden zur Geschichte des Römerzuges Kaiser Ludwig des Baiern und der italienischen Verhältnisse seiner Zeit, ed. J. Ficker (Innsbruck, 1865).

The Valuation of Norwich, ed. W. E. Lunt (Oxford, 1926).

Vatikanische Akten zur deutschen Geschichte in der Zeit Kaiser Ludwigs des Bayern, ed. S. Riezler (Innsbruck, 1891).

'Vatikanische Urkunden zur Geschichte Ludwigs des Bayern', ed. C. Erdmann, *Archivalische Zeitschrift*, xli (1932), 1–47.

Vetera monumenta historica Hungariam sacram illustrantia, ed. A. Theiner. 2 vols. (Rome, 1859–60).

Vetera monumenta Poloniae et Lithuaniae gentiumque finitimarum historiam illustrantia, ed. A. Theiner. 4 vols. (Rome, 1860–4).

ii. Narrative and Literary Sources, Treatises etc.

Andrew of Hungary, 'Descriptio victoriae a Karolo Provinciae comite reportatae', *MGHS*, xxvi. 559–80.

'Annales altahenses', *MGHS*, xvii. 351–427.

'Annales de Burton', ed. H. R. Luard, in *Annales monastici*. Rolls Series, xxxvi. 5 vols. (London, 1864–9), i. 183–500.

'Annales mantuani', *MGHS*, xix. 19–31.

'Annales mediolanenses', *RIS*, xvi, cols. 641–840.

'Annales placentini Gibellini', *MGHS*, xviii. 457–581.

'Annales sanctae Justinae patavini', *MGHS*, xix. 148–93.

'Annali genovesi di Caffaro e de' suoi continuatori', ed. L. T. Belgrano and C. Imperiale di Sant'Angelo, *Fonti per la storia d'Italia*. 5 vols. (Rome, 1890–1929).

Augustinus Triumphus, *Summa de potestate ecclesiastica* (Rome, 1584).

Bartholomew of Neocastro, 'Historia sicula', *RISNS*, xiii[3].

Bernard Desclot, *Chronicle of the Reign of King Pedro III of Aragon. A.D. 1276–1285*, tr. F. L. Critchlow (Princeton, 1928).

Bernard Gui, 'De secta illorum qui se dicunt esse de ordine apostolorum', *RISNS*, ix[5]. 17–36.

—— *Manuel de l'inquisiteur*, ed. G. Mollat and G. Drioux. Les classiques de l'histoire de France au Moyen Âge, viii–ix. 2 vols. (Paris, 1926–7).

Chronica et chronicorum excerpta historiam Ordinis Praedicatorum illustrantia, ed. B. M. Reichert. Monumenta Ordinis Fratrum Praedicatorum historica, vii (Rome, 1904).

'Chronicon Girardi de Fracheto et anonyma eiusdem operis continuatio', *RHGF*, xxi. 3–70.

'Chronicon parmense', *RISNS*, ix[9].

'Chronique anonyme des rois de France', *RHGF*, xxi. 81–102.

'Chronique rimée dite de Saint-Magloire', *RHGF*, xxii. 82–7.

'Continuatio chronici Guillelmi de Nangiaco, a monacho benedictino abbatiae S. Dionysii in Francia', *RHGF*, xx. 584–646.

'Cronaca di Morea', ed. C. Hopf, in his *Chroniques gréco-romanes inédites ou peu connues* (Berlin, 1873), 414–68.

'Cronaca senese attribuita ad Agnolo di Tura del Grasso detta la Cronaca maggiore', *RISNS*, xv[6].

'Cronicon suessanum', ed. A. A. Pelliccia, in his *Raccolta di varie croniche, diari, ed altri opuscoli cosi italiani, come latini, appartenenti alla storia del regno di Napoli*. 5 vols. in 4 parts (Naples, 1780–2), i. 51–78.

Dante Alighieri, *The Divine Comedy*, ed. and tr. J. D. Sinclair, 2nd edn. 3 vols. (London, 1948).

'Directorium ad passagium faciendum', *RHC, Documents arméniens*, ii. 367–517.

'E chronico Normanniae ab anno 1169 ad annum 1259, sive potius 1272', *RHGF*, xxiii. 213–22.

Eude Rigaud, *Regestrum visitationum archiepiscopi Rothomagensis*, ed. T. Bonnin (Rouen, 1852).

'Ex annalibus normannicis', *MGHS*, xxvi. 512–17.

'Ex continuatione gestorum episcoporum Autissiodorensium', *MGHS*, xxvi. 584–6.

'Excerpta e chronico Gaufridi de Collone', *RHGF*, xxii. 2–11.

Le Garçon et l'aveugle. Jeu du xiiie siècle, ed. M. Roques. Les classiques français du Moyen Âge (Paris, 1912).

'Georgii Stellae Annales genuenses', *RIS*, xvii, cols. 951–1226.

'Gesta Boemundi archiepiscopi Treverensis', *MGHS*, xxiv. 463–88.

Gesta Dei per Francos, sive orientalium expeditionum et regni Francorum Hierosolymitani historia, ed. J. Bongars. 2 vols. (Hanover, 1611).

Gilles le Muisit, *Chronique et annales*, ed. H. Lemaître. La Société de l'histoire de France (Paris, 1906).

Giovanni Villani, *Cronica*, ed. F. Gherardi Dragomanni. 4 vols. (Florence, 1845).

Hostiensis, *Summa aurea* (Venice, 1570).

John of St. Victor, 'Memoriale historiarum, excerpta', *RHGF*, xxi. 633–76.

'Maius chronicon lemovicense, a Petro Coral et aliis conscriptum', *RHGF*, xxi. 763–88.

Marino Sanudo Torsello, 'Liber secretorum fidelium crucis', ed. Bongars, in *Gesta Dei*, ii.

Marsilius of Padua, *Defensor pacis*, ed. R. Scholz. Fontes iuris germanici antiqui (Hanover, 1932).

Martino da Canale, 'Cronaca veneta', in *Archivio storico italiano*, viii (1845), 268–766.

Matteo Villani, *Cronica*, ed. F. Gherardi Dragomanni. 2 vols. (Florence, 1846).

Matthew Paris, *Chronica maiora*, ed. H. R. Luard. Rolls Series, lvii. 7 vols. (London, 1872–84).

Nicolaus Speciale, 'Historia sicula', *RIS*, x, cols. 917–1092.

Peter Dubois, *De recuperatione terre sancte*, ed. C. V. Langlois (Paris, 1891).

—— *Summaria brevis et compendiosa doctrina felicis expedicionis et abreviacionis guerrarum ac litium regni Francorum*, ed. H. Kämpf. Quellen zur Geistesgeschichte des Mittelalters und der Renaissance, iv(Leipzig–Berlin, 1936).

Poesie provenzali storiche relative all'Italia, ed. V. De Bartholomaeis, Fonti per la storia d'Italia. 2 vols. (Rome, 1931).

Ptolemy of Lucca, 'Tractatus de jurisditione ecclesiae super regnum Apuliae et Siciliae', ed. S. Baluzio and G. D. Mansi, in their *Miscellanea novo ordine digesta et non paucis ineditis monumentis opportunisque animadversionibus aucta*. 4 vols. (Lucca, 1761–4), i. 468–73.

Raymond Muntaner, *Chronicle*, tr. Lady Goodenough. Hakluyt Society, 2nd series, 47, 50. 2 vols. (London, 1920–1).

Rolandino Patavino, 'Chronica', *MGHS*, xix. 32–147.

Rutebeuf, *Onze poèmes concernant la Croisade*, ed. J. Bastin and E. Faral. Documents relatifs à l'histoire des Croisades, i (Paris, 1946).

Saba Malaspina, 'Rerum sicularum libri sex', *RIS*, viii, cols. 785–874.

Salimbene de Adam, 'Cronica', *MGHS*, xxxii.

Thierry de Vaucouleurs, 'Vita Urbani IV', *RIS*, iii², cols. 405–20.

Vita Edwardi secundi monachi cuiusdam Malmesberiensis, ed. and tr. N. Denholm-Young (London, 1957).

William of Nangis, 'Gesta Philippi regis Franciae', *RHGF*, xx. 466–539.

—— 'Gesta sanctae memoriae Ludovici regis Franciae', *RHGF*, xx. 312–465.

3. Printed Secondary Works

Altmann, W., *Der Römerzug Ludwigs des Baiern. Ein Beitrag zur Geschichte des Kampfes zwischen Papsttum und Kaisertum* (Berlin, 1886).

Amari, M., *La guerra del Vespro siciliano*. A cura di F. Giunta. Edizione nazionale delle opere di Michele Amari, 2nd series. 2 vols. in 3 parts (Palermo, 1969).

Amiani, P. M., *Memorie istoriche della città di Fano*. 2 vols. (Fano, 1751).

Atiya, A. S., *The Crusade in the Later Middle Ages* (London, 1938).

Baethgen, F., 'Der Anspruch des Papsttums auf das Reichsvikariat. Untersuchungen zur Theorie und Praxis der potestas indirecta in temporalibus', *Zeitschrift der Savigny-Stiftung für Rechtsgeschichte*, xli, Kanonistische Abteilung, x (1920), 168–268.

—— 'Quellen und Untersuchungen zur Geschichte der päpstlichen Hof-u. Finanzverwaltung unter Bonifaz VIII.', *QFIAB*, xx (1928–9), 114–237.

Belperron, P., *La Croisade contre les Albigeois et l'union du Languedoc à la France (1209–1249)* (Paris, 1942).

Berger, É., *Saint Louis et Innocent IV. Étude sur les rapports de la France et du Saint-Siège* (Paris, 1893).

Bevere, R., 'Ancora sulla causa della distruzione della colonia saracena di Lucera', *ASPN*, NS, xxi (1935), 222–8.

Biscaro, G., 'Dante Alighieri e i sortilegi di Matteo e Galeazzo Visconti contro papa Giovanni XXII', *Archivio storico lombardo*, 5th series, xlvii (1920), 446–81.

Bloch, M., 'The Problem of Gold in the Middle Ages', in his *Land and Work in Mediaeval Europe. Selected Papers*, tr. J. E. Anderson (London, 1967), 186–229.

Boase, T.S.R., *Boniface VIII*, Makers of the Middle Ages (London, 1933).

Bock, F., 'Kaisertum, Kurie und Nationalstaat im Beginn des 14. Jahrhunderts', *RQ*, xliv (1936), 105–22, 169–220.

De Boislisle, A., 'Projet de Croisade du premier duc de Bourbon (1316–1333)', *Annuaire-bulletin de la Société de l'histoire de France*, ix (1872),

230–6, 246–55.

Borsari, S., 'La politica bizantina di Carlo I d'Angiò dal 1266 al 1271', *ASPN*, NS, xxxv (1956), 319–49.

Bourel de la Roncière, C., 'Une Escadre franco-papale (1318–1320)', *Mélanges*, xiii (1893), 397–418.

Bowsky, W. M., 'Clement V and the Emperor-Elect', *Medievalia et Humanistica*, xii (1958), 52–69.

—— *The Finance of the Commune of Siena, 1287–1355* (Oxford, 1970).

— *Henry VII in Italy. The Conflict of Empire and City-State, 1310–1313* (Lincoln, Nebraska, 1960).

—— 'Italian Diplomatic History: a Case for the Smaller Commune', in W. C. Jordan *et al.* (eds.), *Order and Innovation in the Middle Ages: Essays in Honor of Joseph R. Strayer* (Princeton, 1976), 55–74.

Boyle, L. E., *A Survey of the Vatican Archives and of its Medieval Holdings*. Pontifical Institute of Mediaeval Studies, *Subsidia mediaevalia I* (Toronto, 1972).

Brentano, R., *Rome before Avignon. A Social History of Thirteenth-Century Rome* (London, 1974).

Brucker, G. A., *Florentine Politics and Society, 1343–1378*. Princeton Studies in History, 12 (Princeton, 1962).

Brundage, J.A., *Medieval Canon Law and the Crusader* (Madison, 1969).

—— 'Recent Crusade Historiography: some Observations and Suggestions', *Catholic Historical Review*, xlix (1964), 493–507.

Busson, A., 'Die Schlacht bei Alba zwischen Konradin und Karl von Anjou, 1268', *Deutsche Zeitschrift für Geschichtswissenschaft*, iv, 2 (1890), 275–340.

Cadier, L., *Essai sur l'administration du royaume de Sicile sous Charles Ier et Charles II d'Anjou*. Bibliothèque des Écoles françaises d'Athènes et de Rome, fasc. 59 (Paris, 1891).

Caggese, R., *Roberto d'Angiò e i suoi tempi*. 2 vols. (Florence, 1922–30).

Canz, O., *Philipp Fontana, Erzbischof von Ravenna—ein Staatsmann des xiii. Jahrhunderts (1240–1270)* (Leipzig, 1911).

Capasso, C., 'La signoria viscontea e la lotta politico-religiosa con il papato nella prima metà del secolo xiv', *Bollettino della Società pavese di storia patria*, viii (1908), 265–317, 408–54.

Cardini, F., 'La crociata nel Duecento. L'"Avatāra" di un ideale', *Archivio storico italiano*, cxxxv (1977), 101–39.

Carucci, C., 'Le operazioni militari in Calabria nella guerra del Vespro siciliano', *Archivio storico per la Calabria e la Lucania*, ii (1932), 1–17.

Castruccio Castracani degli Antelminelli. Miscellanea di studi storici e letterari edita dalla Reale Accademia lucchese. Atti della R. Accademia lucchese, NS, iii (Florence, 1934).

Chroust, A., *Beiträge zur Geschichte Ludwigs des Bayers und seiner Zeit. I. Die Romfahrt* (Gotha, 1887).

Ciaccio, L., 'Il cardinal legato Bertrando del Poggetto in Bologna(1327–1334)', *Atti e memorie della R. Deputazione di storia patria per le provincie di Romagna*, series 3, xxiii (1905), 85–196, 456–537.

Cipolla, C.M., 'Une Crise ignorée. Comment c'est perdue la propriété ecclésiastique dans l'Italie du nord entre le xie et le xve siècle', *Annales*, ii (1947), 317–27.

Claeys-Bouvaert, F., 'Légat du pape', in R. Naz (ed.), *Dictionnaire de droit canonique*, vi (Paris, 1957), 371–7.

Constable, G., 'The Second Crusade as seen by Contemporaries', *Traditio*, ix (1953), 213–79.

Cramer, V., *Albert der Grosse als Kreuzzugs-Legat für Deutschland 1263–4 und die Kreuzzugs-Bestrebungen Urbans IV.* Palästina-Hefte des deutschen Vereins vom Heiligen Lande, Heft 7 bis 8 (Cologne, 1933).

Croce, B., 'Filippo di Fiandra, conte di Chieti e di Loreto', *ASPN*, NS, xvi (1930), 5–40.

Cross, F.L. and Livingstone, E.A. (eds.), *The Oxford Dictionary of the Christian Church.* 2nd edn. (London, 1974).

Davidsohn, R., *Geschichte von Florenz.* 3 vols. in 4 parts. (Berlin, 1896–1912).

Delaville le Roulx, J., *La France en Orient au xivᵉ siècle.* Bibliothèque des Écoles françaises d'Athènes et de Rome, fasc. xliv-xlv. 2 vols. (Paris, 1886).

Delisle, L., 'Mémoire sur les opérations financières des Templiers', *Mémoires de l'Institut national de France. Académie des inscriptions et belles-lettres*, xxxiii, pt. 2 (1889).

Digard, G., *Philippe le Bel et le Saint-Siège de 1285 à 1304.* 2 vols. (Paris, 1936).

Douie, D.L., *The Nature and the Effect of the Heresy of the Fraticelli* (Manchester, 1932).

Durrieu, P., 'Études sur la dynastie angevine de Naples. Le liber donationum Caroli primi', *Mélanges*, vi (1886), 189–228.

—— *Les Gascons en Italie. Études historiques* (Auch, 1885).

Egidi, P., 'Carlo I d'Angiò e l'abbazia di S. Maria della Vittoria presso Scurcola', *ASPN*, xxxiv (1909), 252–91, 732–67, xxxv (1910), 125–75.

—— 'La colonia saracena di Lucera e la sua distruzione', *ASPN*, xxxvi (1911), 597–694, xxxvii (1912), 71–89, 664–96, xxxviii (1913), 115–44, 681–707, xxxix (1914), 132–71, 697–766.

Ehrle, F., 'Der Nachlass Clemens' V. und der in Betreff desselben von Johann XXII. (1318–1321) geführte Process', *Archiv für Literatur-und Kirchengeschichte des Mittelalters*, v (1889), 1–166.

Eitel, A., *Der Kirchenstaat unter Klemens V.* Abhandlungen zur mittleren und neueren Geschichte, i (Berlin–Leipzig, 1907).

Erdmann, C., *The Origin of the Idea of Crusade*, tr. M. W. Baldwin and W. Goffart (Princeton, 1977).

Eubel, K., 'Vom Zaubereiunwesen anfangs des 14. Jahrhunderts', *Historisches Jahrbuch*, xviii (1897), 608–31.

Fawtier, R., *The Capetian Kings of France. Monarchy and Nation (987–1328)*, tr. L. Butler and R. J. Adam (London, 1960).

—— 'Documents négligés sur l'activité de la chancellerie apostolique à la fin du xiiiᵉ siècle. Le registre 46A et les comptes de la chambre sous Boniface VIII', *Mélanges*, lii (1935), 244–72.

—— 'Un Grand Achèvement de l'École française de Rome. La publication des registres des papes du xiiiᵉ siècle', *Mélanges*, lxxii (1960), i–xiii.

Fliniaux, A., 'La Faillite des Ammanati de Pistoie et le Saint-Siège (début du xivᵉ siècle)', *Revue historique de droit français et étranger*, 4th series, iii (1924), 436–72.

Fop, M. P., *Il comune di Perugia e la Chiesa durante il periodo avignonese con particolare referimento all'Albornoz. BDSPU*, 1970, Appendix ii (Perugia, 1970).

Forey, A. J., *The Templars in the 'Corona de Aragón'*, University of Durham Publications (London, 1973).

Franceschini, G., *I Montefeltro* (Milan, 1970).

De Frede, C., 'Da Carlo I d'Angiò a Giovanna I (1263–1382)', in E. Pontieri *et al.* (eds.), *Storia di Napoli iii: Napoli angioina* (Naples, 1969), 5–333.

Fryde, E. B. and M. M., 'Public Credit, with Special Reference to North-Western Europe', in M. M. Postan *et al.* (eds.), *The Cambridge Economic History of Europe*, iii (Cambridge, 1963), 430–553.

Gabrieli, F., 'Le ambascerie di Baibars a Manfredi', in *Studi medievali in onore di Antonino de Stefano* (Palermo, 1956), 219–25.

Gasnault, P., 'La Perception dans le royaume de France du subside sollicité par Jean XXII "contra haereticos et rebelles partium Italiae"', *Mélanges*, lxix (1957), 273–319.

—— 'Le Subside caritatif de 1326. Note additionnelle', *Mélanges*, lxxviii (1966), 187–90.

Geanakoplos, D., 'Byzantium and the Crusades, 1261–1354', in Setton (ed.), *History of the Crusades*, iii. 27–68.

—— *Emperor Michael Palaeologus and the West 1258–1282. A Study in Byzantine–Latin Relations* (Cambridge, Mass., 1959).

Giunta, F., *Aragonesi e Catalani nel Mediterraneo*. 2 vols. (Palermo, 1953, 1959).

Göller, E., 'Aus der Camera apostolica', *RQ*, xv (1901), 425–7, xvi (1902), 181–5.

Gottlob, A., *Kreuzablass und Almosenablass. Eine Studie über die Frühzeit des Ablasswesens*, Kirchenrechtliche Abhandlungen, xxx–xxxi (Stuttgart, 1906).

—— 'Päpstliche Darlehenschulden des 13. Jahrhunderts', *Historisches Jahrbuch*, xx (1899), 665–717.

Guillemain, B., *La Cour pontificale d'Avignon (1309–1376). Étude d'une société*. Bibliothèque des Écoles françaises d'Athènes et de Rome, fasc. cci (Paris, 1962).

Guiraud, J., *Histoire de l'Inquisition au Moyen Âge*. 2 vols. (Paris, 1935–8).

Hale, J. *et al.* (eds.), *Europe in the Late Middle Ages* (London, 1965).

Hampe, K., *Geschichte Konradins von Hohenstaufen* (Innsbruck, 1894).

—— *Urban IV. und Manfred (1261–1264)*. Heidelberger Abhandlungen zur mittleren und neueren Geschichte, xi (Heidelberg, 1905).

Heers, J., *Parties and Political Life in the Medieval West*, tr. D. Nicholas. Europe in the Middle Ages. Selected Studies, 7 (Amsterdam, 1977).

Henneman, J. B., *Royal Taxation in Fourteenth Century France. The Development of War Financing 1322–1356* (Princeton, 1971).

Hennig, E., *Die päpstlichen Zehnten aus Deutschland im Zeitalter des avignonesischen Papsttums und während des Grossen Schismas* (Halle, 1909).

Herde, P., 'Carlo I d'Angiò', in *Dizionario biografico degli Italiani*, 20 (Rome, 1977), 199–226.

—— 'Gerardo Bianchi', in *Dizionario biografico degli Italiani*, 10 (Rome, 1968), 96–101.

—— 'Die Legation des Kardinalbischofs Gerhard von Sabina während des Krieges der Sizilischen Vesper und die Synode von Melfi (28. März 1284)', *Rivista di storia della Chiesa in Italia*, xx (1967), 1–53.

Heymann, F. G., 'The Crusades against the Hussites', in Setton (ed.), *History of the Crusades*, iii. 586–646.

Heywood, W., *A History of Perugia* (London, 1910).

Hillgarth, J. N., *The Spanish Kingdoms 1250–1516. Volume I. 1250–1410. Precarious Balance* (Oxford, 1976).

Hofmann, W., 'Antikuriale Bewegungen in Deutschland in der Zeit Ludwigs des Bayern (1314–1346)', *Forschungen und Fortschritte*, xxxv (1961), 79–82.

Housley, N. J., 'The Franco-Papal Crusade Negotiations of 1322–3', *Papers of the British School at Rome* (forthcoming).

Hyde, J. K., 'Contemporary Views on Faction and Civil Strife in Thirteenth and Fourteenth Century Italy', in L. Martines (ed.), *Violence and Civil Disorder in Italian Cities, 1200–1500*. UCLA Center for Medieval and Renaissance Studies. Contributions, 5 (Berkeley, California, 1972), 273–307.

—— *Padua in the Age of Dante. A Social History of an Italian City-State.* (Manchester, 1966).

—— *Society and Politics in Medieval Italy. The Evolution of the Civil Life, 1000–1350*, New Studies in Medieval History (London, 1973).

Jordan, E., 'La Faillite des Buonsignori', in *Mélanges Paul Fabre* (Paris, 1902), 416–35.

—— *De mercatoribus camerae apostolicae saeculo xiii* (Rennes, 1909).

—— 'Notes sur le formulaire de Richard de Pofi', in *Études d'histoire du Moyen Âge dédiées à G. Monod* (Paris, 1896), 329–41.

—— *Les Origines de la domination angevine en Italie* (Paris, 1909).

Kaeuper, R. W., *Bankers to the Crown. The Riccardi of Lucca and Edward I* (Princeton, 1973).

Kedar, B. Z., 'The Passenger List of a Crusader Ship, 1250: towards the History of the Popular Element on the Seventh Crusade', *Studi medievali*, 3rd series, xiii (1972), 267–79.

Kennan, E., 'Innocent III and the First Political Crusade: a Comment on the Limitations of Papal Power', *Traditio*, xxvii (1971), 231–49.

Kienast, W., 'Der Kreuzkrieg Philipps des Schönen von Frankreich gegen Aragon', *Historische Vierteljahrschrift*, xxviii (1933–4), 673–98.

Klüpfel, L., *Die äussere Politik Alfonsos III. von Aragonien (1285–1291)*. Abhandlungen zur mittleren und neueren Geschichte, xxxv (Berlin–Leipzig, 1911–12).

Lambert, M. D., *Franciscan Poverty. The Doctrine of the Absolute Poverty of Christ and the Apostles in the Franciscan Order 1210–1323* (London, 1961).

—— *Medieval Heresy. Popular Movements from Bogomil to Hus* (London, 1977).

La Monte, J. L., *Feudal Monarchy in the Latin Kingdom of Jerusalem 1100 to 1291*. The Medieval Academy of America. Monograph no. 4 (Cambridge, Mass., 1932).

Langlois, C. V., *Le Règne de Philippe III le Hardi* (Paris, 1887).

Larner, J., *The Lords of Romagna. Romagnol Society and the Origins of the Signorie* (London, 1965).

Lecoy de la Marche, A., 'L'Expédition de Philippe le Hardi en Catalogne', *Revue des questions historiques*, xlix (1891), 62–127.

—— 'La Prédication de la Croisade au treizième siècle', *Revue des questions historiques*, xlviii (1890), 5–28.

Lefebvre, C., 'Hostiensis', in R. Naz (ed.), *Dictionnaire de droit canonique*, v (Paris, 1935), cols. 1211–27.

Leff, G., *Heresy in the Later Middle Ages. The Relation of Heterodoxy to Dissent c. 1250–c.1450*. 2 vols. (Manchester, 1967).

Lemerle, P., *L'Émirat d'Aydin, Byzance et l'Occident. Recherches sur 'La Geste d'Umur Pacha'*. Bibliothèque byzantine. Études 2 (Paris, 1957).

Léonard, E. G., *Les Angevins de Naples* (Paris, 1954).

Linehan, P., 'The *Gravamina* of the Castilian Church in 1262–3', *EHR*, lxxxv (1970), 730–54.

Lunt, W. E., 'Clerical Tenths levied in England by Papal Authority during the Reign of Edward II', in C. H. Taylor (ed.), *Anniversary Essays in Medieval History by Students of Charles Homer Haskins* (Boston, Mass., 1929), 157–82.

—— *Financial Relations of the Papacy with England*. Studies in Anglo-Papal Relations during the Middle Ages, i–ii. 2 vols. (Cambridge, Mass., 1939, 1962).

—— 'The First Levy of Papal Annates', *American Historical Review*, xviii (1912–13), 48–64.

—— *Papal Revenues in the Middle Ages*. Records of Civilization. Sources and Studies, xix. 2 vols. (New York, 1934).

—— 'Papal Taxation in England in the Reign of Edward I', *EHR*, xxx (1915), 398–417.

Luttrell, A., 'The Crusade in the Fourteenth Century', in Hale *et al.* (eds.), *Europe in the Late Middle Ages*, 122–54.

—— 'The Hospitallers at Rhodes, 1306–1421', in Setton (ed.), *History of the Crusades*, iii. 278–313.

Magnocavallo, A., *Marin Sanudo il vecchio e il suo progetto di crociata* (Bergamo, 1901).

Mallett, M., *Mercenaries and their Masters. Warfare in Renaissance Italy* (London, 1974).

Marchetti-Longhi, G., *Gregorio de Monte Longo patriarca di Aquileja (1251–1269)* (Rome, 1965).

Mayer, H. E., *The Crusades*, tr. J. Gillingham (London, 1972).

Mazzoleni, J., *Le fonti documentarie e bibliografiche dal secolo x al secolo xx conservate presso l'Archivio di Stato di Napoli* (Naples, 1974).

McNamara, J. A., 'Simon de Beaulieu and *Clericis laicos*', *Traditio*, xxv (1969), 155–70.

Merkel, C., 'L'opinione dei contemporanei sull'impresa italiana di Carlo I d'Angiò', *Atti della R. Accademia dei Lincei*, 4th series, *Classe di Scienze morali, storiche e filologiche*, iv (1888), pt. i, 275–435.

Michel, R., 'Le Procès de Matteo et de Galeazzo Visconti', *Mélanges*, xxix (1909), 269–327.

Minieri-Riccio, C., *Cenni storici intorno i grandi uffizii del Regno di Sicilia durante il regno di Carlo I. d'Angiò* (Naples, 1872).

Mollat, G., 'Benoît XII et l'Italie', in Benedict XII, *Lettres closes et patentes intéressant les pays autres que la France*, ii, pp. v–xxi.

—— *The Popes at Avignon 1305–1378*, tr. J. Love (London, 1963).

—— 'Procès d'un collecteur pontifical sous Jean XXII et Benoît XII',

Vierteljahrschrift für Social-u. Wirtschaftsgeschichte, vi (1908), 210–27.

Monti, G. M., 'L'Albania e la guerra di Sicilia: trattative diplomatiche', in his *Nuovi studi angioini*, 577–87.

—— 'Gli angioini di Napoli negli studi dell'ultimo cinquantennio', in his *Nuovi studi angioini*, 3–102.

—— *Le confraternite medievali dell'alta e media Italia*. 2 vols. (Venice, 1927).

—— *Nuovi studi angioini* (Trani, 1937).

Moorman, J., *A History of the Franciscan Order from its Origins to the Year 1517* (Oxford, 1968).

Nicolini, N., 'Sui rapporti diplomatici veneto-napoletani durante i regni di Carlo I e Carlo II d'Angiò', *ASPN*, NS, xxi (1935), 229–86.

Nitschke, A., 'Carlo II d'Angiò', *Dizionario biografico degli Italiani*, 20 (Rome, 1977), 227–35.

Offler, H. S., 'Empire and Papacy: the Last Struggle', *Transactions of the Royal Historical Society*, 5th series, vi (1956), 21–47.

Orioli, R., *L'eresia dolciniana*. Part 2 of L. Paolini and R. Orioli, *L'eresia a Bologna fra xiii e xiv secolo*. Istituto storico italiano per il medio evo. Studi storici, fasc. 93–96. 2 vols. (Rome, 1975).

Otto, H., 'Benedikt XII. als Reformator des Kirchenstaates', *RQ*, xxxvi (1928), 59–110.

—— 'Zur italienischen Politik Johanns XXII.', *QFIAB*, xiv (1911), 140–265.

Partner, P. D., 'Camera papae: Problems of Papal Finance in the Later Middle Ages', *Journal of Ecclesiastical History*, iv (1953), 55–68.

—— 'Florence and the Papacy, 1300–1375', in J. Hale *et al.* (eds.), *Europe in the Late Middle Ages*, 76–121.

—— *The Lands of St. Peter. The Papal State in the Middle Ages and the Early Renaissance* (London, 1972).

Paulus, N., *Geschichte des Ablasses im Mittelalter vom Ursprunge bis zur Mitte des 14. Jahrhunderts*. 2 vols. (Paderborn, 1922–3).

Pissard, H., *La Guerre sainte en pays chrétien* (Paris, 1912).

Pontieri, E., 'Un capitano della guerra del Vespro: Pietro (II) Ruffo di Calabria', *Archivio storico per la Calabria e la Lucania*, i (1931), 269–310, 471–530.

Powicke, F. M., 'Pope Boniface VIII', in his *The Christian Life in the Middle Ages* (Oxford, 1935), 48–73.

Prawer, J., *The Latin Kingdom of Jerusalem. European Colonialism in the Middle Ages* (London, 1972).

Prestwich, M. C., *War, Politics and Finance under Edward I* (London, 1972).

Previté-Orton, C. W., 'Marsilius of Padua and the Visconti', *English Historical Review*, xliv (1929), 278–9.

Purcell, M., *Papal Crusading Policy. The Chief Instruments of Papal Crusading Policy and Crusade to the Holy Land from the Final Loss of Jerusalem to the Fall of Acre, 1244–1291*. Studies in the History of Christian Thought, xi (Leiden, 1975).

Queller, D. E., *The Fourth Crusade. The Conquest of Constantinople 1201–1204* (Leicester, 1978).

Rapisarda, M., *La signoria di Ezzelino da Romano* (Del Bianco-Udine, 1965).

Re, E., 'La compagnia dei Riccardi in Inghilterra e il suo fallimento alla fine del secolo xiii', *Archivio della R. Società romana di storia patria*, xxxvii (1914),

87–138.

Renouard, Y., *The Avignon Papacy 1305–1403*, tr. D. Bethell (London, 1970).

—— 'Comment les papes d'Avignon expédiaient leur courrier', *Revue historique*, clxxx (1937), 1–29.

—— 'Une Expédition de céréales des Pouilles en Arménie par les Bardi pour le compte de Benoît XII', *Mélanges*, liii (1936), 287–329.

—— 'Les Papes et le conflit franco-anglais en Aquitaine de 1259 à 1337', *Mélanges*, li (1934), 258–92.

—— *Recherches sur les compagnies commerciales et bancaires utilisées par les papes d'Avignon avant le Grand Schisme* (Paris, 1942).

—— *Les Relations des papes d'Avignon et des compagnies commerciales et bancaires de 1316 à 1378*. Bibliothèque des Écoles françaises d'Athènes et de Rome, fasc. cli (Paris, 1941).

Reydellet-Guttinger, C., *L'Administration pontificale dans le duché de Spolète (1305–1352)*. Studi dell'Accademia spoletina (Florence, 1975).

Riley-Smith, J. S. C., *The Knights of St. John in Jerusalem and Cyprus c. 1050–1310* (London, 1967).

—— *What were the Crusades?* (London, 1977).

Robinson, I. S., *Authority and Resistance in the Investiture Contest. The Polemical Literature of the Eleventh Century* (Manchester, 1978).

—— 'Gregory VII and the Soldiers of Christ', *History*, lviii (1973), 169–92.

Rodenberg, C., *Innocenz IV. und das Königreich Sicilien. 1245–1254* (Halle, 1892).

Rohde, H. E., *Der Kampf um Sizilien in den Jahren 1291–1302*. Abhandlungen zur mittleren und neueren Geschichte, xlii (Berlin–Leipzig, 1913).

Roscher, H., *Papst Innocenz III. und die Kreuzzüge*. Forschungen zur Kirchen-u. Dogmengeschichte, 21 (Göttingen, 1969).

Rousset, P., *Les Origines et les caractères de la première croisade* (Neuchâtel, 1945).

Runciman, S., 'The Crusader States, 1243–1291', in Setton (ed.), *History of the Crusades*, ii. 557–98.

—— 'The Decline of the Crusading Idea', in *Relazioni del X Congresso internazionale di Scienze storiche. Storia del medioevo, iii*. Biblioteca storica Sansoni, NS, xxiv (Florence, 1955), 637–52.

—— *A History of the Crusades*. 3 vols. (Cambridge, 1951–4).

—— *The Sicilian Vespers. A History of the Mediterranean World in the Later Thirteenth Century* (Cambridge, 1958).

Russell, F. H., *The Just War in the Middle Ages*. Cambridge Studies in Medieval Life and Thought, 3rd series, viii (Cambridge, 1975).

St. Clair Baddeley, R., *Robert the Wise and his Heirs 1278–1352* (London, 1897).

De Saint-Priest, A., *Histoire de la conquête de Naples par Charles d'Anjou frère de Saint Louis*. 4 vols. (Paris, 1847–8).

Salavert y Roca, V., *Cerdeña y la expansión mediterránea de la Corona de Aragón, 1297–1314*. 2 vols. (Madrid, 1956).

Samaran, C. and Mollat, G., *La Fiscalité pontificale en France au xivᵉ siècle (période d'Avignon et Grand Schisme d'Occident)*. Bibliothèque des Écoles françaises d'Athènes et de Rome, fasc. xcvi (Paris, 1905).

Sassi, R., 'La partecipazione di Fabriano alle guerre della Marcà nel decennio 1320–1330', *Atti e memorie della R. Deputazione di storia patria per le Marche*, series 4, vii (1930), 57–129.

Scarisbrick, J. J., *Henry VIII* (London, 1968).

Schäfer, K. H., 'Geldspenden der päpstlichen Kurie unter Johann XXII. (1316–1334) für die orientalischen Christen, insbesondere für das Königreich Armenien', *Oriens christianus*, iv (1904), 184–7.

Schneider, F., 'Zur älteren päpstlichen Finanzgeschichte', *QFIAB*, ix (1906), 1–37.

Schneider, G., *Die finanziellen Beziehungen der florentinischen Bankiers zur Kirche von 1285 bis 1304* (Leipzig, 1900).

Setton, K. M., 'The Catalans in Greece, 1311–1380', in his *History of the Crusades*, iii. 167–224.

—— *A History of the Crusades*. 4 vols. so far. Vols. i and ii 2nd edn.; vol. iii 1st edn. (Madison, 1969–).

Smail, R. C., 'Latin Syria and the West, 1149–1187', *Transactions of the Royal Historical Society*, 5th series, xix (1969), 1–20.

Smalley, B., 'Church and State, 1300–77: Theory and Fact', in Hale *et al.* (eds.), *Europe in the Late Middle Ages*, 15–43.

Soldevila, F., 'L'amistat catalano-veneciana en 1283–1285', in *Miscellanea in onore di Roberto Cessi*, i. Storia e letteratura. Raccolta di studi e testi, lxxi (Rome, 1958), 233–8.

Soranzo, G., *La guerra fra Venezia e la Santa Sede per il dominio di Ferrara (1308–1313)* (Città di Castello, 1905).

Sternfeld, R., *Ludwigs des Heiligen Kreuzzug nach Tunis 1270 und die Politik Karls I. von Sizilien.* Historische Studien, iv (Berlin, 1896).

Stickel, E., *Der Fall von Akkon. Untersuchungen zum Abklingen des Kreuzzugsgedankens am Ende des 13. Jahrhunderts.* Geist und Werk der Zeiten, xlv (Bern–Frankfurt-M., 1975).

Strayer, J. R., *The Albigensian Crusades* (New York, 1971).

—— 'The Crusade against Aragon', *Speculum*, xxviii (1953), 102–13.

—— 'The Crusades of Louis IX', in Setton (ed.), *History of the Crusades*, ii. 487–518.

—— 'Defense of the Realm and Royal Power in France', in his *Medieval Statecraft*, 291–9.

—— 'The First Western Union', in his *Medieval Statecraft*, 333–40.

—— 'France: the Holy Land, the Chosen People, and the Most Christian King', in T. K. Rabb and J. E. Seigel (eds.), *Action and Conviction in Early Modern Europe* (Princeton, 1969), 3–16.

—— *Medieval Statecraft and the Perspectives of History. Essays*, ed. J. F. Benton and T. N. Bisson (Princeton, 1971).

—— 'The Political Crusades of the Thirteenth Century', in Setton (ed.), *History of the Crusades*, ii. 343–75.

—— and Taylor, C. H., *Studies in Early French Taxation.* Harvard Historical Monographs, xii (Cambridge, Mass., 1939).

Tabacco, G., *La casa di Francia nell'azione politica di papa Giovanni XXII.* Istituto storico italiano per il medio evo. Studi storici, fasc. 1–4 (Rome, 1953).

—— 'La tradizione guelfa in Italia durante il pontificato di Benedetto XII', in P. Vaccari and P. F. Palumbo (eds.), *Studi di storia medievale e moderna in onore di Ettore Rota* (Rome, 1958), 97–148.

Testa, F., *De vita, et rebus gestis Federici II, Siciliae regis* (Palermo, 1775).

Thier, L., *Kreuzzugsbemühungen unter Papst Clemens V. (1305–1314)*. Franziskanische Forschungen, xxiv. (Werl, Westf., 1973).

Throop, P. A., *Criticism of the Crusade: a Study of Public Opinion and Crusade Propaganda* (Amsterdam, 1940).

Tomacelli, D., *Storia de' reami di Napoli e di Sicilia dal 1250 al 1303*. 2nd edn. 2 vols. (Naples, 1864–6).

Trexler, R. C., *The Spiritual Power. Republican Florence under Interdict.* Studies in Medieval and Reformation Thought, ix (Leiden, 1974).

Ullmann, W., *The Growth of Papal Government in the Middle Ages. A Study in the Ideological Relation of Clerical to Lay Power.* 3rd edn. (London, 1970).

—— Historical Introduction to H. C. Lea, *The Inquisition of the Middle Ages, its Organization and Operation* (London, 1963).

—— *Law and Politics in the Middle Ages. An Introduction to the Sources of Medieval Political Ideas* (Cambridge, 1975).

—— *A Short History of the Papacy in the Middle Ages.* Corrected reprint (London, 1974).

Vaughan, R., *Matthew Paris.* Cambridge Studies in Medieval Life and Thought, 2nd series, vi (Cambridge, 1958).

Vehse, O., *Die amtliche Propaganda in der Staatskunst Kaiser Friedrichs II* (Munich, 1929).

Villey, M., *La Croisade. Essai sur la formation d'une théorie juridique.* L'Église et l'État au Moyen Âge, vi (Paris, 1942).

—— 'L'Idée de la Croisade chez les juristes du Moyen Âge', in *Relazioni del X Congresso internazionale di Scienze storiche. Storia del medioevo, iii.* Biblioteca storica Sansoni, NS, xxiv (Florence, 1955), 565–94.

Volpe, G., *Movimenti religiosi e sette ereticali nella società medievale italiana secoli xi–xiv.* Biblioteca storica Sansoni, NS, xxxvii (Florence, 1926).

Waley, D. P., 'The Army of the Florentine Republic from the Twelfth to the Fourteenth Century', in N. Rubinstein (ed.), *Florentine Studies. Politics and Society in Renaissance Florence* (London, 1968), 70–108.

—— '*Condotte* and *Condottieri* in the Thirteenth Century', *Proceedings of the British Academy*, lxi (1975), 337–71.

—— *The Italian City-Republics.* 2nd edn. (London, 1978).

—— 'Papal Armies in the Thirteenth Century', *English Historical Review*, lxxii (1957), 1–30.

—— *The Papal State in the Thirteenth Century* (London, 1961).

Watt, J. A., *The Theory of Papal Monarchy in the Thirteenth Century. The Contribution of the Canonists* (London, 1965).

Wieruszowski, H., *Vom Imperium zum nationalen Königtum. Vergleichende Studien über die publizistischen Kämpfe Kaiser Friedrichs II. und König Philipps des Schönen mit der Kurie* (Munich–Berlin, 1933).

Wilks, M. J., *The Problem of Sovereignty in the Later Middle Ages. The Papal Monarchy with Augustinus Triumphus and the Publicists.* Cambridge Studies in Medieval Life and Thought, 2nd series, ix (Cambridge, 1963).

Willemsen, C. A., *Kardinal Napoleon Orsini (1263–1342).* Historische Studien, clxxii (Berlin, 1927).

Winkler, F., *Castruccio Castracani Herzog von Lucca.* Historische Studien, ix (Berlin, 1897).

Yver, G., *Le commerce et les marchands dans l'Italie méridionale au xiiie et au xive siècle.* Bibliothèque des Écoles françaises d'Athènes et de Rome, fasc. lxxxviii (Paris, 1903).

4. Unpublished Dissertation

Beebe, B., 'Edward I and the Crusades'. St. Andrews University, 1970.

Index

ISBN 0–19–	Author	Title
8143567	ALFÖLDI A.	The Conversion of Constantine and Pagan Rome
6286409	ANDERSON George K.	The Literature of the Anglo-Saxons
8219601	ARNOLD Benjamin	German Knighthood
8228813	BARTLETT & MacKAY	Medieval Frontier Societies
8111010	BETHURUM Dorothy	Homilies of Wulfstan
8142765	BOLLING G. M.	External Evidence for Interpolation in Homer
814332X	BOLTON J.D.P.	Aristeas of Proconnesus
9240132	BOYLAN Patrick	Thoth, the Hermes of Egypt
8114222	BROOKS Kenneth R.	Andreas and the Fates of the Apostles
8203543	BULL Marcus	Knightly Piety & Lay Response to the First Crusade
8216785	BUTLER Alfred J.	Arab Conquest of Egypt
8148046	CAMERON Alan	Circus Factions
8148054	CAMERON Alan	Porphyrius the Charioteer
8148348	CAMPBELL J.B.	The Emperor and the Roman Army 31 BC to 235 AD
826643X	CHADWICK Henry	Priscillian of Avila
826447X	CHADWICK Henry	Boethius
8219393	COWDREY H.E.J.	The Age of Abbot Desiderius
8148992	DAVIES M.	Sophocles: Trachiniae
825301X	DOWNER L.	Leges Henrici Primi
814346X	DRONKE Peter	Medieval Latin and the Rise of European Love-Lyric
8142749	DUNBABIN T.J.	The Western Greeks
8154372	FAULKNER R.O.	The Ancient Egyptian Pyramid Texts
8221541	FLANAGAN Marie Therese	Irish Society, Anglo-Norman Settlers, Angevin Kingship
8143109	FRAENKEL Edward	Horace
8201540	GOLDBERG P.J.P.	Women, Work and Life Cycle in a Medieval Economy
8140215	GOTTSCHALK H.B.	Heraclides of Pontus
8266162	HANSON R.P.C.	Saint Patrick
8224354	HARRISS G.L.	King, Parliament and Public Finance in Medieval England to 1369
8581114	HEATH Sir Thomas	Aristarchus of Samos
2115480	HENRY Blanche	British Botanical and Horticultural Literature before 1800
8140444	HOLLIS A.S.	Callimachus: Hecale
8212968	HOLLISTER C. Warren	Anglo-Saxon Military Institutions
8219523	HOUSLEY Norman	The Italian Crusades
8223129	HURNARD Naomi	The King's Pardon for Homicide – before AD 1307
8140401	HUTCHINSON G.O.	Hellenistic Poetry
9240140	JOACHIM H.H.	Aristotle: On Coming-to-be and Passing-away
9240094	JONES A.H.M	Cities of the Eastern Roman Provinces
8142560	JONES A.H.M.	The Greek City
8218354	JONES Michael	Ducal Brittany 1364–1399
8271484	KNOX & PELCZYNSKI	Hegel's Political Writings
8225253	LE PATOUREL John	The Norman Empire
8212720	LENNARD Reginald	Rural England 1086–1135
8212321	LEVISON W.	England and the Continent in the 8th century
8148224	LIEBESCHUETZ J.H.W.G.	Continuity and Change in Roman Religion
8141378	LOBEL Edgar & PAGE Sir Denys	Poetarum Lesbiorum Fragmenta
9240159	LOEW E.A.	The Beneventan Script
8241445	LUKASIEWICZ, Jan	Aristotle's Syllogistic
8152442	MAAS P. & TRYPANIS C.A .	Sancti Romani Melodi Cantica
8142684	MARSDEN E.W.	Greek and Roman Artillery—Historical
8142692	MARSDEN E.W.	Greek and Roman Artillery—Technical
8148178	MATTHEWS John	Western Aristocracies and Imperial Court AD 364–425
9240205	MAVROGORDATO John	Digenes Akrites
8223447	McFARLANE K.B.	Lancastrian Kings and Lollard Knights
8226578	McFARLANE K.B.	The Nobility of Later Medieval England
9240205	MAVROGADO John	Digenes Akrites
8148100	MEIGGS Russell	Roman Ostia
8148402	MEIGGS Russell	Trees and Timber in the Ancient Mediterranean World
8142641	MILLER J. Innes	The Spice Trade of the Roman Empire
8147813	MOORHEAD John	Theoderic in Italy
8264259	MOORMAN John	A History of the Franciscan Order
9240213	MYRES J.L.	Herodotus The Father of History
8219512	OBOLENSKY Dimitri	Six Byzantine Portraits
8116020	OWEN A.L.	The Famous Druids
8131445	PALMER, L.R.	The Interpretation of Mycenaean Greek Texts
8143427	PFEIFFER R.	History of Classical Scholarship (vol 1)
8143648	PFEIFFER Rudolf	History of Classical Scholarship 1300–1850